Who reads academic histories? Should historians reach out more beyond academia to the general public? Why do Hollywood films, historical novels and television histories prove more successful in presenting the past to a wider audience? What can historians do to improve their effectiveness in reaching and engaging their target audience in a digital age?

The way history is presented to an audience is often taken for granted, even ignored. *Presenting History* explores the vital role played by presenters in both establishing why history matters in today's world and communicating the past to audiences within and outside academia. Through case studies of leading historians, historical novelists, Hollywood filmmakers and television history presenters, this book looks critically at alternative literary and visual ways of presenting the past as both academic history and popular history.

Historians discussed include Stephen Ambrose, Niall Ferguson, Eric Hobsbawm, Robert A. Rosenstone, Simon Schama, Joan Wallach Scott and A.J.P. Taylor. Chapter topics include Hollywood and history; Michael Bellesiles' controversial history of gun rights in the USA; Philippa Gregory's historical novels; historians and the David Irving trial; and Terry Deary's 'Horrible Histories'.

Raising serious questions about the nature, study and communication of history, *Presenting History* is an essential text for historians and history students, as well as anyone involved in listening to, reading, or watching presenters of the past.

Peter J. Beck is Emeritus Professor of History at Kingston University, Kingston upon Thames, UK, and a Fellow of the Royal Historical Society. His publications include *Using History, Making British Policy: the Treasury and Foreign Office, 1950–76*. He has contributed to a wide range of publications, including newspapers, *History Today* and the *BBC History Magazine*, as well as to radio and television programmes in the UK and internationally.

Also By Peter J. Beck

Using History, Making British Policy: the Treasury and the Foreign Office, 1950–76

Scoring for Britain: International Football and International Politics, 1900–1939

British Documents on Foreign Affairs. Reports and Papers from the Foreign Office Confidential Prints: The League of Nations 1918–1941

The Falkland Islands as an International Problem

The International Politics of Antarctica

Presenting History

Past and Present

Peter J. Beck
Kingston University

First published 2012 by
PALGRAVE MACMILLAN

Palgrave Macmillan in the UK is an imprint of Macmillan Publishers Limited, registered in England, company number 785998, of Houndmills, Basingstoke, Hampshire RG21 6XS.

Palgrave Macmillan in the US is a division of St Martin's Press LLC, 175 Fifth Avenue, New York, NY 10010.

Palgrave Macmillan is the global academic imprint of the above companies and has companies and representatives throughout the world.

Palgrave® and Macmillan® are registered trademarks in the United States, the United Kingdom, Europe and other countries.

ISBN 978–0–230–24207–4   hardback
ISBN 978–0–230–24208–1   paperback

This book is printed on paper suitable for recycling and made from fully managed and sustained forest sources. Logging, pulping and manufacturing processes are expected to conform to the environmental regulations of the country of origin.

A catalogue record for this book is available from the British Library.

A catalog record for this book is available from the Library of Congress.

10   9   8   7   6   5   4   3   2   1
21   20   19   18   17   16   15   14   13   12

Printed in Great Britain by the MPG Books Group, Bodmin and King's Lynn

Contents

List of Boxes

Preface

Having long explored alternative ways of teaching 'the nature of history', during the late 1990s I developed a course using individual historians to focus upon presenting history to diverse audiences. In part, this book draws upon the teaching materials produced to fill gaps in the existing literature as well as upon staff and student feedback about the course. In part, the text benefits from my recent publications on history and public policy, as detailed at http://fass.kingston. ac.uk/faculty/staff/cv.php?staffnum=34. Also relevant is my longstanding interest in public history, which was reinforced after meeting Wesley Johnson and Bob Kelley at the 1982 Public History Conference in Chicago. These exchanges led to my delivery of a paper at the 1983 Public History Conference held at the University of Waterloo, Canada, and the publication of an article entitled 'History goes public' in the *Times Higher Education Supplement* (1983).

This book draws upon original research – the government's rejection of two FOI requests concerning the 'U-571' controversy limited its scope – but is primarily a work of synthesis. Highlighting a central but largely overlooked historical issue, *Presenting History: Past and Present* takes advantage of the high public profile of today's presenters to illuminate the nature of the historian's craft in taking the past to audiences within and outside academia.

As ever, my family provided a supportive home environment for undertaking this project. This book has benefited from the constructive role performed by Kate Haines, my editor, Juanita Bullough, the book's copyeditor, and the referees advising on the draft manuscript. I acknowledge also the help of Robert A. Rosenstone, Joan Wallach Scott, Sarah Bower and Sarah L. Johnson as well as of library staff at Kingston University, the British Film Institute, the National Theatre Archive, and Special Collections at the University of Birmingham's library.

Acknowledgements

I am grateful to Lady Avon for permission to quote from Lord Avon's private papers and to Professor Sir Keith Thomas for permission to quote from his Wolfson prize speech in 1997. Extracts from *Horrible Histories: The 20th Century*, Text Copyright © Terry Deary, 1996; *Horrible Histories: The Terrible Tudors*, Text Copyright © Terry Deary, 1998; *Horrible Histories: The Vile Victorians*, Text Copyright © Terry Deary, 1998; *Horrible Histories: The Frightful First World War*, Text Copyright © Terry Deary, 1998; *Horrible Histories: The Frightful First World War*, Text Copyright © Terry Deary, 1998; *Horrible Histories: The Barmy British Empire*, Text Copyright © Terry Deary, 2002; and *Horrible Histories: Rotten Rulers* (2005), Text Copyright © Terry Deary 2005, are reproduced with permission of Scholastic Ltd.

List of Abbreviations

AHA	American Historical Association
AP	Lord Avon Papers
BAFTA	British Academy of Film and Television Arts award
BBC	British Broadcasting Corporation
CBBC	Children's BBC
CEO	Chief Executive Officer
CiTV	Children's ITV
CND	Campaign for Nuclear Disarmament
CPGB	Communist Party of Great Britain
CPHG	British Communist Party Historians' Group
FOI	Freedom of Information
GCE	General Certificate of Education
GMTV	Good Morning Television (ITV's breakfast show)
HA	Historical Association, UK
HBO	Home Box Office
ICT	Information and Communication Technology
ILP	Independent Labour Party
IPUP	Institute for the Public Understanding of the Past, University of York
ITV	Independent Television
KPD	Kommunistische Partei Deutschlands (Communist Party of Germany)
MORI	Market & Opinion Research International
MP	Member of Parliament
NAACP	National Association for the Advancement of Colored People
NRA	National Rifle Association
Ofsted	The Office for Standards in Education, Children's Services and Skills
PBS	Public Broadcasting Service (USA)

Introduction

Why publish yet another book on 'the nature of history'? Surely there are enough publications covering the topic already. Yes, there are several existing books, many of them extremely good. However, like the numerous teaching courses covering 'the nature of history', their prime focus is often directed towards such issues as defining history, justifying history, and studying the nature of the historian's craft with special emphasis upon historical research techniques and the nature and value of sources. By contrast, the actual process of presentation responsible for communicating history to an audience is taken for granted, and hence frequently glossed over, even ignored. Nor does the nature, changing character, and potential responsiveness of audiences attract much attention, perhaps in part because the continued growth of higher education has always promised historians, at least on paper, a captive audience of fellow academics and students.

Against this background, the fundamental aim of *Presenting History: Past and Present* can be expressed in three words: 'Presentation, Presentation, Presentation'. The intention is to encourage and enable readers to engage with and reflect upon in an informed manner the varying ways in which the past is presented to diverse audiences within and outside academia. For historians and history students, the book's central message is to move on from discussing such questions as 'What is history?' and 'How to conduct historical research?' to a broader range of issues. These include 'Who reads academic histories?'; 'To what extent does the target audience actually access and engage with academic histories?'; and 'Do alternative ways of presenting the past offer a more effective way of reaching the intended audience?' There are, of course, many other possible debating issues, but the key point is to ensure that both presentation and audiences receive as much attention as earlier stages of the historical process.

Despite claims about the intrinsic merit of doing historical research, any historian's findings will only enhance historical knowledge and understanding if they reach an audience. Indeed, most present-day definitions of research, such as those adopted for research assessment exercises conducted for British universities, assume publication and impact. Nor should history students ignore this book's message. After all, throughout school and college, they are expected to write essays, dissertations and theses for an audience composed of academic markers/examiners.

Other questions posed increasingly frequently during recent decades have been along the lines of 'Can movies, television histories and historical novels teach history?' This trend reflects the fact that a growing number of people are accessing history, or what they are led to believe is history, from Hollywood filmmakers, television programme makers and historical novelists, not professional historians. Apart from raising serious questions about how far such alternative presentations rate as 'history', their popularity with audiences challenges historians to think seriously about engaging a wider audience, and particularly to consider 'How far should historians reach out from academia to a wider public in order to enhance public understanding of the past?' At first sight, presenting history to a wider audience might seem less demanding, but from personal experience – this point is confirmed by presenters featured in this book – it is not as easy as it appears.

Setting the scene for the main section of the book, **Part I** foregrounds the vital role played by history presenters in establishing why history matters and communicating the story of the past to diverse audiences within and outside academia. In **Part II** case studies centred upon individual presenters based on both sides of the Atlantic are used to explore critically and in depth alternative literary and visual ways of presenting the past as academic history and public history to diverse audiences. Presentation proves central throughout, but the fact that most chapters cover also the communication of history to a wider public means that Part II possesses also a strong public history dimension. Individual case studies cast light also on the nature of the historian's craft, including the use and abuse of sources, the translation and mistranslation of historical documents, historical methodology, theory and history, historical revisionism, different types of historical writing, history and literary style, referencing, and historical standards. Finally, **Part III**, framed by Alan Bennett's *The History Boys*, draws together key points raised throughout the book regarding history, presentation, and audiences within and outside academia.

Selecting presenters for inclusion was no easy task. For most case studies, it was possible to identify several presenters possessing strong academic and/or public profiles within and outside Britain. Ultimately, the final choice was guided largely by the extent to which individual presenters promised not only to illuminate the key issues for discussion but also to offer readers a sound foundation for further study about presentation and audiences.

At the individual level specific reasons proved important. A.J.P. Taylor (chapter 4) died over two decades ago. Although he might appear a somewhat remote figure for today's history students, Taylor remains still an important reference point for many historians, as evidenced by the manner in which Niall Ferguson, Simon Schama and David Starkey acknowledge his pioneering role presenting the past to a broader audience on radio and television as well as in the press. Moreover, over time changing perspectives upon Taylor's career establish the way in which historical revisionism affects historians' reputations as well as historiography. **Eric Hobsbawm** (chapter 5) has never made any secret of his admiration of Karl Marx or membership of the British communist party. Thus, he offers an excellent example of the impact of Marxist theory upon presenting the past, such as by highlighting capitalism's troubled history and prioritising 'history from below'. Communist party membership explains both his reluctance to write a history of the Soviet Union and belief in taking history beyond the ivory tower. However, whereas he reached out from academia chiefly through lecturing and writing, **Simon Schama** (chapter 6), a self-confessed populariser of history, has proved a highly successful television historian setting a new course from that associated with Ken Burns, the producer of *The Civil War* television series. **Niall Ferguson** (chapter 7) followed Schama onto television, but here his studies of alternative pasts are central to a discussion about the historical merit of studying the past's 'what ifs?'

Significantly, given her role in helping to qualify Part II's apparent maleness, **Joan Wallach Scott** (chapter 8) has spent much of her career presenting histories challenging history's masculinist nature and recognising women's place in the past. Moreover, she found postmodernist theory, especially poststructuralism, useful in understanding and presenting the history of power, knowledge and gender. Scott's political activism means that she possesses also a lengthy track record as a public historian, most notably using history to support feminism or to intervene in French debates about national identity. Postmodernist theory appealed also to **Robert A. Rosenstone** (chapter 9), the leading historian of film as history and history as film. For most historians, Hollywood's history films, though playing an influential role in carrying historical messages to the general public, fall well short as 'history'.

However, Rosenstone has adopted an alternative line when arguing that historical films remain capable of taking the past as history to cinema audiences.

During recent decades historical novels have not only proved remarkably popular but also acquired greater historical and literary gravitas. **Philippa Gregory** (chapter 10), one of Britain's most popular historical novelists, has boosted public interest in the Plantagenets and the Tudors. Selling in large numbers on both sides of the Atlantic, her novels have inspired adaptations for film and television. Reportedly **Terry Deary** (chapter 11), whose target audience is young children, has sold more histories than any presenter studied in this book. Furthermore, over time his 'Horrible Histories' have been adapted for a wide range of alternative forms of presentation – these include a computer game, museum exhibitions, plays and television programmes – to reach out to new audiences.

For academic historians, a high public profile can prove a double-edged sword, as highlighted when **Stephen Ambrose** and **Michael A. Bellesiles** (chapter 12) attracted unwelcome widespread media and public attention for alleged shortcomings in their histories. For some readers, the inclusion of **David Irving** (chapter 13) will appear problematic. In reality, the Irving–Lipstadt High Court trial, held in 2000, offers an illuminating case study centred upon a presenter whose use and abuse of the Nazi and Holocaust past for political reasons led to his ostracism by academia but failed to prevent him reaching a substantial popular audience. Moreover, this episode raised interesting questions about public history, memory laws, and the courts and history.

Highlighting the need to attach a higher priority to both presentation and audiences, hopefully this study will encourage readers to think more seriously about the alternative ways in which the past is presented within society in general and academia in particular, especially given ongoing debates about the future of both academic history and public history. In the present-day world mantras are frequently employed to encourage, empower, and give a sense of purpose to an audience. For historians and history students, the challenge is to ensure that the 'Presentation, Presentation, Presentation' mantra does not remain mere historical rhetoric, but is matched by action guided by the following maxim: 'The better their presentation of the past, the more effective their history will prove in accessing, engaging and impacting upon the target audience.'

Part I
Presenting Academic and Popular History

Arguing that history really matters in today's fast-moving world, Part I foregrounds the central role performed by presenters in communicating the past to audiences within and outside academia. Written and oral presentations remain predominant in academia. However, alternative aural, literary and visual presentations, most notably radio programmes, historical novels, Hollywood films and television histories, prove increasingly important in taking the past to the broader public audience. Apart from raising questions about how far such alternative presentations rate as 'history', their popularity challenges historians to think seriously about reaching out more widely from academia, or risk leaving public understanding of history to radio and television producers, Hollywood filmmakers and historical novelists.

1
Why History and Presenters of the Past Matter

July 2006 saw the launch in Britain of the 'History Matters' campaign. Supported by leading historians – including Bettany Hughes, Tristram Hunt, Andrew Roberts and David Starkey – and several prominent public figures, the campaign helped raise public awareness of the need to know and value Britain's history. Over one million Britons pledged their support. Some 46,000 people wrote 'One Day in History' diaries. Moreover, Tony Blair (2007), a prime minister (1997–2007) not renowned for his historical credentials, acknowledged how the 'overwhelming response' to the campaign established that Britons 'have an enormous appetite for their culture and their history'.

'History is Everywhere'

Against this background, history has often been depicted as not only essential and relevant but also all-pervasive in contemporary British culture, more popular than ever. Indeed, the 'History Matters' campaign was launched on the back of a MORI opinion poll in which 73 per cent of those polled indicated an interest in history as compared with 48 per cent for football (Fenton 2006; National Trust 2008: 1).

In Britain today, it seems, 'history in public is everywhere' (Jordanova 2000: 21; de Groot 2009a: 11–13, 181–3), even inescapable. Examples of history's present-day visibility include:

- the commemoration of anniversaries, like November's Day of Remembrance for the war dead or Holocaust Memorial Day;
- box-office returns for history feature films, including *The History Boys* (2006), *The Other Boleyn Girl* (2008) and *The King's Speech* (2010);

- lengthy theatre runs by such plays as *The History Boys* (2004–) and *War Horse* (2007–), quite apart from the enduring impact of Shakespeare's history plays;
- highly regarded BBC radio programmes such as *Document* and Melvyn Bragg's *Voices of the Powerless*;
- impressive audience ratings for television histories presented by Niall Ferguson, Bettany Hughes, Simon Schama and David Starkey, among others;
- the popularity of channels such as the History Channel and Yesterday;
- circulation figures for *History Today* and *BBC History Magazine*;
- sales and public library borrowing figures for popular histories, such as Antony Beevor's *D-Day: the Battle for Normandy* (2009);
- best-selling historical novels, including Philippa Gregory's *The Other Queen* (2009) and Hilary Mantel's *Wolf Hall* (2009);
- visitor numbers to museums, historical exhibitions (e.g. 'Henry VIII: Man and Monarch' at the British Library in 2009), historic houses and gardens, and historical re-enactments;
- and the vogue for family history, as reflected by BBC TV's *Who Do You Think You Are?* and the crash of the 1901 British census website in January 2002 after receiving 1.2 million hits per hour!

Using this framework readers should be able to compile similar lists for other countries, given the fact that – to quote Jörn Rüsen (2002: vii) – everywhere popular history has returned 'with a vengeance'. Thus, readers in the USA, where Princeton's Sean Wilentz (2001: 36) pointed to a 'new golden age of historical popularization', might list such examples as Independence Day, the Fourth of July; the popular histories of Stephen Ambrose, David McCullough and Jon Meacham; Ken Burns's television documentaries; the historical fiction of Jean Auel, Sharon Kay Penman and Jeff Shaara; family history programmes like *Faces of America with Henry Louis Gates, Jr.*; and the 50 million hits taken on its first day in April 2001 by Ellis Island's immigrant records website.

Historians' Worries

At the same time, the perceived need for the 'History Matters' campaign reflected genuine worries about history's place in a forward-looking digital age seemingly obsessed with the new and bereft of any sense of the long time frame (C. Anderson *et al.* 2006). Indeed, many present-day Britons, it is often argued, suffer from historical illiteracy, as evidenced by complaints made by David Cannadine (2008: 7) and Christopher Andrew (2004) about living in an 'increasingly amnesiac and ahistorical' society suffering from 'Historical Attention Span Deficit Disorder'. For Eric Hobsbawm (1995: 3), young people grow up 'in a sort of permanent present lacking any organic relation to the public past of the times they live in'. Nor is the problem confined to this side of either the Channel – Hobsbawm's comment was directed also at continental Europe – or the Atlantic, where Wilentz (2001: 38) criticised the lack of real historical substance to the popularisation process.

Indeed, in 2000 *Losing America's Memory: historical illiteracy in the 21st Century*, a report published by the American Council of Trustees and Alumni (2000: 1), pointed to the 'profound historical illiteracy' and 'collective amnesia' displayed by American college students about their national past. Despite scoring top marks for contemporary popular culture – 99 per cent correctly identified the cartoon figures, Beavis and Butt-Head – students displayed an 'alarming ignorance' about leading American historical personalities and events. Prompting presidential, congressional and media concern, the report encouraged the introduction of the federally funded 'Teaching American History' programme to improve the teaching of US history (Meléndez 2008).

There has been no comparable comprehensive British study, but occasional surveys have reaffirmed repeatedly that the position in Britain is no better, where Britons, especially the young, have displayed an appalling ignorance of the major landmarks and personalities in their country's history (Garner 2001; Leonard 2004). For example, one survey of 1600 state school pupils revealed that 36 per cent did not know who Winston Churchill was, as indicated by answers that he was an American president, even an insurance salesman (Burke and Wavell 1995)! The last response indicated greater exposure to television – Churchill Insurance was a frequent advertiser – than history teaching. Nor, according to recent reports (Rees 2010), have things improved.

Understanding the Problem

What reasons have been put forward to explain – to quote an editorial in the *Sunday Times* (1996) – why 'Britain's sense of history is a thing of the past'? Following Raphael Samuel (1999: 214–23), Britons' sense of the past, most notably their awareness of personal and national identities, is strongly influenced by school history. In part, therefore, history's problem results from its declining place in an over-loaded educational curriculum prioritising english, mathematics and science. In 2010 the

Historical Association (HA) (2010), a British organisation supporting the study and enjoyment of history, reported widespread evidence that history was being marginalised in secondary education, even becoming a virtual non-subject. Indeed, Ofsted (2011: 14), the Office for Standards in Education, Children's Services and Skills, reported that in 2010 only 20 per cent and 30 per cent of students in academies and state secondary schools respectively took history for GCSE (General Certificate of Secondary Education), the exam taken by 14–16-year-olds. Reportedly, many school managers, parents and pupils – to quote Ofsted (2007: 29) – 'do not perceive history as either relevant or important'. School history was viewed as 'too bookish', comparing unfavourably with the manner in which history was presented on television.

Moreover, even those opting to study history often left school with what Starkey (quoted, Jardine 2006) described as detached 'gobbets' of information focused excessively upon the Tudors and Nazi Germany. Starkey has proved critical also of the failure of teachers to present the subject in an exciting and engaging manner. Admittedly, history retains a prominent place in universities, but higher education's specialist nature means that students leaving school with little or no history lack any opportunity to fill their knowledge gap about the past. As mentioned in chapter six, in 2010 the new British Conservative-Liberal Democrat government began to grapple with the crisis affecting school history.

Nor is the situation helped by the failure of most historians to bridge the gap between academia and the lay public. Few Britons are exposed directly to the fruits of professional historians, most of whom have a low public profile and write principally for their fellow historians. The resulting lengthy, densely argued and heavily footnoted histories, rooted in historiographical debates and using a specialist vocabulary and jargon, are essential for an academic audience, but normally prove inaccessible for other readers. Reviewing John Walton's *The British Seaside: holidays and seaside resorts in the twentieth century* (2000) for the *Sunday Times*, Lynne Truss (2000) acknowledged its merits as a 'a worthy piece of popular culture scholarship', but highlighted the problem faced by a lay reader in taking on an academic history, even one promising 'so much in the way of narrative and fun'.

> Of straining canvas windbreaks and dazzling water, of burying dad in the sand and forgetting to dig him up, of accidentally trapping your arm in your deck chair. Ah, but that's not the real story of the British seaside, of course – not to a professor of social history who has built a career on Blackpool … So there is no candyfloss in this book? No whiff

of donkey saddle, no echo of steam-organ carousel music, no screams from the roller-coaster?

For Truss, whose prize-winning *Eats, Shoots & Leaves* (2003) sold more than three million copies, Walton offered 'bone-dry' passages, lengthy recitals of facts and figures, and unfriendly jargon focused upon the 'resort product cycle' and 'liminality' (transitional stage).

Walton gained national media visibility, but was unfortunate to be judged by reference to the perceived requirements of a popular audience rather than those of his target academic readership. By contrast, reviewers (Huggins 2002; Croll 2003) in academic journals commended Walton's presentation in terms of being based on in-depth research drawing upon political, economic, social and cultural perspectives, challenging the existing declinist historiography, and stressing the constant reinvention of the British seaside experience. For both Mike Huggins (2002: 235) and Jeffrey Richards (2000: vi), Walton's book was not only 'elegantly written' but also distinguished by its 'combination of scholarship and readability'.

Unsurprisingly, the current state of play in academia on specific historical topics, as presented by Walton and his fellow historians, rarely reaches the general public directly. This point is highlighted by the example of Neville Chamberlain, the British prime minister (1937-40) facing Hitler during the closing days of peace and the initial phase of the Second World War. Depicted negatively still in popular histories and the media as a 'Guilty Man' appeasing Hitler, Chamberlain is presented as bringing nearer the very war he had tried to prevent at Munich in 1938. By contrast, since the late 1960s the opening up of the archives led historians to present a far more sympathetic portrait of Chamberlain as peacemaker, most notably proving the victim of circumstances arising from Britain's overstretch and growing lack of power. But such revisionist texts made little or no impression upon the wider public, as evidenced by the continuing pejorative depiction of 'appeasement' and 'Munich' in contemporary political vocabulary (Beck 2006: 20–1). Pointing to the seemingly 'unbridgeable divide' between lay and historians' perceptions, David Dutton (2001: 191–2) conceded that 'the popular image of Neville Chamberlain is deeply ingrained, and it may well be that the historian is engaged in a losing battle if he thinks he is capable of changing it'.

In any case, as discussed in the next chapter, the lay audience has proved, and remains, a low priority for most academic historians. As a result, popular knowledge of the past is shaped largely by radio and television programme makers, filmmakers, journalists, museum curators, historical novelists and popular historians, who not only possess a very different agenda from that of academic historians but also demonstrate varying degrees of awareness of good historical practice and the latest scholarship. Simon Jenkins (2002) is prominent among those lamenting this trend:

> Popular history has boomed ... Histories and biographies jam best-seller lists. Starved of modern history at school, young people turn to books, television and movies, especially for knowledge of the recent past. They learn of the Great War from 'Birdsong' and of the Holocaust from 'Schindler's List'. For Normandy, they watch 'The Longest Day' and 'Saving Private Ryan'. For Vietnam they go to 'The Deerhunter' and 'Apocalypse Now'. For the death of Kennedy, heaven help them, they rely on 'JFK'. For Ireland they turn to 'In the Name of the Father' and 'The Crying Game'. Films give them history. Television gives them history. Old buildings give them history. Fiction gives them history. History gives them none.

The problem, Jenkins complained, is that such 'distorted, biased, glamorised and perverted' accounts are not really 'history', 'but to young people it is the closest that they get to the past'. An emerging concern centres upon the quality of accounts presented as history on the internet by multifarious contributors. Lacking any grasp of historical reference points, people are easily taken in by such accounts, which rarely deserve the descriptor 'history' at all regarding their mode of production, historical accuracy or presenters' qualifications.

The active role performed by heritage groups in the 'History Matters' campaign reflected the manner in which 'history' has become viewed increasingly as synonymous with 'heritage'. Organisations like English Heritage and the National Trust have proved remarkably successful in engaging public interest in the past by presenting 'the historic environment', defined as comprising material objects like country houses or Victorian kitchens and gardens, in an attractive and entertaining light as a kind of present-day 'anaesthetized theme park' (Snowman 2007: 5, 9–10). For historians, the resulting assimilation of past and present blurs the marked contrast between 'them' and 'us', thereby resulting in a flawed history. In 2010 Richard Overy (2010) followed Robert Hewison, the author of *The Heritage Industry* (1987), and John Tosh (2010: 17–19), among others, when warning historians about the serious threat posed to history's academic status by society's growing tendency to treat 'history' as 'heritage'. Pointing also to ongoing governmental attempts to enhance history's socio-economic utility, Overy feared that the subject's intellectual and scholarly impact no longer seemed to matter.

Conclusion

The 'History Matters' campaign highlighted contemporary Britons' ambivalence about history. As Tosh (2008a: 6) observed in *Why History Matters*, 'we are confronted by the paradox of a society which is immersed in the past yet detached from its history'. Present-day Britons, like their counterparts across the Atlantic or the Channel, give out mixed messages about history. Simultaneously valued, marginalised, and forgotten, at times history has even been rejected, as happened after 1997 when Blair's 'New Labour' government cast off much of the Labour Party's historical baggage, turned its back on the imperial past by refusing to fund the Museum of the British Empire and Commonwealth, and marked the millennium with a domed exhibition largely ignoring the national past.

Unsurprisingly, the sharpening debate about history's present-day role means that historians, though accepting the case for an improved interface with the wider public, have felt the constant need to articulate why history matters as an academic discipline. In particular, as Overy argued (2010), history must be neither treated as heritage studies nor subjected to the demands of the market place. In turn, the continued enhancement of history's academic credentials will provide a stronger base of historical expertise enabling historians to make what Peter Mandler (2002: 163) has described as 'a central contribution' to national life. Today's fast-moving world 'needs' historians in order not only to push back the frontiers of knowledge but also to act as society's memory providing roots, historical perspective, reference points, and a sense of personal and national identity. Moreover, 'thinking with history', Tosh (2008a: 142; 2008b) claimed, plays a crucial role in being an active citizen by 'exposing politically slanted myth, placing our concerns in more extended narratives, testing the limits of analogy, and above all showing how familiarity with the past can open the door to a broader sense of the possibilities in the present'.

In brief, people everywhere need historians to produce and present sound histories of their past. Of course, historians would be expected to say this, especially as history does not emerge automatically from the sources in a ready-made form. Rather 'the past' has to be researched, reconstructed, and then presented as 'history' in writing, orally or visually to present-day academic and/or general audiences. Required to link past and present as well as to encourage people to think historically, this presentational role makes historians – to quote Daniel Snowman (2007: 1, 13) – 'Very Important People' occupying centre stage in this book.

2
Presenting History in Academia

For A.J.P. Taylor (1950: v), the perennial difficulty facing any historian is 'the problem of presentation': 'The historian has to combine truth and literary grace; he fails as a historian if he is lacking in either.' As Taylor demonstrated better than most of his fellow historians, history is intended to be read, listened to or watched on screen. No historian wants the fruits of his or her labours to be ignored. For historians, therefore, the guiding maxim must be 'The better their history communicates to the target audience(s), the better it works as history.' Or, as Starkey (quoted, *Daily Telegraph* 2002) asserted, 'What matters is the product – the history, the writing, the big picture.' As Sir Charles Firth (1938: 29–30), Regius Professor of History at the University of Oxford (1904–25), advised, the historian needs to be far more than a skilful researcher:

> When a man puts his pen to paper and proceeds to print the result, he is attempting to convey his ideas to some other man. He presupposes the existence of a reader. It is therefore essential that he should arrange his ideas clearly, that he should state them so that they may be understood, and express them so that they may leave a lasting impression on the mind of the person to whom they are addressed. If he fails to achieve this, he has done only half of his work. Thus, the historian's task is two-fold: he has first of all to find out the truth ... and then to state the truth for the information of other people.

Against this background, this chapter studies the presentation of history in academia.

Presenting 'the Past' as 'History'

Despite employed frequently to describe what actually happened in 'the past', strictly speaking 'history' should be defined as the representation of 'the past' by historians: 'what historians write *is* history' (Marwick 2001: 29). Or rather, to quote Arthur Marwick (1989: 13) again, 'History is the past as we know it from the interpretations of historians based on the critical study of the widest possible range of relevant sources, every effort having been made to challenge, and avoid the perpetuation of, myth'. For Tosh (2010: 1–2, 6–12), presenters must possess also 'historical aware-ness' in terms of:

1.   acknowledging the 'otherness' of 'the past'. Rather than being viewed through present-day spectacles, 'the past' should be treated as – to follow L.P. Hartley's often quoted phrase in *The Go-Between* (1953) – 'a foreign country' where people did things differently;
2.   studying 'the past' in its distinctive contemporary context; and
3.   recognising the nature of the historical process over time, particu-larly the continuities and discontinuities of 'the past'.

'The past' is dead and gone for good. As a result, we can neither view the past through a glass window, an impression encouraged by museum exhibits, nor use Hollywood-type time machines to travel back in time. The gulf separating past and present can only be bridged, historians argue, by the use of sound historical methodology. During the late nine-teenth century professionalisation radically reshaped history on both sides of the Atlantic. Seeking to establish the subject in universities as an academic discipline, historians followed Leopold von Ranke in pressing the need for a rigorous research-based methodology. Rejecting the long-standing emphasis upon a usable past, they studied the past in its own terms to show '*wie es eigentlich gewesen*' [author's note: as it actually was]. Eschewing narrative for a more analytical approach, historians, who were usually employed henceforth in universities, prioritised writing specialist, fully referenced histories for professional colleagues, not a wider public.

Key questions raised about the work of historians include:

1. why do historians disagree?
2. how theoretical are historians' presentations?
3. do historians present the absolute truth?
4. do historians present definitive histories?
5. are historians' presentations objective?

Why Do Historians Disagree?

Despite admitting that much had been learned about the coming of war in 1914, Samuel Williamson, Jr and Ernest May (2007: 386–7) conceded that even nearly one century on 'we will never know everything, and we will probably never achieve 'identity of opinion,' but we keep clarifying the relevant questions and issues – and that is, after all, the essence of the scholarly enterprise'. As a result, as stated by William Lamont (1998: xiii), 'we should look to it [history] for contribution to debate rather than for the transmission of certainties'. Notwithstanding the unity implied by the term 'history', the historical profession is far from representing a homogenous group sharing a common approach to the past, let alone an agreed view thereof. Perhaps the only thing historians can agree about is their propensity to disagree with each other. Get six historians together, and you must expect at least seven different viewpoints!

But why do historians disagree? Basically, the answer comes down to the subject's dependence upon individual historians, who construct, revise and present history in the light of their own attitudes, time and experiences. In this sense, as Benedetto Croce claimed, all history is contemporary. Historians, even those studying the same problem and having access to the same evidence, will always struggle to produce an agreed presentation thereof. Evidence will be processed, ordered, interpreted and presented in contrasting ways by different historians. There are, and will be – to quote Raphael Samuel (1991) – 'always competing histories' of the same event, just as rival football fans will have contrasting opinions about any referee.

Viewing the past in varying ways coloured by a range of conscious and unconscious assumptions and preoccupations, history's presenters are individual products of their respective backgrounds (Cannadine 1987: 169–91). Key influences include:

- **personal factors** – class, education, gender, generation, political affiliation, race and religion;
- **grasp of historical skills** –
  - literary and verbal capabilities, most notably an ability to communicate clearly in writing and/or orally;
  - an eye for detail;
  - mastery of sources, including an ability to perceive the relatedness of events and to abstract patterns from complex, frequently contradictory, evidence;
  - critical acumen;

- capacity to engage imaginatively with the mentality and atmosphere of the past;
- and linguistic, quantitative and ICT skills;
- **geography** – varying local, regional, national and global perspectives;
- **context** – the world in which the historian grew up and lives;
- **theoretical position** – e.g. empirical, feminist, Marxist, postmodernist, etc.;
- **hindsight bias** – knowing what happened next renders it tempting
  to see successive events as part of one continuing trend rather than
  as a series of disconnected one-off moves.

Unsurprisingly, E.H. Carr (2001: 38) advised, 'Before you study the
history, study the historian ... Before you study the historian, study his
historical and social environment.' Regarding Holocaust history, Don
Guttenplan (2002: 68) pointed to the prudence of checking 'a historian's known prejudices, political engagements, and sources of funding'.
Looking back to the novel way in which his book *The Fatal Environment:
the myth of the frontier in the age of industrialization, 1800–1890* (1985)
focused on black troops and Pennsylvania coalminers, not the political
and economic elites, Richard Slotkin (2005: 223) conceded that:

> I brought to the study a historical consciousness that had been
> formed by the political and social upheavals of the 1960s, and the
> new revisionist forms of history writing developed between 1965
> and 1973. In particular, the 'New Social History' had made visible to
> historians the lives, beliefs, words and thoughts of those 'invisible
> classes' who make history 'from the bottom up'.

There is a need also to allow for switches of direction through any career.
Historians change, as does the contextual framework within which they
work. For example, chapters 8 and 9 record the mid-career postmodernist conversions of Joan Wallach Scott and Robert A. Rosenstone,
respectively. Likewise, living through the 1989–91 Revolutions led Eric
Hobsbawm to reshape radically his history of the twentieth century
published as the *Age of Extremes* (1994).

Traditionally, historians have drawn their professional ideas and
beliefs from empiricism, the view that historical knowledge is derived
from experience or observation. Thus, most historians employ the
empirical methodology, which involves:

1. identifying the nature of the problem under investigation, the project's
   aims, possible hypotheses for investigation, and the target audience(s);

2. undertaking a literature review to survey the existing historiography, that is, what historians have already written on the topic;
3. conducting the research:
   - finding and selecting relevant primary and/or secondary sources;
   - treating the evidence in a critical and sceptical manner by testing the authenticity of sources; making and checking translations; disrupting mythologies; dealing with fragmentary, imperfect and contradictory evidence;
   - using critical and analytical skills to arrive at a balanced, accurate and reasoned interpretation of the evidence regarding the problem being studied – what happened, how, why and with what consequences; relating findings to initial hypotheses and existing historiography;
4. presenting the findings to an audience in writing, orally and/or visually;
5. impacting upon the topic's historiography by providing new knowledge, fresh perspectives or a revised synthesis supporting, undermining or conflicting with existing interpretations;
6. contributing to popular historical knowledge directly and/or indirectly through other presenters.

Although the whole question of presentation is ideologically positioned and underpinned by long-running philosophical controversies, most historians prove reluctant to describe what they do as theorising. Rather they prefer a looser descriptor, like historian's method or craft, possibly involving little more than the formulation of a hypothesis along the lines of, say, the Turner thesis about the frontier in American history or the Fischer thesis about Germany's *Weltpolitik* ambitions in 1914 (Marwick 2001: 88–9, 105–6).

How Theoretical Are Historians' Presentations?

For Keith Jenkins (1991: 2; 1997: 1), history is 'theoretically backward', particularly as compared to the natural and social sciences. As mentioned above, most historians, though prepared to reflect upon the nature of their craft, prove reluctant theorisers, given their apparent unwillingness to subscribe to a system of ideas shaping and ordering a series of complex relationships between facts or phenomena over time and space. Denouncing theorisers as 'devilish tempters', Geoffrey Elton (1991: 41; G. Roberts 1998: 29) wrote about the nature of history more as an account of what working historians did, not as philosophy.

Viewing philosophical speculation as doing little to help, perhaps even hindering, the historical process, most historians prefer to practise history rather than to debate its nature because of:

• the perceived problem of applying abstract theory to a humanities subject concerned with real people, not natural phenomena;
• the tendency for theory to be imposed upon the past through a 'pick-and-mix' approach looking back selectively through present-day spectacles at events detached from their specific historical context;
• the belief that history's role is to explain the past, not to project trends over time in a deterministic manner, making no allowance for accidents and contingencies; and
• the alleged failure of theory to make sense when actually applied to the past.

Hugh Trevor-Roper pointed to the fundamental problem. Looking back in 1981 to his student days at Oxford in the 1930s, Trevor-Roper (1981b: 358–9; Sisman 2010: 202) recalled one tutor extolling the virtues of Marxist history:

He explained that, theoretically, it should be possible to discover the objective laws of historical change, and that the way to test such laws, once discovered, was to see whether they enabled one to predict the next stage in the historical process. The Marxist interpretation, he assured us, had survived this test: it had predicted the course of events since Marx's own time with remarkable accuracy; and therefore it could now be regarded as scientifically valid ... this was what impressed me most. The vast pageant of history, hitherto so indeterminate, so formless, so mysterious, now had, as it seemed, a beautiful, mechanical regularity, and modern science had supplied a master-key which, with a satisfying click, would turn in every lock, open all its dark chambers, and reveal all its secret workings. This was very exciting.

But for Trevor-Roper, Marxist theory failed to live up to the hype: 'Unfortunately, when I began to apply the key, I soon encountered some difficulties ... I found it difficult to accept the authority of Marxist historical science.' As indicated in chapter 4, A.J.P. Taylor underwent a similar transformation. By contrast, Hobsbawm (chapter 5) remained loyal to Marx, whose ideas impacted also upon Joan W. Scott (chapter 8) and Philippa Gregory (chapter 10).

More recently, postmodernism lent a new sharpness to this issue. Drawing heavily upon literary theory and cultural studies, particularly the thinking of Jacques Derrida and Michel Foucault, postmodernists launched a serious epistemological [author's note: questioning the nature and validity of historical knowledge], intellectual and methodological challenge to prevailing historical practices. Pointing to the manner in which historians present the past in a literary form, they claimed that the production of history was comparable to that of any other literary output, including works of fiction. Thus, historians were viewed as performing essentially an imaginative literary task. Treating texts as 'discourses' unencumbered by a single fixed meaning, postmodernists argued that there could be no 'true' objective account of the past, but merely an infinitely flexible combination of 'discourses' created by historians as imaginative writers rather than objective researchers (Munslow 2006: 191–4; W. Thompson 2004: 6–26). The resulting 'cultural turn' – another common descriptor is 'linguistic turn' – led both primary sources and historians' presentations to be dismissed as subjective literary constructs, as recorded by Evans (1998: 29): 'In the postmodernist world, meanings are shifting and uncertain, truth unattainable, objectivity a meaningless concept.'

Attracting support from historians in both Britain and North America, such as from Keith Jenkins, Alun Munslow, Joan W. Scott (chapter 8) and Robert Rosenstone (chapter 9), postmodernism proved influential in certain specialisms like cultural history and women's history (Eley 2005: 122–33). Conversely, its challenge prompted strong hostility in some quarters. Indeed, historians like Hobsbawm (1998: vii) and Marwick (1995: 29) felt compelled to go public, confront postmodernists as a serious menace to historical study, and spell out hitherto unarticulated assumptions about practising history through an accepted methodology focused upon people, not abstract discourses. Another target for critics was what Niall Ferguson (1997b) described as postmodernism's 'impenetrable jargon' and obscurantism. For some today, as claimed by Simon Gunn (2006: 189–93), cultural theory's moment has passed.

In reality, historians, even those least philosophically minded, cannot write history – to quote John Warren (1998: iv) – 'without taking a stance, implicit or explicit, on what history actually is, and what it is for'. Inevitably, the way in which historians present the past reflects, to varying degrees, their views about history's nature, methodology and purpose. Thus, historians subscribing to, say, feminist, Marxist or postcolonial theories will shape and impart meaning to the past very differently from each other, just as responses from readers, reviewers, listeners and viewers to any history will be influenced by not only their own attitudes but also their awareness of the presenter's perceived stance. Whereas some readers will be drawn towards histories authored by, say, a Marxist historian, those of a right-wing disposition might deliberately avoid them.

In this sense, 'all history is theoretical' (K. Jenkins 1991: 70), even if some approaches prove more theoretical than others. History may appear 'an undertheorised discipline' (S. Davies 2003: 1–6, 126–9), but even the empirical method outlined above and favoured by most academic historians is underpinned by theory, in the sense that their histories are constructed and presented around preconceived ideas and assumptions about studying the past through the sources using an accepted Rankean-influenced approach. As Sue Morgan (2006a: 3) observed, 'All history-writing is therefore intrinsically theoretical because it cannot escape being artificially organised; formulated through particular intellectual explanatory frameworks or epistemologies (theories of knowledge).'

Do Historians Present the Absolute Truth?

Historical research should be conducted with an open mind, with interpretations following from the evidence. Any initial hypothesis should be capable of amendment, even replacement, in the light of research. In fact, history is often used and abused, most notably by governments, pressure groups and their supporters. Just as 'there are lies, damned lies and statistics', so 'history' is capable of being squeezed, even invented, to fit a *predetermined conclusion* supportive of a present-day cause, like Scottish (Trevor-Roper 2008) and Welsh nationalism (P. Morgan 1992: 43–100), or government policy. For instance, the Argentine and Iraqi governments deployed the past as part of their case for invading the Falklands/Malvinas (Beck 1988: 61–81) and Kuwait (Yapp 1990) in 1982 and 1990, respectively.

Falling well short of good practice, the resulting purposive accounts exploiting the power of the historian's pen must be dismissed as propaganda, not 'history'. Nor, as implied by such accounts, is history a simple matter of being right or wrong. Historical studies are bound to be grey, not black and white, in nature, given the limitations imposed by gaps in the evidence or rules preventing access to government records for 30 years. Recently, in 2010 the British government announced plans to move to a less restrictive 20-year rule. Despite claims to the contrary, it is difficult to accept the absolute truths proclaimed by invented histories. Indeed, any history promising historical truth must be treated with extreme caution. Rather, one needs to stress the relative accuracy of any history, even concerning topics attracting a vast literature. Looking back in 2007 at 'the enormous literature' on the origins of the First World War, Williamson and May (2007: 386–7) concluded that 'large uncertainties still exist': 'We still have little understanding of most of the major decision makers ... we are still very far from being clear as to what men in power understood to be happening, why they thought it mattered, or how they assessed their action choices.'

Do Historians Present Definitive Histories?

Moreover, any historian's presentation should be treated as merely interim in character, subject to constant re-evaluation tending either to reaffirm existing interpretations or to advance alternative views, which then take over as the accepted line, subject to further challenge. Historians move constantly towards a definitive conclusion through a continuing process of revisionism, but without ever actually arriving there.

Why is history, in effect – to quote Pieter Geyl (1964: 15–16) – an 'argument without end'? Carr (2001: 24) famously depicted history as an unending dialogue between past and present. Despite static images, history proves a dynamic subject. Thus, it is often said that God cannot change the past, but historians can. Of course, 'the past' itself does not change. What changes over time and between countries are the historians' representations of the past, which is constantly being viewed from new perspectives and alternative vantage points. Just as, at any one time, each nation looks at the past differently, so each generation writes and presents its own history. Moreover, as Hobsbawm (1998: vii) admitted, historians often display a combative nature when dealing with each other's writings; indeed, for some – today Niall Ferguson (chapter 7) is seen as following in A.J.P. Taylor's (chapter 4) footsteps – going against the conventional historical tide proves a prime career motivator.

Revisionism reflects also the changing focus of historians, who like Hobsbawm (chapter 5) and Scott (chapter 8) have looked increasingly beyond political elites to study the people – these include workers, women, the colonised, or the subalterns – previously marginalised by, even excluded from, the historical record. In turn, the availability of fresh evidence, resulting from, say, archival releases or Freedom of Information (FOI) requests, published memoirs, or oral testimony, ensures that the door to the past is never closed. Finally, the computer, the internet and carbon dating highlight the impact of new techniques and methodologies, such as in terms of creating vast databases, accessing sources, or dating and authenticating evidence.

Are Historians' Presentations Objective?

Let us begin by posing (but leaving you to answer) the following questions by way of background:

* How far can Marxist historians present sound histories of the labour movement or right-wing governments?
* Was Elton (1986) correct when asserting that 'the best women's history is written by men'?
* How far can Scottish historians present an unbiased history of Scotland, given George Gömöri's (1985: 7) claim that 'each nation interprets its own history and the history of its neighbours in the manner most advantageous to itself'?
* Was Fernand Braudel (1988: 15) right to argue that only French historians were capable of writing a history of France? Or, following Richard Evans (1997: 214), is French history too important to be left to the French?

Despite acknowledging the subjectivity displayed by many historians, Elton (1986) argued that objective history – in brief, an account unaffected by prejudice, bias, or wishful thinking – was not only possible but also the preferred goal. But for many historians, history's reliance upon interpretation introduces a personal element fostering subjectivity. Historians might claim to act in a detached and balanced manner, but no presentation 'is proof against the values of the enquirer' (Tosh 2010: 50). As Hobsbawm (quoted, Elliott 2010: 103) conceded, 'all of us inevitably write out of the history of our own times when we look at the past and, to some extent, fight the battles of today in period costume'. Unsurprisingly, postmodernism's uncertainties gave renewed momentum to this controversy.

Writing History

There are several alternative ways – these include radio and television programmes, films, lectures and conference papers – of reaching an audience, but for most historians, particularly those targeting an academic readership, the act of writing is central to their work.

Writing enables historians to record and make sense of their research; process thoughts about the problem under investigation; identify interconnections, discontinuities and gaps in the work to date; and present their findings to an audience. In particular, written composition proves 'more precise' (Kershaw 2008) than verbal communication. Inevitably, the impact of any history, no matter how well researched, will depend in part upon the quality of presentation, which is determined by far more than sound historical methodology and referencing. Literary style is vital, since written presentations are expected to be well organised, structured and ordered; clearly focused, relevant and coherent; and most importantly engaging and readable. Even so, Cannadine (2002: xi), Tosh (2010: 149) and Wilentz (2001: 36), among other historians, continue to complain that too much unreadable history written in dismal prose or impenetrable jargon is being published on both sides of the Atlantic, particularly by scholars working in what Dominic Sandbrook (2007) called 'a jargon-spouting ghetto'.

Box 2.1 outlines the three main literary modes for presenting history: description; narrative; and critical analysis (Judd 1997: 2–9; Marius 1999: 49–71). For certain types of history, most notably demographic, economic and social history, a quantitative approach may prove preferable, even if a literary format is required still to explain datasets and charts.

In practice, the three modes of historical writing, though different from each other, tend to be complementary, and all are often used in any one study. Whereas description and narrative help to re-create the past at any one period and over time, analysis is important for the purposes of exposition, explanation, discussion, interpretation and argument. Much academic historical writing today is characterised by the flexible use of analytical and narrative modes, 'sometimes in alternating sections, sometimes more completely fused throughout the text' (Tosh 2010: 158). Claiming that the three forms differ in purpose and manner, not quality, Elton (2002: 109; G. Roberts 2001: 133) preferred 'narratives thickened by analysis', stories of human activities over time punctuated by in-depth discussion and explanation. Even so, one type of writing is likely to predominate. Whereas academic historians incline towards a critical analytical approach, the writers of popular histories rely more heavily upon description and narrative. Furthermore, language and grammatical style differ. Employing shorter sentences and simpler words, popular historians avoid the academic jargon and terminology criticised by Truss (chapter 1): 'the scaffolding of scholarship is pared down to a minimum. Documentation and analysis are less rigorous' (Tosh 2008b).

Referencing

This book is referenced according to the Harvard system, where sources are cited in a bracket inserted in the text, as happens with the Grafton

---

Box 2.1   Presenting history in writing

1. Description
   - describes what people, events and developments in the past were like through an account of sensory experiences, that is, the way things and events looked, felt, tasted, sounded and smelt or people looked, spoke, moved or acted;
   - requires literary style, including an eye for detail and imaginative powers to cover gaps in the evidence;
   - proves less helpful in showing the passage of time or why things happened and with what consequences.

2. Narrative
   - relates the complex sequence of events as they happened one after another, thereby offering readers a sense of continuity and change through time alongside an awareness of the role of chance and accident;
   - offers an engaging story representing something more than 'one darn fact after another', possibly by establishing some kind of tension to encourage readers to read on to see what happened next and at the end;
   - proves less effective in indicating either structural factors, the relationship between complex events, or why things happened and with what consequences.

3. Analysis
   - presents an ordered, reasoned, informed and relevant critical account about specific historical problems;
   - presses a definite line of argument regarding points of controversy;
   - identifies the significance of events and offers a coherent exposition of the causation, context and connectedness of events over time;
   - takes forward the historiography by reaffirming or challenging existing viewpoints;
   - needs added narrative to provide an appreciation of the sequencing and unpredictability of events.

---

reference later in this paragraph. Alternative styles employ footnotes or endnotes. Referencing, including the use of quotation marks for attributing quotes, developed as a literary device employed to enhance the credibility and authority of historical writing as an inductive and empirically grounded procedure (Grafton 1999: 4–24; 143; AHA 2005). In addition, it protects historians against accusations of plagiarism, that is, the unattributed use of someone else's prose. However, for postmodernists, like Alun Munslow (2006: 35), the 'massive empiricist overkill in the footnotes' merely dupes readers to believe that historians' presentations offer something more than mere literary constructs.

Referencing remains a vital presentational requirement for historical monographs, journal articles and higher-degree theses, enabling readers and reviewers to place any academic history in the existing historiography as well as 'to repeat and verify the process through which the knowledge in question was constituted' (Feldner 2003: 14–15). As Stephen Davies (2003: 29) recorded:

> The point of the citation was that any reader could follow the 'directions' given in the footnote to the *precise* source for the statement being made. They could then judge for themselves whether the statement was justified. This was one of the things that made it possible for scholars to check each other and to correct their mistakes or misinterpretations, an essential element of the cumulative growth of knowledge.

In effect, 'scholarship came to be measured out in footnotes' (Ferguson 1999: 218). Normally those writing for an audience outside academia avoid referencing, but the lack thereof should not necessarily be viewed as compromising the academic integrity or authority of such histories.

Do Not Forget the Audience

Nor can any presenter, even those accustomed to a captive academic audience, overlook the target readership, whose nature and interests prove a prime concern for any publisher. Indeed, Leslie Howsam (2009: 5–6, 100) has recorded the crucial, albeit often overlooked, role of publishers and editors in bringing 'a good deal of influence' to bear upon any history from initial conception to publication.

Quite apart from being produced in an appropriate historical manner, history must be presented in a form accessible to the intended audience(s), and hence judged at least in part by its effectiveness in reaching and exerting meaningful impacts thereupon. Despite claims by Elton (2002: 105–7) and Hobsbawm (1962: xv; 1987: xi) that any written history should be capable of reaching diverse audiences, most historians and publishers accept the need to target readers more precisely, as recorded by Tosh (2008b): 'Writing for one's peers and writing for a non-specialist readership are two different registers.'

Notwithstanding this book's focus upon presenters, the audience, though extremely difficult to identify, let alone to research, cannot be totally ignored. After all both the presenter's approach and success in communicating history are influenced by the audience's nature, expectations and response. Indeed, as recorded in Part II, broadcasters and filmmakers judge the success of television histories and Hollywood films by reference to media coverage, audience ratings and box-office returns, not historical standards. For publishers of historical novels, sales figures, lending-library data and film rights prove paramount. Nor, as stressed by Antony Beevor (chapter 3), Philippa Gregory (chapter 10) and Simon Schama (chapter 6), should presenters ignore the varying nature of audiences over time.

Whatever one's views about postmodernism, history's 'cultural turn' pointed to the need also to study the audience in the light of ongoing debates about whether meaning is inherent in the presenter's text and/or created by audiences. Stressing the active role performed by readers in creating textual meaning – readers are viewed as free to treat any historical text as an imaginary literary construct whose meaning remains open to diverse, even subversive, readings – postmodernism challenged what Munslow (2006: 37–8, 84, 207) has described as the 'take-it-or-leave-it' attitude fostered by empirical histories.

Unsurprisingly, the profession's aversion to theory in general and postmodernism in particular means that most historians – notable exceptions include Jonathan Rose (2002: 1–7) and Reba Soffer (2009: 1–39, 303–5), who have studied working-class and conservative audiences, respectively – have shown little or no interest in taking on this message. Nor have they been attracted by audience and reception theory, which focuses upon the interaction between written/visual texts and readers/viewers. However, such theory, as articulated in film studies publications and journals, reminds presenters that their 'histories' are not accepted passively by any audience. Indeed, as argued by Stuart Hall (1980: 128–38), audiences, influenced by a range of personal, political, economic, social and cultural factors, exhibit varying reactions when consuming and decoding any history. Whereas some readers might accept the presenter's viewpoint, or a part thereof, others might reject his/her reading of the past. Alternatively, the text might never reach the target audience, and remain largely unread or unseen.

Conclusion

Most historians will continue to talk principally to each other, not the general public. Indeed, for Richard Overy (2010), this remains the preferred future objective, given both his anxiety to protect history as an academic discipline and belief that popular history is a very different beast from academic history. Despite denying any wish for historians to turn their backs on a public audience, Overy advised that 'the reference points for the historian must remain the intellectual framework within which research is generated and the body of academic opinion at which it is directed'.

By contrast, Gordon Wood (2010) described academic history writing, the type of presentation favoured by Overy, as in a state of crisis: 'Historical monographs pour from the university presses ... and yet have very few readers.' Most people, it seemed, are not interested in reading history, at least not the history written by academic historians, and yet the latter proved reluctant to write the more readable and accessible popular histories that the general public apparently wanted to read. Rejecting a narrow vision of historians' target audience, Wood wondered whether academic historians have forgotten that there is, as claimed by the late Samuel Eliot Morison, the bestselling Harvard historian, an art to writing history, let alone ever fully appreciated either the need or the way to capture and hold an audience. In part, this problem reflects the fact that hitherto the numerous publications about the nature of history have devoted far less attention to presentation, most notably how to engage and retain the interest of diverse audiences, than to the other stages of the historical process.

Within academia there has been little systematic effort to consider why and how to present history in popular and/or non-written formats. Despite the rapid growth of alternative forms of presentation and frequent claims that historians should target a wider readership outside academia, the historical profession continues to prioritise presenting the past to fellow academics through articles, chapters, monographs, and higher-degree dissertations. Writing such specialist histories judged in terms of academic originality, significance and rigour is regarded still as history's gold standard, even if the resulting outcomes accessed principally through university libraries reach only a narrow captive audience of academics and students plus a very limited readership outside academia. Of course, for Overy, among others, this is not seen necessarily as a problem, given history's character as an academic discipline and the accumulative nature of historical knowledge. Indeed, Wood (2010), though urging historians to reach out from the ivory tower, conceded the continued value of academic histories in extending historical knowledge and understanding.

Also, it might be argued that the derivative nature of popular history means that academic historians often reach a lay audience indirectly, since their publications provide essential building blocks for those conducting research for history feature films, historical novels, popular histories and television documentaries. Indeed, the historical quality of such popular histories is largely a function of the extent to which reference has been made to relevant recent academic histories. Nor, according to Roy Rosenzweig (2011: 6–7), should we overlook the impact of modern digital technologies upon 'the ancient practice of history' in terms of not only conducting research and word processing but also rethinking modes of presentation and access to audiences. Pointing to the way in which online resources like Google Scholar and JSTOR's digital archive have made historical monographs and scholarly journals suddenly more accessible within and outside academia, Rosenzweig identified an ongoing 'fundamental paradigm shift from a culture of scarcity to a culture of abundance': 'the Internet has dramatically expanded and, hence, blurred our audiences'.

Strong support for peer review – whether in approving research for publication, reviewing publications, or conducting periodic research assessment exercises – highlights the historical profession's belief in focusing upon research quality rather than quantitative impact measures, such as citation counts [author's note: the number of times a publication is cited by other authors], book sales or journal circulations. Of course, there is no reason why any academic history should not attract a wide audience and become a bestseller, as happened to Paul Kennedy's *The Rise and Fall of the Great Powers: economic change and military conflict from 1500 to 2000* (1988). His book was very long, totalling 678 pages, and included over 80 pages of endnotes! But perhaps serendipitously the topic struck a contemporary chord, arising from western angst about the implications of the continuing rise and fall of the major powers, most notably American concerns that the USA was entering a period of decline relative to the rapid emergence of Japan and China. As discussed in chapter 12, Michael Bellesiles's *Arming America: the origins of a national gun culture* (2000), though allegedly aimed at an academic audience, also attracted a large public audience by impacting upon the ongoing debate about gun rights in the USA. Alternatively, as stressed in the next chapter, academic historians, particularly those anxious to enhance public knowledge and understanding of the past, have specifically targeted a popular readership.

3
Reaching Out to a Popular Audience

Written histories remain still a favoured format for popular histories. However, during recent decades the visual media have become – or so Robert A. Rosenstone (1995: 3; 2007a: 13) claimed – 'the chief carrier of historical messages in our culture', particularly when presenting the past to a general audience. Indeed, the makers of history films and television histories have often represented themselves as rescuing history from scholars reluctant to take their subject outside academia. For Ken Burns (quoted, Thelen 1994: 1032; Cripps 1995: 742–3), the American documentary filmmaker discussed in chapter 6, the historical profession's adoption of the Rankean model 'really spelled the end of popular history' as far as most academic historians were concerned: 'Somewhere along the line our history has been murdered by an academic academy dedicated to communicating only with itself and unconcerned not only with how one wrote, that is to say, the art of writing history, but also who was listening.' Over time the resulting gap has been filled by Burns, among others, presenting varying forms of popular history. Unsurprisingly, most, if not all, formats struggle to satisfy academic historians in terms of ticking all the boxes for treatment as proper 'history'. As Justin Champion (2003: 154–5) commented about history feature films, historians would like to fill the screen with 'verbal footnotes and narrative-clogging qualifications'.

Public History

During recent decades 'public history' has proved a significant growth area. In the USA 'public history', centred upon 'the core concept of public engagement by historians' making the past accessible and useful to the public (Babal 2010: 79; Beck 1983: 13; Tyrrell 2005: 153–69), dates back at least to the late 1970s, if not much earlier. By contrast, in Britain a strong focus on 'public history', defined by Ludmilla Jordanova (2000: 20) 'to include all the means, deliberate and otherwise, through which those who are not professional historians acquire their sense of the past', emerged more recently (Jordanova 2006: 126–49; Hoock 2010: 7–19). Key indicators include the series of conferences following the 2001 Royal Historical Society Conference on Historians and their Publics; the History & Policy website; MAs in Public History at Ruskin College, Oxford, and Royal Holloway, University of London; and the University of York's Institute for the Public Understanding of the Past (IPUP).

Despite public history's seemingly novel nature, history has a lengthy track record in addressing a wider audience, even if the Rankean professionalisation of the subject led academia to marginalise this role until recent decades. Thus, Schama (1993: 23–4; Gewertz 2001), a prominent advocate and practitioner of public history, has frequently made the point by citing such examples as Herodotus and Thucydides communicating historical knowledge to civic elites in ancient Greece, or Thomas Macaulay and Thomas Carlyle presenting history to the nineteenth-century reading public. In this vein, Cannadine (2008: 7), Champion (2008: 171–2) and Tosh (2008a; 2010: 148) view any failure in public communication as an abdication from historians' claims to social relevance, such as in terms of preserving public memory, overcoming the tyranny of present-mindedness, participating in public debate, offering an informed historical perspective on today's world, and confronting mythologies.

Arthur Marwick (2001: 32, 85) articulated a clear belief in the historian's public role: 'The closer the contact between the history of the historians and the history that is widely diffused, the greater the awareness of how history actually comes to be written, the better .... It is also necessary that what is already known should be widely known.' For Marwick, George Macaulay Trevelyan offered a good example of an academic populariser treating historical study as citizenship training. Indeed, Trevelyan (1968: 152) reminded his Cambridge colleagues that 'if historians neglect to educate the public, if they fail to interest it intelligently in the past, then all their historical learning is valueless except in so far as it educates themselves'. David Cannadine's (1992: 226) biography highlighted Trevelyan's role as the great communicator leading by example to present history to both academic and popular audiences, with *English Social History* (1942) selling over half a million copies.

Over time, Trevelyan's thinking about historians' essential public function, for him their prime justification, has been echoed by not only Cannadine himself (1987: 176–8) but other historians, like Taylor (chapter 4). Trevor-Roper (1981a: 8) warned colleagues not to lose touch with 'the laity', the non-professional audience, or else they were 'condemned to perish'. Schama (2001c; 2010a: 142–5), like John Burrow (2007: 475–8), pointed to the influential role performed by John Plumb in passing on Trevelyan's view of history as 'a public craft', not 'arid scholasticism':

> From the beginning of his career to its end he [Plumb] never wavered from the view that history's vocation might begin in the academy, but it should not end there; that as an illumination of the human condition, the 'interpreter of its destiny', it was too important to be confined to the intra-mural disputes of the professionals.

Notwithstanding a fundamental professional reluctance to cater for any audience other than their peers, many of Plumb's students at Cambridge continued his legacy in their own distinctive ways. Thus, several former students – apart from Burrow and Schama, these included David Cannadine, Linda Colley, Niall Ferguson, Roy Porter, Quentin Skinner, Norman Stone and John Vincent – have been prominent in reaching out from academia to a wider public with boldly conceived, carefully researched and elegantly written histories attracting a substantial readership within and outside academia and achieving critical and commercial success.

The Challenge of Writing Popular History

Frequent exhortations urging academic historians to write for a popular readership overlook the nature of the challenge. First, personal preferences, professional and career expectations, and research assessment pressures combine to ensure that academic history writing remains the prime focus for most historians working in academia. Protective of their academic status and 'intellectual ownership of the discipline' (Champion 2003: 155), they prove reluctant to follow in the footsteps of Trevelyan, Plumb and company. In particular, reaching out beyond academia always raises the risk of being accused of 'dumbing down', since there remains – to quote Tosh (2008b; 2010: 162) – 'much snobbish disparagement of those who write for the general reader'. Within academia popular histories are frequently stigmatised as 'journalistic' or 'coffee-table books' diluting historical standards and falling well short of proper history.

Secondly, the presentational style adjudged essential for popular histories – media descriptors of a history as 'academic' imply that it is boring, even unreadable, as far as a popular audience is concerned – makes special demands in the sphere of descriptive and narrative writing beyond the reach and/or inclinations of many academic historians. For example, the *BBC History Magazine* (Origin Publishing 2005) instructs authors 'to engage and inform, and provide an accessible read, without of course talking down to the reader at any time', or making assumptions about readers' knowledge. Looking back to his bestselling biography of Hitler (2008), Kershaw (2008) admitted that 'literary flourishes, often displayed through colorful adjectives, are difficult to combine with exact historical scholarship'. Even a banal sentence, such as 'It was a hot sunny day as Hitler's train pulled out of the Pomeranian railway station', introduced to give the story colour, could not be written without checking that day's weather bulletin.

Thirdly, popular history requires academic historians to cater for an extraordinarily diverse audience within and outside academia, including many people who have little or no existing historical knowledge. As Truss's review (chapter 1) indicated, it is never easy to make research-based publications accessible to diverse audiences. What is expected, indeed demanded, by an academic readership will often appear abstruse, jargonistic and incomprehensible when viewed as public history. Quantitative histories introduce yet another potential barrier, particularly for readers lacking ICT, mathematical and statistical skills. For presenters, a fine balance needs to be achieved in terms of going far enough towards the perceived needs of a lay audience, but not so far as to alienate an academic audience. Reviewing *The Second Crusade: extending the frontiers of Christendom* (2007), Susan Edgington (2009) questioned whether Jonathan Phillips's 'scholarly and well-researched' monograph had achieved the professed aim 'to relate the story of the crusade in an accessible fashion': 'I certainly found some of the densely detailed passages hard to assimilate, and I suspect this may apply to a general readership too. There is probably still room for a "popular" history of the Second Crusade.'

Finally, for academic historians achieving success as a public historian, the resulting pressures of book-a-year deadlines can result – critics have pointed to the example of Stephen Ambrose (chapter 12), among others – in a temptation to cut corners and infringe historical standards. Moreover, the financial rewards and public recognition resulting from success as a public historian can be guaranteed to bring out the worst in any historian's professional colleagues.

Academic Historians and Popular Histories

For Tosh (2010: 150, 333), the recent revival of readable popular history written by academic historians has been spearheaded by a few 'accomplished communicators', most notably Hobsbawm, Schama and Starkey. However, in Tosh's view, 'too few' historians have shown themselves capable of writing histories reaching both academic and public audiences.

Schama will be discussed in chapter 6. Certainly Starkey has been to the fore in showing fellow historians how to reconcile academic scholarship with populist storytelling in books, lectures, television programmes and museum curating for London's 2009 Henry VIII exhibition. Complaining that history had become increasingly 'a private conversation' amongst academics, Starkey (2001: 14; J. Thompson 2004) urged academic historians to reconsider their relationship with the general public, most notably the need to write enjoyable and marketable books rather than 'unreadable books about "isms" and "ists"'. Critiquing the usual distinction drawn between academic and popular histories, Starkey (quoted, Baxter 2001) claimed that 'the real distinction is between books that sell and books that don't, between popular and unpopular books'. Apart from regularly attracting good audiences for his television histories screened in prime-time slots in Britain as well as on PBS across the Atlantic, Starkey has achieved strong sales and positive reviews for his written histories, combining – to quote John Guy (2008), a Tudor specialist – 'tabloid verve and original scholarship, peppering every page with pungent wit and yet never skimping on the detail'.

Tosh (2010: 333–4) pointed also to Hobsbawm (chapter 5) as an academic historian presenting major historical themes to a lay audience. Introducing one of his world histories, Hobsbawm (1987: xi) claimed that: 'Though written by a professional historian, this book is addressed not to other academics, but to all who wish to understand the world and who believe history is important for this purpose … I have done my best to make it accessible to non-historians.' For Hobsbawm, there seemed no reason why scholarly histories should lack lay appeal, even if such *haute vulgarisation* (making popular from on high) makes its own demands upon the presenter, including the perceived need to scale down the usual academic apparatus. Furthermore, Hobsbawm (1962: xv) thought seriously about his target reader:

> Its ideal reader is that theoretical construct, the intelligent and educated citizen, who is not merely curious about the past, but wishes to understand how and why the world has come to be what it is today and whither it is going. Hence it would be pedantic and uncalled-for to load the text with as heavy an apparatus of scholarship as it ought to carry for a more learned public.

Published in 1962, *The Age of Revolution*, the first of his world histories, sold well within and outside academia. Nearly fifty years on, it remains in print, and, excepting the usual reservations articulated about Hobsbawm's Marxist credentials, was well received by academic reviewers. For Cannadine (2008: 235), it represented a major history 'of lasting importance, exceptional quality and widespread appeal'. Indeed, its success led Weidenfeld & Nicolson, the publisher, to commission further volumes taking the story up until the 1990s, especially as Hobsbawm's populist sentiments failed to prevent the series becoming widely used in schools and universities.

Popular Historians and Popular Histories

Whereas Schama and Starkey tend to work across both academic and popular audiences, popular historians working as professional writers, not historians, often emphasise the distinctiveness of their approach and audience. The late Christopher Hibbert, the author of such books as *The Destruction of Lord Raglan* (1961), *Redcoats and Rebels: the war for America 1770–1781* (1990) and *Napoleon: his wives and women* (2002), provides a typical example. Despite acknowledging the influence of Plumb, Taylor and Trevelyan in writing for a public audience, Hibbert (quoted, Bati 1990), an Oxford history graduate, articulated a clear notion of both his methodology and target audience in Britain and beyond.

> The main aim is to entertain and tell a good, accurate story, without attempting to make historical discoveries or change historical opinion in any way. You've got to make the reader want to know what's going to happen next, even if you're writing about something the outcome of which is well known. You have to build up an atmosphere, almost like writing a novel or detective story. An academic historian doesn't have to do that. He usually has to write a reformist [author's note: revisionist] book which a popular historian doesn't have to bother with. The chap like me has to keep asking, 'Will the reader be bored by this? Will he understand this? Is it strictly necessary?' The popular historian's books are almost invariably narrative – which in many academic quarters is considered not the way to write history. They want analysis: that's something I don't do, and my readers wouldn't want me to.

On paper, there is no reason why any historical topic should not work as a popular history, as demonstrated by the way in which Hibbert's publications ranged widely by country and period as well as topic.

Even so, books on Hitler's Germany (BBC 2011), warfare, kings and queens or 'upstairs–downstairs', like film/television tie-ins, notch up the strongest sales. In fact, according to one British commissioning editor (quoted, Morris 2002), 'Ask any history publisher and they'll tell you candidly: a bad book on Hitler will sell better than a good book on almost anything else.' Over 65 years after Hitler's death, the Nazi regime remains one of the bestselling book topics in Britain and a substantial source of income for publishers, as evidenced by the 850 books published about the Third Reich in 2010 (BBC 2011). Indeed, David Irving's alleged short-comings as a presenter of Hitler's Germany failed to prevent him building up a lucrative career working outside academia (chapter 13).

Of course, there are highly regarded popular historians of Hitler's Germany. Indeed, in 2009 one of Britain's bestselling popular histories was yet another book about the Second World War. Published in May 2009, *D-day: the Battle for Normandy* had sold nearly 150,000 hardback copies in Britain by the end of the year and was placed eleventh in the year's top 20 non-fiction hardback chart (*Bookseller* 2010: 21). This time the story, though told many times before, such as by Stephen Ambrose (chapter 12), received the Antony Beevor treatment. Beevor, a former army officer educated at the Royal Military Academy, Sandhurst, has established him-self as a highly successful popular military historian. Global sales exceed five million books, with *Stalingrad* (1998) alone selling two and a half million copies. *Berlin: the Downfall 1945* (2002) was the most borrowed history book in public libraries during the 'noughties' (Clee 2010). Critical acclaim has led to several awards, including the Wolfson Prize for History and the Longman–*History Today* Trustees' Award.

Although he achieved only limited success as a novelist, the experi-ence of writing imaginative literature, alongside the inspiration of John Keegan's teaching at Sandhurst and publications in overturning military historians' traditional top-down approach, helped Beevor (2002) to strike a chord with readers by bringing 'to life the fate of individuals caught up helplessly in the maelstrom of the war'. Reviewing *D-day: the Battle for Normandy*, Max Hastings (2009), a fellow military historian, praised Beevor's 'powerful and authoritative account' of war's human dimen-sion: 'Nobody knows better than Beevor how to translate the dry stuff of military history into human drama of the most vivid and moving kind. His book offers a thousand vignettes of drama, terror, cruelty, compas-sion, courage and cowardice.' Seeking to provide 'the view from above and below', Beevor (von Maier and Glantz 2008: 48; Holgate 2009) used an engaging and well-researched narrative to juxtapose the broader military overview with the human drama of a ferocious battlefield. For

Allan Mallinson (2009), 'Beevor tells it all with the soldier's eye for what matters on the ground as much as with the historian's for the broader understanding of events.' There were also two marked differences of approach as compared to Stephen Ambrose's 1994 bestseller *D-Day: June 6 1944*. Unlike Ambrose, who relied heavily upon veterans' evidence, Beevor (von Maier and Glantz 2008: 57–8) distrusts oral testimony. Moreover, he avoided Ambrose's jingoistic flag-waving stance, even treating Britain far more critically than the USA in *D-Day*.

Beevor (2002), though recognising the Hitler effect, believed that the popularity of his books was largely a matter of timing: 'We have reached a moment when historians, novelists and filmmakers are at the right distance in time to be able to recreate the Second World War without the distortion of propaganda or myth. We also have a far wider variety of sources on which to draw.' Pointing to a dramatic change in the attitudes and expectations of readers during the 1990s, Beevor (2002; von Maier and Glantz 2008: 48–9) represented his histories as moving on from 'the old-fashioned corporate version of events' characteristic of books marking the fiftieth anniversary of the end of the Second World War: 'a generation which had shrugged off the ideals of collective loyalty suddenly wanted to know about the experiences and suffering of the individual'. For readers, moral dilemmas – for example, how would they respond to the face of battle or to orders to shoot civilians? – provided much of the drama in Beevor's books.

Untypically, Beevor, like Hibbert, references his well-researched histories. Normally, as Hobsbawm admitted above, histories targeted at a wider audience drop, or at least reduce, the scholarly apparatus of referencing. Thus, Schama (1993: 23; J. Thompson 2004) deliberately omitted footnotes from *Citizens: a chronicle of the French Revolution* (1989) and *The American Future: a history* (2008). As a result, Gertrude Himmelfarb, depicted by Schama as one of Clio's 'self-appointed constables' strictly upholding traditional ways of writing history, confronted him on the issue lest footnotes become 'an endangered species'. Conversely, it is worth noting that historical novelists, like Philippa Gregory (chapter 10), have begun to include bibliographies by way of enhancing their books' historical authority as research-based publications. Indeed, some historical novelists even include footnotes.

Conclusion

Present-day tensions between academic and popular historians are not new. The divide, albeit proving somewhat fluid, has always been there, even if both academic and popular historians are united by the need for communication to an audience. Hitherto, contemporary academic culture on both sides of the Atlantic and Channel has proved largely indifferent to the needs of the man or woman in the street interested in knowing more about the past. Although Jordanova (2000: 20; 2008) described this attitude as 'more marked in Britain than elsewhere', there is no reason why historians should resist following Trevelyan, Plumb, Taylor and Schama, among others, in reaching out beyond academia to a large lay audience. After all, not all scholarly monographs, journal articles and conference papers are dull, jargonistic and inaccessible as public history. One historian concerned about the specialist jargon of historians and their resulting reluctance and/or inability to communicate with a popular audience is Norman Davies (1996: 36–7), whose *Europe: a history* (1996) proved a bestseller in spite of totalling nearly 1400 pages and including 65 pages of references. Presented in a readable style by a historian acknowledging Taylor's influence, Davies's panoramic and populist account of a continent divided and united by history chimed also with the contemporary world's focus on the European Union project. Indeed, *The Times* (1996) not only made his 'must-read' history the subject of an editorial, but also published extracts from Davies's 'great book'.

In many respects, Davies was following Norman Stone, professor of modern history at the University of Oxford. When justifying his regular *Sunday Times* column, Stone (1990) asserted that 'this is precisely what a professor of modern history ought to do: to set contemporary matters in a historical perspective'. More recently, Stone (2011), who is currently based at Ankara's Bilkent University, published a popular history of Turkey. Covering 1000 years of history, he sought to liberate Turkey's past from present-day western prejudices and – to quote one reviewer (Seal 2011) – 'to redeliver it in digestible style, to a wider readership'. Offering an alternative historical perspective regarding such mainstream events as the Ottoman Empire's takeover of Christian Constantinople (1453) and sieges of Vienna (1529 and 1683), or the Armenian genocide (1915), Stone's readable revisionist study was praised by Jeremy Seal (2011) for introducing readers 'to a place beyond their presumptions'. Clearly, such a history possesses contemporary relevance at a time when Turkey's future role *vis-à-vis* Europe and Asia, most notably its accession to the European Union, is high on the global agenda and the Armenian genocide remains a source of contemporary controversy.

Hobsbawm's (2002a: 303–4) acknowledgment of the manner in which David Higham, his literary agent, ensured that he continued to reach out from the ivory tower to a wide readership at home and overseas raises questions about how far such agents can ease the way for academics seeking to identify and access new audiences. Indeed, Niall Ferguson, the focus of chapter 7, has three agents, covering his literary, public speaking and television work.

For academic historians, fellow academics will remain their principal audience. As a result, their research findings will feed into public history only if consumed, read, absorbed, and used by writers of popular histories, filmmakers, television presenters or historical novelists. Meanwhile, Davies, Hobsbawm, Jordanova, Schama, Starkey and Stone are prominent among those championing a more outgoing approach. Significantly, when asked if he was a populariser of history, Schama (2011) responded that 'there's no nobler label'. Nor should popular history be dismissed necessarily as bad history. When written with scholarly integrity, it is simply history written and presented in a different way for a lay audience. Indeed, Jordanova (2006: 126–31), who has been proactive in apprising fellow historians about public history, claims that its core intellectual issues are central to the discipline of history. Nobody wants academics to strip out history's complexities, depth, and ongoing historiographical controversies, but 'reaching out would be nice', as urged by Sandbrook (2007), who left his university post to write 'the kind of book that the public might read' in preference to journal articles 'that only a few people will read'. After all, as Elton (2002: 99–100) advised, 'the way to combat bad popular history is to write good popular history, not to retreat from the world'.

Finally, Ambrose (quoted, Bacon 1998; 2002b: xv–xvi), a renowned public historian, offered a useful reference point for those seeking guidance on how to engage a wider audience through the storytelling power of history: 'I like imagining myself at a campfire when I teach, and I want those students who are out at the outer edge of the light from the campfire where I can just see them, I want them leaning forward just a little bit to make sure they don't miss what happens next.' As mentioned above, this technique underpinned his writing as well. Inspiring storytellers of the past cited in this chapter have a strong track record in engaging readers. Nor should responses be confined to aural and written histories on account of the visual media's high-profile role in popularising history.

Part II
Presenters of the Past: Case Studies

Part II has three main objectives:

To identify and discuss the nature of alternative and increasingly varied ways of presenting the past to an audience(s).

As outlined in the introduction, most publications and courses about 'the nature of history' have concentrated on 'doing history'. Against this background, Part II concentrates upon the often overlooked process of actually presenting history to an audience. Within academia written presentations prove the norm, and hence figure prominently but not exclusively throughout this book. Popular histories are still often written, but outside academia recent decades have witnessed the enhanced role played by alternative written and non-written modes – these include historical novels, Hollywood feature films and television histories – in communicating the past to an audience.

To examine critically the presentation of the past to academic and public audiences

Notwithstanding a continuing focus upon presenting history to an academic audience, most chapters possess a broader dimension, given the emergence of public history and the way in which alternative forms of presentation have taken history to a wider audience. Space constraints allow only a selection of alternative approaches to be explored.

To illuminate and discuss critically these themes through case studies based on individual presenters of the past, with particular regard to the acceptability of their presentations as 'history'.

4
A.J.P. Taylor: The People's History Man

> It is more than 30 years since A.J.P. Taylor published his *English History, 1914–1945*, but I can still remember the occasion on which I first encountered it. I was visiting the house of a Birmingham school friend, and happened upon Taylor's book, which had been given to my friend's father as a present. Having begun by turning the pages in rather a desultory way, I soon found myself so engrossed that I could not put it down. It was the most compelling and exciting history I had yet read (I must have been 15 at the time), and by the end of the evening, at which I must have been an unconscionably anti-social guest, I had decided that I wanted to become an historian myself. (Cannadine 1998)

There could be no more striking recognition of the skill, indeed the narrative power, of Taylor as a presenter of history than this comment by David Cannadine, who by the time of writing in 1998 had followed Taylor to become one of Britain's leading historians. Nor is Cannadine, who is currently based at Princeton University, the only historian on record as being inspired by Taylor in one way or another. For most, Taylor was – to quote Niall Ferguson (quoted, Riding 1999) – 'the first historian I had ever heard of as a schoolboy'.

In his prime, 'AJP' attracted – and captivated – a wider following than any other historian. He became a national figure, a household name, whose fame was highlighted during the early 1970s by a character named 'A.J.P. Historian' in the *Monty Python's Flying Circus* television series and a mention in the 1974 film *Monty Python and the Holy Grail*. The *Times* (1990) obituary described him as 'the most controversial, and certainly the best known, historian in the English-speaking world'. A prolific and bestselling author, a gifted journalist, and a radio and television celebrity,

Taylor was far more than just an academic historian. Indeed, the readability of his publications, alongside his extensive media work, meant that he took history to a large audience outside academia. Pioneering the presentation of history on television, Taylor is widely acknowledged – to quote Ferguson (1999: 213–14) – as the first 'telly don', leading the way for others to follow. For Schama (2002d: 44), Taylor was 'the granddaddy of all television historians'. Taylor died in 1990, but his histories continue to be read today, still proving central building blocks for the historiography of major topics. Moreover, his presentational skills were acknowledged as recently as 2008, when *The Times* (2008) listed him among the fifty greatest post-1945 British writers.

Background Influences

Like many historians, Taylor was a complex character full of contradictions. Acknowledged as an individualist, a loner and an outsider, he was renowned also as a great communicator and showman for his ability to relate easily to a diverse range of audiences. Despite making the University of Oxford a central part of his life and career, he fitted in uneasily with his colleagues and never received the academic recognition and status many, including Taylor himself, felt he deserved. Fascinated by powerful men, Taylor (1956: vii) took pride in presenting himself as the people's historian displaying 'little respect for men in positions of power'. Describing himself as an enlightened radical historian, Taylor failed nevertheless to keep pace with the fast-changing nature of his discipline. Claiming to be detached and impartial, his histories were opinionated and subjective, even occasionally somewhat propagandist. Despite substantial media earnings on top of his academic salary, Taylor worried constantly about money.

Born at Birkdale, Southport, in 1906, Taylor used his 1980 television journey around the *Edge of Britain* to highlight his Lancastrian roots. Prosperous parents, whose wealth came from the family cotton textile firm, provided a comfortable upper-middle-class lifestyle both as a child, when Taylor was sent to public school, and after. At Oxford, where he drove an open-top Rover, he was one of the few undergraduates with a car. Even so, Taylor acquired a reputation for being very careful with money, even downright mean.

Taylor grew up in what he described as a very political household. Despite their wealth and initial Liberal Party sympathies, his parents shifted to the left politically in the wake of the First World War and the 1917 Bolshevik Revolution. Reportedly his parents' house acted as a meeting place for a wide range of political figures from the left, including Arthur Henderson, George Lansbury and Harry Pollitt. Nor was the family overly religious. Taylor soon lost his religious faith. Invited by a dean at Oxford to discuss his religious doubts, Taylor (1983: 67) responded in his typically forthright manner, 'I have none.' Arguably, nonconformism, together with his northern background, contributed to Taylor's efforts to present himself as a 'convinced individualist' (Kennedy 1986: 12), an outsider fighting for unfashionable causes against the 'Establishment', a term that Taylor did much to popularise during the early 1950s.

A significant formative influence derived from Taylor's stay at Bootham School, a Quaker public school located at York: 'the five years between 1919 and 1924 when I was at Bootham created me as an individual' (Taylor 1983: 45). Given descriptors of Taylor as an idiosyncratic historian doing his own thing, this seems a revealing observation, while exposure to Quaker ideals helps to explain his subsequent involvement in the disarmament and anti-war movement. Bootham developed Taylor's interest in history, seemingly more through fostering an interest in church architecture than the quality of history teaching.

Subsequently Oxford represented an enduring feature of Taylor's life and career. Awarded a scholarship at Oriel College, he studied medieval history. Taking pride in claiming never to have attended many lectures, Taylor graduated with a First in 1927. Initial thoughts about a legal career were soon dropped following a boring spell working as an articled solicitor's clerk for his uncle. Instead, Taylor returned to Oxford to undertake postgraduate research providing the basis for his first book, *The Italian Problem in European Diplomacy, 1847–1849* (1934). Based in Vienna and guided by Professor Alfred Pribram, Taylor extended his education. He learnt German, took up music and riding, and discovered women. Reportedly (Sisman 1994: 76–7), he went out with his first serious girlfriend, met Margaret Adams, his first wife, and had sex for the first time, with a prostitute.

Starting his academic career in 1930 as an Assistant Lecturer in Modern History at the University of Manchester, Taylor developed his presentational and research skills. Lewis Namier (quoted, Burk 2000a: 144), professor of history at Manchester, described him as 'a man of first-class ability', even 'one of the coming men for diplomatic history in this country'. In turn, Namier continued to act as a mentor, a kind of academic father figure, for a substantial part of Taylor's career (Colley 1989: 99–100); indeed, one of his sons was named Lewis. The denouement in their relationship came in 1957 when Taylor's journalism led Namier to refuse support for his nomination for Oxford's regius professorship in history. Feeling 'betrayed', Taylor broke off their friendship. They never spoke again. Revealingly, praise for Namier as a 'great historian' in an obituary written for the *Observer* was countered by Taylor's (1960) admission that 'I was his colleague at Manchester for eight years; and for twenty-six years [1931–57] his close friend.'

Despite enjoying life living in the Peak District while working at Manchester, Oxford always beckoned, and in 1938 Taylor travelled down Manchester's Oxford Road, where the university was located, to become a tutorial fellow at Magdalen College. Showing himself to be a good teacher and college man, Taylor played an influential role in pushing Oxford's history teaching and research into the modern period. At the same time, he experienced difficulties fitting in at Oxford, where his position was not helped by the reservations, even outright hostility, of fellow academics about his 'trashy' (Wheatcroft 2006: 49) journalism and divorce. Unsurprisingly, he faced several disappointments, most notably his failure to secure a professorship, let alone the regius professorship in 1957. In this case, Hugh Trevor-Roper, an unsuccessful candidate for the Magdalen fellowship in 1938, pipped Taylor to the post.

A Very Political Historian

No historian is insulated from the period during which she or he grew up and lived. Taylor, though claiming to be a detached and impartial scholar, was no exception. Throughout his life Taylor's thinking and writing about the past reflected the impact of the present. Despite denying that he had strong political opinions but merely 'extreme views, weakly held', Taylor (1977a: 7–8; quoted, Sisman 1994: 87) proved a very political animal, commenting upon and involving himself actively in current affairs, even admitting that as a historian he learned 'a good deal' from contemporary events. Two world wars, the rise of the Soviet Union, the 1926 General Strike, the Great Depression, the threat of Hitler's Germany, the Cold War, the danger of a nuclear holocaust, and the Common Market loomed large in his thinking, and helped explain his concentration on the history of diplomacy and war; pro-Soviet, anti-American and anti-German mindset; support for disarmament; and sympathy for the working man. Blending past and present, Taylor's histories, like his media work, pressed strong opinions upon readers, listeners and viewers.

Taylor followed his parents in adopting a pronounced left-wing outlook. Although he joined the Independent Labour Party (ILP) in 1921, Oxford witnessed a brief flirtation with the Communist Party of Great Britain (CPGB) alongside a lengthy visit to the Soviet Union in

1925. Strong support for the General Strike led Taylor to use his car to drive around members of the Preston strike committee, although the CPGB's relative inaction therein prompted a move back to the university's Labour Club. Reportedly, Taylor (1983: 80), accompanied by Tom Driberg, a fellow student and future Labour Party politician, drove round to the CPGB's headquarters for strike instructions, but found the building locked! Only the caretaker could be found.

During the 1930s defence and foreign policy issues fuelled Taylor's political activism. In particular, his emergence as a public speaker – he spoke for the Manchester Anti-War Council and the Labour Party – yielded both national visibility and invaluable experience in addressing a non-captive audience outside academia. For Taylor, the 'German problem' was a prime worry, as evidenced by not only his active participation in the 'Stand up to Hitler' campaign but also the anti-German line adopted in his early histories. Just as *Germany's First Bid for Colonies* (1938) was framed by contemporary debates about colonial appeasement, so *The Course of German History* (1945) was a product of the Second World War. As Adam Sisman (1994: 153) noted, it was in effect 'an indictment, Alan the prosecuting counsel'. Developed from a chapter written for (but not used by) the British government's Political Warfare Executive, Taylor (1951: 7, 13–14, 146, 223) urged a re-think of Germany's past: 'No civilised nation has such a record of atrocity.' Exploiting wartime prejudices, he targeted the book at a wide readership, with some 6000 copies being sold in six months.

During the Cold War Taylor's longstanding pro-Soviet sympathies led him to present the USA as the prime threat to global peace. Refusing ever to set foot in the USA, Taylor (1983: 238) visited North America only once, in 1961, when he went to Canada's University of New Brunswick at Fredericton at the specific request of Lord Beaverbrook, the proprietor of *Express* newspapers. Despite looking across the bay from St. Andrews towards the USA, Taylor refrained from crossing into the nearby state of Maine. Meanwhile, the threat of nuclear holocaust proved a profound worry, given what Taylor (1969a: 121; 1977c: 140) saw as deterrence's poor track record: 'In 1914 ... the deterrent failed to deter. A deterrent may work ninety-nine times out of a hundred. On the hundredth occasion it produces catastrophe. There is a contemporary moral here for those who like to find one.' In this vein, in 1957 *The Troublemakers* took up the unfashionable but innovatory theme of dissent in foreign policy, foregrounding those providing what Taylor (1969b: 15) called the 'noises off' stage in support of an alternative foreign policy. Clearly, the book reflected Taylor's belief that he knew best about Britain's nuclear option.

Between 1958 and 1962 Taylor worked tirelessly for the Campaign for Nuclear Disarmament (CND). Looking back, Taylor (1977a: 13; 1983: 225–30) opined that this was 'the one worthy thing I have done in my life'. Certainly, CND espoused a cause in which he believed deeply, a belief influenced by both his Quaker schooling and fears, informed by history, that it was easy 'to sleepwalk into war' almost by accident. Convinced that he could help change the fate of the world, in February 1958 Taylor spoke at the CND's inaugural meeting held at Westminster's Central Hall, and then travelled the country speaking at a wide range of venues, including London's Albert Hall and Manchester's Free Trade Hall. In April 1960 he addressed a 60,000-plus crowd in Trafalgar Square at the end of the annual Aldermaston to London 'Ban-the-bomb' march (*The Times*, 1960). For Taylor, Britain should set an example to the world through unilateral disarmament. In any case, Britain's apparent decline, as signalled by the 1956 Suez Crisis, rendered nuclear weapons an unnecessary luxury: 'if we threw away our bombs, who'd notice?' (quoted, Sisman 1994: 310). Nor did Taylor (quoted, Sisman 1994: 396–7) moderate his views, as evidenced in 1982, when giving the Romanes lecture at Oxford: 'The deterrent starts off only as a threat, but the record shows that there comes a time when its reality has to be demonstrated – which can only be done by using it. So it was in August 1914 and so it will be again.' When using history to make a present-day point, Taylor found it difficult treading the fine line between acting as a detached historian and a CND propagandist.

A Historian of Politics

Taylor's love of history, though fostered by his schoolboy interest in church architecture, derived largely from his fascination with reading what happened in the past, and especially discovering what happened next. For Taylor (quoted, Wrigley 2006: 215), the subject was central to the humanities:

> History is the one way in which you can experience at second hand all kinds of variations of human behaviour; and ... understand how other people behave ... it makes the reader, and ... the historian too, somebody with a fuller, much wider life than he could possibly have merely by his own private experience.

Within this context, the historian's task was to present an accurate view of the past based upon a critical assessment of the evidence. Although his first book, *The Italian Problem in European Diplomacy*, was an archival study, Taylor's histories increasingly took the form of syntheses based upon published primary and secondary, not archival, sources.

As a political historian, Taylor focused principally upon power, diplomacy and war as well as major political figures, like Bismarck, and ruling elites, like the Hapsburgs. Acknowledging his preoccupation with war, in 1982 Taylor (quoted, Wrigley 2000: xvi) conceded that 'For fifty years I had been teaching history and writing books about it. All my books and all my lectures had been implicitly about war, from the Napoleonic Wars to the shadow of the final war under which we now live.' Even so, when delivering Oxford's 1982 Romanes lecture, he confessed to being somewhat embarrassed by his lack of actual military experience, excepting membership of the Home Guard in 1940! Over time his elitist, male-centred political historical approach began to appear old-fashioned, even surprisingly conservative, in the light of his radical reputation. Generally speaking, the rapid emergence of cultural, economic and social history passed him by, as recorded by Keith Thomas (1966: 276) when describing Taylor's *English History 1914–1945* as 'a brilliant swansong for the dying concept of history as past politics, and social history as undemanding subsidiary'. In fact, Taylor (quoted, Wrigley 2000: xxvi) had already acknowledged changing realities when conceding in 1962 that 'Like an ageing music hall artist, I can't perform new tricks.'

The late 1950s and 1960s signalled also Taylor's move away from the history of continental Europe towards that of England. Notwithstanding Thomas's critique, Taylor's *English History*, the final volume in the prestigious 'Oxford History of England', won wide praise for its strong story line. Compulsively readable, *English History* sold well – reportedly in ten years sales totalled around 55,000 – and helped to override concerns about Taylor's scholarship prompted by his recent book about the origins of the Second World War. In 1998 Cannadine (1998) echoed Thomas's views about Taylor's shortcomings, but still selected *English History* in the *Guardian*'s 'I Wish I'd Written ...' series because it offered a 'dazzling display of the historian's narrative art': 'it coruscates with wit and fire, life and warmth, it is a paean of praise to the English people, and it concludes with one of the most memorable paragraphs ever written. It is Taylor's history of Taylor's times.' At one time, the book's success fostered plans for a second edition, but he lacked enthusiasm for what promised to be an onerous task. In any case, for Taylor (1983: 244), the book proved 'a period piece in both sources and outlook': 'it can only be written differently by someone of a different generation'.

A Historical Revisionist

Taylor's reputation as an individualist, even a maverick historian, derived from his willingness, indeed determination, to confront current historical thinking. Following one HA branch lecture, a schoolboy asked him what could be learned from history. Taylor (quoted, Sisman 1994: 311, 387) answered in one word: 'scepticism'. Like Namier, he regarded iconoclasm as the mark of a great historian, and saw himself as 'the great propagator of doubt', a revisionist *par excellence*. Reluctant to accept received opinions about the past, Taylor (1977a: 2; Cole 1993: 1) took pride in presenting himself as 'a traitor within the gates'. Rather than worrying about driving against the traffic flow, Taylor, a lover of fast cars and hater of speed limits, was only too anxious to drive off fast in a new direction. In any case, as Taylor (1957: 743) admitted, the historical method often swept historians in unexpected directions: 'The facts get up, hit the historian on the head, and make him go where he did not intend to go at all.'

Perhaps the most striking example of Taylor's contrarian character occurred during the early 1960s, when his *Origins of the Second World War* (1961) rewrote the history of the war's origins. Until then the topic had attracted relatively little historical controversy. Framed by the 1945 Nuremberg war crimes trials and Winston Churchill's *The Gathering Storm* (1948), responsibility for causing war in 1939 was placed firmly upon Hitler, whose long-term plans were facilitated by the blunders of the appeasers. Inevitably, as Taylor (quoted, Wrigley 2000: xix) predicted, there were risks attached to challenging received notions about such a sensitive issue: 'I think it will annoy the old boys who thought they had settled everything about the Second World War years ago.' Rather, he presented Hitler as the arch-opportunist employing in successive crises bluff, threats and improvisation to secure his leadership and advance German interests.

Henceforth, Taylor was condemned as an apologist for both Hitler and the appeasers, regardless of his anti-appeasement credentials during the 1930s and the anti-German line characteristic of his early histories. In 1963 Taylor's 'Second Thoughts', published in a revised edition of the book, denied any intention either to excuse Hitler or to vindicate appeasers. For Taylor (1964: 26), the historian's 'sole duty is to find out what was done and why', not to say what ought to be done. Bitter academic controversy followed, as epitomised by a clash with Trevor-Roper given added poignancy by their recent rivalry for Oxford's regius professorship. Responding to Trevor-Roper's claim that the book 'will do harm, perhaps irreparable harm to Mr. Taylor's reputation as a serious historian', Taylor (1971: 102) asserted that 'The Regius Professor's methods of quotation might also do harm to his reputation as a serious historian, if he had one.' Nor was debate confined to academia, as the battle spilled over into the press – influential debates were conducted in the *Times Literary Supplement* and *Encounter* – as well as radio and television programmes. In July 1961 Robert Kee chaired a much-anticipated clash on BBC television between Taylor and Trevor-Roper. Neither landed a knock-out blow, but Taylor's debating skills led many to conclude that he won on points (Sisman 2010: 332–4).

Whatever one's view, Taylor's revisionist approach proved academically liberating. The book opened up major topics, most notably the causes of the Second World War and the course of pre-1940 British foreign policy, to new perspectives and debate at a time when the war was increasingly distant, many of the principal actors were either dead or in retirement, and archival sources were becoming available. Moreover, Taylor's thesis impacted also upon the emerging historiographical controversy sparked off in 1961 by Fritz Fischer about the origins of the First World War and the continuities and discontinuities in German foreign policy. However, for many historians, the book raised serious questions about Taylor's scholarship, including whether or not he had actually read Hitler's *Mein Kampf*. For Tim Mason (1964), as Taylor (1983: 233) himself admitted, the book seemed 'a period piece' produced by an old-fashioned diplomatic historian guilty of not only overlooking the economic dimension, but also adopting a eurocentric approach focused upon the outbreak of a limited European war in September 1939.

Nevertheless, on balance, Taylor's *Origins of the Second World War* represented, and still represents, an invaluable reference point. Apart from extending his reach to a wider international audience, the book sparked off a veritable publications industry centred upon the debate, while inspiring numerous teaching modules thereupon. Selling over 10,000 copies in Britain within a year, the book proved a significant commercial success. Nor was its success short-lived, as shown by the sale of 23,000 copies in the USA between 1985 and 2000.

Pressing the Role of Accident

Pressing the role of contingency, Taylor (1977a: 1; 1983: 97) asserted that 'most things in history happen by accident'. Statesmen, Taylor (1967: 70) argued, rarely followed preconceived plans: 'historians err when they describe even the most purposeful statesman as though he were marching down a broad high-road with his objective already in sight'. In this vein, his biography of *Bismarck* (1955) confronted the Prussian minister's claims about following a master plan to unify Germany. The coming of the two world wars was presented in similar terms. Speaking on BBC Radio in 1954, Taylor (1954: 234) claimed that the outbreak of war in 1914 was an accident, with the key decision-makers proving 'the victims of circumstances'. As Taylor (1969a: 45) wrote subsequently, suddenly in July 1914 peace broke down: 'In much the same way, a motorist who for thirty years has been doing the right thing to avoid accidents makes a mistake one day and has a crash ... The only safe explanation in history is that things happen because they happen.' Re-thinking the outbreak of war in 1939 in the *Origins of the Second World War* (1961), Taylor (1964: 269) argued that Hitler, far from following a preconceived step-by-step plan for war, reacted pragmatically and opportunistically to unforeseen contingencies: 'The war of 1939, far from being premeditated, was a mistake, the result on both sides of diplomatic blunders.'

Although critics accused him of glossing over the impact of profound forces, Paul Kennedy (1986: 9, 12) believed that any problems arose from the fact that Taylor, albeit not actually overlooking profound forces, failed to spell out his overall view of historical causation, thereby 'leaving many a reader with the impression that he has encountered two different historians at work: one who points to the longer-term shifts in the balance of power as the key to understanding great-power diplomacy; and another who is deeply sceptical of "profound causes"'.

By implication, he was no advocate of learning from history. History, Taylor (1969b: 22–3; Wrigley 2006: 229) argued, merely told us about the past, not the future: 'We learn nothing from history except the infinite variety of men's behaviour. We study it ... for pleasure, not for instruction ... The present enables us to understand the past, not the other way round.' Or, as Taylor (quoted, Sisman 1994: 306) asserted when discussing the two world wars, 'men learned from past mistakes how to make new ones'. Unsurprisingly, he was guilty of the occasional deviation, especially as outlined above when using deterrence's past failings to validate the CND message.

Taylor's emphasis upon the role of accident worked also against historical determinism. As Hugh Thomas (1975: 537) noted, according to Taylor, 'Practically nobody has any idea of what they are doing ... This is, of course, the reverse of Marxist history.' Notwithstanding his reading of Marxist classics and brief flirtation with the CPGB, Taylor (1983: 60) admitted that 'Somehow I never managed to bring Marxism into my historical work.' Indeed, Eric Hobsbawm (quoted, Brivati 1993: 607), the Marxist historian discussed in the next chapter, remarked that 'one cannot think of one single left-wing historian who is less influenced by Marxism, than A.J.P. Taylor'. Prioritising short-term diplomatic manoeuvring, in *Germany's First Bid for Colonies* (1938) Taylor (1983: 123) took 'a jab at the fashionable theories of economic imperialism' advocated by Marxist historians, just as his *Origins of the Second World War* ignored 'the dreadful logic of German economic development' (Mason 1964: 87).

Presenting History to Diverse Audiences

For Taylor academic acclaim was not enough. As revealed by successive biographers, he proved a self-centred, vain, opinionated, quarrelsome and competitive individual constantly seeking more. From an early age, a 'driving desire to gain national recognition' (Wrigley 2000: xxi) led him to target a wider audience in order to develop a high public profile outside academia. To some extent, he was inspired also by Trevelyan's example in securing a large readership within and outside academia, but unlike Trevelyan focused more directly upon the way in which substantial sales of his histories would maximise his income (Burk 2000a: 369–70; Wrigley 2006: 2, 37).

At Manchester and Oxford, he undertook a considerable amount of media work, especially as fame in one sphere threw up opportunities elsewhere; thus, during the early 1950s the *Sunday Pictorial* advertised Taylor as the man seen on television's *In the News*. Indeed, following the end of his Oxford lectureship and fellowship in 1963, Taylor became in effect a professional writer and broadcaster. Then, between 1967 and 1975 he served also as Honorary Director of the Beaverbrook Library, as well as Lord Beaverbrook's biographer, even his 'court historian', given Taylor's somewhat uncritical, indeed controversial, admiration of the press baron.

Also, although much of his journalism focused upon everyday issues, Taylor's newspaper columns, editorials and book reviews provided a strong base for presenting public history. In this vein, in 1951 he played a supportive role in the launch of *History Today*, a monthly periodical targeted at a popular audience, while acting also during the late 1960s as editor-in-chief of Purnell's successful part-work, *History of the Twentieth Century*. Extensive extra-academic work contributed to Taylor's wealth. Freelance earnings, boosted by celebrity appearances on television talk shows, rapidly overtook his academic salary; indeed, by 1958 they exceeded the latter threefold, and continued to rise (Burk 2000a: 416–19).

At Manchester Taylor (1983: 104; Radice 2004: 94) learnt how to teach history, and particularly how to reach an audience. As Namier (quoted, Burk 2000a: 144) recorded, he was 'a first-class teacher, interesting and stimulating'. Presented clearly, confidently and effectively, his lectures, punctuated by witticisms and epigrams, proved equally popular with students at Oxford, and were famed for attracting large audiences, even at 9.00am! Indeed, Taylor, the great performer, liked to claim that no hall would have been large enough for a lecture delivered at a more popular time. In particular, Taylor (1977a: 6) was renowned for not only reaching his conclusion dead on time but also lecturing without notes: 'After delivering my lectures once … I threw away my notes and thereafter lectured without notes as I have done ever since … I taught myself history, literally on my feet.' Performing before a live audience stimulated Taylor intellectually, and he claimed to re-think topics as he talked. Éva Haraszti (quoted, Wrigley 1997: 21), his third wife, described one lecture given in 1978 at the University of St. Andrews: 'What is extremely important to him is the way he formulates his thoughts and gets newer and newer inspiration for his own thoughts. At the end, when great applause followed his lectures, his face becomes sweet and flushed with happiness and looks twenty years younger.'

But were Taylor's lectures really impromptu? Was their seemingly spontaneous nature merely an act, one element in a carefully crafted theatrical performance delivered by a master history craftsman? Or were they well prepared *in advance*? Whatever the answer, Taylor's lectures evoked positive responses from most audiences. For Sisman (1994: 86), 'Alan seemed to have a marvellous grasp of everything he was talking about … he brought a fresh independent approach to otherwise tired old themes.' Highlighting the power of a spoken presentation, his lectures proved accessible and interesting to a lay audience. John Irwin (quoted, Wrigley 2000: xxiii), a television producer, attended one of Taylor's Ford lectures delivered at Oxford in 1956: 'I've seen nothing like it. That audience was hypnotized by Taylor's dynamic personality, his passionate sincerity, his wit, his command of words, his brilliant sense of timing, and his complete mastery of the subject – *without a single note* [author's emphasis].' Fame failed to diminish Taylor's loyalty to the HA – he first lectured to an HA branch in December 1930 – and he continued to lecture regularly to branches around the country for another 50 years. Naturally, Taylor was always guaranteed a large and varied audience, drawing in students from nearby schools as well as local people attracted by a celebrity historian.

The First 'Journodon'

Writing for tabloid and quality newspapers on both the left and right of British politics gave Taylor direct access to a large national audience. When working in Manchester, he began writing book reviews for the *Manchester Guardian*, and then moved on to write articles and occasional editorials. During the post-1945 period he continued to write for the *Manchester Guardian*, but also contributed regular columns for the five million-plus circulation *Sunday Pictorial* (1951–2) – now called the *Sunday Mirror* – the *Daily Herald* (1953–6) and Beaverbrook's *Sunday Express* (1957–82), while publishing articles and book reviews in the *New Statesman* and the *Observer*.

The press gave Taylor a public platform upon which not only to propound his opinions on matters of the day but also to illuminate the value of the historical dimension in understanding today's world. Working for the press, especially under the guidance of A.P. Wadsworth (assistant editor, and then editor of the *Manchester Guardian*, 1944–56), honed Taylor's presentational skills, most notably his ability to work quickly and incisively, meet tight deadlines, and communicate effectively with diverse audiences through a strong narrative combined with a provocative approach to received opinions. Carefully crafted opening lines captured the reader's attention straight away. Short, sharp sentences, interspersed with paradox and humour, enhanced readability. As Taylor (1950: v) advised, it was vital to avoid 'flabby sentences' and 'tired metaphors'. In this vein, presenting history through the written word became a literary form combining accuracy and style. Worrying as much about style as scholarship, Taylor (1977a: 7) believed that 'a work of history misfires unless readers get the same pleasure from it that they do from a novel'. Of course, as Taylor (1936) conceded, this was easier said than done: 'The most important works of history often seem to the general reader rather dull and technical, while the popular successes usually merit the censure of the historian. It is no easy task to be both interesting and accurate.'

More recently, journalism has become more acceptable, even sought after, within academia, thereby causing Taylor to be seen as leading the way as the first 'journodon' (Wheatcroft 2006: 49), even 'the greatest media don of all' (Ferguson 1999: 213–14). However, during the 1950s and 1960s Taylor's enthusiasm about writing for Fleet Street was not widely shared in academia, as shown when Namier (quoted, Sisman 1994: 245) accused him of 'journalistic prostitution', even refusing to support his candidature for the regius professorship unless he ended such work. Taylor's fellow dons at Oxford proved equally censorious, as recorded by Beaverbrook (quoted, Sisman 1994: 326):

> Taylor writes an enormous amount, and much of it is written for ordinary, intelligent people who make no claim to be scholars. This is highly distasteful to the kind of don who writes a little monograph once every ten years to be read only by other dons and maybe a few young men who are trying hard to become dons themselves.

Indeed, at one time during the early 1950s, an abortive attempt was made to use Taylor's journalism to prevent the renewal of his Oxford fellowship.

Attracting a substantial contemporary readership within and outside academia, Taylor's journalism and histories frequently prompted criticism from politicians unhappy with his presentation of their careers. Prominent among complainants about Taylor's penchant for what Lord Chandos (1962) called 'throwing stones at the windows of the great' was Anthony Eden, who became Lord Avon in 1961. Following his resignation as prime minister after the 1956 Suez debacle, Eden's hypersensitivity about his reputation at the bar of history led him to devote retirement to presenting a very personal view of his political career (Beck 1998: 397–402). Taylor became something of a *bête noire*, since his *Origins of the Second World War* (1961) and *Observer* (Taylor 1962) review of the Avon memoirs were seen by Lord Avon as undermining both his carefully cultivated anti-appeaser image and strong belief in Hitler's responsibility for causing the Second World War. Avon (1963a) found it 'exasperating' to read Taylor's (1962) assertion that, far from taking a tough stance towards Hitler and Mussolini as Foreign Secretary (1935–38), 'he did not resist them', but merely used 'hard words'. As Avon (1968) informed a former diplomat, 'I am not happy at the increased prevalence of the A.J.P. Taylor school of thought who seem to me completely wrong-headed, to put it mildly.' For Avon (1963b; 1964), 'the writings of A.J.P. Taylor', who was also 'the hero of our television programmes', had to be confronted: 'it would perhaps be healthy for a corrective to be produced within the next few years'.

A Radio and Television Star

In his autobiography, Taylor (1983: 132, 203) proudly admitted becoming 'a television star'. More importantly, as recognised by Janice Hadlow (quoted, Hill 2005), when Controller of BBC4 (2004–8), Taylor is widely credited as pioneering the presentation of history on television by proving 'the model for the modern TV don'. Ian Kershaw (2004: 120), who presented BBC Television's *The Nazis: A Warning from History* (2000), acknowledged that:

> The stars of a much more elaborate (and expensive) present-day television history, the Schamas, the Starkeys and Fergusons, follow in Taylor's footsteps and have inherited the mantle of those who believed long ago that the historian's job was to use their skills and knowledge to bring big and important themes to the attention of a mass audience.

From the late 1950s onwards Taylor was British television's 'History Man', history's counterpart of Kenneth Clark (art) or Sir Mortimer Wheeler (archaeology).

All this started on radio during the Second World War, when Taylor began working for the British Forces Network and appeared on the BBC's *Brains Trust*. Following the end of the war Taylor continued to give occasional radio talks – for example, in spring 1947 he spoke about Lord John Russell and Lord Salisbury in the British prime ministers series – as well as to contribute book reviews for the BBC Third Programme (now Radio 3). During the 1950s he proved a frequent speaker for the BBC's Home and Overseas Services, and in 1956 the BBC broadcast a shortened version of his six Ford lectures. Nor was Taylor's radio work lacking in controversy, given his uncanny knack of annoying government ministers. Thus, in December 1946 Herbert Morrison (1946: 1237–40, 1285), the Lord President of the Council, was among those complaining in Parliament about the prejudiced and damaging anti-American tone of his broadcasts. Then in July 1950 the BBC refused to broadcast Taylor's 'As I see it' talk on the Korean War because of his advocacy of appeasement and condemnation of UN intervention (Sisman 1994: 197).

Quite apart from raising questions about BBC neutrality, such episodes prompted debate about appropriate ways of presenting history on radio. Following his contributions to the British prime ministers series, George Barnes (quoted, Wrigley 2006: 228–9), Controller of BBC Radio's Third Programme (1946–50), complained that Taylor's polemical approach 'contributed nothing ... to the very difficult question of how to treat history over the radio'. Barnes claimed that, unlike university students, the radio audience possessed widely differing knowledge of any topic, and hence proved unlikely to respond critically to Taylor's tendency to present controversial opinions as objective facts. Taylor disagreed. Acknowledging his sharply opinionated approach, Taylor expressed the hope that 'my talk would succeed in starting people off thinking about the subject, and my aim ... was to stimulate by new thought not merely by provocation'.

But it was television which brought Taylor fame as a presenter of public history through successive series of lectures delivered between 1957 and 1984. His lectures gave him an entrée into the lucrative world of the media celebrity, as signalled by several appearances on the high-profile *Parkinson* show – he appeared alongside such guests as Fanny Cradock, the celebrity cook; Kim Novak, a Hollywood star; and Bernard Manning, the controversial comedian – and *The Late Clive James* show. Taylor's television work began in 1950 with BBC's *In the News* programme (1950–4), a 'brains trust' using Taylor as part of a relatively regular panel including two MPs, Robert Boothby and Michael Foot, and a former MP, W.J. 'Bill' Brown. The cut-and-thrust of fierce debate proved good television, and attracted a substantial audience. Depicted as the 'TV don', Taylor became a national celebrity, consciously cultivating his reputation as a clever, witty and strongly opinionated arguer. But not everyone was impressed by his television persona, as demonstrated by Randolph Churchill's (quoted, Wrigley 2006: 221) claim that Taylor had only to see a television camera 'to lose resemblance to a human being. He then becomes an angry mountebank and buffoon.' Some BBC staff also articulated doubts about Taylor's qualities as a broadcaster, even dismissing him as second-rate after the 'sulky don' episode in November 1952 when he stopped talking in protest at the overtly political approach of his fellow panellists (BBC 1995).

In fact, it was ITV (Independent Television) which brought Taylor national prominence. Lew Grade, the Head of ATV (Associated Television), was looking for a programme for Sunday afternoons, but feared that a straight history lecture – this had been suggested by John Irwin after attending Taylor's Ford lectures – would be unsuitable for viewers. However, Grade changed his mind after meeting Taylor, who was already appearing on ITV reprising his *In the News* role for ITV's *Free Speech*. Taylor proposed a Russian history topic. Born in Russia, Grade was 'enthralled' by Taylor's ability to put things so simply and clearly, and knew that he was a star, 'an unusual type of star' (BBC 1995).

On 12 August 1957 Taylor delivered the first of three 30-minute programmes produced by Irwin. Already, the *TV Times* of 9 August had previewed the programme in terms of 'Alan Taylor starts a "Revolution" on ITV'. Taking up this theme, the programme's announcer challenged viewers right at the start:

Can a brilliant historian talking about a fascinating subject hold the attention of a television audience of millions for half an hour? That is the question, and the answer lies with you. Our subject is the Russian Revolution, this evening's theme The End of the Tsars, our historian, Alan Taylor, fellow of Magdalen College, Oxford. (BBC 1995)

Taylor (quoted, Wrigley 2000: xxiii) opined that history lecturing on television was on trial: 'It's not only me on trial but the whole idea of lecturing on TV.' When looking forward to the opening programme, Taylor expressed optimism that 'the British public has an appetite for things which are intellectually interesting and stimulating on the mind'. If the experiment worked, he anticipated 'a tremendous university of the air in no time'. The success of the opening programmes led ITV to commission a 13-programme series, *When Europe was the Centre of the World*. Further series followed, but Taylor's presentational role was not confined to ITV. Beginning in 1962, he made five series, totalling 30 lectures, for the BBC. Once again, political subjects, especially diplomacy, revolution and war, figured prominently. Transcripts of several television lecture series have been published, but when assessing presentation there is of course no substitute for watching an actual programme, such as held on video in a university library.

Generally speaking, Taylor's TV lectures, described by Jonathan Meades (1978) as 'illustrated radio', were well received in terms of conveying the pleasures of history to the British people. Success was indicated by the fact that he was asked back repeatedly to do more. A brilliant storyteller, Taylor made history matter for the man in the street, while demonstrating that 'an intelligent talking head' (Isaacs 2004: 37) could be both '*visually* compelling' and entertaining. Such a lecture format would not be adjudged suitable for today's television audience, given the limited attention span of viewers and the perceived need to entertain as well as to educate. However, during the period between the 1950s and 1970s, many television viewers had grown up in households where the radio was prominent, and hence accustomed to listen to the spoken word. Evoking the past with a light touch, Taylor was not scared to voice his own opinions and sympathies as a man of the left sympathetic to the people but attracted by men of power. Taylor (quoted, Wrigley 1980: 160) refused to countenance claims that his TV lectures, though requiring some lightening of both the subject matter and content, involved any compromising of historical standards through dumbing down to a mass audience:

> These lectures are intended as serious history, or as serious as I can make it. They are exactly like the lectures which I give at Oxford University except they are shorter and faster ... The lectures are taken

out of books and records as they would be on any earlier period. They are not presented as anecdotes or personal recollections.

Looking back, members of the studio audience recalled finding Taylor's lectures refreshing, especially as compared to school textbooks (Wrigley 2006: 273). Alan Sked (1996), a LSE-based historian, admitted that 'I came under his spell as a teenager watching his television lectures.' Even so, their actual historical impact remains debatable. For Roger Spalding (2002), Taylor's 'much-referred-to television lectures were, in reality, "turns". Viewers remember that he spoke without notes, and finished bang on time. They do not remember what he said.'

More importantly, his TV lectures secured good viewing figures despite being transmitted normally at non-peak hours, early (6.00–6.30pm) or late (10.35pm) evening. Many viewers, it appeared, carried on watching Taylor rather than change channels or switch off the television. The estimated audience for the second series was 0.75 million, a respectable figure for a non-peak programme at a time when relatively few (around 2.66 million) homes were able to receive ITV, which had only begun transmission in 1955 (Wrigley 2000: xxiii). Initial series were released also as gramophone records. During the early 1960s audience figures continued to improve to around four million as ITV extended its reach across the country. Such work proved extremely lucrative for Taylor – for example, in 1962 his fee was around £131 per lecture – but represented cheap television for the BBC and ITV.

Taylor was still lecturing on television during the early 1980s, even if by the late 1970s he was already showing occasional signs of age. He was still able to put on a good show and continued to attract an audience. But straight lectures, lacking visual aids, maps and dramatic re-enactments, were perceived increasingly by broadcasters as a somewhat dated mode of presentation – to quote the BBC's television controller (quoted, Wrigley 2006: 340) in 1979 – 'not suitable for television'. Despite participating in a less formal capacity in Granada's *Edge of Britain* series, designed in part to retrace his roots, Taylor refused to change the format, as evidenced by the final series on *How Wars End* undertaken for the new TV Channel 4 in the mid-1980s.

2006 and All That

According to Jeremy Popkin (2005: 183), historians writing auto-biographies face a difficult task, that is, 'to tell at least some of the truth about a life in academe without appearing smug about one's accomplishments, bitter about one's frustrations, jealous of the rewards reaped by others, or disloyal to one's discipline, and at the same time to make the story stimulating'. Perhaps the biggest problem, Popkin (2005: 6) feared, arose from the fact that historians' life stories always risked 'falling into the category of books deemed uninteresting' by readers.

Claiming that 'we historians are dull creatures, and women sometimes notice this', Taylor (1983: ix; quoted, Sisman 1994: 349) planned originally to entitle his memoirs *An Uninteresting Story*. In the event, his 'horribly revealing' (Wheatcroft 2006: 47) autobiography, entitled *A Personal History* (1983), ticked few of Popkin's boxes – Taylor revealed an arrogant, malicious, resentful character only too anxious to settle old scores – but few readers, listeners or viewers found either his personal story or histories 'uninteresting'. Indeed, one of his principal qualities as a presenter of history was an easy ability to reach out to a large and responsive audience within and outside academia.

Nor was Taylor's personal history dull. On the contrary, he had a somewhat striking, albeit complex and chaotic, private life involving three wives, six children, and multiple households, a situation aggravated by his alleged lack of understanding of the expectations of being a husband and/or father. Having suffered from his parents' marital difficulties, Taylor (1983: 106) experienced 'almost indescribable misery' from his first wife's affairs with Robert Kee, one of his students, and Dylan Thomas, the poet. Then, despite his second marriage to Eve Crosland, the sister of the Labour politician, Taylor still spent two days each week with his first wife for the sake of the children. Following their separation, Eve took two Israeli tennis coaches as lodgers, and then taunted Taylor (quoted, Sisman 1994: 81), who had observed after his first night in bed with Margaret that 'nothing was achieved as often happened with me', with their sexual prowess. Moreover, Eve threatened to sue if she were mentioned in Taylor's autobiography. Notwithstanding his remark that 'no intellectual woman attracted me sexually' and his repeated advocacy (in the *Daily Herald*) of seven-year marriages, Taylor (quoted, Burk 2000b) claimed to have found happiness through his third marriage to a Hungarian historian, Éva Haraszti. Even so, she took time to adjust to Taylor's domestic arrangements concerning his former wives. Obviously, our focus must be placed upon his career and reputation as a history presenter, but Taylor's extensive extra-academic activities were motivated in part by his substantial domestic commitments and expensive tastes, such as for fast cars and fine wines.

Speaking in March 1986 at Taylor's eightieth birthday party, Michael Foot (quoted, Wrigley 2006: 361), who led the Labour Party between 1980 and 1983, predicted that:

> Alan Taylor has introduced us to the great historians – Macaulay and others. Alan himself is among them. In a hundred years' time – that is if Alan's gloomy predictions about The Bomb have not come true – then the people of this country will be reading Alan Taylor's books just as people now still read Macaulay.

Inevitably, during the two decades since his death in 1990, Taylor's reputation as a major British historian responsible for expanding, even transforming, ways of presenting history has been subject to continual reassessment. According to Chris Wrigley (1980), by the late 1970s Taylor had written 23 books, edited and/or introduced 26 books, and published 45 historical essays, 459 press articles and 1550 book reviews. Several books remain in print, and are listed still on student reading lists or read for pleasure and interest by general readers. Three biographies, written by Kathleen Burk (2000a), Adam Sisman (1994) and Chris Wrigley (2006), have been published already, while Robert Cole (1993) produced an in-depth analysis of Taylor's histories. Taylor has been the subject of special issues of academic journals, the *Journal of Modern History* (1975) – for Taylor (quoted, Sisman 1994: 375), this represented his 'intellectual biography' – and the *International History Review* (2001); three festschrifts published in 1966, 1976 and 1986; and several radio and television programmes, most notably *A.J.P. Taylor, History Man* (BBC 1981), *Reputations: A.J.P. Taylor – An Unusual Type of Star* (BBC 1995), and *AJP at the BBC* (BBC 2010).

Taylor has attracted more attention from biographers than any other recent historian. Quite apart from helping to preserve his visibility as both a historian and public figure, most notably prompting numerous commentaries and book reviews in academic journals and the national press, biographers have presented a somewhat mixed impression of their subject. Generally speaking, praise for his skills as a narrative historian presenting history to both academic and popular audiences has been qualified by revelations about Taylor's spiteful nature, bitterness about the regius chair episode, harsh treatment of Namier, cringing praise of Beaverbrook, and eccentric private life.

The centenary year of Taylor's birth, 2006, saw yet another biography – the author was Chris Wrigley (2006) – as well as the publication of several commentaries marking the anniversary and/or reviewing Wrigley's book. Frequently commentators adopted a critical line suggesting the ephemeral impact of Taylor's books and television performances. Writing as a former admirer, indeed someone who still acknowledged Taylor's 'intensely readable' writing, in March 2006 Geoffrey Wheatcroft (2006: 46–9) painted an extremely negative portrait. Viewing Taylor's reputation predominantly in terms of decline and fall, he pointed to the way in which the personal failings highlighted by biographers were compounded by his shortcomings as a historian: 'I have myself come close to feeling that almost nothing he says can ever be accepted without collaboration.' In this vein, Wheatcroft cited historical distortions arising from Taylor's 'bigoted Germanophobia', dogmatic hostility towards the USA, and uncritical approach concerning the Soviet Union. Even worse was his 'utterly disgraceful' admiration of Beaverbrook.

Building upon Wheatcroft's critique, Cannadine (2006) – it will be recalled that Taylor had inspired his interest in history – feared that Taylor's standing as a historian had been 'in irretrievable decline' since his death:

> Taylor's reputation has fallen still further: with three well-meant but unflattering biographies; his pioneering television lectures have been largely forgotten, his books no longer sell, and his journalism seems embarrassing ... When Taylor stopped publishing, there was nothing else: he stood, or rather fell, by what was already in print.

His image has not been helped by the lack of a Taylor school of history. For Sisman (1994: 368; Brivati 1993: 602), there was, and is, no one quite like Taylor, whose individualism means that the concept of an A.J.P. Taylor school must be dismissed as a contradiction in terms.

> He was magnificently oblivious to orthodoxy, and deeply distrusted 'confederated learning'. Nothing was more likely to set him on the opposite course than an expression such as 'it is generally held that ...'. Other historians moved in schools, like fish swimming together; when they clashed, it was *en masse*, like army battalions. He fought his battles single-handed. He was an individualist, an iconoclast, an independent.

Nor is Taylor's status as a public figure secure. Despite devoting a whole chapter to him as one of Britain's leading twentieth-century intellectuals in *Absent Minds: intellectuals in Britain*, Cambridge's Stefan Collini (2006: 392) concluded that Taylor was better at exercising his voice to articulate prejudices rather than saying something worthwhile for a wider audience.

But Taylor still has many supporters. Norman Davies (2007: 62–3), a former pupil, conceded the negatives revealed in biographies and recent commentaries, but concluded that nonetheless 'Taylor must be rated an academic heavyweight.' Perhaps the most robust defence emanated from Richard Vinen. As Vinen (2006) complained, critics judged Taylor against standards higher than those applied to any other historian, even writing as though he never had a reputation worth considering. Describing Taylor's *The Struggle for Mastery in Europe, 1848–1918* (1954) as 'erudite and authoritative', Vinen praised *Origins of the Second World War*: 'it redefined the subject so dramatically that it is hard now to imagine how subsequent histories would have been written without it'. Pointing to criticisms of Taylor for being old-fashioned, Vinen noted with pleasure that 'narrative history designed for a wide public is back in fashion': 'In part, Taylor is a victim of his own success. Professional historians may not read Taylor much, but they are uncomfortably aware that the reading public still does, and this provokes their resentment.' Indeed, in 2008 *The Times* (2008) listed Taylor as one of Britain's leading post-1945 writers. Moreover, as mentioned above, Taylor is recognised still by today's broadcasters, 'journodons' and TV historians as leading the way in the press and on radio and television.

For many historians, Taylor remains a good read, a historian worth recommending to students, and a role model regarding the adoption of a sceptical revisionist mindset towards the past. Let me illustrate the last point with a brief anecdote. In 2008 I published a book review strongly critiquing the author's fundamental thesis. Nevertheless, the review concluded by stating that the book was still worth reading, since the author, like A.J.P. Taylor, encouraged readers to re-think their position on the whole topic. Soon after the review appeared, the author sent me an email recording that the comparison made in print with Taylor was one of the biggest compliments he had ever received!

Conclusion

Less than 40 years ago Taylor was both Britain's best-known historian and a prominent public figure, a celebrity historian famous for his fame as much as for his professional status. Clearly, there remains scope for further reassessments of Taylor's reputation, particularly given the unduly pessimistic view articulated by Cannadine and Wheatcroft.

Taylor's qualities as a history presenter – for Tosh (2006: 154), he was 'the narrative historian *par excellence*' – renowned for his readability is complemented by his status as a revisionist historian encouraging, even forcing, other historians to re-think existing versions of the past in a fresh light and providing the basis for historiographical debates which continue to resonate today. Writing in 1953, Martin Wight (1953: 639) pointed out that Taylor, 'our most distinguished international historian', is 'distinguished from so many professional historians by possessing not only a trenchant style but also a historiographical personality. This is the reason why he is so readable and worth reading.' Several decades later, Norman Stone (1991; 1998) echoed such thoughts, when observing that Taylor's histories 'will be read as long as historians are read': 'his best books will belong in English literature – the only way for any historian to survive the obsolescence of his facts'.

Impatient with received opinions about the past, Taylor took pleasure in providing a fresh reference point for major historiographical controversies. Like any other historian, Taylor (quoted, Sisman 1994: 400–1) saw himself as merely presenting one version of the past: 'The fact that there are other versions does not make any one of them wrong. It is just like taking different views about a human being.' Unsurprisingly, Taylor presented himself somewhat arrogantly as offering a better version arising from his critical and informed questioning of existing histories, as well as from his ability to view past events in a new light. Even so, his revisionism resulted largely from taking an alternative view based on wide reading rather than presenting new knowledge based upon extensive archival research. Claiming that his mind was 'too anarchic to be fitted into any system of thought', Taylor (1956: vii; 1977a: 4) asserted that:

> I am not a philosophic historian. I have no system, no moral interpretation. I write to clear my mind, to discover how things happened and how men behaved. If the result is shocking or provocative, this is not from intent, but solely because I try to judge from the evidence without being influenced by the judgments of others.

Of course, this was mere spin, given his technicolour personality, deliberately opinionated nature, revisionist mindset, and strongly held moral feelings. Taylor proved to be – to quote Ferguson (1999: 213) – 'an inveterate troublemaker'; indeed, his support for a line of argument 'grew in more or less direct proportion to the number of people it annoyed'.

Naturally, the qualities characterising Taylor's writing were reflected in his lecturing. For Paul Addison (1990: 3–4), another former pupil, Taylor proved an inspiring spoken presenter of history:

> It was like being spirited away in a time-machine. To say that he brought the past to life would be true but quite inadequate. What he conveyed was the sense that the past was an unexplored country in which the traveller was always on the brink of fresh discoveries.

A confident and impressive grasp of his subject was reinforced by an ability to make complex topics clear and comprehensible. A skilled, authoritative and effective oral communicator, Taylor led the way in taking up the challenging task of presenting history to a wide range of audiences outside Oxford. Generally recognised as the public face of a subject confined previously to the ivory tower, he 'made history a somewhat less serious business than it otherwise would have been' (Kennedy 1986: 12) when reaching out to readers, listeners, and viewers.

For many Britons, their historical knowledge was heavily influenced by Taylor's presentation of the past on television. For several decades, he proved 'the wizard of the television studios' (Addison 2001). When introducing Taylor's opening television lecture in 1957, the voiceover presented the programme as an experiment. The fact that Taylor was asked back repeatedly by both the BBC and ITV for over two decades to deliver further series of history lectures indicated that, far from remaining experimental, history came to be regarded as an established feature of TV programming in Britain, capable of attracting a substantial viewing audience. As such, Taylor, albeit perhaps remembered more for the style rather than the content of his TV lectures, pioneered what Addison (2001) has described as the 'new and important medium of public history', and set the benchmark for today's tele-dons. Where Taylor led, Schama, Starkey and Ferguson, among others, have followed. Of course, as detailed in chapter 6, today's presenters of history on television adopt a very different approach. Faced by viewers possessing limited attention spans, they avoid a lecture-type format, have scripts, incorporate considerable visual resources, and use dramatic re-enactment, but build upon foundations laid down by Taylor over 50 years ago in what Schama (2009b: 696) described as 'a different cultural universe'. Moreover, most specifically acknowledge their debt to Taylor's early forays on the box.

Despite his fame within and outside historical circles – admission as a Fellow of the British Academy in 1956 was taken as validating his status as a serious academic historian – Taylor was not showered with major distinctions. Nor was he recognised nationally through a knighthood or peerage, such as received by Trevor-Roper, Taylor's professional rival and antagonist in the debate about the origins of war in 1939, who became Lord Dacre. Typically, Taylor (1983: 223, 244) claimed he would never have accepted a knighthood. Repeated use of the title 'Mr Taylor' in reviews of his work – one example by Trevor-Roper was quoted above – was revealing in terms of highlighting Taylor's lack of professorial status and failure to lay claim to a doctoral title. Despite securing a pass for his doctoral thesis at Manchester, Taylor never presented himself for the award of the degree. Instead, he secured a range of honorary doctorates including Bristol, Manchester, New Brunswick, Warwick and York. Taylor was never made a professor by Oxford, even if many people assumed he must be a professor. Taking much pleasure in being hailed as the 'Plain Man's Historian', Taylor (1983: 196, 220) is perhaps best described as the 'people's professor', whose histories, journalism and TV lectures made him at the time the most popular presenter of public history: 'These lectures gave me individual fame. No longer was I addressed at random as Bill Brown or Sir Robert Boothby. To taxi drivers, bus conductors, coal miners everywhere I was unmistakably "Alan". This was truly popular education. I was taking history to ordinary people.' As Andrew Roberts (2000c) remarked.

A.J.P. Taylor popularised history for the masses as no historian had done since Macaulay ... Taylor made history come alive for hundreds of thousands, perhaps millions of people ... Taylor encouraged people to reawaken their latent but untutored interest in history, and no historian can hope for a finer epitaph than that.

Alan John Percivale Taylor (1906–90): Select Bibliography

Histories

1934	*The Italian Problem in European Diplomacy, 1847–1849*
1938	*Germany's First Bid for Colonies, 1884–85: a move in Bismarck's European diplomacy*
1941	*The Hapsburg Monarchy, 1815–1918: a history of the Austrian Empire and Austria-Hungary* (rev.ed. 1948)
1945	*The Course of German History*
1954	*The Struggle for Mastery in Europe, 1848–1918*

→

1955	*Bismarck: the man and the statesman*
1957	*The Troublemakers: dissent over foreign policy 1792–1939*
1961	*Origins of the Second World War* (rev. edn. 1963)
1965	*English History 1914–1945*
1969	*War by Timetable: how the First World War began*
1972	*Beaverbrook*
1979	*How Wars Begin*
1985	*How Wars End*

Autobiography

| 1983 | *A Personal History* |

Television series

[number of programmes given in brackets]

1957	*Russian Revolution* (ITV)	[3]
1957–58	*When Europe was the centre of the World* (ITV)	[13]
1960	*Prime Ministers* (ITV)	[6]
1962	*The Twenties* (BBC)	[6]
1963	*Men of the 1860s* (BBC)	[6]
1966	*World War* (ITV)	[10]
1967	*Revolution 1917* (ITV)	[5]
1976	*The War Lords* (BBC)	[6]
1977	*How Wars Begin* (BBC)	[6]
1978	*Revolution* (BBC)	[6]
1980	*Edge of Britain* (ITV)	[4]
1984–5	*How Wars End* (TV Channel Four)	[6]

Reference work

| 1980 | Chris J. Wrigley (ed.), *A.J.P. Taylor: a complete annotated bibliography* |

5
Eric Hobsbawm: The Marxist Historian

In October 2008 Eric Hobsbawm was interviewed at length on BBC Radio 4's flagship *Today* programme about the resurgence of interest in Marx's writings during the global economic and financial crisis. Introduced as 'perhaps our greatest living historian' (BBC 2008a), Hobsbawm argued that capitalism, an inherently unstable system, was facing its greatest test since the Great Depression of 1929. In this manner, as argued by Gregory Elliott (2010: xi, 143–9), Hobsbawm acted as a public intellectual, using his professional authority to pronounce on issues of the day. Not every listener welcomed the BBC's decision to give Hobsbawm, a self-confessed Marxist and former long-time member of the Communist Party of Great Britain (CPGB), a 15-minute slot on prime-time radio. Writing in *The Times*, Michael Gove (2008), the Shadow Cabinet spokesman for schools (Secretary of State for Education, 2010–), attacked 'Moscow-liner' Hobsbawm as 'our greatest living apologist': 'He is not, as the BBC argued this week, perhaps our greatest living historian. He's an apologist for totalitarianism ... I am convinced that only when Hobsbawm weeps hot tears for a life spent serving an ideology of wickedness will he ever be worth listening to.'

Even during his nineties, Hobsbawm remains capable of making a national, even global, impact, as a historian, given the divergent opinions about the extent to which his Marxist credentials enable him to offer an informed historical perspective upon recent developments, let alone affect his qualities as a detached presenter of history. Only a few days before his BBC interview, Hobsbawm attracted further international media visibility as a lead signatory of the *Appel de Blois* (chapter 13) identifying the threat posed to historians by memory legislation. One month later, Hobsbawm, introduced as 'one of the foremost historians in international terms of the 20th Century' responsible for revolutionising social history, was in Germany to receive the Bochum History Prize (Ritscher 2008).

Hobsbawm is best known for his four-volume history of the world from 1789 to 1991. Indeed, the final volume, *Age of Extremes* (1994), proved his most successful book to date in terms of critical reception, sales, and foreign editions. Within a decade it had been translated into over 36 languages. Inevitably, the book further enhanced his reputation as a skilled history presenter capable throughout his career of reaching a large global audience within and outside academia through his written histories, journalism, lectures and broadcasts. In 1996 Hobsbawm's 'distinguished contribution to the writing of history over a long period of time', with specific reference to writing for the general public, was recognised by the award of the Wolfson History Prize (Wolfson Foundation 2010). Histories of jazz, like jazz reviews published for the *New Statesman*, written as 'Francis Newton', a pseudonym inspired by the American trumpeter Frankie Newton, provide an added popular dimension to his career.

Drawing upon his multilingual skills, Hobsbawm (quoted, Hunt 2002; quoted, 'Making History' 2008) has achieved considerable global reach, targeting 'educated but non-specialist' readers 'curious about the past' and anxious 'to understand how and why the world has come to be what it is today'. Rationalising his role as a public historian, Hobsbawm pointed to the example set by Trevelyan and Taylor, among others: 'Choosing to write for a broad public isn't only my personal choice. I regard it as part of a long English tradition. After all, this is a country in which even the most important thinkers have expressed their views for the broad public.' When taking on such a task there was, he admitted, always a 'risk of people saying well, of course, he's talking down, you know', but for Hobsbawm the role of public historian was a function of being a Marxist historian: 'We reacted against a tradition of historians between the wars who were suspicious of talking to the public for fear of talking down.'

A Marxist Historian

For Eugene Genovese (1984: 13), 'to be "Hobsbawmian" means to be Marxist'. Hobsbawm has made no secret of either his treatment of Karl Marx and Friedrich Engels as sources of intellectual inspiration, adoption of a Marxist approach to history or lengthy membership of the CPGB. Hobsbawm (1998: 208) believed that Marx, though failing to write much history as understood by historians, viewed the world historically in the sense that everything he wrote was 'impregnated with history'. Lecturing in 1983 at San Marino's 'Marx Centenary Conference', Hobsbawm

(1998: 223) represented Marxism as a prime factor 'modernizing' the writing of history. Far from being embarrassed by the Marxist tag and the inevitable taunts about ideological bias, historical distortions, and so on, Hobsbawm has taken pride in representing himself as a 'Marxist historian' or 'Marxist intellectual'. Apart from joining the Marxist-inspired communist party 'to change the world in association with the labour and socialist movements', Hobsbawm (1998: ix–x; 2002a: 97; 2005) saw Marxism as providing the best way of understanding the history of the world in general and of modern capitalism in particular.

Drawing historians closer to the social sciences, Marxism, as articulated in the *Communist Manifesto* (1848) and *Das Kapital* (1867), offered a comprehensive theoretical framework for understanding, ordering, interpreting and presenting the past. In effect, as asserted by E.P. Thompson (1978: 212), the Marxist approach to history prescribed 'a *programmed* succession of historical "stages", motored towards a pre-determined end by class struggle' (Perry 2002: 29–46; Eley 2003: 63–7). Impressed by the rise of science, Marx claimed to offer an objective approach based upon scientific laws predetermining the past, present and future. Applying Georg Hegel's dialectical process, as used to explain philosophical development, to political and socioeconomic developments (Box 5.1), Marx presented history as a series

---

Box 5.1   Marx and the dialectical process

i)   The dialectical process was used by Hegel to explain philosophical development. Conflicting ideas (thesis and antithesis) produced a synthesis, which became the new thesis:
THESIS → *ANTITHESIS* → *SYNTHESIS* → ... *THESIS* (the old *SYNTHESIS*) → *ANTITHESIS*, and so on.

ii) Marx applied the dialectical process to political and socioeconomic developments, past, present and future. Class struggle provided the basis for revolutionary change to a new type of society. The existing regime (*Thesis*) came into increasing conflict with the emerging class (*Antithesis*). The resulting conflict led to a new form of society (*Synthesis*), which then became the new *Thesis*.

   – Marxist theory explained the historical development of present-day society, while predicting the inevitability of a classless socialist society:
   Feudalism v Bourgeoisie → CAPITALISM
   Bourgeoisie v Proletariat → SOCIALISM

of stages following on inevitably from each other. Thus, the bourgeoisie's (capitalists') struggle against the feudal aristocracy would be followed in time by that of the workers preparing the way for the eventual
emergence of a classless socialist society.

For Marx, the driving force in history was historical materialism, the
struggle of human society to meet material needs. Providing a critique
of capitalism stressing the inevitability of success, Marxism armed
the working class with an understanding of how it could achieve its
own emancipation and how capitalism contained the seeds of its
own destruction. Class consciousness as, say, a 'capitalist' or 'worker',
and struggle led to revolutionary change, as stated in *The Communist
Manifesto* (1848): 'The history of all society up to now is the history of
class struggles. ... Oppressor and oppressed stood in continual conflict
with one another ... a struggle that finished each time with a revolutionary transformation of society as a whole.'

Encountering Marx

Hobsbawm's longstanding support for Marxist history and 50-year
plus membership of the CPGB can be understood only by knowing his
personal history. Significantly, Hobsbawm (1998: 1), who has often been
depicted as 'so pre-eminently cosmopolitan yet also so unmistakably
English' (Snowman 1999: 16), has described himself as 'an outsider who
is also an insider'. Born in Alexandria, Egypt, in 1917 and subsequently
resident in Austria and Germany between 1919 and 1933, Hobsbawm
has lived most of his life in Britain. Throughout his childhood postwar
economic difficulties meant that his family, like many others, moved on
constantly in search of work. Perhaps the key constant was Hobsbawm's
stress upon his status as both an Englishman – his mother was Austrian
but his father was English – and, albeit to a lesser extent, a Jew.

Living through an era steeped in politics, Hobsbawm (2002a: 11, 13)
admitted that he was 'seized so young and so long by that typical twentieth-century passion, political commitment'. Growing up in Vienna
and Berlin during the late 1920s and the early 1930s, a period of sharp
ideological conflict conducted against the background of political insta-
bility, economic depression and social dislocation, 'one acquired political consciousness as naturally as sexual awareness'. Despite recording
that he became a communist in 1932, Hobsbawm (2002a: 127) did
not actually join the communist party itself until 1936. Berlin's
Prinz-Heinrichs-Gymnasium offered the young man his window on what

proved a decisive moment in world history. The brief period spent in Berlin between July 1931 and April 1933, when Hobsbawm (1998: 304–5; 2002a: 55-6; 2008: 34–5) witnessed at first hand the rise of both the Nazi Party and the Communist Party of Germany (KPD), 'determined my politics and my interest in history'. Events, most notably news of Hitler's coming to power, became 'a part of the past which is still part of my present': 'I can still see the scene.'

Rejecting the Nazi option – Hitler's stress on German nationalism and anti-Semitism lacked appeal to an English Jew – Hobsbawm (2002a: 58, 71–4, 137–40) gravitated almost inevitably towards the KPD through membership of the *Sozialistischer Schülerbund* (SSB), a Young Communist organization engaged in endless hours of marching, waving red flags, and singing party songs. Quite apart from the fact that the KPD was perceived to be part of a global movement hostile to fascism, Hobsbawm was attracted by the party's emphasis upon the idea of revolution with the industrial working class as the agency of change. At a time of severe depression, despair ruled, and the old world seemed doomed. Whereas his Aryan schoolmates talked about national rebirth under the Nazis, Hobsbawm (2002a: 73: 2008: 35) believed that only a 1917 Bolshevik-type revolution offered the prospect of a better future: 'we dreamed of great tomorrows'. Henceforth, he faced the present-day world, 'always with the confidence, derived from Marxism, that our victory was already inscribed in the text of the history books of the future'.

Offering an intellectual underpinning for his political convictions, Marx's writings reinforced Hobsbawm's interest in history. At school in Berlin, he told a teacher about his growing support for the KPD. Unimpressed, the master questioned whether Hobsbawm knew what he was talking about, and sent him off to the library. As Hobsbawm (2002a: 54) recalled, 'I did so, and discovered the Communist Manifesto.' For Hobsbawm (1998: ix–x, 207; quoted, Snowman 2007: 16), this discovery 'was a knockout!', and was to prove significant for his life and career, given the uninspiring nature of history teaching in both Berlin and London: 'Without Marx I would not have developed any special interest in history ... I would almost certainly not have come to earn my living as a professional academic historian.'

'An Aged Extremist'

Admissions of Marx's influence upon both his political thinking and historical methodology have ensured that Hobsbawm's presentation of the past has attracted not only close attention as an example of the impact of theory on the presentation of history but also frequent criticism from historians and the media accusing him of presenting audiences with a distorted and biased left-wing version of events for political reasons.

Challenging descriptors of Hobsbawm as an academic historian, in 2003 David Pryce-Jones (2003: 9), the senior editor of the USA-based *National Review*, criticised Hobsbawm as 'someone who has steadily corrupted knowledge into propaganda, and scorns the concept of objective truth'; thus, he was 'neither a historian nor professional'. Pointing to lapses into Marxist dialectic, Andrew Roberts (1994) complained that Hobsbawm's histories read like a communist manifesto written by 'an Aged Extremist'. Readers, he advised, should steer clear of them 'unless you want to understand the mind-set that ensured communism was allowed to soil this century's history for so long'. Arguably, these critiques tell readers as much about Pryce-Jones and Roberts as Hobsbawm, but such right-wing diatribes highlight the controversies surrounding his role as a presenter of the past, as well as the fact that many historians and media commentators have worried, and worry still, about the fundamental merit of a Marxist presentation of history.

In this vein, over time, numerous historians, including Elton (2002: 33), Himmelfarb (1987: 90), Marwick (2001: 267) and Trevor-Roper (1981b: 358–9), have asserted that Marxist theory offered a fundamentally flawed basis for studying the past, because presenters were imprisoned by an ideology claiming to provide a predetermined schema applicable to all periods and events. Taylor (1977a: 4) joined the CPGB briefly in the 1920s, but soon rejected the Marxist approach to history:

> I called myself a Marxist ... But reading more history at Oxford, I began to feel that Marxism did not work. Consider the famous sentence in the Communist Manifesto: 'The history of all hitherto recorded society is the history of class struggles.' Very impressive, but not true ... There have been long periods of class collaboration and many struggles that were not about class at all ... I have tried to be a Marxist but common sense kept breaking in.

By contrast, Hobsbawm remained loyal to the CPGB, even after the serious crisis of conscience consequent upon the Soviet Union's brutal suppression of the 1956 Hungarian Revolution. Even so, over time Hobsbawm began to accept political realities, most notably the fact that in the west there was not going to be any communist revolution from below.

From Berlin to London and Cambridge

Three months after Hitler came to power Hobsbawm, whose parents had both died by 1931, moved to London with his uncle, who migrated in search of work, not as a refugee from Nazism. Hobsbawm (2008: 34) was underwhelmed by his new home:

> Imagine yourselves ... as a newspaper correspondent based in Manhattan and transferred by your editor to Omaha, Nebraska. That's how I felt when I came to England after almost two years in the unbelievably exciting, sophisticated, intellectually and politically explosive Berlin of the Weimar Republic. The place was a terrible letdown.

The jazz scene was one of London's few redeeming features.

History teaching at St Marylebone Grammar School proved no better than that offered in Berlin, but this failed to deter Hobsbawm from moving on to study history at King's College, Cambridge. At Cambridge, where he edited *Granta*, the student weekly, he joined the CPGB in autumn 1936 and attended the Cambridge Apostles, a secret debating society. Other members included Guy Burgess and Anthony Blunt, who were later exposed as Soviet spies. Paris became a regular holiday location; indeed, Hobsbawm (2002a: 315) confessed to losing his virginity in a Paris brothel during this period.

CPGB membership determined Hobsbawm's (2002a: 129, 134) attitude to contemporary events, given the need to follow, or at least not to appear as dissenting from, the party line: 'The Party had the first, or more precisely the only real claim on our lives. Its demands had absolute priority. We accepted its discipline and hierarchy.' Apart from making it unthinkable to have a serious relationship with an outsider – in 1943 Hobsbawm married a fellow party member – CPGB membership ruled out acceptance of contemporary reports about the brutal and repressive, even genocidal, nature of the Stalinist regime (BBC 1994; Price 2003). Recently, what Robert Conquest (2000: 50, 295) described as Hobsbawm's 'addiction to Marxism' and denials of knowledge about harsh Soviet realities have attracted considerable flak, even prompting comparisons with Holocaust deniers like David Irving (Pryce-Jones 2001; 2003: 9; Gove 2008).

Following graduation in summer 1939 with a starred first – he was the only student given a distinction in the History tripos – Hobsbawm stayed on at Cambridge to conduct postgraduate research on French

North Africa. But the Second World War soon intervened. CPGB membership ensured that his war – Hobsbawm served in the Royal Engineers and Army Educational Corps – was mundane, since his politics ensured exclusion from sensitive areas, like the intelligence services. Subsequently, Hobsbawm has been unable to secure FOI access to his MI5 file (Levy 2009). Wartime experience of public speaking for the Educational Corps led Hobsbawm to realise that he was no mass orator, no A.J.P. Taylor.

After the war Hobsbawm returned to his doctorate, but the postwar difficulties of visiting North Africa forced a change of topic to the history of the Fabian Society. In 1947 he obtained a lecturing post at Birkbeck College, University of London, and remained there until his retirement in 1982. Promotion to a professorship came in 1970. Completing his doctorate successfully in 1950 while working at Birkbeck, Hobsbawm (2003) saw himself increasingly as a 'labour historian' specialising in the late nineteenth-century labour movement. Although there was no McCarthyite-type purge against communists in Britain, the Cold War ensured that it was a challenging time for CPGB members working in the intellectual professions. Certainly, Hobsbawm, albeit invited to deliver talks on BBC radio in 1947, believed that party membership helped explain both his delayed promotion to a readership – this came eventually in 1959 – and failure to secure a lecturing post at Cambridge. For Hobsbawm (2002a: 183-4; quoted, 'Making History' 2008), it was as much victimisation as exclusion. In particular, in 1954 he suspected that Hutchinson's rejection of his manuscript for a contracted book entitled *The Rise of the Wage Worker* was prompted by political rather than academic reasons, and even contemplated legal action. Such discrimination, alongside the west's crusading global anti-communism, served merely to reaffirm, not shake, Hobsbawm's (2002a: 180) political beliefs.

The Communist Party Historians' Group

Following the breakdown of his marriage during the early 1950s in circumstances which left him wounded and depressed, Hobsbawm filled his time with writing, teaching, travel, and party work. In 1962 he remarried. 'Party work' largely involved operating in intellectual groups, most notably the British Communist Party Historians' Group (CPHG), not political activism. For Hobsbawm, the group represented an essential part of his formation as a historian, and hence his presentational role should be viewed also as part of a collective CPHG contribution to historical knowledge and understanding. This group, which included Christopher Hill, Rodney Hilton, Victor Kiernan, George Rudé, Raphael Samuel, John Saville and E.P. Thompson, conducted a regular Marxist seminar held normally in an upper room of Camden's Garibaldi Restaurant or at Marx House, Clerkenwell (Schwarz 1982: 44–9). The year 1956 proved a crisis year for the CPHG. Several participants, including Hill and Thompson, resigned their party membership in protest at the Soviet Union's suppression of the Hungarian uprising. Hobsbawm (BBC 1994) had his doubts, but remained in the party because of his continuing belief in the communist ideal.

Apart from highlighting the politics of intellectual activity and the growing influence of Marxist thought in academia, during its brief lifetime the CPHG made a substantial impact upon history, particularly economic and social history. According to Phillipp Schofield (2004: 182), 'in no other country in the West did the critical mass of Marxist historiography generated in the immediate postwar period match that to be found in Britain'. In particular, the CPHG championed novel approaches like 'history from below': 'History was not words on a page, not the goings-on of kings and prime ministers, not mere events. History was the sweat, blood, tear and triumphs of the common people, our people' (Thomson *et al.* 1954: 8).

One enduring legacy, reflected also by Hobsbawm's current presidency of the Past and Present Society, is the prestigious journal *Past and Present*, launched in 1952 to reach out beyond the group to foster – to quote Hobsbawm (2003) – 'the international modernization of historiography in the 1950s and 1960s'. A commemorative *Past and Present* portrait, including Hobsbawm, is held by London's National Portrait Gallery (Farthing 1999). By contrast, the CPHG encountered less success in popularising communist party history. As Hobsbawm (1978: 29) recalled, during the late 1940s a four-volume collective documentary history entitled 'History in the Making' was produced for 'the public of trade union and adult education readers, which did not take them up, and for a public of students which did not yet exist'. Clearly, the early phase of the Cold War provided too hostile a climate for such a venture.

Paradoxically, yet understandably, given the strict party line constraining the presentation of such topics, the CPHG's members avoided writing histories of the Soviet Union and the Communist Party. Despite claiming to be unaware of the extent of the horrors of Soviet camps in the Gulags, Hobsbawm was not alone in expressing scepticism, albeit only in private, about official Soviet histories. Nor was he impressed by the Soviet model in practice. In December 1954 Hobsbawm (2002a: 196, 200), accompanied by other CPHG members, visited the Soviet Union, but returned 'depressed, and without any desire to go there again'. In fact, he did not make another visit until 1970, and then undertook several tourist-type visits during the 1980s when working in Helsinki.

Presenting World History

For Hobsbawm (2003), the defining events in European and world history during the 'long nineteenth century' between 1776 and 1914 were the 1789 French Revolution, the Industrial Revolution and the 1848 Revolutions.

> Anyone who is attracted to history by the Communist Manifesto is likely to be interested, first and foremost, by the emergence of the modern world, what Marx called 'modern bourgeois society that has sprouted from the ruins of feudal society', and the unprecedented and revolutionary process of globalisation and social transformation inherent to its development. Indeed, most of my writing as a professional historian was to be concerned with this process in one way or another, and specifically with the period since the political and industrial revolutions of the late eighteenth century.

Subsequently, Hobsbawm moved on to 'the short twentieth century', defined as the period between 1914 and 1991, including the 1917 Russian Revolution and the collapse of the Soviet bloc in 1989–91.

Such thinking underpinned Hobsbawm's *magnum opus*, that is, a four-volume history of the world since the French Revolution published between 1962 and 1994: *The Age of Revolution: Europe 1789–1848* (1962); *The Age of Capital, 1848–75* (1975); *The Age of Empire, 1875–1914* (1987); and *Age of Extremes: the short twentieth century, 1914–91* (1994). Despite the apparent overall unity of the series, the initial volume was treated as a one-off publication. For Hobsbawm (2002a: 185), the commissioning of a book on *The Age of Revolution*, supported by a £500 advance, offered the opportunity to write an ambitious historical synthesis in Weidenfeld & Nicolson's internationally co-produced 'History of Civilization'. In turn, the academic and commercial success of this book, drawing in part upon drafts tested in his teaching, encouraged the commissioning of three further volumes, taking the story up until the 1990s.

The tetralogy's unifying theme came not so much from its sequential nature but rather from an underlying Marxist methodology viewing developments in terms of a pattern of mutually incompatible binary opposites. Class-consciousness and class-conflict proved enduring but not overpowering features. For Perry (2002: 157), Hobsbawm applied Marxist history with an ever-lighter touch, as revealed by 'the virtual absence of the working class as an agent of historical change' in the *Age of Extremes*. What particularly interested Hobsbawm (1987: xi; 2003) was the search for synthesis, enabling readers to see the past as a coherent whole and 'to know how all these aspects of past (or present) life hang together, and why'. Seeking 'to understand and explain a world in the process of revolutionary transformation', Hobsbawm (1987: xi; 2003) presented the transition from a pre-capitalist to a capitalist society 'not as a continuous process but as a series of advances broken by periods of crises and restructurations'. Thus, in *The Age of Revolution* Hobsbawm (1962: 1) viewed the revolutions of 1789–1848 as 'the triumph of *capitalist* industry' and middle-class liberal society, with subsequent volumes centring upon the global advance of industrial capitalism and society. Over time, the series, though continuing to highlight his focus upon the common people living through periods of political, economic and social upheaval, reflected changes in Hobsbawm's approach. Once primarily a labour historian, he devoted relatively more attention to cultural issues in later volumes.

Presenting 'History from Below'

Traditionally, historians concentrated upon the elites and great men, and said relatively little about the common people. Specialising in economic and social history, Hobsbawm (1988: 13–28; Kaye 1984: 136–45), like his CPHG colleagues, prioritised 'history from below'. Also he treated labour history less as institutional and organisational history centred upon trade unions but more as the totality of working-class experience.

Despite glossing over the role of women – a 1980 article co-authored with Joan W. Scott (Scott and Hobsbawm 1980), the feminist historian, studied shoemakers, not women – Hobsbawm interpreted the 'common people' broadly, as evidenced by the way in which *Labouring Men* (1964) was complemented by publications on *Primitive Rebels* (1959), *Bandits* (1969) and *Revolutionaries* (1973). As such, his work complemented that of fellow CPHG members, like Rudé's *The Crowd in the French Revolution* (1959), Thompson's *Making of the English Working Classes* (1963) and

Hill's *The World Turned Upside Down* (1972). Excepting *Primitive Rebels* and *Labouring Men*, the key strength of Hobsbawm's work was in terms of theoretical analysis and synthesis, not original archival research, a task handicapped by the lack of any ready-made body of source materials detailing the thoughts and deeds of the 'people' (Hobsbawm 1988: 17–19). Nor did he see oral testimony as filling the gap. When interviewing former members of the Fabian Society for his doctorate, Hobsbawm (1998: 273, 307–8) soon discovered that oral evidence was 'a remarkably slippery medium' for the historian: 'memory is not so much a recording as a selective mechanism, and the selection is, within limits, constantly changing'. Moreover, he realised that for any independently verifiable fact memory was invariably wrong.

Presenting a History of His Own Times

For much of his career Hobsbawm (1995: 9; 2002a: 291) deliberately avoided working on the post-1914 period: 'Given the strong official Party and Soviet views about the twentieth century, one could not write about anything later than 1917 without the likelihood of being denounced as a political heretic ... My history finished at Sarajevo in June 1914.' However, when moving on to complete his four-volume world history, he found himself, whether he liked it or not, writing about events during his own lifetime. For Hobsbawm (1988: 26; 1995: x; Elliott 2010: 100–34), the main purpose of the *Age of Extremes* was not to tell the story, but rather to explain the past, 'and in doing so to provide a link with the present'.

Hobsbawm identified three factors influencing historians writing the history of their own times: personal experience; changing perspectives; and presentism. First, Hobsbawm (1998: viii, 302–4) openly admitted that his histories bore 'the marks of a man of my age, background, beliefs and life-experience'. Varying chronological, geographical, ideological, political and socioeconomic contexts – these were outlined above – ensured that *his personal angle of vision* was different from that of other historians, even from that of fellow Marxist historians, working in the same field.

The fact that Hobsbawm (1995: x, 4; 1998: 304) had lived through much of the period proved as much a disadvantage as an advantage. On the one hand, there were benefits from having lived through the events as 'a participant observer', as demonstrated by his frequent references to 'I was there' in Berlin when witnessing a newspaper headline announcing Hitler's accession as German chancellor. For Hobsbawm, the past became part of his permanent present, and hence presenting the period's history possessed elements of an autobiographical endeavour amplifying and correcting his memory. On the other hand, living through events, combined with the constraints imposed by CPGB membership, resulted in a natural tendency to view events subjectively from his 'private perch'. Having lived through the Great Depression, the Second World War and the Cold War, Hobsbawm (1995: ix, 4–5) found it difficult to remain detached: 'My own lifetime coincides with most of the period with which this book deals, and for most of it, from early teen-age to the present, I have been conscious of public affairs, that is to say I have accumulated views and prejudices about it as a contemporary rather than as a scholar.' This point is, of course, true for many other presenters, but applies with greater force to a Marxist historian living through a period of ideological conflict as a member of the CPGB.

Secondly, over time Hobsbawm viewed the century from different historical perspectives. Like any other period, continuity and change proved enduring features of twentieth-century history. What was unprecedented was the escalating speed of change, as Hobsbawm (1998: 308) acknowledged in the 1990s: 'The past thirty or forty years have been the most revolutionary era in recorded history.' Inevitably, the passing years altered Hobsbawm's perspectives when viewing the past, particularly as he discovered what actually happened next. However, by the early 1990s, he believed that it was now possible to stand back and to see the period in historical perspective. Recent events – these included the formal end of the Cold War in 1989; the disintegration of the communist bloc and the Soviet Union between 1989 and 1991; and speculation about the advent of a 'new world order' – had transformed Hobsbawm's (1995: ix; 5; 1998: 311) view: 'Whoever we are, we cannot fail to see the century as a whole differently from the way we would have done before 1989–91 inserted its punctuation mark into its flow.' For Hobsbawm, the period between 1914 and 1991 possessed a distinctive structure and coherence as 'the short twentieth century'.

Moreover, any history written in the early 1990s was bound to be very different from one completed prior to the events of 1989–91. Having begun writing the *Age of Extremes* during the 1980s, Hobsbawm (1998: 311–13; Box 5.2) was forced to rethink the book's shape: 'What had changed was not the facts of world history since 1973 as I knew them, but the sudden conjunction of events in both East and West

---

Box 5.2   Hobsbawm's changing perspectives on the twentieth century

i)   View prior to the 1989–91 revolutions
The period was a diptych (two parts):
– **1914–45**: age of catastrophe, two world wars, near-breakdown of world economy, threat to liberal democratic institutions;
– **late 1940s onwards**: liberal capitalism reformed, advance of world economy, socialist sector no longer a feasible economic alternative.

ii)   View after 1989–91
The period was a triptych (three parts; a sandwich)
– **1914–45**: two world wars, breakdown of western civilisation, serious crises for capitalism; rise of communist system as alternative to capitalism;
– **1945–73**: golden age when capitalism surged forward; communism offered an alternative;
– **1973–90s**: new era of uncertainty, even catastrophe for some regions.

---

since 1989 which almost forced me to see the past twenty years in a new perspective.' Depressed about recent trends, he saw the twentieth century as ending badly, the most murderous century on record, a period marked by a significant regression in standards as well as by increased individualism and the disintegration of old patterns of social relationships.

Thirdly, Hobsbawm (1998: 309) attempted to avoid presentism, that is, viewing the past through present-day spectacles. Notwithstanding the Marxist emphasis upon taking the concept of class back into the past, he upheld repeatedly the Rankean approach about treating the past in its own terms. In particular, the unexpected nature of events led Hobsbawm (1998: 317) to incline towards Taylor's emphasis upon contingency: 'The fundamental experience of everyone who has lived through much of this century is error and surprise. What has happened has been, far more often than not, quite unexpected.' Certainly, what happened between 1989 and 1991 was not in accord with communist party beliefs, thereby compelling Hobsbawm to acknowledge his support for a failed cause.

Hobsbawm the History Presenter

During recent decades Hobsbawm has enhanced his reputation and visibility through further publications: *The Age of Extremes* (1994), the final volume in the world histories series; *On History* (1997), a collection of essays articulating his approach to history; and the autobiographical *Interesting Times* (2002). However, these years have proved also an extremely challenging period for him. The revolutionary events occurring between 1989 and 1991, most notably the collapse of the Soviet bloc, led many to follow Francis Fukuyama's *The End of History and the Last Man* (1992) by assigning Marx's philosophical insights to the historical dustbin alongside Soviet-style Communism.

For Niall Ferguson (2002), Hobsbawm's autobiography helped to answer a puzzling question: 'why did so many otherwise intelligent people become Communists?' Writing therein, Hobsbawm (1998: 317; 2002a: 127) recalled with pride his long-term commitment to the communist party – his membership lapsed shortly before the CPGB dissolved itself in 1991 – before acknowledging that 'Communism is now dead.' Admitting that much of his life was devoted to what had proved an abortive cause, he believed that this improved his work as a historian because of the greater need to explain failure. Nevertheless, Hobsbawm (1998: ix; BBC 2008a), though conceding that aspects need 'junking' in the light of both events and the postmodernist challenge to Marxist determinism, remains loyal to Marx as his 'intellectual master'. Despite communism's failure in practice, Marx's ideas remain deeply embedded in his thinking today, as highlighted in 2011 by his *How to Change the World: tales of Marx and Marxism*. Nor, according to Hobsbawm (2011: 3–15, 419), has Marx lost his contemporary relevance, most notably in terms of his vision of capitalism as 'a historically temporary mode of the human economy'. Pointing to the recent global economic crisis, Hobsbawm concluded that 'once again the time has come to take Marx seriously'.

Raphael Samuel and Gareth Stedman-Jones (1982: ix–x) described Hobsbawm's histories as distinguished by 'the marriage between Marxism and Hobsbawm's sustained and imaginative historical curiosity and the particular'. Undoubtedly Hobsbawm's politics impacted upon his role as a presenter of history, as evidenced by his espousal of Marxist theory, choice of subject, and lengthy attempt to avoid writing about either his own times or the Soviet Union. Paradoxically, his histories, though published virtually everywhere except in the former Soviet bloc, have been well received in the USA, where he has held visiting posts at such prestigious institutions as the Massachusetts Institute of Technology, New York's New School of Social Research (1982–97) and Stanford University. By contrast, he made few visits to the Soviet Union, but proved a frequent visitor to the USA in spite of requiring special visa arrangements consequent upon CPGB membership.

Despite fears that a 'ghetto reputation' might limit his readership, Hobsbawm has never minded being described as 'Hobsbawm the Marxist historian'. The extent to which a Marxist approach has affected, even distorted, his presentation of the past in the manner remains an issue, as highlighted by the above-mentioned critiques advanced on both sides of the Atlantic by Pryce-Jones and others. By contrast, Snowman (1999: 18) assumed a sympathetic view: 'Does Hobsbawm's Marxism skew his history? No more so, probably, than the work of anyone guided by an overall vision – and you surely can't write about several hundred years of world history without one.' Similarly, for Evans (2009: 128) and Keith Thomas, Hobsbawm's Marxism has always proved – to quote Thomas (n.d.) – 'supple, undogmatic and highly individual' in nature.

Writing one of his final book reviews in 1984, A.J.P. Taylor (quoted, Wrigley 2000: 286, 290) praised Hobsbawm, the author, as 'a clever man' providing 'intellectual entertainment of a superior order'. Notwithstanding strong reservations expressed about his Marxist approach, Hobsbawm has established a global reputation in capitalist societies as a leading British historian vastly enriching labour and social history, even if – to quote Genovese (1984: 13) – 'no "Hobsbawmian School" has arisen'. Indeed, as Stuart Hall (quoted, Jaggi 2002) asserted, Hobsbawm has been one of the few left-wing historians 'taken seriously by people who disagree with him politically'. Thus, Ferguson (2002), who is often depicted as a right-wing historian, described Hobsbawm as 'so politically wrong', and yet also as 'one of the great historians of his generation' when recommending the quartet of world histories as the best starting point for anyone studying modern history. Peter Burke (2009: 276), Cannadine (2009), Evans (2009: 128), Orlando Figes (1997), Marwick (2001: 5, 251, 267) and William Palmer (2001: 292, 296) have proved prominent in acknowledging Hobsbawm's impact, most notably his synthesising skills when presenting big themes and complex problems from a wide range of perspectives and contexts. As Samuel and Stedman-Jones (1982: ix–x) recorded, Hobsbawm's histories displayed an 'unusual combination of theoretical clarity, large generalising capacity and an uncanny eye for suggestive detail'. For Sandbrook (2011), few historians can match either 'his elegant, lapidary style' or 'the epic sweep' of his books.

Moreover, as recognised by the 1996 Wolfson History and 2003 Balzan European History prizes, Hobsbawm's histories have proved both scholarly and accessible to the lay reader as public history. In July 2004 a readers' poll conducted by *Prospect* magazine listed him as one of Britain's top five 'public intellectuals'. Even so, despite occasional BBC radio broadcasts (e.g. *Desert Island Discs*, 1995) and television interviews (e.g. BBC 1994), his public profile never matched that of television dons like Schama or Taylor. Presenting Hobsbawm with the Wolfson Prize, Keith Thomas (n.d.) summarised his qualities:

> He brings to his historical writing some outstanding gifts: remarkable linguistic facility, exceptional analytic power, a vast reservoir of knowledge and a superb historical imagination. Above all, he is a cosmopolitan of very broad culture, and that very rare and suspicious thing among British historians: an intellectual.

Snowman (1999: 17) pointed to Hobsbawm's presentational range:

> Whether writing about the Industrial or the French Revolution, bandits or the bourgeoisie, Count Basie or Count Bismarck, Wellington or Ellington, Vienna, Venice or Venezuela, Hobsbawm's erudition was dazzling and his breadth of allusion encyclopaedic. It is a rare historian who can draw upon so wide a variety of sources – in at least five languages – while yet remaining in total intellectual control of his material. With Hobsbawm, you never feel that ... a structural straitjacket is imposed upon the facts. Rather, the detail and the analysis appear to run together.

Hobsbawm Today

Emphasising the need to conform to sound historical methodology, Hobsbawm joined other historians in confronting the challenge from postmodernism, which specifically targeted Marxist historians' scientific determinism. Denying that history is a literary creation – 'it isn't and can't be fiction' because 'we cannot invent our facts' – Hobsbawm (1998: 7, 258; 2005) critiqued postmodernists for not only erecting linguistic barriers supposedly limiting historical understanding but also failing to recognise history's empirical methodology and reliance upon evidence.

For Hobsbawm (2003), equally 'damaging' historically is the fashionable tendency of new states and contemporary collective identity groups to invent a past propagated through textbooks, historical museums, and 'heritage' for present-day purposes. Within this context, Hobsbawm (2005; quoted, Hunt 2002; 'Making History' 2008), who co-edited and contributed to the *Invention of Tradition* (1983) and wrote *Nations and Nationalism since 1780: programme, myth, reality* (1990), views himself as a polemicist acting as 'a pain in the arse for national myths' at a time when 'it's more important to have historians, especially sceptical historians, than ever before': 'The worrying thing at the moment is that history – including tradition – is being invented in vast quantities ... the world is today full of people inventing histories and lying about history.' Nor were such invented presentations of the past necessarily harmless. Frequently they proved 'dangerous' (Hobsbawm: 1998: 7, 365–6):

> In this situation historians find themselves in the unexpected role of political actors. I used to think that the profession of history, unlike that of, say, nuclear physics, could at least do no harm. Now I know it can. Our studies can turn into bomb factories like the works in which the IRA [Irish Republican Army] has learned to transform chemical fertiliser into an explosive.

Recent developments, most notably present-day society's ambiguous attitude towards history, have led Hobsbawm repeatedly to assert that historians, whose task is to remember what others forget, are more essential than ever. Retaining a strong interest in the future of history as a discipline alongside its role in tracing the roots of the present-day world, Hobsbawm worries about society's declining grasp of history. Indeed, right at the start of *Age of Extremes*, Hobsbawm (1995: 3; 2002b) complained that society's 'historical memory was no longer alive' because of the destruction of social mechanisms linking today's society with earlier generations.

Against this background, Hobsbawm has remained active as a public historian, particularly offering media commentaries upon contemporary events with a historical twist or making occasional presentations such as at the 2007 Cheltenham Literature and Hay Book Festivals. Reportedly (Rusbridger 2007; Shankleman 2008) at Hay he was introduced by Simon Schama 'in tones of genuine admiration, bordering on awe' – as a young historian Schama admitted being spellbound by the staggering breadth and humanity of Hobsbawm's writing – as the man who 'defined agelessness'.

The perceived historical illiteracy of present-day society, alongside his lifetime 'attempt to find a way forward in left politics through historical reflection', helps explain why Hobsbawm (quoted, Pickering 2011) remains a strong advocate of public history, using his histories and journalism to provide a sense of historical perspective. For Hobsbawm (2002a: 282, 300; Snowman 1999: 18), good 'communication is the essence both of teaching and of writing'. Too much history, he complained, was targeted at a limited academic audience: 'Historians should not write only for other historians.' Deliberately aimed at a broader public, *The Age of Revolution* followed Hobsbawm's first monograph, *Primitive Rebels* (1959), in spawning translations accessible to an international audience. Indeed, *The Age of Revolution*'s commercial success led to an approach from David Higham, a leading literary agent, who ensured that Hobsbawm continued to write for this broader market at home and overseas. Translations and foreign editions served both to reflect and boost Hobsbawm's global reputation, which was in part also a function of the way in which his multilingual abilities enabled him to present history directly in their own language to a diverse range of foreign audiences through books, media work, lectures and conference papers.

Using history to offer informed comment as a public intellectual on today's world followed on naturally from Hobsbawm's belief in public history. Historical reference points frame his reflections upon the contemporary world. Pointing to the USA in the wake of 9/11, the 2001 terrorist attacks in the USA, in 2002 Hobsbawm (quoted, Hunt 2002) compared the USA, 'a world propagandist power', with Revolutionary and Napoleonic France:

> The French under Napoleon ... said they were doing a lot of good to the countries they conquered, but they were regarded by the rest of the world as a conquering empire ... The Americans are in a position to do what the French did after the Napoleonic period ... The United States would have to learn that there are limits even to its own power ... but right now the learning process has only just begun.

Then, when reviewing developments in Afghanistan and Iraq, history, Hobsbawm (2004) advised, indicated 'scant chance of success' of reinforcing world order by spreading democracy to those countries: 'The 20th century demonstrated that states could not simply remake the world or abbreviate historical transformations.' Nor has the passage of time dented the force of his observations, as shown in 2007, when Hobsbawm (quoted, Rusbridger 2007) reiterated that western interventions to impose 'democracy' or a 'superior' value system were doomed in the present-day world: 'The age of empires and foreign interventions was over. We would have to find alternative ways of ordering the world. But so far we haven't found it and I can't tell you how it is going to be found.'

Conclusion

Reviewing his life story, Hobsbawm (2002a: 263) saw himself as more a Marxist historian presenting his version of the past than a communist activist seeking to change the world: 'Looking back, I am surprised how little direct political activity there was in my life after 1956, considering my reputation as a committed Marxist.' Unlike E.P. Thompson, Hobsbawm did not address large crowds in support of issues like nuclear disarmament. Nor did he march at the head of demonstrations: 'Essentially, apart from a lecture here and there, my political activity consisted of writing books and articles ... as a historian or a historically minded journalist, a Marxist one, which obviously gave my writings a political dimension.'

Hobsbawm, the historian, has always proved a controversial figure, attracting both high praise for influencing the way we think about history and strong hostility for espousing a Marxist approach glossing over the Soviet bloc's unsavoury past. Even so, over time his standing as one of Britain's leading living historians has been recognised by an extremely wide range of historians, including many who disagree profoundly with his politics. Fellowships of both the British Academy (1978) and the American Academy of Arts and Sciences (1971) highlight the high regard in which he is held on both sides of the Atlantic. Despite working as a historian in Britain throughout his career, Hobsbawm's reputation is truly international, extending across continental Europe as well as North and South America and beyond.

Believing that the present-day world could have been different and better, Hobsbawm looks back to the past with melancholy while looking forward with considerable unease (Crace 2007). When asked in 2002 if the twenty-first century would see the 'interesting times' witnessed by him in the twentieth century, Hobsbawm (quoted, Hunt 2002) hoped not: 'I don't look forward to the next 30 to 40 years with any kind of pleasure (although I won't see very much of them).'

Eric John Ernest Hobsbawm (1917–): Select Bibliography

Histories

1959 *Primitive Rebels: studies in archaic forms of social movement in the nineteenth and twentieth centuries*
1962 *The Age of Revolution, 1789–1848*
1964 *Labouring Men: studies in the history of labour*
1968 *Industry and Empire: an economic history of Britain since 1750*
1969 *Bandits*
1969 (with George Rudé) *Captain Swing*
1973 *Revolutionaries: contemporary essays*
1975 *The Age of Capital, 1848–1875*
1980 (with Joan W. Scott) 'Political shoemakers', *Past and Present*
1984 *Worlds of Labour: further studies in the history of labour*
1987 *The Age of Empire, 1875–1914*
1990 *Nations and Nationalism since 1780: programme, myth, reality*
1990 *Echoes of the Marseillaise: two centuries look back on the French Revolution*
1994 *Age of Extremes: the short twentieth century, 1914–91*
1997 *On History*
1998 *Uncommon People: resistance, rebellion and jazz*
2007 *Globalisation, Democracy and Terrorism*
2008 *On Empire: America, war and global supremacy*
2011 *How to Change the World: tales of Marx and Marxism*

Edited/co-edited works

1948 *Labour's Turning Point, 1880–1900: extracts from contemporary sources*
1982 (trans.) *The History of Marxism: Marxism in Marx's Day, vol.1* (1982)
1983 (with Terence Ranger) *The Invention of Tradition*
1998 *The Communist Manifesto: a modern edition*

Autobiography

2002 *Interesting Times: a twentieth-century life*

Television broadcasts/videos

1988 *Interviews with historians: Eric Hobsbawm with Pat Thane* (Institute of Historical Research)
1989 *Timewatch: An Age of Empire*, BBC2, 8 February

→

1994   *Late Show Special*, BBC2, Eric Hobsbawm interviewed by
        Michael Ignatieff, 24 October
2004   *Eric Hobsbawm Talks to Kirsty Wark*, BBC4, 29 November

Reference work

1982   Keith McClelland, 'Bibliography of the writings of Eric
        Hobsbawm', in Raphael Samuel and Gareth Stedman-Jones
        (eds.), *Culture, Ideology and Politics: essays for Eric Hobsbawm*

6
Simon Schama: The Television Historian

Writing in 2001, John Willis (2001), the managing director of Worldwide Production for Granada Media, claimed that:

> Three years ago history on television in Britain was on death row. As a self-evident health warning for viewers it had been corralled into a Saturday night History Zone on BBC2, was almost non-existent on ITV and being re-evaluated at Channel 4. Now everything has changed. Given lift-off by the helium of David Starkey and Simon Schama, TV history is hot.

Notwithstanding typical journalistic exaggeration, history's position in media culture in general and on British television in particular had been transformed. Nor was this transformation confined to Britain. As Pat Ferns (quoted, BTF 2001b), the director of the Inaugural World Congress of History Producers held at Boston in October 2001, told some 400 broadcasters, television and new media producers from 20 countries, 'We're the new rock'n'roll and we're going to keep on rocking.' Previously such an event could well have been held in a couple of phone boxes, not Boston's Park Plaza Hotel.

The 2001 Congress reflected history's growing global presence on terrestrial, cable and satellite television channels, most notably on dedicated channels like the History Channel. Television broadcasters, though still obsessed with celebrity, crime, sex and sport, woke up to the fact that history was popular, particularly with the affluent ABC1 audience attractive to advertisers, relatively cost-effective to produce, and capable of tapping new audiences from those reluctant to pick up a history book and feeling 'disenfranchised by "old school" history teaching' (Champion 2003: 169).

Despite inevitable professional reservations, historians have begun to write and present, even to watch and praise, television histories. Indeed, for Nigel Spivey (quoted, Membery 2002), who presented a TV Channel 5 series on *Kings and Queens of England*, 'television is perfect for relating history'. For Kershaw (quoted, Crace 2002), 'the best TV programmes add something that straightforward historical writing can't achieve'. During the past decade, television has made several historians better known nationally, even globally – and frequently the highest-paid presenters of history – than any since Taylor some forty or so years ago.

At the 2001 Congress of History Producers the keynote speaker was Simon Schama, the focus of this chapter. The invitation reflected Schama's international standing as a television history presenter responsible for the BBC's *A History of Britain*, first shown the previous year in both Britain and the USA. As Schama (2001b) told delegates, 'what has drawn us all here in the first place is the relatively recent discovery of history's appeal as mass entertainment'. 'The business we're in', he observed, 'is time travel', offering armchair viewers a round trip to the past without any of its discomfort; indeed, television was now 'the medium through which more history is consumed and absorbed than any other'. Far from hiding out in 'the dusty stacks of academia', Schama became – to quote one American journalist (Gwinn 2000) – 'a leather-jacketed, fast-talking history star' whose television series attracted new audiences for history: 'Millions of Brits and Americans discovered the history teacher they'd always dreamed of, a pyrotechnically entertaining lecturer who can resurrect long-dead Angles, Saxons and Normans in all their blood-lusting, power-mad glory.' Indeed, Schama's celebrity status as 'the man who made history sexy' (Billen 2003) was epitomised by the manner in which his presentational style was satirised on radio and television, such as by the British comedy series *Dead Ringers*.

For de Groot (2009a: 17, 27, 154), Schama's 'personality-led, populist narrative histories' proved the catalyst transforming both television history programming and the historian's place in the present-day public imagination. His landmark role in establishing history's present-day visibility and popularity on television was recognised by both a 'Forum' on *A History of Britain* in the *American Historical Review* in 2009 and a conference entitled 'Televisualizing the Past: Simon Schama and "A History of Britain", Ten Years On' held at IPUP, the University of York, in 2010. Significantly, in January 2011 Schama returned to the Congress of History Producers – or rather to History Makers: International Summit of History and Current Affairs Producers (History Makers 2009) as it has been called since 2007 – as the keynote speaker to mark the organisation's tenth anniversary. Apart from Schama's more recent series, history's television presence has been further enhanced by programmes contributed by an ever-widening circle of presenters, including Niall Ferguson, Richard Holmes, Tristram Hunt, Ian Kershaw, Neil Oliver, David Reynolds, David Starkey and Michael Wood.

Generally speaking, television history has remained a predominantly male preserve – reportedly, one would-be female presenter was told by a television executive that 'no one wants to be lectured at by a woman' (quoted, Bell 2008: 4) – but Bettany Hughes, Amanda Vickery (2011) and Fiona Watson, among others, have already given women a tenuous foothold in a man's world. As Erin Bell (2009: 11–15) reported, rightly or wrongly many media professionals view women historians as lacking the authority required of television history presenters. Such attitudes recall the manner in which publishers, like Humphrey Milford (quoted, Howsam 2009: 83, 123), the London publisher of Oxford University Press from 1913 to 1945, once disparaged the concept of women as writers of academic histories.

Moreover, television history, albeit still attracting less attention than Hollywood history films and yet to find its historian, is emerging also as a serious topic for academic research (Bell and Gray 2007). In this vein, Hunt (2004a: 89; 2006: 846–7), an experienced television history presenter and currently a Labour MP (2010–), pointed to the need for fellow academics to appreciate the multiplicity of television histories as well as to approach the subject with greater sophistication: 'The question is no longer one of validity but of progress; not whether television history is a good thing, but how do we make it better.'

Ken Burns's Television Histories

Concluding his history of histories, John Burrow (2007: 517) recognised that 'in the presentation of history, the chief new medium is obviously television'. Apart from being guilty of overlooking the emerging role of the internet, Burrow should have been more specific by pointing to the Schama-led transformation in *the way* history was presented on television. As detailed below, his approach contrasted vividly with Taylor's somewhat limited and dated lecture format discussed in chapter 4. More significantly, Schama moved on as 'author-presenter' from the formulaic dependence of recent historical documentaries upon an archive photograph/film and 'talking head' (one-on-one interviews) alternation, with a voice-over narration from some unseen omniscient presence. The key contemporary exponent of such historical documentaries was the American filmmaker Ken Burns, whose principal achievement was *The Civil War* (1990).

Burns has proved a highly successful maker of television histories telling stories about the past to prime-time nationwide audiences in the USA and beyond. Inevitably, his distinctive style, as sketched out above, offered a model for emulation by other documentary filmmakers. In effect, Burns established that – to quote Gary Edgerton (2001: 4) – 'history is no longer the principal domain of specialists, as it had been for nearly a half-century, but now is relevant and compelling for everyone – only this time on TV'. As such, Burns (quoted, Cripps 1995: 742; Thelen 1994: 1032) saw himself as helping 'to rescue history from those who teach it and the scholars who only wish to talk to themselves about it, and to return history to kind of a broad dialogue'.

Seeking to break 'the stranglehold the Academy has had on historical exchange for the last hundred years', Burns (1991; quoted Edgerton 2001: 14) used television to tap fresh audiences for popular history:

> The historical documentary filmmaker's vocation is not precisely the same as the historian's, although it shares many of the aims and much of the spirit of the latter ... The historical documentary is often more immediate and more emotional than history proper because of its continual joy in making the past present through visual and verbal documents.

In particular, Burns (quoted, Edgerton 2001: 19, 99, 166), who graduated in film studies from Hampshire College, Massachusetts, stressed repeatedly that he was 'primarily a filmmaker', not a historian, but merely 'an amateur historian at best'. Moreover, Burns (quoted, Weisberger 1990) admitted that television histories were 'not equipped to do what a book does, which is to attain profound levels of meaning and texture'. Made-for-television histories were deemed unsuitable for debating issues critically and analytically, challenging mythologies and conventional historiography, or creating new knowledge and perspectives. Rather, Burns prioritised engaging the audience by telling gripping stories about the past viewed through present-day spectacles.

Apart from retelling the story of the 1861–5 conflict to a new generation of Americans, *The Civil War* established Burns's reputation as a history documentary filmmaker making America's past accessible and comprehensible to a vast prime-time television audience through the PBS. Some 38.9 million Americans tuned in to at least one episode when the nine-programme series was premiered in September 1990, with over 12 million viewers watching at any one time (Attie 1992: 95–6; Edgerton 2001: 5). Reportedly, many viewers would not have been watching television at all but for this programme. Regular repeats increased viewer numbers for a series shown outside the USA, such as by the BBC in Britain.

Both videotapes and the companion book sold well, and were used extensively in the nation's schools and colleges. Inevitably, historians' commentaries exhibited the usual tensions existing between history filmmakers and academic historians (Attie 1992: 95–104). As Robert Brent Toplin (1996a: vi) commented, controversy centred upon '*which stories* about the Civil War ought to be told and *which conclusions* should be drawn from the evidence'. In particular, Burns was criticised for presenting an old-fashioned master narrative focused on military battles and heroes, while ignoring the manner in which the 'new' social history written from below viewed the Civil War as a social revolution transforming the position of common soldiers, women and slaves. Thus, the series, though attracting many academic admirers like Burrow (2007: 518), revealed yet again 'the chasm between professional historians and public representations of history' (Higashi 1998: 87–9; Wilentz 2001: 38).

The American Civil War had always fascinated Americans, but, as Burns (quoted, Edgerton 2001: 7) claimed, the series led to that interest becoming 'higher than it has ever been'. Reflecting upon television's growing contribution to public history, including the national memory, Burns (1991) observed that:

> As we gradually become a country and a society without letter writing and diary keeping, more and more dependent on visual signs and language, television will become more and more an important part of the making of history. More and more we will be connected to the past by the images we have made, and they will become the glue that makes memories.

Indeed, Shelby Foote (Thelen 1994: 1050), one of the 'talking heads', claimed that the series made him a millionaire, since 100,000 sets of his Civil War publications were sold during the succeeding six months as compared to 30,000 sets in the previous 15 years. In part, Burns (1991) attributed the popular appeal of the series to the fact that a nineteenth-century conflict was presented as an event 'that continues to speak to central questions of our present time' through a focus upon the imperial presidency, civil rights, new military technology, and the horrors of war. For some commentators, the series' contemporary military resonance was accentuated by the fact that it premiered soon after the USA's involvement in the first Gulf War (1990–1) consequent upon Iraq's invasion of Kuwait in August 1990.

Burns continues to make television histories in the same format – *Forbidden Fruit: Prohibition in America* was released in 2011 – but during the past decade or so Schama emerged as prominent among those presenting history televisually in an alternative way to that mapped out by Burns (Burns n.d.; Peck 2009: 683). In this sense, Schama's *A History of Britain* was to prove genre-changing in impact. But first, let us look at Schama as a historian, and particularly at how he became involved in a television history of Britain.

Simon Schama as a Historian

Born in London and educated at the University of Cambridge, Schama has spent most of his academic career across the Atlantic, first at Harvard University (1980–93) and since 1993 at Columbia University in New York. Despite a lengthy residence in the USA, during which the history of continental Europe proved his central focus and baseball replaced cricket in his sporting affections, Schama (2009a) retained close links with Britain through family ties and media commitments.

When asked why he became a historian, Schama (1995: 3–7; 2000b: 3; 2000c: 10–13) admitted being 'a hopeless addict of the past' for as long as he could remember:

> Through a fascination with trying to reach people who were once separated from us by unbridgeable distances and time but who in some ways are very like us ... History is the best way I know of having the outrageous luxury of time travel, of being able to live in other people's worlds as well as your own. It's a bit like gate-crashing the great parties of the past.

Schama recalled the received notions of British history as they were mediated to his post-Second World War generation growing up in a country seeking both to hang on to and let go of the past. Thus, whereas in 1953 Queen Elizabeth II's coronation exploited links drawn between the two Elizabeths to emphasise the unbroken continuity of British history, 12 years later Churchill's funeral took place in a very different Britain, a country looking forwards, not back, and led by a Labour government espousing the 'white heat of technology'. For Schama (quoted, Appleyard 2006), 'the 1960s were fantastic, never-ending, on edge ... There was something about growing up in the Britain of Harold Macmillan [prime minister, 1957–63] and ending up in the Britain of Mick Jagger.'

As a history presenter, Schama has won praise for writing readable narrative histories, proving an effective oral presenter, establishing the historical utility of visual sources and supporting public history in theory and practice. All contributed to Schama's transformation of television history presentation, and will be discussed briefly in turn.

In 2010 Schama's daughter, Chloë, dedicated *Wild Romance* (2010), her well-reviewed first book, 'to my father, who taught me how to tell a story'. Despite acknowledging the manner in which his showmanship and 'torrential eloquence' had transformed him into a television celebrity, Andrew Marr (2004) opined that Schama's power with words was 'best imbibed' on the printed page. In many respects, the common features linking Schama's diverse range of historical outputs and enabling him to reach out beyond academia have been good prose and engaging stories. Schama (2010a: xvii; 2011) admits also to adjectival overload, a surfeit of adjectives. For Champion (2002), words represent Schama's 'primary tool of enchantment and persuasion'. Snowman (2004: 34; 2007: 258) agreed, giving Schama high praise for harnessing a literary imagination to personal experience and scholarship: 'his writings are packed with evocative detail: rich fruitcakes crammed with raisins, currants, nuts and glacé cherries all mulled in brandy sauce'.

Prior to undertaking *A History of Britain*, Schama specialised in pre-1800 continental Europe. Significantly, his first book, *Patriots and Liberators* (1977), about the Dutch Republic during the French Revolution, won the £4000 Wolfson Prize for History, an award recognising 'standards of excellence in the writing of history for the general public'. Subsequently, in 1989 the bestselling *Citizens: a chronicle of the French Revolution*, published to celebrate the event's bicentenary, consolidated Schama's reputation as a highly readable academic historian, using what Richard Evans (1997: 244–5) described as a 'brilliantly written narrative' to lend history dramatic and poetic power. Personal histories and revealing anecdotes, informed by extensive use of documentary and visual sources, offered readers a sense of immediacy, indicating what it was like living through revolution whether as a member of the elite or merely one of the people.

Conceding that the book was an 'old-fashioned piece of story-telling' downplaying analytical frameworks and displaying a vivid literary imagination, Schama (1989: xv–xvi) opted deliberately for a chronological narrative:

If, in fact, the Revolution was a much more haphazard and chaotic event and much more the product of human agency than structural conditioning, chronology seems indispensable in making its complex twists and turns intelligible. So *Citizens* returns, then, to the forms of the nineteenth-century chronicles, allowing different issues and interests to shape the flow as they arise.

In this manner, Schama (quoted, Klepp 1995: 57), though attracting criticism from Roger Chartier, a French historian writing in *Le Monde*, for taking an allegedly right-wing Reaganite (Ronald Reagan was the American president, 1981–9) line, distanced himself from Marxist historians presenting the French Revolution in terms of the bourgeoisie clearing the way for capitalism by overthrowing the old order.

Secondly, Schama's qualities as a television historian built also upon his track record as an inspiring oral presenter of history. According to Jonathan Cole (quoted, Marshall 2001), Columbia University's provost, 'Columbia students flock to Simon's courses because he uses gripping stories to bring history to life.' Reportedly, the *Times Literary Supplement* (quoted, Carnegie Library 1996) praised Schama as 'Fizzing with vitality and insight, bubbling over with ideas and perceptions, buzzing with gossip, anecdote and a sense of drama'. For the *New York Magazine*'s Lawrence Klepp (1995: 56), Schama resembled 'Robin Williams with a highbrow database'.

Thirdly, Schama, whose professorship at Columbia University covers history and art history, believes that words are not enough when presenting a frequently illiterate past. Visual imagery proves equally powerful. His longstanding belief in the power of art and imagery has been reflected in both his publications, like *The Embarrassment of Riches: an interpretation of Dutch culture in the Golden Age* (1987) and *Rembrandt's Eyes* (1999), and television work. Indeed, on certain topics, he claims that televisual history proves superior to its written variant in terms of presentation and impact.

Fourthly, Schama has proved increasingly supportive of public history in theory and in practice. Acknowledging the influence of historians like Trevelyan, Plumb and Taylor, Schama (2009b: 693) has proved a prominent advocate of public history, most notably by delivering regular public lectures on the subject, teaching a postgraduate course at Columbia University called 'History beyond the Academy', and acting as a public historian. Confronting Henry Ford's dismissal of history as 'bunk', Schama (2000a; 2000c: 16) argued that public history was vital in the contemporary world: 'Cultures without history doom themselves to remain trapped in the most illusory tense of all, the present, akin to small children who know neither whence they have come nor whither they go.' Frequently Schama (quoted, Gewertz 2001) has represented public history as 'an extremely ancient tradition' dating back to ancient

Greece, but had 'seldom been taken care of by academics' during the past century. As a result, Schama (2009b: 693) has repeatedly urged historians to *recover* a lost sense of public vocation: 'our calling not only invites us but requires us to reach beyond the academy'.

Like other historians active in popularising history, Schama has undertaken regular work for the media, including the *Sunday Times*, *The New Yorker*, *Vogue* and *GQ* magazine. At Cambridge he acknowledged the influence of academics possessing journalistic experience. When writing his first article for a popular magazine, Schama (quoted, Gewertz 2001) recalled the warning from Plumb, his mentor, that '"This will be the hardest thing you've ever done" – and it was.' Over time he has thought seriously about, experimented with, and practised alternative ways of communicating history to diverse audiences in writing, orally, visually, televisually and dramatically on stage. Eschewing the scholarly apparatus of the historian, in 1991 Schama's *Dead Certainties* offered readers multiple stories about Wolfe's capture of Quebec and the murder of George Parkman in Boston in 1759 and 1849, respectively. In brief, Schama (1998: 319–28) experimented with historical fiction by way of not only testing the boundaries between history and fiction but also suggesting ways of filling the resulting gap. More recently a stage play, adapted by Caryl Phillips from Schama's *Rough Crossings* (2005), premiered at the Birmingham Repertory Theatre in 2007 to mark the bicentenary of the Abolition of the Slave Trade Act.

However, Schama's (2002b) achievements as a public historian derive principally from his television histories, perceived as a kind of 'History Lite' contributing to what Michael Burleigh (2002) described as the 'democratisation of knowledge' against the Bastille of the Academy.

Schama's Television *History of Britain*

The BBC's multimedia *A History of Britain* project (Box 6.1), commissioned to mark the millennium, was designed to illuminate televisually Britain's lengthy past. Involving several years of preparation, writing and production (Rubin 2009: 664–6; IPUP 2010), the project eventually comprised fifteen BBC Two programmes accompanied by three books intended to be far more than either programme transcripts or television tie-ins. Reflecting Schama's (2000c: 9) 'life as a writer', the books treated the subject matter and issues at greater length and in closer detail than allowed by television. In addition, the internet offered viewers the opportunity for interactive discussion with Schama as well as online access to additional materials and exercises.

Box 6.1   *A History of Britain* multimedia project

i)   Television
    3 series: 15 programmes (2000–2)
ii) Videotapes/CDs/DVDs of the television series
iii) Books
    A History of Britain, vols.1–3 (2000–3)
iv) Internet resources and Interactive discussions with Schama

---

Notwithstanding his longstanding advocacy of public history and proven ability to exploit the power of visual sources, Schama was initially unenthusiastic about involvement in the project when first contacted by the BBC during the mid-1990s. On the one hand, Schama (1999a; 2000c: 8; Bremner 2001: 68–72) admitted that the proposed series was a 'terrific' idea, especially as hitherto there had never been any attempt on television to tell the whole story of Britain's past. On the other hand, he pointed to his lengthy residence in the USA and lack of publications on British history when disclaiming his personal qualifications for what would prove a demanding and time-consuming job. Claiming that other historians seemed more suitable choices, Schama feared that a returning expatriate, whose vision was clouded by sentimentality, might not prove the most dispassionate presenter of Britain's history:

> On reflection, perhaps Mickey Mantle's upscale burger joint on Central Park South wasn't the best place for the BBC producer to talk me into writing a television history of Britain. The Venerable Bede, the Cromwells (Thomas and Oliver), and Mrs. Pankhurst all felt a long, long way away and so did I. Flattered, but unpersuaded that I was the right person for the job, I tried to point out this distance to the producer, Janice Hadlow.

Janice Hadlow, joint head of the BBC's history department (1995–9), proved instrumental in approaching Schama, who had already presented a BBC television series on *Landscape and Memory* in 1995. Reportedly, Hadlow (quoted, Rowan 2004; IPUP 2010) who had worked with him on BBC Two's *The Late Show*, had been impressed by the manner in which Schama's *Citizens*, 'a fantastic book', gave a human face to the French experience of revolution. Subsequently, Hadlow, who is described frequently as the 'queen of television history', was responsible for putting Ferguson and Starkey on screen when Channel 4's Head of History (1999–2004).

Two years later, and with the series already in preparation, the BBC repeated the offer. Schama (1999a) eventually agreed, especially as it became clear that his excuses were in fact the reasons for being offered the assignment. In particular, his distance from Britain and writing its history was seen as a strength, not a liability. Thus, the production team, urging him to treat the project as a homecoming, hoped that Schama's detachment, reinforced by the excitement of his own rediscovery of Britain's past, would provide a meaningful link with viewers. Moreover, residence in the USA enabled him to view Britain's past from an external perspective, and more importantly, help sell the series to the American market.

Schama as 'Author-presenter'

Like any television history, *A History of Britain* was a team project. But for viewers Schama occupied centre stage. As Starkey (quoted, Hironson 2009) has frequently advised, there needs to be a personal voice that viewers recognise and trust. Represented as the 'author-presenter', Schama (2000c: 8–9; 2009b: 693–4) was responsible for conceptualising, researching, writing, narrating and presenting programmes, even if other historians were consulted to cover gaps in his expertise as well as to help identify key issues and recent scholarship.

When asked why he agreed eventually to take on the project, Schama (2001a; 2009b: 693–5) responded with the phrase 'crazed optimism'. More specifically, as 'author-presenter', he aimed to:

- inject fresh energy and drama into stories about Britain's past;
- exploit television's potential to take history outside academia to a large public audience 'starved' of history at school;
- foster broader interest in history, something not remote from people's lives today but fully a part of it. Anxious to avoid treating the past as a form of mass entertainment and cultural escapism merely involving 'a stroll down memory lane', a kind of 'Antiques Roadshow with ruins', Schama (2000c: 8; 2001b; 2002a) sought to encourage viewers to see history as 'a shared public enthusiasm', a way of feeling 'connected' with pressing contemporary issues such as national identity, cultural pluralism and civic tolerance. Inevitably his desire to help viewers 'to know where we are, who we are' possessed resonance at a moment when the whole issue of national allegiance, identity and citizenship was the subject of intense public

debate due to ongoing developments appertaining to devolution in
Britain, European Union integration, and globalization. At the same
time, Schama (IPUP 2010) conceded that the series was an unapologetic return to an unfashionable type of history that joined up past
and present and gave the audience a narrative chronological sweep;
- challenge the ingrained prejudices of historians about television
  histories by showing that history could be popularised without compromising its scholarly integrity; and
- offer an alternative way from Burns of presenting television history.

Moving on from Burns

Reportedly (Bremner 2001: 64, 70), *A History of Britain* was intended
originally to follow a Burns-type format. Despite the success enjoyed by
Burns's television histories, Schama (1999a) pressed the case for a re-think
of what had become a tried-and-tested, albeit seemingly tired, formula:

> The effect ... was a striving for a kind of consensual inoffensive-
> ness, leaving only the talking heads to supply the occasional note
> of eccentric nonconformity or dispute ... the approach seems to me
> occasionally to take the sting out of history. And the enduring his-
> torical voices ... have, I've thought, been stingers.

Confessing 'impatience' with Burns's assumption that a multiplicity of
voices ensured balance, Schama (2009b: 693) set out on a new course
by assuming the instrumental role of 'author-presenter' seeking to
engage, inform, educate and entertain a television audience. In fact,
for de Groot (2009a: 154), it was more a case of reviving the authored
approach employed by Jacob Bronowski and Kenneth Clark for *The
Ascent of Man* (1973) and *Civilisation* (1969), respectively.

Employing a voice-over commentary, complemented by his visual
presence where he is shown on location delivering numerous 'pieces
to camera' offering viewers context, description and narrative, Schama
plunged viewers deep into Britain's past. His authority as a presenter,
though underpinned by an academic imprimatur, was enhanced by
'speaking in locations ('it happened here"), handling artefacts ("this
branding iron was used for") and pointing to sources ("these letters
say" or "Magna Carta argued")' (Champion 2003: 165). As a televisual
historian, Schama benefited also from expert camera-work and editing,
enabling him to present viewers with a powerful montage of images,
spoken commentary, music, and dramatic reconstruction.

Conceding that no historian was bias-free, Schama (2000a) asserted that 'the main thing is to try and tell the truth as best an historian can with the evidence at his command' in the light of the existing historiography. However, fundamentally, the series reflected Schama's (2000b: 1) personal interpretation of Britain's past, as highlighted by opting for *A History of Britain* as the title, not *The History of Britain*: 'Here's my take on this event ... and I'm going to try and persuade you to my view – but you're free to accept or reject it after I've laid out the evidence.' Far from suppressing his own beliefs, Schama (2001a) conceded the need to be honest and up-front about them:

> Mine is the only narrating voice you hear. So the programmes are inevitably very much my own vision and my own interpretation. The unavoidably opinionated nature of the storytelling is, I hope, going to provoke all kinds of disagreement and alternative stories – but that's all to the good since one of my favourite historians, Pieter Geyl, described history as an argument without end.

At the same time, Schama (2000a) stressed that Britain's past had to be approached critically and sceptically, paying due regard to both positives and negatives: 'history should never be just an exercise in self-congratulation. But nor could it possibly be the realistic truth if it was a blanket condemnation.' Schama (1998: 320) acknowledged also the usual limitations imposed upon historians, who were left always chasing shadows because of their inability ever to reconstruct the past in its completeness.

A Challenging Assignment

For Schama (2001b), *A History of Britain* was not only the most rewarding but also the most exacting assignment he had ever undertaken as an historian. Inevitably, the series brought its own difficulties, an appreciation of which had contributed to his initial reluctance to present the series.

First, as Schama feared, the series took considerable time and effort. Despite joining in 1997 when the series was already in preparation, he devoted some four to five years to the project. Apart from the tedium of filming with lots of breaks because of bad weather and having to say the same lines repeatedly in various positions for any one scene, there were chastening moments in the production process for a historian accustomed to presenting history in a university lecture hall or a book. Prior to the first shoot Schama (1999a) received a BBC 'Hazard Assessment

Sheet' recording risks to which the presenter might be exposed: 'Falling into Roman bath' with risk of meningitis, 'Falling overboard from boat in rough Scottish and Irish waters' or 'Falling over cliffs'. Proposed remedies included 'Take presenter immediately to hospital' or carry him to a stomach pump as quickly as possible. Unsurprisingly, Schama worried when filming in Bath, at sea, or on Beachy Head.

Secondly, Schama faced the problem of covering televisually the huge sweep of British history; indeed, his mentor, Plumb (quoted, Grainger 1986: 12), once likened Britain's past to 'a great heap of Himalayas'. There was never sufficient time for Schama (2001a) to do justice to key topics, especially when the original plan for 25 episodes was downsized to 15 programmes: 'We've had to omit all kinds of big stories for the sake of telling even bigger ones. I would certainly have liked to have dealt with the Wars of the Roses [1455–85] in rather more than the two minutes it got in programme five!' For Schama, there was an enduring need for what Hadlow (quoted, Hill 2005) described as 'constant creative compression', that is, 'the ability to identify the heart of a proposition, or to convey an idea in its most dilute and focused sense'. Therefore, at the end of each programme as well as online, Schama indicated ways in which the audience could pursue any topic, in the hope that the series would act as a prompt and portal for further study.

Thirdly, Schama (2001a; 2009b: 695–6), though conceding the constraints, claimed to provide a television history of 'the people' as well as of the ruling elites: 'We neither set out to be purely political nor to deliver an overwhelmingly social history of Britain. How much social history – the history of ordinary people's experience – you can bring to television depends crucially on sources, and since we're talking about television, how to make those sources *visually compelling*.' Inevitably, it proved difficult to focus on, say, the life of the early medieval peasant – 'there are only so many shots of ploughs and oxen that people will want to see in any given programme' – but the problem eased during more recent centuries, when the greater availability of appropriate source materials enabled more time to be devoted to ordinary people's lives.

Fourthly, the series had to be pitched at an appropriate level for a television audience. When discussing documentaries as popular history, Schama (1999a) recalled the basic dilemma raised at the 'Telling the Story: the Media, the Public, and American History' Conference, held at Boston in 1993. 'It's nice but it ain't history,' was the typical refrain of academics about film histories. 'It's scholarship but it won't do in a visual medium,' was the frequent response of filmmakers. Historians' complaints about 'dumbing down' were invariably countered by filmmakers' worries about depicting scholarship as well as events lacking visual sources. Schama (quoted, Grice 2010) has never concealed his irritation about academics accusing him of 'dumbing down':

> You want to say to them, as I do: 'Try it, Buster. See how unbelievably demanding it is.' Anyone can write an academic piece directed at other academics. To write something that delivers an argument and a gripping storyline to someone's granny or eight-year-old takes the highest quality of your powers.

Nor did Schama (2001a) see any real conflict of interest between demands for good history and good television:

> The whole point of our series is that we believe that those two goals are not mutually incompatible and that it's possible to tell a really gripping story without doing damage to the complexity of historical truth. The challenge we set ourselves week after week is bringing the result of academic debate and scholarship into a form that will grip the imagination of the viewer.

Even so, the need to avoid making programmes sound like university classes meant that Schama (2001a; 2001b) had 'to find ways to bring all these issues before our viewers without making them feel they're about to take an exam'. As Schama (IPUP 2010) admitted, much of what was put on the screen for the viewer had been 'emptied out' of historical complexities; thus, 'less was always more' in terms of allowing viewers to find their own ways of acting upon the programmes' verbal and visual cues.

Reflecting upon the experience of making the series and receiving feedback from viewers, Schama (2001b; 2002d: 42–4) codified the qualities required of an 'author-presenter' seeking to make engaging, instructive and serious television histories:

- 'immediacy' – the dramatic flow of history should be punctuated by historical voices allowing contemporary witnesses to become an integral part of the narrative, with the presenter acting as an 'interlocutor between audience and protagonists': 'If you [the author-presenter] manage to convey immediacy, it's because you're experiencing it yourself';
- 'imaginative empathy' – one significant contrast with Burns's *The Civil War* concerned Schama's reliance upon re-enactment to cover gaps in the story, as well as to give colour and dramatic effect to the

storyline. In particular, the reconstruction of action overlaid onto authentic locations and landscapes helped the immersion of viewers into the distant past. For example, the second programme used blurred and unsteady footage of dramatic reconstruction, cut with images from the Bayeux Tapestry and accompanied by a soundtrack of battle noise, to encourage viewers to imagine themselves acting out the 1066 Battle of Hastings. Locations of past events were equally important: 'place can be made to speak, to be its own presenter; or even a kind of re-enactor'. Widespread use was made of artefacts, buildings, music and paintings. Only the final two programmes used archive film footage;

- 'candid moral engagement' – rather than sitting on the fence, Schama sought to engage viewers by praising, criticising, and identifying turning-points. Avoiding complex historiographical issues, priority was placed upon a narrative storyline and visual storyboard introducing 'debate by stealth', that is, submerging arguments and issues into the presenter's narrative. Rather than cutting to a 'talking head', programmes were 'thickly seeded' also with contemporary voices, sometimes articulating contrasting viewpoints. Even so, in a ratings-led medium, there was no room for historical controversy. Viewers must not be left baffled and confused by a 'salad of opinions', as happened, Schama (quoted, Bell and Gray 2007: 130) claimed, with Burns's 'talking heads'; and
- 'poetic connexion' – the aim was to demystify the past and animate events in order to persuade viewers to suspend their disbelief so as to imagine living in a past world.

Fifthly, a central question was how to present a relatively familiar story in a novel and interesting way for television. In particular, was it possible to offer a television history that would be something more than a teleological Whiggish (viewing the past as leading inevitably to the present), Churchillian narrative centred upon the liberal progress and imperial triumphalism of an island race? Could justice be done to the history of Ireland, Scotland and Wales as well as of England? Given his previous publications on Dutch, French, German and Zionist identities, did the project offer him an opportunity to generate public debate about the historical meaning of British national identity at a time of transition? In the event, Schama (2000a; 2002e: 40; Bremner 2001: 72–5) decided to confront head-on, not evade, the longstanding national issue by covering the troubled history of the different nations of the British Isles in one programme.

In addition, Schama (2000c: 10, 17) opted to present Britain's story as primarily one of 'disruption' and 'persistence': 'Although the great theme of British history seen from the twentieth century is endurance, its counter-point, seen from the twenty-first, must be alteration.' He favoured an approach in which alteration, mutation and flux, not continuity, proved the norm; a history that did not lead inexorably to a unitary British state but saw any period as merely another chapter in an ongoing story, and viewed national identity not as fixed but having a shifting fluid quality:

> This history might be a history respectful of contingency, mistrustful of inevitability, indifferent to any predetermined route or destination; a history refusing to take for granted (as the victors' texts always want) that the way things turned out was the way they were always meant to be; a history that can see, but for a happen-stance – Harold not falling out with his brother; Anne Boleyn giving birth to a healthy son; Oliver Cromwell not dying when he did – an altogether different outcome.

Media Responses

When shown on BBC Two, *A History of Britain* won widespread media praise (Costello 2001: 17–18) for its accessibility as 'public history', and particularly for Schama's ability as 'author-presenter' to convey so-called 'dry' subjects in an original and engaging way through nightly television 'lessons' (Marshall 2001). What has been depicted as 'Schamerisation' (Woodward 2003) brought alive the story of Britain's past for viewers within and outside Britain. Indeed, the series highlighted television history's ability to draw substantial audiences. A weekly British television audience of over four million – over time repeat showings on cable, terrestrial and satellite channels at home and overseas further increased this total – was reinforced by the sale of over half a million books and a good level of sales for videotapes/CDs/DVDs. Building upon his long-time interest in taking history beyond the academy and belief that history should provide 'not just instruction but pleasure', Schama (2000c: 17) succeeded in bringing alive the long story about Britain's past – *'our' history*, as he stressed repeatedly – for a large popular audience.

When speaking at the 2001 Edinburgh Television Festival, David Liddiment, ITV's Director of Channels, identified *A History of Britain* as one of the BBC's high points (BBC 2001b). For Max Hastings (2000), then editor of the *Evening Standard*, British history was fortunate to find a populariser as skilled and compulsive as Schama:

> Many modern British academic historians sink ever deeper into arcane specialization and unreadable prose. Schama's superbly literate television series and book are likely to achieve more than the work of any other British historian in this decade, to awaken an interest in the subject among a new generation.

For Pat Ferns (quoted, BTF 2001a), a prime mover in the Congress of History Producers, Schama proved a strong television performer distinguished by 'an undeniable popular touch'. In this vein, Schama won strong praise even from John Walsh (2000), who reviewed the series for *Maxim*, a lads' magazine: 'The presentation is ballsy too. Schama clearly knows and loves his subject, and his history geek's enthusiasm is infectious.' Awarding the series four stars out of five, Walsh compared *A History of Britain* favourably to Burns's 'snoozers' on *The American Civil War*. For Walsh, Burns's television histories proved 'video Valium': 'Two minutes of slow pans over a still photograph and some hack actor reading diary entries in a hushed monotone, and you're out like a light.'

Both the series and Schama received numerous awards (BBC 2001a), including the Richard Dimbleby Award for the Best Presenter – Factual, Features and News. Of course, for the television world, audience ratings and impact (e.g. critical acclaim, awards, perceived legacy), not historical quality, represented the principal performance indicator. In turn, the success of the series, alongside the popularity of television programmes presented by Starkey and other historians, reinforced history's television presence, and fostered media interest in doing more. Greg Dyke (IPUP 2010), who was BBC Director-General between 2000 and 2004, recalled that when the series was transmitted Schama's impact as a presenter was being talked about extensively inside the BBC as well as by the media as a whole. Television's potential for popularising history and engaging the general public in conversation about Britain's history was reaffirmed by regular online exchanges with viewers conducted on the BBC website, where Schama received comments and feedback from people of all ages and abilities. For Schama (quoted, Gewertz 2001), this contact with a substantial learning community, particularly children, proved 'a very democratic experience', and at times exposed him to dissent, 'robustly expressed', about his views.

Apart from audience ratings, reviews and specific feedback made in internet exchanges, we have little hard information explaining why

Schama's television histories struck a chord with a large popular audience. Audience Research Reports for *A History of Britain* have yet to become available at the BBC Written Archives Centre at Caversham Park; thus, pending in-depth research on how and why viewers consumed Schama's series, it is easier to raise questions. For example, was Schama (quoted, Burrell 2007) right in claiming that he was 'very lucky' to catch the moment when British television audiences began to crave history programming? Did viewers respond positively to the manner in which Schama acted as a companion taking them by the hand back to the past? Did the audience merely want 'something they can understand and relate to its period' (Bremner 2001: 66), or did viewers seek something more? Some historians have suggested possible answers. Starkey (n.d.), whose *Six Wives of Henry VIII* (2000) headed sitcoms and soaps like *Friends* and *Brookside* in Channel 4's ratings, opined that

> What I want people to do is to grasp the romance of history, the excitement of history, and to realize that although it seems fantasy and fairy tale, it is true, and that the consequences are still felt not simply in Britain, but in America ... People like the big personalities and big stories. It's a soap opera, but of course, a soap opera that's real and that's true. It's like the great old dynasties of Dallas [a popular American television series about the Ewing family, 1978–91] and the Ewings, but on a much greater scale of drama and even greater scale of violence.

For Andrew Higson (IPUP 2010) and Hunt (2004a: 97–8; 2006: 844–5), in an era of migration, devolution and globalization, television history provided an accessible and clear national narrative satisfying a present-day search for roots and identity – national, familial and racial – by people feeling increasingly detached from the past. Hobsbawm (2002b) agreed, claiming that the popularity of television history reflected 'a protest against forgetting': 'Our society is geared to make us forget. It's about today ... it's about tomorrow ... But human beings don't want to forget ... Relating to the past, their own past and the general past, is part of the DNA.'

Academic Commentaries

Unsurprisingly, academic commentaries proved somewhat mixed, especially as Schama's celebrity status as a television history don was guaranteed to 'invite showers of slings and arrows from his outraged and envious peers' (A. Taylor 2000).

Generally speaking, the series' narrative and visual qualities were widely admired even within academia. For Champion (2003: 153), Schama 'presents the viewer with the experience of the rich diversity of the passage of human time in the British islands'. Patrick Wormald (2001), an Anglo-Saxon historian, admired the series' dramatic and visual impact:

> The show itself was superb ... It is hard to conceive how a historical documentary could have been better illuminated on small screen or large. Visually, 'A History of Britain' was in the class of David Attenborough's 'Life on Earth' two decades back ... Nor is this just a matter of visuals. As drama, Schama's narrative – for film and book alike – is magnificent. Britain's history is made as exciting as his 'Citizens' made the French Revolution.

Likewise the emphasis upon personal confrontations, such as between William the Conqueror and Harold (1064–6) or Elizabeth I and Mary, Queen of Scots (1560–87), made 'damn fine theater': 'Schama can characterize like Tacitus, narrate like Macaulay, quip like A.J.P. Taylor. He should set a fashion for the revival of the art, almost forgotten by professional academics, of good storytelling.'

Echoing such sentiments, John Charmley (quoted, Woodward 2003) and Burrow (2007: 478) praised Schama's sweeping overview of Britain's past and timely reminder about the historian's storytelling skills. For Roger Smither (2004: 56–7), the series showed that television history could offer far more than just Hitler and war.

Most academic critics subscribed to the view that 'proper history' simply was not suitable for television. As Schama (2002e: 40) observed, a deep-seated prejudice against the concept of *serious* television history led many academics to argue that history should remain the monopoly of the academy. Or, as Hunt (2004a: 90) remarked, for most critics the prime problem arose from television history's failure to be a book. For Champion (2003: 169), most academic commentators missed the point because they failed to engage with Schama's series as public history, taking advantage of the highly effective manner in which television allowed presenters to combine the aural, literary and visual dimensions. There were, of course, specific criticisms. These included: Schama's alleged lack of specialised knowledge; 'dumbing down'; the adoption of a teleological approach; an elitist focus; and Anglocentrism.

These points will be discussed in turn.

First, Schama's lack of a track record on British history rendered him vulnerable to critiques from subject specialists (e.g. Vincent 2000: Lenman

2001), who not only recorded that he was, say, no medievalist but also listed factual errors, distortions and misrepresentations in the programmes and/or books. For Patrick Wormald (2001), 'People thoroughly deserve to have their history made exciting. They are also entitled not to be misinformed.' Thus, he recorded that the Lindisfarne monks did not move the body of St Cuthbert when the Vikings attacked in 793, as claimed by Schama (2000c: 54), but 80 years later.

Secondly, 'dumbing down' was another target. Complaining about Schama's popular romps into the past, Wilentz (2001: 38) found it 'hard to think of a sadder scholarly defection to the universe of entertainment'. Will Hutton (2002) admitted that Schama provided 'great television' by making history 'accessible and fun', but questioned 'is it great history?' Was not British history far more complex: 'We are not watching the history of Britain. The programmes are too selective to constitute a true representation of our history.' Claiming that viewers were capable of taking on board the past's complexities and controversies, several commentators (P. Wormald 2001; Cannadine 2004: 4; Rubin 2009: 670) complained about the series' excessively narrative-driven tendencies and oversimplification. Indeed, Simon Ditchfield (2001) argued that an arrogant presumption that the viewing public was unable to cope with complex argument rendered Schama guilty of betraying the trust placed in him by the public as 'the expert' on Britain's past. Worrying about the lack of scholarly density, Bruce Lenman (2001) criticised 'the appallingly limited minds of those who commission and make these films'.

Roy Foster (2000: 50) and Nicholas Vincent (2000) regretted 'the updating spin' placed upon the past, such as Schama's portrayal of William the Conqueror as 'the first database king' responsible for commissioning the Domesday Book, or of Archbishop Thomas Becket as a twelfth-century Cockney wide-boy, to whom 'kit mattered', even in death. Nor did Schama's recourse to re-enactment appeal to Peter Stansky (2009: 689), who attacked 'the abomination of historical reconstruction' for blurring the boundary between fact and fiction.

Thirdly, several critics were unimpressed by Schama's disclaimers about adopting a teleological approach to Britain's past. Patrick Wormald (2001) complained that in reality Schama offered a Whiggish history where things could only get better and where history's purpose was primarily to explain how the past become the present:

There is the inexorable implication of mankind's good sense in moving out of that Other Country, the Past, where lots of people died violently and no one smelled very nice. Clearly, the 19th-Century progressivist Whig still lurks in the crannies of the British-American historical mentality. Ultimately, Schama does nothing to banish it.

Nor did Schama's claims about respecting contingency prevent his narrative attracting criticism (quoted, Bell and Gray 2007: 128–30) as liable to close the minds of viewers to any alternative course for Britain's past.

Fourthly, several commentators – they included Vincent (2000), Ditchfield (2001); Linda Peck (2009: 681) and Miri Rubin (2009: 666–9) – saw the series as providing merely yet another old-fashioned 'kings and battles narrative' treating 'the people', especially women, as largely invisible. Thus, Foster (2000) remarked that 'it cannot be said that the forgotten, the mute, and the inglorious elements in British history get much of a look from Schama'. Admittedly, television history's reliance upon visual presentation was part of the problem, but greater use of computer-generated imagery, it was argued, would have enabled a more striking visual portrayal of the distant past.

Finally, few reviewers were impressed by Schama's approach to the national issue. For Patrick Wormald (2001), 'It might just pass muster as an old-fashioned History of England. As a History of Britain, it is laughable.' Fiona Watson (quoted, Costello 2001: 18), who presented BBC Scotland's *In Search of Scotland* (2002), agreed: 'I was shocked that such an Anglocentric version of British history could be shown in the 21st. century ... What worries me is that he is reinforcing stereotypes, that the public will think "well, if that's what the academics are saying it must be true".'

Prior to the transmission of the opening programme, Schama (1999a) admitted that making *A History of Britain* had been a rewarding experience: 'Whether it will be worthwhile history is another matter.' As indicated above, both academia and media were divided about not only his take on Britain's past but also the fundamental merits of television histories. 'Walls', Schama (2002e: 41; 2009b: 699) complained, were being raised in academia against television history. By way of response, Schama (2001b) has depicted himself as part of the 'demolition squad' attempting to break down these 'walls' while presenting good 'history' to viewers. Unsurprisingly, in 2009 Schama (2009b) drafted a vigorous response to the three historians, Peck (2009), Rubin (2009) and Stansky (2009), critiquing *A History of Britain* in a 'Forum' for the *American Historical Review*.

The Television Presenter's Role

At the same time, Schama's performance offered invaluable insights into the 'entirely new craft' (Vickery 2011: 3) of presenting history on television. Benefiting from skills acquired from journalism, writing narrative histories and using visual images, Schama's user-friendly presentation made the difficult task of popularising history on television look easy. A clear and gripping narrative, reinforced by the use of vivid anecdotes and dramatic reconstruction, a strong focus upon personalities, and recourse to a wide range of visual and non-visual sources, helped explain the series' impact. As Champion (2002) commented, Schama performed his 'instrumental' role as a presenter in a distinctive manner:

> Schama leads the viewer, as it were by the hand, through a first-class tour of 'our' history ... The presenter is the thread that runs though each programme and between each episode, providing continuity and familiarity. Unlike a book, here the historian is a visual presence (rather than a voice submerged in the reader's consciousness). The physicality of this presence, the aspect of performance and engagement is critical to the historical authority of the project.

Indeed, notwithstanding Schama's emphasis upon offering *a personal history of Britain*, the slick and professional way in which the BBC packaged the series on prime-time television and advertised it to viewers enhanced his authority role. Thus, it became easy for viewers to treat the programmes as offering something more, that is *the definitive history* of Britain.

Outlining the initial findings of their 'Televising History' project (2006–2010), Erin Bell and Ann Gray (2007: 123, 125) represented Schama-type 'author-presenters' as crucial to the success of present-day television history programming in terms of accessing audiences and possessing historical authority:

> Although they demonstrate on-screen presence and use their personal style to persuade and captivate, there is a further aspect to their appeal. That is the nature of their address. They are presented as knowledgeable, they are experts and, above all, they are intellectuals. They speak with eloquent fluency, enthusiasm and the certainty that their access to a fund of knowledge affords. Their performances are powerful in visual and literary terms. Add to this both beautifully shot and composed images and we have beguiling television. This power to beguile is afforded to the charismatic author-presenters and is a key component of their authority and legitimacy.

Codifying alternative presentational styles, Bell and Gray (2007: 122, 130) employed Burns's approach as a reference point. David

McCullough, the narrator of *The Civil War*, was merely reading a script written by Geoffrey Ward, Ken Burns and Ric Burns, interspersed by 'editing clusters' composed of 'talking heads'. Despite making extensive use of 'talking heads', Burns severely restricted their contribution, as evidenced by the manner in which footage of, say, Barbara Fields, one of Schama's colleagues at Columbia University, was – to quote Jeanie Attie (1992: 98) – 'carefully spliced, at times cutting her off in mid-thought', thereby ensuring that she never had the last word. This example highlights the fact that historians acting as 'talking heads' have little or no say in how their contributions, inserted to impart academic legitimation, are used in, or more frequently edited out of, television histories. Complaining about 'scissors-and-paste' editing procedures, Kershaw (2004: 122) has described television producers as 'essentially exploitative' in their dealings with academic historians.

By contrast, Schama as the 'author-presenter' occupied a pivotal role in *A History of Britain*, imposing his personal interpretation on the flow of British history. Indeed, his authority as the on-screen all-knowing presenter was accentuated by the way in which Schama (IPUP 2010) was allowed to roam freely on location in front of the camera, as well as to make occasional off-the-cuff comments to camera, imparting a strong sense of immediacy. In this vein, Bell and Gray (2007: 129–30) identified not only the way in which author-presenters moved on from Burns's format but also the fact that their presentational styles, like their modes of dress, prove very different. Thus, they defined Schama's approach as based upon a 'he who knows' format, as compared to, say, the 'he who wants to know' investigative strategy employed by Michael Wood for *In Search of Myths and Heroes* (2005). Dressed more formally in a suit and tie, Starkey appeared – to quote de Groot (2009a: 158) – 'as a serious academic historian on television, rather than a presenter who happens to be an historian', an 'independent recounter of truth rather than subjective interpreter':

> He is not the audience's friend, is not their guide (not for him the inclusive elements of A *History of Britain*, no 'us' or shared history) ... the seriousness he brings to the subject is key to his projected gravitas. Starkey isn't part of the scenery in the way that Schama often is. Indeed, he strides around country houses lecturing the camera with great if distancing authority.

Bell and Gray (2007: 122) pointed also to the way in which author-presenters developed over time: 'The charismatic presenter does not arrive ready formed.' In this regard, *A History of Britain* highlighted the changes in Schama's television persona, particularly as compared to presenting *Landscape and Memory* in 1995. For Snowman (2004: 85), among others, 'Schama's early TV appearances reveal a highly energised, somewhat restless presenter (usually bearded) whose entire body reaches out to share with the viewer his latest enthusiasms.' Nor was Blake Morrison (1995) overly impressed by *Landscape and Memory*; thus, he opined that television did not seem Schama's natural medium:

> In the flesh, Schama is generous and enthusiastic: he waves his arms around, hurls out ideas, reels off reading lists, cracks jokes, is sensitive to criticism but knows how to look after himself. On the screen, budget constraints keeping him to an arty studio, he looks strained, uncomfortable. There is no disguising his intellect, and television is seldom kind to intellectuals.

By contrast, in *A History of Britain* Schama assumed a more confident, relaxed and less formal presenting style while undergoing a makeover in his appearance through, say, the loss of his beard and a switch from spectacles to contact lenses. Schama (Billen 2003) himself acknowledged that his performance improved in the second series after reading Patsy Rodenburg's manual *The Actor Speaks: voice and the performer* (2000): 'If only I'd had this book earlier, the first series would have been so much better.'

Working on television histories helped Schama to think about, even to resolve, some of the problems of presenting such histories, most notably those arising from the nature of the medium itself, with its inevitable demands for compression, simplification and visual presentations. Indeed, the demands of acting as 'author-presenter' and dealing with television production imperatives led Schama (2002c; 2002d: 42; 2011; IPUP 2010) to become something of a filmmaker, or at least more sympathetic to the television filmmaker's perspective when presenting the past. Television history, he appreciated, was 'not just about transcribing learned books onto the small screen'. Programmes were not consumed like books, and hence any presenter was forced not only to treat scriptwriting as an entirely different exercise from book writing but also to prove constantly responsive to the visual sequences shown to viewers.

Leading Historians into the Digital Age

During the past decade or so Schama has proved instrumental in establishing presenter-led histories as a highly popular format enabling the general public to engage with the past in today's multi-platform media world. For Adrian Gill (2009), the *Sunday Times*'s acerbic television critic, Schama's authored documentaries, alongside his liveliness and erudition as a presenter, has made historical knowledge attractive and addictive to a wide audience. Blurring the boundary between culture, education, and entertainment, televisual histories have become the principal means by which a growing number of people on both sides of the Atlantic learn about the past or top up what they studied at school. In fact, for most viewers, the inadequate provision of history at school means that an increasing proportion of their historical knowledge is provided by television.

Inevitably, this development has fed into ongoing debates about popular and academic histories, most notably prompting comparisons between written and televisual histories and exchanges about the extent to which television histories conform to historical standards. After all, the prime focus of television history programme makers is the audience. Programmes are viewer-centred, not history-centred. As a result, for many academic historians, television histories, no matter how well presented, still compare unfavourably with other modes of presenting history. Significantly, this line was taken by Barbara Fields (quoted, Edgerton 2001: 17), one of Burns's 'talking heads in *The Civil War*: 'My job is to convey history to people. No film, however well done, can ever replace that task.' Moreover, the relative ease with which television documentaries can hoodwink viewers through skilful editing of archival film, re-enactments, and so on led Martin Smith (2003: 30), whose television credits include *The World at War* and *Cold War*, to urge fellow filmmakers to make available references for all images and sounds used in any programme.

However, today debate is moving on increasingly from exchanges about television histories as 'good history' or 'bad history' to focus upon broader issues, most notably the style and form of presentation or the role played by television historians in creating and maintaining collective memory through representations of nation, gender and identity (Bell 2007: 5–7; IPUP 2010). One issue centres upon the manner in which the dramatic rise in television history programming has coincided, or so it appears, with growing evidence of modern society's historical illiteracy and history's increasingly tenuous place in the educational curriculum. For some historians, the boom in history programming has been interpreted also as having a detrimental impact on history in schools and universities by encouraging students attracted by the drama of Schama and Starkey-type histories to believe that the subject is merely an exercise in storytelling, a glossy form of edutainment, not a rigorous intellectual discipline (Woodward 2003; Ofsted 2007: 29).

On the other hand, good audience ratings and the healthy level of sales achieved by television tie-in books establish television histories' contribution to public history. In this vein, Columbia University offered an 'e-seminar' entitled 'Liberty and Slavery in the early British Empire' as part of its online educational resources. For Schama (quoted, Marshall n.d; quoted, Sherwin and Owen 2002), the course, developed from one *A History of Britain* programme, highlighted the ability of television and the internet to replace 'formidably dull' history textbooks.

Conclusion

Today Schama, the BBC's 'history man', is one of the best-known and best-paid presenters of history. Following the completion of *A History of Britain*, he moved ahead on several fronts in the wake of a £3 million contract – this followed soon after Starkey's four-year television contract worth £2 million (Wells 2002) – concluded with the BBC and HarperCollins for two television series and three books. Welcomed by Andrew Roberts (quoted, Milner 2002) as 'good for the popularisation of history', the record-breaking deal was justified by Robin Wood (quoted, Milner 2002), the director of BBC Books:

> The reason we paid so much is because we believe in Simon Schama – both for his academic reputation and for his powers as a communicator. I think he is spellbinding ... Maybe it is because we live in an age of great change and uncertainty but history has never been so popular.

Clearly the BBC rates Schama highly as a 'communicator' presenting history to millions of viewers in Britain and overseas. Indeed, in 2009 a leaked BBC memo indicated that he was ranked alongside Jeremy Paxman and Jeremy Clarkson in the 'top tier (highly valued)' category of television presenters (Hastings and Chittenden 2009). For Dyke (IPUP 2010), a former BBC Director-General, Schama proved a brilliant presenter, capable of making history's complexities understandable and engaging to a wide audience.

Like Taylor, Schama (2002f; 2010b) has achieved celebrity status, as evidenced by not only the interview conducted with David Cameron, the British prime minister (2010–), for the *Financial Times* but also media coverage of his culinary and musical interests and appearances on programmes like BBC Radio 4's *Desert Island Discs* and BBC One's *Question Time*. In 2004 Alan Bennett, an admirer of his public histories, invited Schama (2004) to contribute an article for the London theatre programme of *The History Boys*.

Schama's more recent television work has included *The American Future: a history* (2008) and – note the use of his name in the titles – *Simon Schama's John Donne* (2009) and *Simon Schama on Obama's America* (2010). Seeking to explore the 'haunting of the present by the past', Schama (2008) contextualised the 2008 American presidential election as 'a sea-change moment' in *The American Future: a history*:

> It's odd in a country obsessed with the new, that history – its epic figures, its great texts – is treated as a living breathing thing … It's never been more alive than now. Is there any one in America who doesn't call this election historic, a candidate who doesn't reach out to history?

Unsurprisingly, Schama's 'gift for narrative' (Jenkins 2009) and 'unfailingly entertaining' prose was highlighted in reviews of the book accompanying this television series. Schama's presentational qualities were highlighted also in *Scribble, Scribble, Scribble: writings on ice cream, Obama, Churchill and my mother* (2010), a collection of essays and journalism covering art, film, food and history. Offering also a range of autobiographical revelations, Schama (2010a: 140–6, 379–90) reaffirmed Plumb's influence in inspiring his belief in public history, while firing off again the testy response to critiques of *A History of Britain* published as part of the *American Historical Review*'s 'Forum' (Schama 2009b).

Inevitably, Schama's contemporary status as 'the keeper of British history' (Billen 2003) has led him to be treated by the media as a spokesman for present-day historical issues, such as history's place in the educational curriculum or the narrow focus of school history in Britain upon Hitler and the Henrys. For example, during 2002 he was an invited speaker at the Prince of Wales's conference on teaching history in schools. According to Schama (Grice 2010), television histories met a demand for history left unsatisfied by schools, which failed either to engage pupils in the past or to produce historically literate students. Unsurprisingly, when interviewing Cameron in 2010, Schama (2010b) moved on from discussing Britain's past to ways of teaching 'an inclusive but unapologetic version of British community'. Soon afterwards

Michael Gove (2010), the Secretary of State for Education, appointed Schama to advise the government 'on how we can put British history at the heart of a revived national curriculum'. Notwithstanding Schama's (quoted, L. Roberts 2010) hopes as the 'history tsar' of instilling 'excitement and joy' into learning Britain's 'island story', the announcement was not welcomed in all quarters. For Cambridge's Mary Beard, Schama's appointment was merely another example of government exploiting 'celebrity culture' and 'playing to the populist gallery'.

In his keynote lecture delivered to the 2001 Congress of History Producers, Schama (2001b) predicted that:

> Whether scholars like it or not, the future of history, the survival of history is going to depend at least as much, if not more, on the new media and television as on the printed page. Without labouring the point, it's no good simply grousing about the results without being prepared to get into the action.

Although historians continue to prioritise written histories, the general public prefers television. Kershaw (2004: 123), like Philip Taylor (2001: 177), has been prominent among those echoing Schama's view that television history is here to stay: 'If historians do not help to mould and influence it, others will.' At the same time, it is vital for academic historians to acknowledge that television historians employ different presentational methods and instruments for reaching viewers. Certainly, Schama, though uncertain whether the television audience's demand for history has run its course or not, views himself as playing a pioneering role in taking history forward into the digital age, as evidenced by the manner in which his television histories are recognised as providing an 'exemplary model' (Champion 2003: 169–70) of public history.

But does the Schama model meet the needs of all viewers? In fact, as stated by George Entwistle (IPUP 2010), the BBC's Controller of Knowledge Commissioning (2008–11), BBC history programming employs varying formats to access different audiences across its channels. Thus, in 2010, the BBC's belief that a more populist approach was required for a prime-time BBC One audience led to the decision to adapt the CBBC's *Horrible Histories* (chapter 11) for a 2011 series targeted at an adult audience. Inevitably, the proposal attracted mixed views (quoted, Wynne-Jones, 2010; Hickman 2011), with Hunt's critique of an undemanding 'cartoon' approach contrasting with Bettany Hughes's claim that the *Horrible Histories* offered viewers 'a memorable and hilarious hook on which to hang a better understanding of history'.

Notwithstanding criticisms about history's dependence upon pre-senters' egos and their 'informed upfront advocacy', Hadlow (quoted Rowan 2004; Hill 2005; Gibson 2007) described historians 'touched by charisma' and capable of blending showmanship with scholarship as a significant televisual resource possessing 'transformative power'. Indeed, she claimed that Schama, alongside fellow television present-ers like Ferguson and Starkey, have 'changed the way we think about history'. Speaking in 2010, Hadlow (IPUP 2010), Controller of BBC Two (2008–), described *A History of Britain* as an exemplar of history programming giving producers and commissioners confidence that challenging, high-quality, authored history programmes merit a place in today's schedules because they can become critical and popular suc-cesses. For Entwistle (IPUP 2010), the series' concrete practical legacy centred upon an institutional return by the BBC to a commitment to the quality of content and the primacy of ideas as opposed to an exces-sive concentration on visuals. *A History of Britain*, he acknowledged, was also an early milestone on the road to today's multi-platform broadcast-ing landscape.

Meanwhile, Schama continues to urge other historians to follow his lead in acknowledging and exploring the power and reach of television history, and to think about presenting the past through pictures as well as words. Apart from offering a shop window for history in the new media world, television's universality of address and reach means that it offers Schama-type presenters the ability to show a broader audience that history can do far more than provide mere entertainment. In particular, history can tell engaging stories, offer informed and nuanced reflection upon the past, open up debates, and spur further enquiry by encouraging viewers to begin a learning journey through a shared past.

Simon Michael Schama (1945–): Select Bibliography

Histories

1977   *Patriots and Liberators: Revolution in the Netherlands, 1780–1813*
1978   *Two Rothschilds and the Land of Israel*
1987   *The Embarrassment of Riches: an interpretation of Dutch culture in the Golden Age*
1989   *Citizens: a chronicle of the French Revolution*
1995   *Landscape and Memory*

→

1999   *Rembrandt's Eyes*
2000   *A History of Britain, vol.I: At the Edge of the World?, 3000BC–AD1603.*
2001   *A History of Britain, vol.II: The British Wars, 1603–1776*
2003   *A History of Britain Vol.III: The Fate of Empire, 1776–2000*
2004   *Hang-Ups: Essays on painting (mostly)*
2005   *Rough Crossings: Britain, the slaves and the American Revolution*
2006   *The Power of Art*
2008   *The American Future: a history*
2010   *Scribble, Scribble, Scribble: writings on ice cream, Obama, Churchill and my mother*

Historical novel

1991   *Dead Certainties: unwarranted speculations*

Television programmes/series

[number of programmes given in brackets]

1995	*Landscape and Memory* (BBC/PBS)	[5]
2000–2	*A History of Britain* (BBC/History Channel)	[15]
2002	'Television and the trouble with history', Inaugural BBC History Lecture (BBC)	[1]
2003	*Murder at Harvard* (WGBH Boston)	[1]
2004	*Historians of Genius* (BBC)	[3]
2006	*The Power of Art* (BBC/PBS)	[8]
2007	*Rough Crossings* (BBC)	[1]
2008	*The American future: a history* (BBC/PBS)	[4]
2009	*Simon Schama's John Donne* (BBC)	[1]
2010	*Simon Schama on Obama's America* (BBC)	[2]

Radio programmes

2009	*Baseball and Me* (BBC Radio Four)	[2]

Plays

2007   *Rough Crossings* (play adapted by Caryl Phillips from Schama's book)

7
Niall Ferguson: The 'What Ifs?' Historian

Far from being viewed as the inevitable outcome of past events, today's world should be presented more accurately as the product of a road that might not have been. Throughout time people made choices between alternative courses of action. Both past and present could have proved very different. Focusing upon a theme central to Robert Frost's famous poem 'The Road not Taken' (1916), Hugh Trevor-Roper (1981b: 363–4) asked 'how can we *explain* what happened and *why*" if we only look at what happened and never consider the alternatives'. From this perspective, 'History is not merely what happened: it is what happened in the context of what might have happened. Therefore, it must incorporate, as a necessary element, the alternatives, the might-have-beens.' Or, as André Maurois (quoted, Ferguson 1998a: 1) commented, 'There is no privileged past ... There is an infinitude of Pasts, all equally valid ... At each and every instant of Time ... the line of events forks like the stem of a tree putting forth twin branches'.

Studying the roads contemplated in the past, but not taken, allows historians to live – to quote Trevor-Roper (1981b: 365) – 'for a moment, as the men of the time lived, in its still fluid context and among its still unresolved problems'. Presenters failing to take account of the roads not taken risk, it is argued, providing only a partial view of the past. Building upon these views, during the late 1990s Oxford's Niall Ferguson emerged as the most articulate and visible spokesman of the case for exploring alternative scenarios and restoring the past's lost uncertainties. Rather than dumping history's 'what ifs?' in 'the historical dustbin', Ferguson argued that what are described as counterfactual histories – other descriptors include alternate histories or 'allohistories' – should be treated as a central focus for historians. During the recent period counterfactual history has emerged as a fertile field of historical inquiry, as evidenced by the proliferation of alternate histories speculating about a wide range of counterfactual scenarios. For example, 'what if the 1588 Spanish Armada had succeeded in invading England?'; 'what if the South had triumphed in the American Civil War?'; 'what if Britain had stayed out of the First World War?'; 'what if Nazi Germany had won the Second World War?'; and 'what if China, not the West, had dominated the post-1500 world?' Moreover, this trend has proved an effective way for historians to reach out to a popular audience, as highlighted by media coverage of the genre's emergence (Honan 1998; Arnold 2000), the *Sunday Times's* publication of extracts from Ferguson's book, and radio/television series on history's 'what ifs?'

A Public Historian

Reportedly, Ferguson (quoted, Riding 1999) often jokes about becoming a historian by default: 'At Oxford, I discovered that I couldn't be a politician, I wouldn't make a terribly good journalist, I was a very poor double bass player and I was an absolutely appalling actor. I came to realize that what made me happy was to sit in a library reading about dead people.' Born in Glasgow, Ferguson studied history at the University of Oxford. Having obtained a first in history, he moved on to doctoral research, which was completed successfully in 1989. As befits someone acknowledging being inspired by A.J.P. Taylor, Ferguson wanted to be far more than a respected academic historian. The fact that during the past decade or so he has repeatedly proved the subject of articles in *The Times*, the *Guardian*, the *Independent* and the *New York Times* is indicative of his success in securing high media visibility as – to quote the *New York Times* – 'the most talked-about British historian of his generation' (Riding 1999).

Maurice Cowling (1999: 17–18) represented Ferguson as an 'intelligent populist' reaching academic and non-academic audiences on both sides of the Atlantic. Thus, in 2003, the start of his television series on *Empire* was accompanied by the launch of a companion book, the publication of extracts therefrom in *The Times*, and the delivery of a linked lecture series at the University of London. Moreover, in 2004, *TIME Magazine* named Ferguson in the 'TIME 100', a list of people regarded as shaping the thinking of the present-day world (Elliott 2004). More recently, as befits a celebrity historian, in February 2010 the British press focused more on Ferguson's private life following reports about the breakdown of his marriage to Susan Douglas, formerly deputy editor of the *Sunday Times*.

By the late 1990s Ferguson had published several wide-ranging histories, which had helped to establish his media reputation as – to quote the

Guardian – 'one of the most provocative young historians in the country' (Christy 1999). Certainly, his books sold well, and provided the basis for a three-book contract with Penguin reportedly worth half a million pounds, as well as for his switch from a professorship at Oxford to Harvard in 2004 via a brief posting in New York. At Harvard, Ferguson is Laurence A. Tisch Professor of History and William Ziegler Professor of Business Administration. Already in 2003 he had moved on almost inevitably into the rapidly emerging world of television history and tie-in books.

Ferguson as a History Presenter

Significant features of Ferguson's role as a history presenter include:

* the publication of several substantial historical monographs;
* writing readable histories on demanding subjects;
* the adoption of a deliberately revisionist line;
* the assumption of the role of television author-presenter; and
* the championing of counterfactual presentations of the past.

First, Ferguson published within the space of six years four large tomes – *Paper and Iron* (1995), *The Pity of War* (1998), *The World's Banker* (1998) and *The Cash Nexus* (2001) – offering history on a grand scale. Totalling over 3000 pages, these books were also heavily referenced; for example, *The World's Banker* contained 1040 pages of text and 200 pages of footnotes.

Secondly, these monographs, excepting perhaps *Paper and Iron*, which was based on his doctoral thesis, proved eminently readable in spite of covering demanding subjects. Quite apart from again targeting an academic audience through specialist articles in the *Economic History Review*, *Past and Present*, and the *English Historical Review*, he reached out deliberately to an audience beyond academia. Pointing to the inspiration of Plumb and Taylor, Ferguson (1999: 218; quoted, Fulford 2001; Goldstein 1999) has repeatedly urged fellow historians to follow suit: 'What's the point of having knowledge about modern history if you confine yourself to writing monographs for the Oxford University Press?':

> One ought to be able to work in different media to research and write at different levels. Sometimes it is appropriate ... to make no allowances for the lay audience ... And yet the conclusion you may arrive at can be communicated to a wider audience ... And in that sense one has to work from the very academic towards the general reader

in a series of stages ... If your conclusion can't be explained to the general reader ... then your conclusion is probably still confused.

Significantly, Ferguson decided to publish *The World's Banker* (Weidenfeld & Nicolson) and *The Pity of War* (Penguin) with commercial publishers in order to ensure that the books were marketed effectively, read widely, reviewed in the press, and attracted newspaper interviews. For Ferguson (quoted, Riding 1999), the principal difference between them and *Paper and Iron*, his first book, published by Cambridge University Press, *lay in their presentation*:

> Cambridge University Press will produce a book that is intimidating to read, the print is small, the footnotes are on the page. Penguin will produce a book which has pictures, good charts, looks nice, and then they will market it. But if you look at the texts of the two books, it's not that big a shift.

Generally speaking, reviewers, even academic historians critical of content and/or interpretation, have praised the readability and clarity of Ferguson's books, particularly given their challenging subject matter, heavily referenced nature, and frequent focus on economic and financial topics involving a substantial quantitative element. For Alan Clark (1998), *The Pity of War* was 'beautifully written, unpretentious in style'. Jeremy Wormell (2001), though unimpressed by *The World's Banker*'s coverage of debt markets, admired Ferguson's presentation: 'Niall Ferguson has an easy style, the Rothschild story gives great scope, and, between the style and the raw material, he has written one of the most readable and exciting histories of any banking family we have seen thus far.' For Fritz Stern (1999: 34), 'Ferguson's work reaffirms one's faith in the possibility of great historical writing.' Reviewing *Empire*, Stanley Hoffmann (2003: 178–9) praised 'the author's clear writing, his gift for narrative, and his way with words'. Reading the book was indeed 'a pleasure'.

In many respects, Ferguson's skills as a writer presenting public history have built upon his early forays into journalism. Describing his media activities as involving an uneasy union of historian and polemicist, Ferguson (quoted, Moss 2001) followed Schama in viewing himself as reviving an old tradition:

> The idea that the media don is a modern invention is absurd. In many ways the separation of the public from the academic is the real novelty. In the 19th century if you were a historian, you might

not necessarily be an academic. In fact, the best historians in this country weren't.

Even so, the 'collective disdain' displayed by most academic colleagues towards journalism led Ferguson (1999: 207–9) to conceal his initial activities through the use of pseudonyms. Thus, he wrote as 'Alec Campbell' for the *Daily Telegraph* and 'Campbell Ferguson' for the *Daily Mail*, even hiding behind thick-rimmed glasses for the accompanying photograph. Providing access to a broader audience, journalism proved not only lucrative but also a good discipline in forcing him to write clearly, crisply, engagingly, and to a deadline. Writing for the press enabled Ferguson also to present himself as a public thinker contributing to contemporary media debates.

Today, Ferguson, a contributing editor for the *Financial Times*, remains a regular media commentator and reviewer. Indeed, during 2009 he was engaged in a high profile op-ed spat with Princeton's Paul Krugman conducted in the *Financial Times* and *New York Times* about the inflationary impact of American fiscal policies. Reportedly (Bown 2008), Ferguson has also undertaken consultancy and advisory work for investment banks and hedge funds, even securing $100,000 for one presentation at a hedge fund managers' conference!

Thirdly, Ferguson soon acquired, indeed cultivated, a reputation as a revisionist. Despite admiring Ferguson's writing skills as displayed in *Empire*, Hoffmann (2003: 179) claimed there were 'really two Fergusons here ... One is a brilliant economic historian. The other is a political writer who provokes his readers with very dubious theses'. Indeed, Ferguson's image as 'a young don in a hurry' (Christy 1999) attracting good sales and large book advances derived in part from his confrontational revisionist approach. Renowned for taking controversial points of view often possessing a contemporary resonance – as outlined in chapter 14, Ferguson inspired one of the leading characters in Alan Bennett's *The History Boys* – his books were noticed and attracted reviewers and readers within and outside academia.

An accomplished storyteller, Ferguson imposed a strong story line to overcome the perceived shortcomings of narrative studies. According to Ferguson (quoted, Christy 1999), most First World War histories just told the story along the lines of 'Once upon a time there were five great powers, dot, dot, dot and then the Germans lost':

> I've always felt – even going back to A.J.P. Taylor – that they don't explain very much, in fact they don't explain anything because if one reads the First World War as story, most of the time the Germans

are winning. Things go disastrously wrong for Britain in 1915, 1916, in 1917 and in the spring of 1918, and then, lo and behold, the Germans collapse in the summer of 1918. If you tell that as story I don't think that makes much sense.

Rather than writing *The Pity of War* as yet another wartime narrative, Ferguson (1998d) challenged existing historiography by arguing that Britain should have remained neutral, not declared war, in August 1914; that the conflict was prolonged partly because the Allies, including Britain, waged war inefficiently; and that the postwar problem was not that the 1919 Treaty of Versailles was too harsh but rather that the Allies failed to enforce it.

Welcoming a major contribution to the war's historiography, Alan Clark (1998) compared the book's impact to Taylor's *Origins of the Second World War* (chapter 4). Subsequent publications reaffirmed Ferguson's revisionist reputation, as evidenced by the manner in which *The Cash Nexus* (2001) critiqued the accepted view that successful economic policies ensured election victories. Then in *Empire* (2003) he advanced a spirited defence of empire – this view was somewhat out of step with mainstream thinking – based upon the British Empire's contribution to world order and provision of lessons for its successor, the USA.

Inevitably, his revisionist histories have frequently attracted strong reactions from academic historians, as Ferguson (quoted, Christy 1999) has acknowledged: 'One should never underestimate the hatred an author feels for a hostile reviewer. Fair criticism – after the initial red mist has passed – I can take, but it is surprisingly exhausting to get a lot of hostile reviews from a lot of different places.' For example, Wormell's depiction of *The World's Banker* as an 'unsafe' text on debt markets provoked a reasoned but rather bad-tempered response from Ferguson (2001) to the effect that 'Wormell's lop-sided and pedantic jottings are of very little consequence indeed.' Nor has Ferguson (quoted, Moss 2001) welcomed repeated attempts to categorise him in political terms:

> The only thing that's slightly boring is to end up being pigeonholed as a right-wing Thatcherite historian, because those sort of labels don't mean anything any more ... I would rather be seen as radical and revisionist. I'm interested in questioning received wisdom, whether it is from the left or the right.

Fourthly, his proven skills as a presenter of written histories accessible to both academic and non-academic audiences led Ferguson (quoted,

Goldstein 1999) to follow Schama and Starkey into the challenging and lucrative world of television history:

> Too many historians by inhabiting exclusively the academic world ... probably are limiting their own clarity of thought ... If you can get it across to the TV audience, then if nothing else you've arrived at something which is clear ... You may be wrong, but at least it's intelligible.

As author-presenter, Ferguson (quoted, *Daily Telegraph* 2002) has provided his personal version of the past. Like Schama, he recognised the need to avoid confusing viewers by exposing them to conflicting interpretations: 'It doesn't work on television – viewers just want to know what you think.' In turn, his recent publications have tended increasingly to be books accompanying television series. Acknowledging the fact that 'the different formats produced differences in content', Ferguson (n.d.) treated the television series and book as complementary: 'you can provide a great deal more supporting evidence in 800 or so pages than is possible in six 55 minute films'.

Channel 4's Head of History, Janice Hadlow, who had recruited Schama for *A History of Britain* when working for the BBC, was instrumental in arranging Ferguson's first television project. The resulting six-programme series on the seemingly unfashionable subject of *Empire* led to good television audience ratings – significantly, programmes, attracting 2.5 million viewers, occupied a peak-time slot following the high-profile *Graham Norton Show* – and a bestselling book. Adopting a fast-paced format comprising a series of vignettes filmed in exotic locations, *Empire* provided the basis for further series: *Colossus* (2004); *The War of the World* (2006); *The Ascent of Money* (2008); and *Civilisation* (2011). *The Ascent of Money*, which won an International Emmy Award for best documentary in 2009, gave a timely sense of perspective to the escalating global recession centred upon banking failures and the 'credit crunch'. Once again, the companion book reached the charts on both sides of the Atlantic. Significantly, this series was made by Chimerica Media, a company co-founded in 2007 by Ferguson to produce history documentaries. Recent completions include *Civilisation* and *Kissinger* (on Henry Kissinger). A series on China is in preparation.

Finally, Ferguson has been dubbed as – to quote Saul David (2000) – 'the high priest of counterfactual history'. Indeed, in 2004 *TIME Magazine* described Ferguson as 'the impresario of a school of "counterfactual" writers who took seriously the amateur historian's favorite question: What would have happened if ...?' (Elliott 2004: 113). Counterfactual history proved the subject of *Virtual History: alternatives and counterfactuals*, a book conceived and edited by Ferguson. Underpinning his approach to the past, 'virtual history' has proved a recurrent theme in Ferguson's presentation of history in books and television series, and is the central focus of this chapter.

History's 'What Ifs?'

In everyday life most of us find it difficult to resist imagining alternative scenarios, most notably when looking back upon past mistakes or problems in order to understand what went wrong, why, and what to do next time. In practice, we all use counterfactuals when speculating along the lines of 'what if?', 'if only' or 'what might have been?' Moreover, we do this in spite of realising that it is impossible personally to travel back in time to take an alternative path, as happens frequently in the cinema in such films as *Back to the Future* (1985), *Groundhog Day* (1993) or *Sliding Doors* (1998). However, as asserted by Schama in chapter 6, we can travel back through time in our minds using history, even if for most academic historians the emphasis is placed upon returning to the past in order to investigate what actually happened, not to consider 'what might have been'. But for Ferguson, among other historians, 'what if?' is an equally valid and worthwhile area for historical investigation. In effect, counterfactuals prove the historian's virtual equivalent of the laboratory experimentation undertaken by scientists.

Despite the recent surge of both interest and publications, as reflected by the invaluable Uchronia website (http://www.uchronia.net/intro. html), counterfactual history is still far from proving a mainstream historical activity. Admittedly, a growing number of historians have flirted with the occasional counterfactual, but generally speaking 'what if?' approaches to the past have been seen by the profession as neither academically acceptable nor historically useful, as typified by E.P. Thompson's (1978: 69, 299–300) dismissal of them as '*Geschichtenscheissenschlopff*, unhistorical shit'. Why waste precious time and effort on things that never happened? Is it not difficult enough discovering what actually happened? Why not leave alternative histories to historical novelists and science-fiction writers, like Keith Roberts, whose *Pavane* (1968) focused upon an England recovering from the assassination of Elizabeth and a successful Spanish Armada. Alternatively Harry Turtledove's *The Guns of the South* (1997) depicted time-travelling gunrunners securing a southern victory in the 1861–5 American Civil War.

In *Making History* (1997), Stephen Fry offered an imaginative alternate history involving the use of contraceptive pills to prevent the birth of Adolf Hitler!

But times are changing. Notwithstanding the profession's philosophical and practical reservations, a small but growing group of historians have felt called upon to investigate alternative scenarios as a meaningful way of enhancing historical knowledge and understanding. Indeed, for Jonathan Clark (2004: 257), 'counterfactuals implicitly underpin all historical reconstructions of grand events'. Ferguson's *Virtual History* (1997), alongside a 1997 workshop held at Ohio State University's Mershon Center and a special issue of *MHQ: The Quarterly Journal of Military History* (1998), reinvigorated the genre in academia. Apart from inspiring numerous publications, the vogue for counterfactuals led also to 'what if?' series on the History Channel (2000) and BBC Radio 4 (2002–3).

Moreover, the fact that leading historians – they have included Stephen Ambrose, Michael Burleigh, Jonathan Clark, John Keegan, William McNeill, Geoffrey Parker, Paul Preston, Andrew Roberts, Conrad Russell and Norman Stone – have written 'what if?' studies reflects rising academic interest in and acceptance of counterfactual history. More recently Jeremy Black (2008: 188–91), a speaker at the Mershon Center conference in 1997, published *What If?: counterfactualism and the problem of history* (2008), echoing the message advanced by Ferguson's *Virtual History*. Even so, as noted by Ferguson (1998a: 19), some historians have merely flirted with 'a veiled counterfactualism', that is, they have implied the merits of engaging in a counterfactual approach but without going any further. For instance, Ferguson pointed to Roy Foster's *Modern Ireland: 1600–1972* (1988), which repeatedly questioned nationalist teleology centred upon inevitable Irish independence from Britain, but failed to investigate any counterfactual alternative, such as continued membership of the Union. Continuing this Irish theme, a veiled counterfactualism also underpinned the landmark speech delivered in May 2011 at Dublin Castle by Elizabeth II (2011). Looking back on the troubled history of the Anglo-Irish relationship, the Queen encouraged people to consider alternative paths in the past: 'With the benefit of historical hindsight we can all see things we would wish had been done differently or not at all.'

Whereas Ferguson personally has focused primarily on political and economic counterfactuals, Robert Cowley's *What if?* (1999), based on articles previously published in *MHQ*, reflected the concept's appeal for military historians, given the manner in which a chance event such as a change of wind direction might affect the outcome of a battle or war. Other studies focusing on the military dimension include Erik

Durschmied's *The Hinge Factor: how chance and stupidity have changed history* (1999) and the Greenhill anthologies, like Peter Tsouras's *Third Reich Victorious* (2002) and *Cold War Hot* (2003).

Virtual History

Edited by Niall Ferguson (1998a: 89), *Virtual History: alternatives and counterfactuals* (1997) offered 'a series of separate voyages into "imaginary time"',... making explicit what many historians have been doing for years in the privacy of their own imaginations'. Apart from contributing the chapter investigating what if Britain had stood aside from war in August 1914, Ferguson (1998b; 1998c) also wrote the final chapter, entitled 'Afterword: a virtual history, 1646–1996', offering an extended counterfactual version of Britain's past. More importantly, his 90-page opening chapter, described by Andrew Roberts (2004: 8) as a 'magisterial introduction', set out the intellectual case for counterfactual history, even providing something akin to a manifesto for historicising the genre.

Other contributors discussed a range of counterfactual possibilities, such as 'what if Charles I had avoided civil war?', 'what if there had been no American Revolution in 1776?', 'what if Ireland had been given Home Rule in 1912?', 'what if Germany had invaded Britain in May 1940?', and 'what if President John F. Kennedy had not been assassinated in 1963?' The book's impact was enhanced by the fact that it was not only widely reviewed in the press and academic journals but also complemented at the time of publication by Ferguson's (1997a) one-page article in the *Sunday Times*. *Virtual History*'s publication in Germany, Japan, Poland, Spain and the USA extended its geographical reach.

Ferguson's introductory survey focused on three aspects: philosophical reservations about counterfactual histories; their chequered track record; and the case for virtual history. Each will be examined in turn.

Philosophical Reservations

For many historians, negative attitudes towards 'what ifs?' have been moulded by fundamental philosophical concerns. In effect, the Rankean emphasis upon history as a study of what actually happened in the past according to the evidence ruled out serious reflection about alternative scenarios. 'What ifs?' were seen as lying beyond the usual standards of historical proof, and hence – to quote Michael Oakeshott (1933: 128, 139–40) – 'outside the current of historical thought': 'The question in history is never what must, or what might have taken place, but solely what the evidence obliges us to conclude did take place ... The historian ... is never called upon to consider what might have happened had circumstances been different.' From this perspective, historians publishing counterfactual studies risked being accused of presenting accounts falling well short as 'history'. Thus, E.H. Carr (2001: 90–1, 120–1) condemned 'what ifs?' as 'unhistorical', a mere 'parlour game' allowing people to let 'their imagination run riot': 'History is, by and large, a record of what people did, not of what they failed to do ... The historian is concerned with those who, whether victorious or defeated, achieved something.' Or, as asserted by Hobsbawm (1998: 328), 'The past has happened, the match can't be replayed.'

Unsurprisingly, counterfactual history proved anathema to those espousing Marxist and other teleological approaches to the past denying, or at least circumscribing, the ability of individuals to exercise freedom of choice between alternative paths. In this vein, Richard Evans (2002: 23) pointed to the way in which the relative decline of Marxist history during the 1990s, alongside 'a pervasive scepticism about the grand narratives', helped to fuel the growth of 'what if?' history. Moreover, the rise of postmodernism, blurring the boundaries between fact and fiction, served not only to challenge historical verities but also to privilege alternative voices (Rosenfeld 2002: 92). Regretting the decline of social history in the face of cultural history and postmodernism, Hunt (2004b) contextualised counterfactual history in terms of an emerging search for histories of understanding and meaning: 'one narrative is as valid as another. One history is as good as another and with it the blurring of factual, counter-factual and fiction. All history is "what if" history.'

A Chequered Track Record

Counterfactual presentations of the past possess a lengthy history. Significant landmarks include Edward Gibbon's *Decline and Fall of the Roman Empire* (1776) – this offered occasional alternative military scenarios – and Charles Renouvier's *Uchronie* (France: 1876), which outlined 'the development of European civilisation as it has not been, but as it might perhaps have been', say, if Christianity had failed to establish itself in the West. Then in 1907 the *Westminster Gazette* published G.M. Trevelyan's article, 'If Napoleon had won the Battle of Waterloo'. A French victory, Trevelyan argued, would have resulted in Britain's failure to become a liberal democracy.

For many commentators, John Squire's edited book *If It Happened Otherwise: lapses into imaginary history* (1931) represents a key reference point, with contributors like G.K. Chesterton, Winston Churchill, H.A.L. Fisher, Philip Guadella, Harold Nicolson and André Maurois contributing essays studying scenarios like reform avoiding the 1789 French Revolution, or a Confederate success at Gettysburg preparing the way for the South's victory in the American Civil War. Another often quoted publication is Robert W. Fogel's *Railways and American Economic Growth* (1964), which employed cliometrics, a quantitative variant of counterfactual history, to create a model of American economic development without railways in order to evaluate their impact. Subsequently Fogel collaborated with S.L. Engerman in *Time on the Cross: the economics of American Negro slavery* (1974) to investigate whether slavery might have been sustained economically if there had been no American Civil War.

Generally speaking, counterfactual studies have never been highly regarded as 'history'. Inevitably, their variable, frequently low, historical quality did little either to enhance counterfactual history's credibility as 'history' or to commend 'what ifs?' to professional historians, even if this has failed to diminish their appeal to a lay audience. By contrast, during the past decade or so, counterfactual histories have experienced a renaissance within and outside academia, and attracted several well-known historians, frequently upon a repeated basis.

Reviewing previous examples of the genre, Ferguson (1998a: 10) drew attention to Squire's deprecatory comment in *If It Happened Otherwise* (1931) to the effect that counterfactual history 'doesn't help much' in terms of historical understanding and knowledge. Building upon this point, Ferguson's historiographical survey identified the practical difficulties complementing philosophical objections.

First, there was a tendency to pose implausible questions and/or present implausible answers. Although Ferguson found no evidence of authors writing about totally bizarre scenarios – such as what might have happened if Hannibal had possessed nuclear weapons and stealth bombers during the late third century BC – many contributors were adjudged responsible for lightweight studies demonstrating an excessively vivid imagination taking little or no notice of the evidence. For example, Ferguson highlighted Charles McCabe's (1985: 2) contribution in John Merriman's *For Want of a Horse* (1985), based upon Fidel Castro signing a contract to play baseball for the New York Giants – reportedly, the Giants actually received a scouting report on him as a pitcher – rather than becoming Cuban leader in 1959: 'History would have been changed. John F. Kennedy would have been spared the Bay of Pigs and the missile crisis of 1962.'

Secondly, presenters of counterfactuals often offered unrealistic reductive explanations. Thus, a single, often trivial, change was depicted as having momentous consequences. There is no reason why what has been described as 'the beat of a butterfly's wings' should not have major consequences, but reductive explanations proposing trivial causes for great events pose questions about historical realities. For example, Ferguson (1998a: 10) questioned the realism of H.A.L. Fisher's chapter in Squire's book about Byron surviving, not succumbing to, fever to become King of Greece.

Thirdly, normally counterfactual histories have been imbued with a contemporary agenda informed, or rather distorted, by hindsight. Overviewing Squire's *If It Happened Otherwise*, Ferguson (1998a: 11) complained that even the better essays were the products of their authors' present-day preoccupations. Indeed, several chapters seemed a function of the 'never again' mentality fostered by the First World War, with Churchill's essay on Britain's role in reconciling North and South after the American Civil War being used to press the fundamental case for present-day Anglo-American collaboration: 'Rather than approaching past events with a conscious indifference to what is known about later events, each takes as his starting point the burning contemporary question: How could the calamity of the First World War be avoided? The result is, in essence, retrospective wishful thinking.'

Finally, presenters of counterfactual histories were prone to imply that the alternative possibilities were better than they really were. Whereas the course of the path actually taken was known, together with all its negative consequences, the paths not taken were often imagined in terms of a presumption of an improved outcome and without any consideration of the manner in which alternative scenarios could easily go wrong.

The Case for Virtual History

Urging historians to take counterfactual history more seriously, Ferguson (quoted, Goldstein 1999) presented *Virtual History* as a 'manifesto for an approach to the past which wasn't afraid to ask "what if" questions ... which I think many general readers have probably asked themselves ... but which have very rarely, if ever, been taken seriously by historians'. As such, he went further than most, at least publicly, by championing the counterfactual cause in theory and implementing it in practice.

Counterfactual history, Ferguson (1998a: 87, 89) argued, was not only 'a worthwhile thing for historians to do, but actually indispensable':

> There is, then, a double rationale for counterfactual analysis. Firstly, it is a *logical* necessity ... to pose 'but for' questions, and to try to imagine what would have happened ... Secondly, to do this is a *historical* necessity when attempting to understand how the past 'actually was' – precisely in the Rankean sense.

In particular, he presented a counterfactual approach as 'a necessary antidote' to Marxist determinism. As John Lewis Gaddis (2004: 101) commented, 'history is either predetermined or it isn't; and if it isn't then surely some parts of it could have happened in some other way'.

When working on his doctorate, Ferguson (quoted Goldstein 1999) came to appreciate the value of a counterfactual approach for studying interwar German history, most notably when considering whether the hyperinflation of 1922–3 could have been avoided:

> My assumption and the assumption of the literature ... was that this was an inevitable disaster ... My own research suggested ... that hyperinflation was the result of identifiable political mistakes and miscalculations ... I realized that there was really no limit to the way in which counterfactual method could be used.

Ferguson's case for counterfactual history rested on three key claims. First, it enabled a more informed and comprehensive understanding of what actually happened in the past. Overriding the manner in which hindsight and deterministic theories made history seem inevitable, Ferguson (1998a: 86) claimed counterfactual approaches allow a broader and more realistic understanding of the alternative courses of action facing people at the time:

> Most people in the past have tended to consider more than one possible future. And although no more than one of these actually has come about, at the moment *before* it came about it was no more real ... than the others. Now, if all history is the history of (recorded) thought, surely we must attach equal significance to *all* the outcomes thought about.

Moreover, any judgement of the merits of any one action or policy will be helped by drawing comparisons with the other options available at the time.

Secondly, counterfactual history allowed historians to acknowledge the role of chance. Notwithstanding the confidence displayed by economic forecasters, gamblers and fortune-tellers, the future is unpredictable. What actually happened in the past was often not the outcome which informed contemporaries saw as the most likely. Frequently, a battle hinged upon a single point involving, say, a sudden change in the weather or the death of a military commander. Philosophically, a growing acceptance of the part played by accident and contingency in history, such as that pressed by Taylor (chapter 4), has proved instrumental in reinforcing 'what if?' approaches to the past.

Thirdly, counterfactualism underpinned attempts to learn from the past. Regardless of claims about its unhistorical character alongside denials that the historian's role is to say what ought to have been done in the past (Ferguson 1998a: 48), historians, like politicians, frequently draw lessons from history. Resting heavily upon imagined counterfactuals, this practice involves replaying past events, but evaluating the feasibility of alternative courses of action in order to assess whether it was possible to achieve a different, arguably better, outcome. For example, was there a feasible alternative to appeasement for British policymakers confronted by Hitler or Mussolini? When looking back to his role as American Secretary of Defense (1961–8), Robert McNamara (1995: xvi, 320) admitted that, far from waging war in Vietnam – his decision was 'wrong, terribly wrong' – he should have pressed for US withdrawal, 'saving our strength for more defensible stands elsewhere'.

Doing Counterfactual History

Theoretically, at any one point in the past there existed an infinite number of what Jorge Luis Borges (quoted, Ferguson 1998a: 70–2) called 'forking paths'. For the historian investigating 'what ifs?', the chief tasks are to decide which alternative paths to investigate, which counterfactual questions to ask, and which counterfactuals to apply (Ferguson 1998a: 83–4; Cowley 2001: xii).

Seeking to pre-empt objections, most notably allegations that counterfactuals depend upon facts which never existed, Ferguson argued that the academic validity of 'virtual history' would be enhanced if historians adhered to acceptable guidelines, most notably to concentrate principally upon plausible alternatives. There is no point in asking most counterfactual questions, particularly those existing in the realms of fantasy. Rather the choice should be narrowed down to options which are believable in the sense of being shown *by the evidence* to have been

actually available at the time and considered as realistic options contemplated by contemporaries (Ferguson 1998a: 87; Roberts 2004: 5–6).
Prudence dictates the need to prevent wild speculation triumphing over
sober calculation. In addition, historians must understand the way in
which human beings think and act. For example, policymakers, though
capable of exercising reason and judgement, are often influenced by
memories of past actions and events as well as by irrational concerns.

Other historians have suggested additional guidelines. For example,
Gaddis (2004: 101–2), echoing the need to be 'highly disciplined', pointed
to the wisdom of changing only a single variable at a time while keeping the others constant. Stressing the importance of a critical approach,
Donald Kagan (1999: 48–52) advised the need to take account of the fact
that possible alternatives might have unpleasant outcomes, even fail.
'Keep it short', advised Andrew Roberts (2004: 8), given the tendency of
book-length counterfactuals to overstretch writers' imaginations.

Counterfactual Case Studies

Two case studies, based upon Ferguson's presentations, highlight the
ability of counterfactual history to prompt historical controversy, and
perhaps to raise questions as much as to provide answers.

The first case study examines what if Britain had stayed out of
the First World War. *The Pity of War*'s concluding section developed
Ferguson's counterfactual thinking about 1914, as articulated already in
Virtual History (Ferguson 1998b; 1998c). Highlighting history's contin-
gent nature and the range of options open to decision-makers, Ferguson
(1998d: 462; quoted, Goldstein 1999) claimed that the British government's declaration of war in 1914 was 'nothing less than the greatest
error of modern history':

> One of the critical turning points of the 20th century ... is the deci-
> sion of the British Cabinet on the 2nd of August, 1914 to intervene
> in the continental war ... There you have, it seems to me, an abso-
> lutely classic instance of a turning point which could have turned
> in another direction ... And one of the alternatives outcomes of the
> First World War is that Britain stays neutral. And therefore you have
> a continental rather than a world war ... It's clear that the Germany
> of 1914, had it been successful in its objective of defeating its con-
> tinental neighbors, would have created something not unlike the
> European Union ... The Third Reich could never have come about
> without the defeat of 1918 and all the subsequent upheavals.

Claiming that the resulting postwar conditions would not have been conducive to the rise of Nazism, Ferguson (1998b: 278; 1998d: 459–60) argued that Hitler would have remained merely a 'second-rate artist with nothing to complain about'. Moreover, other developments ushered in by war, most notably the collapse of tsarism and the advent of Bolshevism, would have been avoided, leaving Lenin 'scribbling in Zurich, forever waiting for capitalism to collapse – and forever disappointed'. Meanwhile, Britain itself might never have suffered the massive contraction in power arising from fighting not one, but two world wars.

Confronting existing thinking about key events, Ferguson raised interesting points for historical debate, as articulated in critiques written by Evans (2002: 25), Kagan (1999), Thomas Otte (2000: 271–87) and Andrew Roberts (1998):

- If Germany went on to win the 1914 war, would the 'new Germany' actually have been like the European Union?
- Regardless of the rosy picture painted by Ferguson, would it have been possible for Britain to coexist with an enlarged and economically powerful Germany?
- Would Britain really have avoided decline by staying out of the war?

Focusing upon the topic of Ferguson's initial television series, the second case study considers what if there had been no British Empire. In his 2003 television series and book Ferguson (n.d.), who spent part of his childhood in Kenya and was raised on tales of imperial adventure, acknowledged the British Empire's much vaunted sins, but largely foregrounded its 'underplayed' achievements. Pointing to its global role in promoting Western norms of law, order and governance alongside the free movement of goods, capital and labour, Ferguson presented the British Empire as providing the framework for present-day globalization.

Investigating 'what if there had been no British Empire?', Ferguson (2003: xxii–iii) concluded that 'while it is just about possible to imagine what the world would have been like without the French Revolution or the First World War, the imagination reels from the counterfactual of modern history without the British Empire':

> As I travelled around that Empire's remains, I was constantly struck by its ubiquitous creativity. To imagine the world without the Empire would be to expunge from the map the elegant boulevards of Williamsburg and old Philadelphia; to sweep into the sea the squat battlements of Port Royal, Jamaica; to return to the bush the glorious

skyline of Sydney; to level the steamy seaside slum that is Freetown, Sierra Leone; to fill in the Big Hole at Kimberley; to demolish the mission at Kuruman; to send the town of Livingstone hurtling over the Victoria Falls – which would, of course, revert to their original name of Mosioatunya. Without the British Empire, there would be no Calcutta; no Bombay; no Madras. Indians may rename them as many times as they like, but they remain cities founded and built by the British.

Of course, as with any counterfactual history, this might 'have happened anyway, albeit with different names', with another country taking responsibility also for laying telegraph cables across the world as well as inventing and exporting railways. Ferguson's (2003: xxiv, xxviii, 365–81) conclusions illuminated counterfactual history's ability to provoke debate:

> Would other empires have produced the same effects? It seems doubtful ... For better or worse – fair and foul – the world we know today is in large measure a product of Britain's age of Empire. The question is not whether British imperialism was without blemish. It was not. The question is whether there could have been a less bloody path to modernity. Perhaps in theory there could have been. But in practice?

Rising to the challenge, Jon Wilson (2003) complained about Ferguson's 'glossy' and 'retro-chic defence' of imperialism. Focusing upon 'the acceptable face of imperial brutality', he accused Ferguson of presenting 'a version of the history of empire that is simply wrong', particularly when 'using Britain's imperial past to justify America's imperial future'. Echoing Wilson's critique, Andrew Porter (2003) expressed surprise that Ferguson had not gone even further in exploring imperial 'what ifs?':

> Ferguson seems to believe that for most areas of the world the experience of imperial rule offered the only way to the future. This begs many questions. Why, for example, should one assume that eighteenth-century India could not have evolved its own economic path, with distributions of capital, labour and goods 'optimal' in the eyes of its own elites however different from the criteria of liberal western political economists? The work of regional historians gives grounds for disputing such an assumption, and thus for questioning perceptions of backwardness and modernity conditioned in the west, but Ferguson does not pay it any attention.

Hobsbawm, Schama and Starkey on 'What Ifs?'

Notwithstanding ongoing controversies about their historical merits, several historians, including those studied in other chapters, have been tempted to speculate about the past's 'what might-have-beens', even if some, like Hobsbawm and Schama, have expressed contradictory views on the subject.

Given the manner in which counterfactual history's indeterminacy confronts Marxist determinism, Hobsbawm is often cited (Roberts 2004: 2–3) alongside E.H. Carr and E.P. Thompson as being fundamentally hostile to 'what if?' approaches to the past. In fact, despite the occasional critical comment, as cited earlier in this chapter, Hobsbawm (1998: 150, 322–3, 328), as acknowledged by Ferguson (2002) himself, has proved relatively flexible on the subject, particularly following the mindset-challenging events of 1989–91: 'Unlike some other historians I am ready to welcome its [history's] excursions into imaginary or fictional history known as "counterfactuals" ... All history is full of implicit or explicit counterfactuals. They range from speculation about alternative outcomes ... to more specific might-have-beens.' In particular, Hobsbawm (1998: 149–51) praised Fogel's work using cliometrics, 'the school which transforms economic history into retrospective econometrics', to quantify the economic contribution of the American railways.

For Hobsbawm, the major historical controversies concerning twentieth-century Russian and Soviet history focused largely upon what might have happened, not what actually happened. Pointing to the Soviet Union's central role in post-1917 international affairs, Hobsbawm's *Age of Extremes* (1994) raised the question, 'what if there had been no Stalin's Russia to defeat Germany in the Second World War?' For Hobsbawm (1995: 7), this period, including the crucial wartime capitalist–communist alliance against fascism, 'forms the hinge of twentieth-century history and its decisive moment': 'Without it the Western world today would probably consist (outside the USA) of a set of variations on authoritarian and fascist themes rather than a set of variations on liberal parliamentary ones.' Nor was this the only area identified by Hobsbawm for counterfactual debate. Others included: 'what if tsarism's overthrow in 1917 was not inevitable?'; 'what if Lenin had been unable to return from Switzerland to lead the revolution?'; 'what if the Bolsheviks had employed other means to take power?'; 'what if there had been a Europe-wide revolution after the First World War?'; and 'what if Lenin had not died in 1924?'

Despite acknowledging their contribution to any informed presentation of Russian and Soviet history, Hobsbawm (1998: 322–9) conceded the limitations of counterfactual histories in processing questions which 'cannot be answered on the basis of evidence about what happened, because they are about what did not happen'. As he admitted, historians could do little more than speculate: 'The problem is that speculation involves writing what we think today; thus, any counterfactual will reflect our present-day mindset, not viewpoints of those at the time.' More recently, Hobsbawm (2006: 3) employed a counterfactual perspective when marking the fiftieth anniversary of the 1956 Hungarian Revolution:

> Counterfactual history can tell us in principle that history has no predetermined outcomes, but nothing about the likelihood of any other than the actual ones. The tragedy of the Hungarian uprising is that what did happen was always as close to a certainty as makes no matter. Yet its history is full of alternative political choices, major and minor, considered and taken, reconsidered and altered, in Moscow and Budapest, notably by a changeable Khrushchev [the Soviet leader]. Nevertheless, in retrospect, given their historical context, there is an air of inevitability about the flow of events, as there is about the direction of a great river.

Likewise Schama (2000b), though recorded (quoted, Roberts 2004: 1) as dismissing 'what ifs?' as 'fairy stories', has not been averse to indulging in counterfactual speculation:

> The lottery of birth, marriages and deaths in the English ruling class could change the whole culture of the country in a very dramatic way. It certainly wasn't the beat of a butterfly's wing but the ovarian cancer which killed Mary Tudor made the difference between a Catholic and a Protestant England, and a lot certainly hung on that. It's interesting, too, to wonder what would have happened if 'poor Fred', the eldest son of King George II, had not been hit on the head – and killed – by a cricket ball [1751]. By all accounts, he was a Prince of Wales of unusual intelligence and common sense. Had not that lethal cricket ball struck, who knows – the American colonies might still be singing God Save the Queen!

In fact, there remains uncertainty about the actual cause of death, but this does not remove the value of discussing what if Frederick had become king in 1760. More extravagantly, when considering one of the most common counterfactuals, 'what if?' Franz Ferdinand had not been assassinated at Sarajevo in June 1914, Schama (1999b: 152) speculated 'no First World War, no Hitler, no Stalin, no nuclear weapons, no Sarajevo crisis (1990s)'.

Nor has Starkey, Ferguson's fellow television history presenter, proved an exception. For instance, in November 2002 his programme on *Edward and Mary: the unknown Tudors* floated the question of what would have happened if Edward and Mary, history's 'great might-have-beens', had not suffered untimely, and heirless, deaths.

Conclusion

Reportedly Ferguson's current research remains focused on post-1800 economic, financial and international history, with a projected book entitled *Kissinger: a life* (2012). Significantly, Ferguson's (2011a) personal website specifically records his continued interest 'in the use of counterfactuals in historical explanation'. Thus, the defining narrative of 'Civilisation', Ferguson's (2011b: xx) latest television/book project, is underpinned by the concept of forking paths and the 'what ifs?' explaining why the West, not China, dominated world history during the past 500 years. Exploiting the ubiquity of 'apps' in today's computers and mobile phones to present his case, Ferguson argued that the West developed six 'killer apps' that the rest of the world lacked: competition, science, democracy, medicine, consumerism and the Protestant work ethic.

Certainly, Ferguson has proved one of the most influential and prominent enthusiasts for 'what if?' history, challenging those who do not think the past could be any different; indeed, as asserted by Andrew Roberts (2004: 8), *Virtual History* 'stands as the undisputed *Ur*-text of the philosophy behind counterfactual history'. In turn, successive publications have shown that the views expressed in *Virtual History* remain at the core of Ferguson's thinking and presentations of history. The past, he reminds historians as well as his many readers, listeners and viewers, was not pre-ordained, but rather riddled with choice, chance and contingency.

Virtual History highlighted also Ferguson's desire to reach a wider public. It was, as acknowledged by Snowman (2007: 273), 'a book that would display his name in airport outlets. It was not to be his last.' In this vein, Robert Cowley (2002: xviii), who has edited several 'what if?' histories, has pointed to the manner in which counterfactuals, underpinned by fine writing and good storytelling, offer historians another means of engaging with a broad audience as public historians: 'There is no reason why history can't entertain, especially when the object is to turn people on to a subject whose presentation at some point early in their lives may have turned them off.' In particular, 'what ifs?', Cowley (2008: 116) claimed, 'can help to awaken and nourish our historical imaginations':

> Students ... are left with the impression that history is inevitable, that what happened could not have happened any other way. Where in their textbooks are the drama of clashing wills, motives and ideas, of opposing economic and social forces, of accidents and contingencies? ... A rigorous counterfactual examination has a way of making the stakes of a confrontation or a decision stand out in relief ... Too, it can focus on moments that were true turning points.

Of course, even counterfactuals based upon specific guidelines, such as proposed by Ferguson, involve an element of imaginative speculation on unknowable subjects, thereby raising the risk of reflecting present-day mindsets, not the viewpoints of those at the time. Indeed, reviewers of *Virtual History* frequently dismissed chapters as 'wish-fulfilments by predominantly conservative intellectuals venting their regret at the turns history had in fact taken' (Snowman 2007: 273). For this reason, much counterfactual history is frequently dismissed as little more than wishful thinking. Thus, when reviewing *The Pity of War* and 'The Kaiser's European Union', a chapter in *Virtual History*, Thomas Otte (2000: 286–7) pointed to Ferguson's apparent desire 'to sit in judgement over the past': 'Rather than aiming at a more sophisticated understanding of history *wie es eigentlich gewesen* [a quote from von Ranke, meaning 'as it actually was'], he uses "counterfactuality" as an elaborate pretext to write history how it ought to have been (in accordance with his preconceived notions).' Unimpressed by his 'purposively controversial' views about the First World War, Otte complained that Ferguson's 'speculative gymnastics lacked what Clausewitz called "the tact of judgement".' For Evans (2002: 25):

> 'What if' is really little more than 'if only'; and in this form it contributes nothing to our understanding of what actually did happen ... History in the end is and can only really be about finding out what happened and what was, and understanding and explaining it, not positing alternative courses of development or indulging in bouts of wishful thinking about what might have been.

According to Gavriel Rosenfeld (2002: 93–4, 98), the author of *The World Hitler Never Made: alternative history and the memory of Nazism* (2005), such presentism possessed a historical value in terms of enabling

counterfactual histories published over time to cast light upon historical memory, most notably illuminating 'how the past takes shape in
remembrance':

> On the whole, American alternate histories of a Nazi wartime victory
> say just as much about Americans' view of their own present as about
> their views of the past. American views of Nazism have fluctuated
> along with the nation's postwar fortunes. In ascending periods of sta-
> bility and prosperity, the scenario of a Nazi victory has been utilized
> to validate the present, while in declining periods of crisis it nurtured
> fantasies that all could have been different.

Whether or not counterfactual scenarios contribute anything to
our understanding of what actually happened in the past, and hence
should be treated as either 'history' or – to quote Hunt (2004b) – 'reac-
tionary and historically redundant', remains controversial (Bunzl 2004:
845–58). If nothing else, counterfactuals provoke endless possibilities
for debate within and outside academia, thereby not only fostering
interest in ways of presenting the past but also reaffirming history's
nature as an argument without end. For instance, in June 2007 Andrew
Roberts, who edited *What might have been: leading historians on twelve
'What Ifs' of history* (2004) and contributed chapters to both Ferguson's
Virtual History and Cowley's *What If?*, presented an article in the *Daily
Mail* investigating 'What if we had lost the Falklands?'. Britain's defeat
in the 1982 war, Roberts (2007) speculated, would have led to the 'collapse in British power and prestige in the world', a more active British
role in Europe, a Labour government under Michael Foot, and the
strengthening of anti-democratic forces in Latin America. His counterfactual account offers scope for fruitful debate in the light of what
actually happened, most notably regarding prime minister Margaret
Thatcher's claim after regaining the Falklands that 'Great Britain is great
again', her successive election victories in 1983 and 1987, and Britain's
increasingly difficult position in Europe.

Far from representing escapist literature, counterfactual histories
undertaken in a responsible manner represent an intellectual tool capable of use in many contexts to enhance our historical knowledge and
understanding. In particular, 'what ifs?' encourage us to look again at
the past with a heightened sense of its infinite complexity; investigate
alternative possibilities, appreciating the openness of historical situations, including the role of contingency and accident; challenge, even
refute, historiographical orthodoxies; and hence dismiss any notion of

inevitability or hindsight bias. Even so, these arguments cannot disguise the fact that most members of the profession still believe that – to quote Saul David (2000) – 'historians should stick to the facts after all'.

Niall Campbell Douglas Ferguson (1964–): Select Bibliography

Histories

1995	*Paper and Iron: Hamburg business and German politics in the era of inflation, 1897–1927*
1998	*The World's Banker: the history of the House of Rothschild*
1998	*The Pity of War*
1999	'On media dons', in Stephen Glover (ed.), *Secrets of the Press: journalists on journalism*
2001	*The Cash Nexus: money and power in the modern world*
2003	*Empire: how Britain made the modern world*
2004	*Colossus: the rise and fall of the American empire*
2006	*The War of the World: history's age of hatred*
2008	*The Ascent of Money*
2010	*High Financier: the lives and time of Siegmund Warburg*
2011	*Civilisation: the West and the rest*

Edited/co-edited works

1997	*Virtual history: alternatives and counterfactuals*
2010	(with Charles S. Maier, Erez Manela & Daniel J. Sargent) *Shock of the Global: the 1970s in perspective*

Television series
[number of programmes given in brackets]

2003	'Empire: how Britain made the modern world' (Channel 4)	[6]
2004	'Colossus: the rise and fall of the American empire' (Channel 4)	[6]
2006	'The War of the World: history's age of hatred' (Channel 4/PBS)	[6]
2008	'The Ascent of Money: a financial history of the world' (Channel 4/PBS)	[6]
2011	'Civilisation' (Channel 4)	[6]

8
Joan Wallach Scott: The Feminist Historian

In December 1985 Joan Wallach Scott delivered a groundbreaking paper at the American Historical Association's (AHA) conference in New York. Expressing her growing belief in the value of theory for historians, she argued the case for treating 'gender' as a critical category of historical analysis. Resulting in an article in the *American Historical Review* (1986) and a book entitled *Gender and the Politics of History* (1988), the paper reflected Scott's transformation as a history presenter, most notably in terms of acknowledging that Jacques Derrida and Michel Foucault, among others, provided theoretical ways of thinking about the past worthy of exploration and application by historians. Moreover, the article appeared at what Scott (1989a: 682) depicted as 'one of the moments of great contest about the meaning of history', an emerging intellectual cleavage in the historical profession explored by an AHA Forum on 'The Old History and the New' held at Cincinnati in December 1988. Unsurprisingly, Scott (1989a: 689–91; 1989b: 699–700) used her presentation at Cincinnati to place herself firmly in the 'new history' camp.

Twenty years on from the Cincinnati Forum, the *American Historical Review* published a 'Forum' section in which contributors reviewed the impact of Scott's 1986 article, described by the editors (*American Historical Review* 2008a: xiv–xv) as 'one of the most important and influential articles ever published in this journal'. Repeatedly referenced by other historians, listed extensively on teaching syllabi and student reading lists, and translated into several languages including French, Italian, Polish, Portuguese and Spanish, the study easily headed the *American Historical Review*'s list of most accessed (38,093 times) and printed (25,180 times) online articles for the period 1997–2007 (Meyerowitz 2008: 1346). The significance of these figures is accentuated by the extremely limited readership and shelf life of most journal articles, as well as by the fact that Scott's study had been available already for over a decade before going online. In May 2011 Scott's article still topped the *American Historical Review*'s list for the most accessed article during the previous three years. It was also the journal's most cited article over the same period.

Of course, statistical data must always be interpreted in the broader perspective. However, such impressive totals, when viewed alongside the fact that many of her other publications have become seminal texts translated for publication throughout the world, confirm Scott's global reach and influence upon debates about history and theory in general, and feminist and gender history in particular. For Marnie Hughes-Warrington (2008: 308–16), Scott warranted inclusion among her 50 key thinkers on history. Apart from helping to give women a place in history by illuminating the way in which power operates in society, Scott's critique of the discipline's nature and methodology helped to alter and radically reshape our understanding and presentation of history. In particular, her career highlights the fact that – to quote Bonnie Smith (2010: 727), the author of *The Gender of History: men, women and historical practice* (1998) – 'the writing of women's history has continued despite the seemingly permanent deposit of professional disapprobation' and the highly gendered nature of the historical profession.

Background Influences

Born in 1941, Joan Scott, née Wallach, grew up in Brooklyn, New York. Both her parents were history teachers. Eli Wallach, her father's brother, became a leading actor. During her postgraduate studies at the University of Wisconsin-Madison, she married Donald Scott, a fellow student, who collaborated subsequently on some of her publications. They are now divorced.

Like any historian, Scott's approach, and particularly changes thereto, are difficult to understand without an appreciation of the broader context. This is especially true regarding a self-confessed political activist who lived through the Cold War and the Vietnam War and participated in 'Ban the Bomb' and women's liberation campaigns. Moreover, as Scott (1996a: 170) acknowledged, her education and career occurred during a period when history's nature as a discipline was thrown open to question by repeated epistemological challenges to its fundamental assumptions, as well as by heated controversies about the politics of history.

Key background factors included Scott's:

* appreciation of the intertwining of history and politics;
* awareness of the role of ideas and exposure to the 'new social history';
* focus on French history; and
* academic and political activism.

Each factor will be examined in turn.

Attracted by neither the history of war nor the lives of the famous, at school Scott (2009: 26) preferred literature and French language to history. History proved merely another subject. What Scott (2009: 27–30; Abelson *et al.* 1989: 42) acquired from her highly political parents was a belief that history was a way of 'doing politics', becoming politically engaged, and transmitting ideas and knowledge to change present-day society: 'I decided to become a historian in the heat of my own political activism in the 1960s ... Becoming a historian was not a consolation for politics, but a companion to it.'

During Scott's undergraduate studies at Brandeis University, Frank Manuel was instrumental in inspiring her emerging appreciation of the importance of the history of ideas alongside the meaning of language and texts. When moving on to postgraduate research on French history at the University of Wisconsin-Madison, she continued to prioritise the contribution of intellectual history. Even so, perhaps the most valued part of her postgraduate studies at Wisconsin-Madison was a Comparative Social History Seminar acquainting Scott (2009: 33) with the 'new social history', represented by Eugene Genovese, Eric Hobsbawm, E.P. Thompson, Charles Tilly and the Annales School. Believing that she was participating in a 'disciplinary reformation', Scott dropped her planned doctorate on Paul Lafargue, Marx's son-in-law, for a nineteenth-century 'community study' investigating the political effects of proletarianisation on the glassworkers of Carmaux, a mining town in southern France. An active mentoring role was performed by Tilly, the author of *The Vendée: a sociological analysis of the counter-revolution of 1793* (1964). Indeed, for Scott (n.d.), he filled the gap left by an unhelpful supervisor 'absorbed by his own narcissism'.

Scott's doctoral dissertation established her identity as a social and labour historian specialising in France and adopting an interdisciplinary approach bringing together history, sociological theory and quantitative methods. Archival research conducted in France strengthened the appeal of all things French, while exposing her to alternative ways of thinking about history imbued with philosophical and interpretative approaches.

Inevitably, Scott's work as a historian has reflected a strong sense of political commitment. Throughout her career Scott's work as an academic historian extended into the sphere of public history. Writing for student newspapers, joining picket lines, and organising petitions and rallies, Scott (2009: 29, 37; Abelson *et al.* 1989: 43) proved the typical student activist. Strong support for civil rights campaigners was combined with opposition to nuclear weapons and Vietnam. However, the prime focus for her political activism and historical scholarship was the women's movement. Scott (1996a: 163) developed also a strong commitment to academic freedom, as evidenced by both her publications and representation on the Committee on Academic Freedom of the American Association of University Professors. This proved in part a legacy of the early 1950s, when McCarthyism (anti-communist Cold War hysteria) was at its peak and exerting much stronger anti-communist pressures than those experienced by Hobsbawm (chapter 5) in Britain. In 1953, Scott's father, a Marxist, lost his teaching job and pension after refusing to cooperate with a House subcommittee investigating un-American activities.

When presenting her research on French labour history, Scott (1988: 69; 2009: 35) realised that she was not only advancing historical knowledge and understanding but also following E.P. Thompson's example by writing socially relevant history. Thus, her study of glassworkers in Carmaux established that working-class militancy was caused not by socialist ideas or leadership – this was the view of contemporary officials and employers as well as existing historiography – but rather by an occupational crisis resulting in 'the last stand of artisans in the face of mechanization' (Scott 1974: 191).

Establishing the logic and reasonableness of political protest movements, Scott (2009: 35) saw her histories – they included an article (Scott and Hobsbawm 1980) co-authored with Hobsbawm about the political radicalism of shoemakers in Britain and continental Europe – as lending weight to arguments for equality of rights across class, race and sex. Moreover, her purposive approach, presenting as political collective socioeconomic activities treated hitherto by governments and employers as irrational, unnecessary and disruptive, possessed wider implications concerning what counted as history as well as politics. For Scott (1989a: 680–1; 2009: 36–7), the meaning of politics was extended beyond the sphere of government to cover any relationship involving the exercise of power, particularly those involving men and women. The key consequence was her reappraisal of women's role as historical actors.

A Politically Active Historian

Coming from a family reportedly treating women no differently from men meant that Scott always saw herself as a feminist in terms of supporting a cause that was at once both political and scholarly. Inevitably, her attitudes acquired a sharper political edge during the late 1960s when the feminist movement was taking off in western society as a whole, particularly on university campuses, where women occupied only a marginal role, frequently a non-role, in most history departments. Indeed, when taking up her first academic post at the University of Illinois at Chicago, Scott (1996b: 2–3; 2009: 37, 43; Hinds 1985: 50–1) depicted herself as 'a feminist historian' seeking to present women's role in history, albeit not necessarily their right to a separate 'herstory', to meet an ever-growing demand from a largely feminist audience within and outside academia: 'we shared a commitment to making women visible and to legitimizing their presence as objects of scholarship and subjects of inquiry'.

In many respects, this process was part of a larger debate conducted between the 1950s and the 1980s, when historians undertook a remorseless re-examination of the American past concerning not only women but also civil rights, labour, race and slavery. As Sean Wilentz (2001: 36) recorded:

> Not surprisingly, this historiography of national self-reckoning stirred up intense – at times even ugly – debates among proponents of the clashing methods and interpretations, left, right, and center ... all these historians had in common a dedication to treating history not as a panoramic backward gaze, but as a battleground of contesting views about American life and development ... American history was meant to rattle its readers, not to confirm them in their received myths and platitudes about America.

Quite apart from publishing research expanding factual knowledge and interpretative understanding, Scott joined fellow feminist campaigners in developing teaching programmes, circulating reading lists, sitting on committees, chairing the AHA's Committee on Women Historians (1977–80) and organising and attending conferences attracting surprising numbers of people from within and outside academia. Looking back, Scott (2008: 1422) came to see the Berkshire Conferences on the History of Women held from 1973 onwards as an important formative influence for her thinking about the concept of gender, such as articulated therein by Natalie Zemon Davis, among others.

Challenging existing attitudes was much easier with allies just as the sense of fighting a battle was energising (Scott 2004: 12; 2009: 41–2). One product was Scott's collaboration with Louise Tilly, Charles Tilly's wife. Combining to challenge a conference paper delivered by Edward Shorter about women during the Industrial Revolution, Scott and Tilly (1978) contended in *Women, Work and Family* that increased illegitimacy rates resulted from the problems of re-creating the family in the new urban context, and were not, as claimed by Shorter, the product of sexual liberation and the emancipation of women. Furthermore, they argued that the category of 'woman' needed to be both historicised and pluralised. As Scott (2009: 38, 40) acknowledged, as feminist historians they were producing new knowledge, making women visible as historical actors, and moving on from the traditional perception of 'workers' as male. There was also an emerging conceptual focus arising from the perceived need to pluralise the term 'women' while retaining something of its unity.

For Scott, the linkage between empirical history and contemporary issues proved exhilarating, but she worried whether politics compromised their history. Indeed, the political nature of calls for the inclusion of women in history led her not only to reappraise her existing approach to historical study but also to confront the serious questions raised about historical standards. In particular, she focused upon the constant tension between on the one hand producing 'herstory' as good history and on the other hand providing a consciousness-raising storyline motivating feminist campaigners.

Seeking 'A New Form of History'

During the late 1970s Scott (1988: 4; 2009: 42; Eley 2005: 118) welcomed recent advances in historical knowledge and understanding, but expressed growing dissatisfaction with existing social historical approaches, given the continued failure of historians to take women's history seriously. Nor had answers been provided to key questions raised by feminist campaigners.

For Scott, a serious problem arose from the fact that social historians, though framing their histories with Marxist paradigms like class-consciousness and exploitation, treated women like any other workers facing economic change and oppression. The resulting tendency to overlook the distinctiveness of women's experience led Scott (1988: 22, 72) to qualify her initial admiration of Thompson's *The Making of the English Working Class* (1963) because women, though mentioned, occupied only a marginal place in a book treating class as synonymous with the politics of male workers. Nor had the 'add women and stir approach' succeeded in revising previous historiographies in feminist terms. As Mary Spongberg (2002: 2) recorded, 'the new women's history accumulated a wealth of detail about women's lives in the past', but exerted only a limited impact on history, especially as the tendency of 'herstory' to isolate women's past experience served merely to reaffirm their marginalisation, even ghettoisation. However, the principal obstacle was history's masculinist nature. Traditionally history was written by men about men. What was needed, therefore, was a new type of history possessing less restrictive norms as far as women were concerned.

Against this background, Scott (1996a: 170; 2009: 36) accepted the need to challenge canonical teachings, expose their conservative premises, and suggest an alternative way forward based upon the concept of 'gender'. When rethinking her approach, Jacques Rancière, the author of *La nuit des prolétaires: Archives du rêve ouvrier* (1981; trans. *The Nights of Labor: the workers' dream in nineteenth-century France*, 1989) proved influential in critiquing social history approaches and opening up the past to alternative readings, including the idea that women's exclusion from history was integral to the development of the discipline of history. By implication, the history of women could be recognised and presented in an appropriate manner only by fundamentally changing the nature of history.

Scott's 'Intellectual Reorientation'

In 1980 Scott, who had worked at the University of North Carolina at Chapel Hill since 1974, moved on to take up the Nancy Duke Lewis Chair at Brown University, Providence, Rhode Island. Significantly, the post, that of the history department's first tenured woman professor, reflected in part the university's response to a recent sex discrimination case. The job carried substantial administrative and teaching responsibilities, including the creation of a women's studies programme.

At Brown Scott established and then headed the Pembroke Center for Teaching and Research on Women. In turn, the centre's intense and exhilarating intellectual environment accelerated Scott's ongoing change of course as a historian, most notably in terms of a willingness to explore the use of theory. Indeed, the Pembroke Center was distinguished from most women's studies research centres by its specific focus on theoretical issues. For Scott (1988: ix; 2009: 49), the centre's interdisciplinary seminar proved a formative, even 'transformational', experience exposing her to a wide range of thinkers – speakers included Derrida in 1984 – and ideas articulating alternative ways of doing and presenting history. Key intellectual influences included:

- poststructuralism (e.g. Derrida, Foucault) contending that reality, and hence the past, were unknowable, and only language and representations mattered (Passmore 2003: 118–19);
- psychoanalysis (e.g. Sigmund Freud, Jacques Lacan); and
- French feminism (e.g. Hélène Cixous, Luce Irigaray).

Realising the limits of her previous disciplinary reformation based upon the 'new social history', Scott (1988: 4; 2009: 33) acknowledged her lack of exposure to the 'epistemological bombshells' published in the same years by Foucault, among others. Looking back, Scott (2009: 45) recalled that at Brown her thinking acquired its philosophical rationale: 'Poststructuralist theory gave me a language for articulating a feminist critique and for conceiving of how history might serve it.'

Like many historians, Scott had been initially resistant to, even dismissive of, theory. Notwithstanding her reliance upon Marxist paradigms, she saw herself primarily as an empirical social historian, as highlighted by her book on Carmaux glass-makers. Indeed, when beginning to work at Brown with staff, principally literary specialists schooled in theories relatively new to her, Scott (2009: 43) found herself negotiating a 'mutual philosophical incomprehension'. There were, of course, several theoretical positions that Scott (1996b: 10–11; 2009: 43, 45) could have taken when historicising feminism – in her 1986 article Scott (1986: 1057–66) was dismissive of patriarchy, Marxism and even psychoanalysis – but a crucial thinker guiding her 'linguistic turn' was Foucault, whose subversive 'critically engaged, philosophically driven history' interrogated and challenged descriptors hitherto taken for granted by historians. Far from being fixed and stable in meaning, analytical categories like 'men' and 'women' were shown to be constructed, and hence malleable, terms.

For Foucault, discourse – this concept, though difficult to define briefly, refers to a system of beliefs and practices framing the reading of a text – was concerned with the relationship between knowledge and power, most notably the ways in which people and things acquired words to define them. Thus, historical knowledge was represented as a field upon which power was enacted through the use of language. Depiction by historians as, say, 'women', 'workers' or 'ruled' meant being placed in relationships of power vis-à-vis 'men', 'employers' and 'rulers', respectively, thereby acquiring agency, that is, an attribution of traits and responsibilities upon which subjects were expected to act. Reading Foucault, Scott (2007: 26–31; 2009: 38) began to make sense of the notion of power/knowledge, and to treat agency as 'a socially created possibility'. In turn, this discovery, treating women's gender identity as a social construct, possessed significant implications for Scott's (1988: 1; 2009: 47) presentation of feminine and masculine subjects in the past:

> Instead of thinking of resistance as innate, one had to ask what the specific discursive resources of such oppositional agency were. It was the possibility of putting these kinds of political questions to historical materials, the linking through them of feminist critique and feminist history that led me to hail gender as 'a useful category of historical analysis'.

In this manner Scott (2009: 47–8) learned how to think about difference, 'that meanings are always sliding even as they are being declared inviolate':

> Gender is a useful category only if differences are the question, not the answer, only if we ask what 'men' and 'women' are taken to mean wherever and whenever we are looking at them, rather than assuming we already know who and what they are. In this sense, my appropriation of poststructuralism is relentlessly historical – there are no women or men, no classes, no races, outside of the relationships established between them and the ways those relationships are understood.

Drawing upon the writings of Derrida, Scott (1986: 1065–6; 2007: 23–6; 2009: 48) employed deconstructionist theory – in brief, a process of investigative thought interrogating the meaning of discourses – to study difference, and particularly to make the concept work for feminism by challenging the premises upon which things taken to be foundational were based. Believing that at last she had discovered a way for feminist history to achieve its radical potential, Scott (2009: 49) began to intervene in 'the politics of history' to expose the way in which the prevailing professional practice of historians privileged men and downplayed, even overlooked, the role of women. Thus, she proposed – to quote Sue Morgan (2006a: 13) – 'a radical reconceptualisation of existing readings of gender'. Rather than presenting women's history as evidence of sexual difference, Scott concentrated instead on using poststructural theory to study how that difference was produced as a system of knowledge and then applied in practice over time.

Presenting 'Gender' as a Useful Historical Category

Introducing *Gender and the Politics of History*, Scott (1988: 2–3, 7) outlined her view of 'gender' as a system of 'knowledge about sexual difference' established through a range of discursive contexts and offering a way of ordering the world:

> I use knowledge, following Michel Foucault, to mean the understanding produced by cultures and societies of human relationships, in this case of those between men and women. Such knowledge is not absolute or true, but always relative. It is produced in complex ways within large epistemic frames that themselves have an (at least quasi-) autonomous history. Its uses and meanings become contested politically and are the means by which relationships of power – of domination and subordination – are constructed.

Sex, like gender, had to be understood in terms of an attributed meaning, which was a product of culture, not nature. Such oppositions concealed not only the heterogeneity of such categories but also their interdependence.

Moreover, any relationship was normally hierarchical, with one category proving dominant and visible, the other category being subordinate and invisible, as happened with men and women whether in the family, labour market, class, politics or society. Fundamentally positive definitions of 'men' rested on the negation or repression of 'women': 'It follows then that gender is the social organization of sexual difference. But this does not mean that gender reflects or implements fixed and natural physical differences between women and men; rather gender is the knowledge that establishes meanings for bodily differences.' Discussing the history of legislation excluding women from the vote or restricting their employment, Scott (1986: 1072) pointed to the way in which governments legitimated themselves by privileging one group of citizens over another: 'The actions can only be made sense of as part of an analysis of the construction and consolidation of power. An assertion of control or strength was given form as a policy about women.' By treating 'women' as a construct, she suggested an innovatory way for historians to study and present the history of sexual identity through experience and representation.

For Scott, the centrality of gender in determining social organisation required study and explanation. Within this context history proved far more than a way of recording or studying change. Rather it became the object of attention providing a means for analysing the process by which present-day knowledge about gender was produced, legitimated and maintained culturally, socially and epistemologically. Like Judith Allen (1987: 173–4, 187) and Linda Gordon (1988: 91–3), Scott (1986: 1066–8) presented the marginalisation of women's history as a function of conventional historical practice whose deeply gendered nature had led the past to be presented from a heavily masculinist perspective by a profession masculine in its ethos and composition. As Burrow (2007: 465–6) conceded, 'the smell of pipe smoke still clung to it'.

For Scott, new methodologies and theoretical positions were adjudged necessary to overcome the gender blindness characteristic of much historical writing. Drawing on Derrida, Scott claimed that the language employed by historians gave the false impression of universality to a profession which was in fact predominantly male, white, and middle-class. As Mary Spongberg (2002: 1–2) complained, traditionally the title 'historian' was reserved for those engaged in the masculine activity of writing political history. Despite claiming to present all-embracing accounts of the past, in reality the resulting histories, like Thompson's *The Making of the English Working Class*, tended to exclude women, normalise their subordination to men, and ensure their historical marginalisation, even invisibility. Within this context, Scott (2004: 20), whose own histories had established repeatedly that women played a far from insignificant role as 'workers' by acting as skilled employees, calling strikes and organizing unions, presented 'gender' as a device for contesting the claims made for comprehensiveness, objectivity and universality by such 'malestream' histories.

Discounting the need for a separate history of women, she proposed that 'the new history' should focus primarily on 'gender'. Urging historians to disrupt the notion of fixity imparting the appearance of permanence to binary gender representation, Scott (1986: 1068; 1988: 3; 1989a: 690) saw herself as sharing the concerns articulated by those viewing history writing as an expression of cultural hegemony, and hence seeking to represent other groups excluded from the historical record because of, say, class, ethnicity and race. Like those working on labour history, postcolonial history and the history of race, she represented herself as sharing in a project helping to refigure history by reappraising changing identities over time. For example, Scott (1996b: 10–11) pointed to Edward Said and the Indian subaltern historians. Having exposed western histories as part of the process by which imperialism was established, not objective accounts of the colonial past, they used the terms and categories employed by western historians as objects of critical analysis (Tosh 2010: 202–3, 285–97).

Scott's Continuing Intellectual Metamorphosis

Having employed an article in *Past and Present* (Scott 1983) to identify the need to confront critically the politics of existing histories and to reappraise history as a discipline, Scott published the fruits of her thinking from the mid-1980s onwards. Paradoxically, the resulting groundbreaking outputs – a seminar paper delivered at the Institute for Advanced Study, Princeton (1985), an AHA Conference paper (1985), an article in the *American Historical Review* (Scott 1986) and a prize-winning (the AHA's Joan Kelly Memorial Prize for Women's History, 1989) book entitled *Gender and the Politics of History* (1988) – were described by Scott (1988: 1) as her 'Pembroke Center essays', but presented when she was no longer based at Brown. In 1985 she moved on to the prestigious Institute for Advanced Study, where she became subsequently in 2000 the Harold F. Linder Professor. Despite being recruited primarily as a social historian with European expertise, Scott, only the second woman to join the institute's permanent staff, continued what she represented as her metamorphosis towards becoming more of an intellectual historian for whom theory mattered. For Scott (2009: 49), the prime focus became, and this remains true today, the study of difference in history, with specific reference to its uses, applications, justifications, and transformations over time.

At the Institute for Advanced Study, Scott's exploration of new intellectual perspectives was framed by the supportive ethos offered by the School of Social Science. Following the inspiration of Clifford Geertz, the school positively encouraged critical thinking across disciplines challenging prevailing disciplinary norms. One feature arising in part from her active engagement with scholars from a wide range of disciplines as well as from the personal experience of undergoing psychotherapy was Scott's emerging appreciation of the value of psychoanalysis. Having initially downplayed the utility of psychoanalysis, Scott (2009: 50–1; 2010: 12–13) began to rethink her position, particularly in the light of recognising the manner in which the writings of Freud and Lacan, among others, enabled an alternative reading imparting greater flexibility to the notion of gender. Acknowledging theory's limitations in explaining the individual psyche, she came to appreciate the value of interpretative readings of dreams, stories, and fantasies in the context of a particular life experience. A book of her essays on the theme of psychoanalysis and history, *The Fantasy of Feminist History*, is scheduled for publication by Duke University Press in 2012.

Even so, Derrida and Foucault continued to underpin Scott's (2007: 34–5; 2010: 9) belief in history writing as 'critique' in terms of seeking not only to identify what was wrong but also to provide the basis for bringing about change, and particularly 'to make visible the premises upon which the organising categories of our identities (personal, social, national) are based'. During the past decade or so, this approach has framed her presentations of the history of France in general and of French feminism in particular (Scott 2008: 1427–8; 2009: 52). Thus, *Only Paradoxes to Offer: French feminists and the Rights of Man* (1996), *Parité! Sexual equality and the crisis of French universalism* (2005) and *The Politics of the Veil* (2007) were intended primarily to critique the way in which a male, white and heterosexual version of universalism was presented as a major legacy of the French Revolution. Scott's focus upon the construction of differences between the sexes ensured that these publications – hitherto, all except *The Politics of the Veil* have been translated into French – possessed a contemporary resonance, most notably contributing to ongoing debates about identity in France. Thus, in *The Politics of the Veil* Scott critiqued the ban on the *hijab* [headscarf] as symptomatic of France's failure to integrate its former colonial subjects, and pressed the case for a new form of national community recognising diversity.

Scott as a History Presenter

Scott's role as a presenter of history illuminates four key themes:

- the use of theory to present the past;
- the controversial nature of a theoretical approach to history;
- the continued progress of feminist history; and
- the academic historian as public historian.

The use of theory to present the past

In *Postmodernism and History* (2004), Willie Thompson (2004: 45) stressed the manner in which Scott, like other feminist historians, found in postmodernism – this was discussed in chapter 2 – useful approaches for studying, rewriting and presenting history. For Scott (2009: 45, 49) postmodernism, or rather poststructuralism, the approach specifically influencing her thinking, provided the philosophical framework transforming her into a historian for whom theory mattered:

> For me, philosophy only improved my ability to do history by analysing the past in a new way, by clarifying what it meant to be doing history, and by throwing important light on the reasons that mainstream or

traditional historians resisted the validity of, for example, women as subjects of history and objects of historical investigation. It provided both a diagnosis and a way of addressing the problem.

In particular, the resulting intellectual reorientation enabled Scott (1996a: 170; 2009: 44; Eley 2005: 157–9) to expose history's conservative foundational premises, and hence to demand attention from historians in general rather than only from those working on gender:

> Theory made sense, not because it provided me with a reliable explanation for why things happened, but precisely because it didn't. Rather, it enhanced my ability to read differently and made me conscious that I was not just discovering, but producing knowledge. Thinking about myself in those terms brought politics and scholarship together in a new way; it enabled me to begin to address the questions that my earlier work in women's history had left unresolved.

Having started out presenting history to show that women were an essential part of the past and to analyse the factors affecting their role, Scott (quoted, Hinds 1985: 51–2) was attracted by the manner in which theory enabled her to examine the attitudes influencing the possession of power in society, particularly placing women in a subordinate position: 'And that's what gender is all about.' For Scott (1988: 10–11), the concept of gender offered an excellent way of studying the past, theorising feminist politics, and rethinking both the history of politics and the politics of history. Requiring feminist history to be far more than mere knowledge about the past, Scott (1988: 9–10; 1993: 438; 2009: 51) saw poststructuralist theory as providing not only a methodology answering unresolved questions about the production of knowledge but also a firm foundation for 'critical history' demonstrating how history produced gender knowledge: 'critique doesn't work without theory'. Acknowledging that history was not purely referential, Scott (1989a: 681) pointed to the role played by male historians in constructing and presenting the past when depicting history as an interpretive practice reflecting and creating power relationships: 'Its standards of inclusion and exclusion, measures of importance, and rules of evaluation are not objective criteria but politically produced conventions. What we know as history is, then, the fruit of past politics; today's contests are about how history will be constituted for the present.'

Within this context, Scott (2009: 45, 51) joined others in employing theory to contest the bias and other shortcomings of 'old history'.

Nor, as demonstrated by Scott's recent conference papers and publications, has time diminished the intellectual attraction of theory and 'critique'. In 2003, when participating in an AHA panel on 'The future of feminist History', Scott (2004: 24–6) reiterated the case for theory – she has often quoted Stuart Hall's observation that theory 'makes meanings slide' – in furnishing alternative ways of doing and presenting history, overriding existing disciplinary boundaries, providing a common language for critical historical inquiry, and establishing that texts are open to diverse, even subversive, readings.

The controversial nature of a theoretical approach to history

The general antipathy of the historical profession towards theory in general and postmodernism in particular means that Scott's stress upon the imperative need to use theory to study feminist history prompted a critical, occasionally hostile, reaction from many historians, even prompting taunts of preferring 'fancy French theory' to tried-and-tested historical methodology. Scott's approach was anathema to historians like Marwick (2001: 109, 293), who dismissed much of what Foucault and other theorists wrote as 'nonsense' and warranting attention 'if only to come up with adverse responses'.

Looking back to the presentation of her paper on gender at an Institute for Advanced Study seminar in autumn 1985, Scott (2008: 1422) recalled the scowls and 'resounding silence' of Princeton's historians: 'Philosophy, not history, opined Lawrence Stone to all who would listen.' Clearly, the historical profession, believing that gender history was ideological and ahistorical uncovering what was not there or conferring significance on allegedly peripheral topics, was not ready for the theoretical approaches underpinning Scott's thinking. Unsurprisingly, Scott (1989a: 689–91; 1989b: 699–700) clashed with 'conservatives', like Gertrude Himmelfarb (1987; 1989) and Joan Hoff (1994), upholding the traditional view of 'history-as-it-has-always-been-written'. Moreover, the overtly political nature of her belief in 'critical history', driven by feminism, raised questions about bias, subjectivity and intellectual rigour, especially upon the part of those policing the boundaries of the 'old history' in these culture wars. As Scott (2009: 51) recorded, 'conflicting visions of social order and so also of gender are the stuff of politics'.

Quite apart from confronting historians' long-standing resistance to theory, Scott (1993; 2001: 61–4; 2007: 21–3) prompted sharp, often vitriolic, debates among feminist and women's historians, as highlighted by her ill-tempered exchanges with Laura Lee Downs in *Comparative*

Studies in Society and History. Clearly feminist historians were not immune from the disagreements characteristic of the historical profession as a whole. Over time areas of controversy have included:

- Did Scott's shift of focus from the history of women to that of gender represent, as argued by June Purvis (Morgan 2006a: 10–12, 16; 2006b: 124–7), among others, a retrograde step diminishing attention on feminism, thereby limiting history's political value by fostering the study of men and masculinity?
- Did Scott's focus on theory and the language of gender discredit the contribution made to women's history by social historians?;
- Did Scott's reliance on gender as a subjective category for analysis discourage a focus on gender as a historical process, as claimed by Jeanne Boydston (2008: 576–9)? Should gender be treated not as a category for analysis but rather as a question for analysis?
- Did Scott's theoretical position exert little effect upon her actual historical practice, as asserted by Willie Thompson (2004: 46–9, 73, 123)? Or is the force of his criticism undermined by Scott's critique-based histories of France mentioned above?
- Did Scott's presentation of women as cultural constructs deny their historical reality and divorce them from their actual historical experience of oppression (Downs 1993a, 1993b; 2003; 273 6; Scott 1993; Evans 1997: 216 17)?
- Did Scott's adoption of poststructuralism's jargonistic, even 'foreign', language introduce obstacles to presenting women's history (Smith 2010: 733)?
- Did Scott's approach reflect an uncritical acceptance of poststructuralist theory (Hughes-Warrington 2008: 314)? In particular, was Mariana Valverde (quoted, Morgan 2006b: 171) correct when suggesting that Scott exaggerated what Derrida offered historians? Indeed, as stated by Catherine Hall (quoted, Morgan 2006a: 14–15), did feminists need Foucault to recognise history's masculinist nature?

The continued progress of feminist history

During recent decades feminist historical writing has gone from strength to strength. Scott, described by Willie Thompson (2004: 45) as 'the most widely renowned of the feminist historians' and 'representative of some of the very best feminist historians', has proved a central figure in this advance.

In 'The future of feminist History' Scott (2004: 10–11) opined that feminism's key aims, that is, for women to be written into history and to be accepted as historians, had been achieved, *at least up to a point*, since 'neither women's history nor women historians are fully equal players'. Reviewing the broader picture, Scott (2004: 11–18) offered a checklist of past trends and achievements:

- since the eighteenth century feminism had used history as a 'critical' weapon in the struggle for women's emancipation to disrupt present-day certainties: 'Feminism's History is both a compilation of women's experiences and a record of different strategic interventions employed to argue women's cause';
- interdisciplinarity proved the hallmark of feminist scholarship;
- the acceptance of women's history as 'history', albeit only partial, meant that the feminist campaign had lost its subversive critical edge. In turn, academic feminists had loosened their links with political campaigners;
- scholarship was no longer focused on women as a singular category, since differences among women were taken to be axiomatic; and
- 'gender' was increasingly substituted for 'women' as the object of inquiry.

Speaking more generally, Scott (2004: 20–1, 24–6) echoed Liz Faue's claim that women's history had 'defamiliarized' history by engaging critically with existing histories and calling into question their production, comprehensiveness and objectivity. Thus, 'what was once unthinkable – that gender was a useful tool of historical analysis – has become thinkable', albeit subject to an ongoing process of defamiliarisation by postcolonial, ethnic and other historians. Finally, as mentioned above, Scott, though declaring her continued loyalty to the discipline of history, reiterated feminist history's ongoing need for theory.

The academic historian as public historian

Throughout her career Scott has always linked history and politics, particularly concerning her support for academic freedom and feminism. Apart from maintaining her role as a political activist, she acted also as a public historian, meeting demands from an ever-growing audience of feminists within and outside academia for 'herstory' in support of the political campaign for women's emancipation. Arguably, during the 1980s Scott's linguistic turn, though further enhancing her profile as a feminist historian, did result in a less user-friendly type of public history than her previous social-historical publications. Certainly, her exchanges with Downs reflected the latter's concern that women were treated as linguistic abstracts, not real people possessing a gender identity rooted in actual experience. Recently Scott (2009: 52), the presenter of several books on French history published originally in and/or translated into French, has reached out increasingly to a public audience in France by way of intervening in ongoing debates about national identity.

Conclusion

In 2008 Scott's election as a Fellow of the American Academy of Arts and Sciences was complemented by an AHA Award for Scholarly Distinction. In addition, as mentioned above, the *American Historical Review* published a 'Forum' centred upon her 1986 article on 'gender'. When introducing the 'Forum', the editors (*American Historical Review* 2008b: 1344) acknowledged Scott's impact as a historian:

> Over the last four decades, feminist scholars have contributed immeasurably to our understanding of the past, deepening our sense of what history means, widening the purview of what history can be, and redefining the very categories of historical analysis. No one has contributed more in this last sense than Joan W. Scott.

Building upon her publications on labour and social history, Scott, the editors claimed, presented histories using theory to rethink 'gender', challenge the fixity of historical thought, and offer 'a model for scholars wishing to reshape our analytical discourse'. In particular, her 1986 article on 'gender' became 'canonical', exerting an enduring impact upon the ways in which many, *but not all*, historians viewed and presented the past concerning 'gender' and other forms of difference, like class and race.

In the journal's 'Forum' section, five historians identified specific impacts for different chronological periods and geographical regions, thereby encouraging Scott (2008: 1422) to employ her response to reaffirm that 'gender', albeit failing to answer completely all questions, remains a useful concept to interrogate the past. One year on, in May 2010, four of these articles plus Scott's response and the editor's introduction were well placed in the *American Historical Review*'s list of the 20 most accessed online articles in that month. Indeed, the 'Forum' contribution by Yale University's Joanne Meyerowitz (2008) on 'gender' and the history of the USA occupied top spot. 2008 saw also a special twentieth-anniversary issue of the journal *Gender & History* edited by Alexandra Shepard and Garthine Walker. Unsurprisingly, Scott's 1986 article, described by Shepard and Walker (2008: 455) as 'one of the most cited historical works of its time', proved a central reference point for several contributors, one of whom, Jeanne Boydston (2008), offered a thoughtful critique of Scott's approach to 'gender'. Reportedly *The Question of Gender: Joan W. Scott's critical feminism*, edited by Judith Butler and Elizabeth Weed, is scheduled for publication in 2012 to explore the current uses of the term 'gender' and the ongoing influence of Scott's agenda-setting work in history and other subjects.

Reviewing the history of women's history writing since the Renaissance, Spongberg (2002: 1–2) recorded, 'More often than not, women's writings about the past, regardless of their historicity, have not been treated seriously as history.' Within this context, Scott (2004: 21; 2008: 1423), though welcoming feminist history's 'radical refusal to settle down' and to call anywhere 'home' within the historical mainstream, has played an active role in challenging longstanding claims that women were situated outside 'history'. Thus, she advanced an alternative gender-centred approach for critiquing, rethinking, theorising, rewriting and presenting feminist history. Apprising historians about the potential utility of ideas articulated by Derrida and Foucault, Scott focused upon the language of 'gender' to explain how historians' presentation of sexual differences was employed to subordinate and constrain women.

Moreover, as Meyerowitz (2008: 1346–7, 1353) recorded, Scott's impact as a historian, though greatest in the sphere of women's and gender history, 'played a significant part in the broader shift from social to cultural history, from the study of the demography, experiences and social movements of oppressed and stigmatized groups to the study of representations, language, perception, and discourse':

> These perceived differences ... also provided a 'primary way of signifying' other hierarchical relationships. This was the heart of her contribution: she invited us to look at how 'the so-called natural relationship between male and female' structured, naturalized, and legitimated relationships of power, say, between ruler and ruled or between empire and colony. The history of gender could, it seems, inhabit more of the historical turf than could the history of women. It could even enter and remap the most resistant domains, such as the history of war, politics, and foreign relations.

In 2010 Scott (2010: 10–13) reaffirmed yet again that 'gender' remains still a useful category of analysis for 'critical uses'. Even so, Scott's role in prompting a critical rethink of historical discourse by taking poststructuralist theory to 'a discipline of committed empiricists' (Meyerowitz 2008: 1356) needs to be viewed in perspective. Both Bonnie Smith (2010: 734–5) and Tosh (2010: 297–8) have reminded us that such radical critiques do not necessarily become received historical wisdom. Not everyone followed Geoff Eley (2005: 7) in treating 'gender' as a useful, even 'necessary', category of historical analysis promising 'a higher form of understanding'. Indeed even Scott (2007: 21), when noting the continued conflation of 'gender' with women, recognised that most working historians continue to shrink from accepting the full implications of 'gender' theory, let alone from being beguiled by her words and texts.

Joan Scott (*née* Wallach) (1941–): Select Bibliography

Histories

1974	*The Glassmakers of Carmaux: French craftsmen and political action in a nineteenth-century city*
1978	(with Louise Tilly) *Women, Work and Family*
1980	(with Eric Hobsbawm) 'Political shoemakers', *Past and Present*
1983	'Women in History: the modern period', *Past and Present*
1986	'Gender; a useful category of historical analysis', *American Historical Review*
1988	*Gender and the Politics of History* (rev. ed. 1999)
1991	*French feminists claim the rights of 'man': Olympe de Gouges on the French Revolution*
1991	'Women's history', in P. Burke, *New perspectives on historical writing* (2nd ed. 2001)
1996	*Only Paradoxes to Offer: French feminists and the Rights of Man*
2004	'Feminism's history', *Journal of Women's History*
2005	*Parité! Sexual equality and the crisis of French universalism*
2007	*The Politics of the Veil (The Public Square)*
2007	'History-writing as critique', in K. Jenkins, S. Morgan and A. Munslow (eds.), *Manifestos for History*
2008	'Unanswered questions: revisiting gender: a useful category of historical analysis', *American Historical Review*
2009	*Théorie critique de l'Histoire: identités, expériences, politiques*

⟶

| 2010 | 'Gender: still a useful category of analysis?', *Diogenes* |
| 2012 | *The Fantasy of Feminist History* (in press) |

Edited/co-edited Histories

1987	(with Jill Conway and Susan Bourque) *Learning about Women: gender, power and politics*
1992	(with Judith Butler) *Feminists Theorize the Political*
1996	*Feminism and History*
1997	(with Cora Kaplan and Debra Keates) *Transitions, Environments, Translations: feminisms in international politics*
2001	(with Debra Keates) *Schools of Thought: twenty-five years of interpretive social science*
2004	*Going Public: feminism and the shifting boundaries of the private sphere*
2008	*Women's studies on the edge*

Autobiography

| 2009 | 'Finding critical history', in J.M. Banner, Jr., and J.H. Gillis (eds.), *Becoming Historians* |

Reference

| 2008 | Christina Woo, 'Joan Wallach Scott: Bibliography', 2008, http://www.lib.uci.edu/about/publications/wellek/ Wellek2008JoanScott.pdf. |

9
Robert A. Rosenstone: The Historian Meets Hollywood

Writing in April 1915 D.W. Griffith (quoted, Lang 1994: 4), the director of the recently released film *The Birth of a Nation* (1915), looked forward to a time when history would be presented primarily through history films, not written histories:

> The time will come, and in less than ten years ... when the children in the public schools will be taught practically everything by moving pictures. Certainly they will never be obliged to read history again
>
> Imagine a public library of the near future ... Instead of consulting all the authorities, wading laboriously through a host of books, and ending bewildered, without a clear idea of what exactly did happen, you will merely seat yourself at a properly adjusted window ... press the button, and actually see what happened.
>
> There will be no opinions expressed. You will merely be present at the making of history. All the work of writing, revising, collating, and reproducing will have been carefully attended to by a corps of recognized experts.

Although this prediction, based upon a flawed view of history, proved overly optimistic, film has emerged to become – to quote Robert A. Rosenstone (2006: 12) of the California Institute of Technology (Caltech) at Pasadena – 'the chief conveyor of public history in our culture', the prime means for presenting what happened in the past to the general public. Indeed, the omission of any discussion of history films viewed in the cinema, on television or through computers would be to ignore the mechanism through which many people today have come to know about the past. 'Hollywood', a shorthand descriptor of the American film industry responsible for producing and distributing many of the films seen in cinemas and on television on both sides of the Atlantic, has exerted a global impact: 'For many, Hollywood History is the only history' (Carnes 1996: 9). Gerald Kaufman (1985: 25), a prominent British politician, is not alone in admitting that 'in my youngest years all my history lessons were taught me via the cinema screen'. Even so, as stressed in chapter 2, written histories retain their hold within academia, where film histories are regarded still as almost beyond the pale, as conceded by Rosenstone (2006: 2):

> To accept film, especially the dramatic feature film, as being able to convey a kind of serious history (with a capital H), runs against just about everything we have learned since our earliest days in school. History is not just words on a page, but on pages which are for the most part contained in thick tomes ... And film why that's just entertainment, a diversion from the serious business of life.

Rosenstone as the Historian of Film as History

Rosenstone has established a global reputation as the historian of film as history and history as film. His thinking, presented in numerous articles, books, lectures and seminar papers as well as on film as a 'talking head' to a doubting academic audience, has encouraged a growing number of historians to treat the concept of film as history more sympathetically, even to make history and film – to quote Rosenstone (2004: 163) – 'a hot topic in the profession'. Moreover, his career – Rosenstone (S. Cohen 2011: 2) entered academia after a brief spell working as a journalist – provides illuminating insights into how a historian's approach evolves over time through the continued rethinking of the nature of the discipline in the light of personal experience.

Apart from presenting histories about film as history, Rosenstone has authored a series of innovative deconstructionist texts as well as personal and family histories, most notably *The Man who Swam into History* (2002), a mix of fact, fiction, invention, forgetting and myth. Despite starting out as an empirical historian when studying for his doctorate at the University of California, Los Angeles (UCLA), and publishing academic monographs, a relative lack of attachment to any specific historical tradition rendered Rosenstone (2004; 2009a: 17–25) open over time to the deconstructive and decentring spirit of postmodernism. Nor should the impact of Rosenstone's literary background – at UCLA he majored in literature for his first degree – be underestimated in encouraging him to view literature as history and history as literature. Thus Rosenstone

(2004: 149–51) believed that historical novels, by bringing the past to life in a way that historical writing never did, 'made you feel as if you had been there. That was what I wanted from the past. That was what I believed history should do.'

Over time exposure to the writings of Frank Ankersmit and Hayden White, among others, led Rosenstone (2004: 159) to reappraise the intellectual rationale for his approach to the past, and become – to quote Marwick (2001: 239) – 'the most vociferous contemporary exponent of postmodernist approaches to history and film' seeking to make 'meaning (in whatever medium) out of the past'. In many respects Rosenstone, the co-Founding Editor of *Rethinking History: the Journal of Theory and Practice* and Associate Editor of *Film-Historia*, sees himself as helping to drag history and historians into the future by adopting, or at least experimenting with, alternative modes of constructing and presenting the past in a culture where the electronic and visual media are supplementing, in fact increasingly replacing, the written word as the primary means of communication.

Rosenstone's belief that history feature films are capable of representing the past as legitimately as written histories is best understood against the background of Hollywood's presentation of the past, and the reactions of historians thereto. Indeed, as mentioned above, filmmakers prove influential presenters of the past to a mass audience.

Providing 'the Truth of History' through Film

In February 1915 Griffith screened *The Birth of a Nation* at the White House. Reportedly, President Woodrow Wilson (quoted, Rosenstone 2006: 13) was impressed by a vivid new way of knowing the American past capable of evoking a sense of the atmosphere and milieu of the time by re-enacting great events in animated fashion: 'It's like writing history with lightning.' Pointing to supportive feedback from 'educators', Griffith (quoted, Toplin 1996b: 18) asserted that a history film 'can impress upon a people as much of the truth of history in an evening, as many months of study will accomplish'.

Whether or not the 200 million-plus Americans estimated to have watched *The Birth of a Nation* during succeeding decades saw the film as imparting 'the truth' about the 1861–5 American Civil War and post-1865 Reconstruction remains questionable. However, this episode offered an early example of a filmmaker using history to make a point about the present as well as presenting what many contemporary Americans wanted to see. Based upon Thomas Dixon, Jr.'s *The Clansman: an historical romance of the Ku Klux Klan* (1905), *The Birth of a Nation* reflected contemporary pro-South attitudes unsympathetic towards racial integrationist values. Indeed, the film's blatant racial bigotry, most notably its anti-African American message, prompted the National Association for the Advancement of Colored People (NAACP) to picket cinemas, demanding a ban on the film. Nor did the controversies raised by the film disappear over time. Thus, in 1992, when the Library of Congress placed *The Birth of a Nation* on the National Film Registry to acknowledge its classic status, the NAACP made the inevitable protests. James H. Billington (quoted, Litwack 1996: 141), the Librarian of Congress, agreed that the film was 'bigoted and racist' in its treatment of African Americans, but nevertheless warranted preservation as 'an inescapable part of our history'.

Far from presenting a truthful view of events, *The Birth of the Nation* highlighted the motion picture's potential to present propaganda disguised as 'history' for the purposes of art and entertainment. Revealing the extraordinary power of the cinema to 'teach history', or rather to present a flawed version of what happened in the past, Leon Litwack (1996: 140) recorded the way in which Griffith's film highlighted the ability of history films to mould contemporary popular attitudes and stereotypes:

> More than any historian or textbook, the vivid images conveyed by *The Birth of a Nation* shaped American attitudes towards Reconstruction and the 'Negro problem.' With that version of history firmly fixed in their minds, most Americans could readily understand why black southerners were unfit to exercise political rights and why the white South had to go to such extraordinary lengths to control and contain its black population. And for much of the twentieth century, *The Birth of a Nation* molded and reinforced racial stereotypes, distorting the physical appearance of black men and women, and fixing in the public mind the image of a race of inferiors.

At a panel discussion held at the Library of Congress in April 1994 Billington's case for placing the film on the National Film Registry was attacked by John Hope Franklin, the author of several publications on black history and Reconstruction. Pointing to the distorted version of history implanted in the American mindset, Franklin (quoted, Grimes 1994) argued that the film 'presented a picture of black rule that existed nowhere in the South at any time, and of riotous behavior that existed only in the pages of Dixon's *Clansman*'. Even so, *The Birth of a Nation* set the tone for several generations, while helping the rebirth of the Ku Klux Klan: 'More than any single incident, it is to be blamed for the 1994 view of Reconstruction.'

Subsequently David O. Selznick's *Gone with the Wind* (1939), though not quite as flawed historically, reinforced the line mapped out by Griffith by romanticising the South and – to quote James M. McPherson (1990: 22) – 'teaching false and stereotyped lessons about slavery and the American Civil War'. One of the most popular American history films ever made, *Gone with the Wind* further defined the Civil War for a mass audience (Clinton 1996: 132–5; Juddery 2008: 36–41), particularly given the manner in which the film encouraged the impression of historical authenticity such as by inserting dates to introduce key scenes.

Film as Public History

The *Birth of the Nation* controversy indicates that the debate about film as an alternative mode of presenting the past has a long history. Over time film and cinema technology have progressed, such as through the advent of sound, the switch from black-and-white film to colour, the emergence of multiplex cinemas, and the vogue for videocassettes/DVDs/Blu-Rays, but history films have proved an enduring feature of Hollywood's output.

Rosenstone (2006: 14–18) has proposed a threefold classification for history films:

1. mainstream dramatic feature films, including television mini-series, depicting actual and/or fictional people caught up in past events;
2. opposition or innovative history films; and
3. historical documentaries.

Concentrating on Hollywood history films and television mini-series within the first category, this chapter covers only part of Rosenstone's first category. The diverse second category is not discussed. Historical documentaries were studied in chapter 6.

In today's Britain much of the general public's grasp of past events and people is framed and influenced increasingly by what they have seen on the screen at the cinema or at home on their television and computer screens. Presenting the past to present-day audiences through moving images combined with dialogue, sound effects and music, the visual media play a crucial role in both popular culture and public history: 'Historical films shape our historical consciousness and thus become part of our cultural memory of past events ... Increasingly, our memories of past events will be structured by these (filmic) images in our head' (Engelen 2007: 562). Indeed, Nigel Spivey (quoted, Membery 2002) complained that 'It's got to the stage where most people know what they know about someone like Elizabeth I from seeing Judi Dench [Elizabeth I in *Shakespeare in Love*, 1998] or whoever it is playing her in a film, not from what they've learnt at school.' More recently, the 'whoever' playing Elizabeth is more likely to be Helen Mirren, the star of a television miniseries on *Elizabeth I* (2005), or Cate Blanchett, who played the queen in Shekhar Kapur's two films about Elizabeth I (1998, 2007).

Conflicting Agendas

Over time Hollywood has repeatedly shown its skills at turning historical fact into fiction, but then presenting its distorted dramatised version of the past as a true story. In March 2009 surviving British prisoners of war imprisoned in Stalag Luft III at Zagan in the Second World War marked the 65th. anniversary of a daring mass breakout by returning to the camp. Part of their celebrations included watching John Sturges's *The Great Escape* (1963), starring Steve McQueen. Celebrating their story, this film gave the escapees enduring fame. Despite presenting itself as 'a true story' – the film claimed that 'Although the characters are composites of real men, and time and place have been compressed, every detail of the escape is the way it really happened' – the demands of the box office led fictional American characters to be written into the story, even if no Americans had been involved in the actual escape. Likewise the infamous motorcycle escape stunt – undertaken by McQueen on a 1963 Triumph 650 motorbike – depicted an event that never took place (Macintyre 2008; Yeoman 2009).

Historians' concerns about such Hollywoodisation of the past reflect the fact that the agenda of film producers is very different from that of academic historians (Box 9.1). History films rely heavily upon imaginary constructions of the past, that is, fiction not fact, and hence Hollywood films supposedly based on actual events are notorious for offering the audience a visual version of the past that takes massive liberties with the historical record. For historians, it becomes all too easy to point to specific scenes, sections of dialogue or sequences of events as inventions failing to reflect accurately the evidence, as well as to point out that the past itself is equally capable of providing stirring material.

As Mark Carnes (1995; 1996: 10) acknowledged, Hollywood movies, like historical dramas and novels, inspire and entertain, but 'they do not provide a substitute for history that has been painstakingly assembled from the best available evidence and analysis'. Moreover, films offer a linear narrative with a simple storyline, denying historical alternatives, and avoiding complex debates about motivation, causation and

Box 9.1 Historians and Hollywood filmmakers: contrasting agendas	
Academic historians aim to:	Hollywood history filmmakers aim to:
• produce a critical, informed, balanced and reasoned account of the past	• entertain using a story based at least in part upon past events and people
• provide a historically accurate account following from the evidence but challenging mythologies and inventions	• tell a good story capable of engaging the audience through enhancing dramatic effect and human interest, if necessary by being economical with the truth and relying heavily upon myths and inventions; mixing fact and fiction concerning people and events; spicing up the story through a love interest, sex, and emotional highs; and having happy endings
• acknowledge the differences between past and present, and avoid historical anachronism and presentism by placing evidence in context and studying the past as far as possible in its own terms	• make the past familiar by highlighting similarities to today's world and adapting developments to present-day concerns
• write in an appropriate historical manner principally targeting a limited academic audience but possibly reaching a broader audience as public history.	• make money to cover at least the production budget by reaching a large audience and using star names in a manner exploiting their audience strengths.

consequences. Historical presentism, a sin for historians, is recognised as a virtue enabling filmmakers to strike a chord with today's audiences by enabling them to view the past through present-day spectacles. Rather than treating the past as a foreign country, film flattens the differences between past and present, thereby enabling the past to be depicted as a mirror of the present. Historical anachronism, that is, assuming that people in the past thought and behaved as we do, also proves common, as recorded by Schama (2000b):

> I remember a movie about 17th century Europe in which a soldier tells his wife, 'Well, dear, I'm off to fight the Thirty Years' War!' And another wonderful example called 'The Sword of Florence' in which the actor playing Michelangelo leaps off his horse and announces to the electrified crowd: 'Citizens of Florence, the Renaissance is here!' These headlines are of course a posthumous invention.

Historical Accuracy and All That

The contrasting agendas of filmmakers and historians were satirised cleverly in 1986 by *Sweet Liberty*, a film scripted and directed by Alan Alda. An impressive cast list, headed by Michael Caine, Bob Hoskins and Michelle Pfeiffer, included Lillian Gish, who had appeared over 70 years earlier in *The Birth of a Nation*. Alda played the part of Michael Burgess, a history teacher in the small town of Sayeville, North Carolina, and the author of a prize-winning academic history about the 1776 American Revolution turned into a Hollywood movie.

Cast and crew descended on Burgess's home town to shoot the location scenes. Reading the film's script, Burgess was shocked by the way in which his 'history', based upon in-depth research, had been revamped for the big screen: 'This isn't my book ... Where's my book? So far there isn't one single thing in here that looks familiar.' Even worse, his 'history' had been transformed into a lightweight (and historically incorrect) love story. 'I just wrote the book from which the movie has NOT been taken', he fumed. Lacking any real sense of American history, the production team was merely using actual events focused on the Battle of Cowpens of January 1781 and real people – these included Colonel Tarleton and Mary Slocumb – central to Burgess's book to frame a fictional love story given added audience appeal by scenes containing naked women and jokes. Nor was Burgess the only historical malcontent. Proud and knowledgeable about its past, as evidenced by regular re-enactments of events in the 1776–83 War of Independence, the local community shared

Burgess's resentment about the way in which Hollywood filmmakers were playing fast and loose with their heritage.

Burgess voiced his concerns about the script to Bo Hodges, the film's director: 'There are only a couple of things I have a problem with ... the story and the dialogue ... None of it ever happened.' Rejecting Burgess's accusations of misrepresenting the American past, Hodges exclaimed, 'Screw historical accuracy!' Expressing what was seen as the typical Hollywood perspective, he responded, 'Who really knows what happened a coupla hundred years ago?', or rather, 'Who cares?' In turn, the closing scene of *Sweet Liberty* depicted the premiere of the film supposedly based on Burgess's book. A press reporter asked Burgess about the film: 'How accurate is it? Did all those things really happen? ... Does this movie show things the way they really were?' Burgess began to answer, 'Well, what *really* happened was ...', but his words were blanked out by celebratory fireworks, and led deliberately into a freeze-frame showing the usual disclaimer carried in closing credits, 'The characters and events in this film are wholly fictitious. Any resemblance to persons living or dead is purely coincidental.'

In this manner, *Sweet Liberty* articulated many of the problems raised by historians about the Hollywoodisation of the past (Box 9.1). For Hollywood's history filmmakers, their priority is placed upon entertainment, the need for a good story and dramatic effect, such as through the identification of 'goodies' and 'baddies' or the imposition of a love interest, *not to teach people about the past*. Additionally, the demands of the box office are seen also as requiring nods to the modern cinemagoers' frame of reference – action, explosions, nudity, sex and violence. No real effort is made to conform to either historical standards regarding, say, accuracy, balance, coverage, historical presentism and anachronism, or the latest historical scholarship. On the contrary, filmmakers, personified by the Hodges character in *Sweet Liberty*, possess few qualms about accuracy, as stated famously by the film producer, Darryl F. Zanuck (quoted, Suid 2002: 174; Toplin 2002: 119), when defending dramatic licence in *The Longest Day* (1962): 'Anything changed was an asset to the film. There is nothing duller on the screen than being accurate but not dramatic.'

Admittedly, a semblance of historical credibility might be given by basing the story on actual events, as claimed by Roberto Rossellini (quoted, Freeman 2009a: 5) for *The Rise to Power of Louis XIV* (1966): 'It is all in the documents, nothing is invented.' Indeed, for filmmakers, there is perceived box-office value in exploiting history in this manner, as happened with *The Great Escape*. Thus, John Sayles (Foner and Sayles 1996: 17), who has written and directed films based on actual events, including *Matewan* (1987) and *Eight Men Out* (1988), admitted that:

> There's a certain power that comes from history ... I've heard produc-
> ers say many, many times that the only way a movie is going to work
> is if the ad says 'Based on a true story.' Audiences appreciate the fact
> that something really happened. Whether it did or didn't, they're
> thinking that it did or knowing that it did. That gives the story a cer-
> tain legitimacy in the audience's mind.

Another tool employed by filmmakers to enhance authenticity is the production of an accompanying study guide for distribution in schools and universities. Indeed, in 1965 a classroom guide for *Shenandoah* pointed to the film's extensive background research to claim that 'In learning history, nothing beats a good Hollywood film' (Freeman 2009a: 6)! Likewise, in 1991 Oliver Stone produced a study guide to help establish that *JFK* offered a 'higher truth' than existing accounts about President Kennedy's assassination (Toplin 1996b: 68–9). In real-ity, such guides prove little more than promotional press packs.

In theory, the employment of historical consultants/advisers, as evi-denced by Rosenstone's involvement with *Reds* (1981), *The Good Fight* (1983) and *Darrow* (1991), should help authenticity. In reality, consult-ants are frequently marginalised, possessing little or no control over the end product, but will be listed in the film's credits by way of 'promo-tional "window dressing"' (Hughes-Warrington 2007: 17). Recalling his consultancy role for *Reds*, Rosenstone (2009b; S. Cohen 2011: 6–7) admit-ted having 'to sign off on Warren Beatty's many inventions'. Reportedly, Ainslie Embree, who taught the history of India at Columbia University, was asked by Richard Attenborough to read the script of *Gandhi* (1982). Embree sent a lengthy list of errors to Attenborough but – to quote Eric Foner (Foner and Sayles 1996: 18) – 'not a single one of them got changed' because they 'got in the way of his storytelling'. Embree was not mentioned in the film's credits.

Nor are historians alone in highlighting the shortcomings of Holly-wood's presentation of history. This is certainly true of Britain, where Hollywood has been frequently accused by both the media and politi-cians of rewriting the past in a manner disadvantageous to the British national interest. Reviewing Roland Emmerich's *The Patriot* (2000) for the *Daily Express*, Andrew Roberts (2000b) acknowledged the visual power of Hollywood while lamenting Britain's declining ability to shape its own national identity at home and abroad: 'As educational standards decline,

British schoolchildren learn a greater and greater proportion of history from movies. Yet most of the ones Hollywood currently produces seriously misrepresent the motivations and achievements of our forefathers.' In 2001 the *Daily Mail* was to the fore in the campaign attacking the way in which Steven Spielberg's television series *Band of Brothers* largely ignored Britain's war effort (Hudson 2001). Nor is this a new concern, as highlighted in 1945 by the furore outlined below surrounding *Objective, Burma!* As the British Board of Film Censors (quoted, Chapman 2005: 6) recorded in 1947, 'It is known that some American films have twisted and adapted OUR history to suit THEIR needs.'

In fact, *Sweet Liberty* demonstrated that the history of other countries, including that of the USA itself, is treated no differently by Hollywood. Indeed, Robert Brent Toplin subtitled his study of history and Hollywood as 'the use and abuse of the American past'. For example, Toplin (1996b: 26) pointed to the manner in which Alan Parker's *Mississippi Burning* (1988) related 'Hollywood's distorted version' of events in 1964, when members of the Ku Klux Klan murdered a black civil rights campaigner and two white companions near Philadelphia, Mississippi. Despite claiming to offer an authentic account of 1964's 'Freedom Summer' centred upon the actual murders, the film's manipulation of facts through fictionalising events and people failed to do justice to the active role African Americans played in the civil rights campaign. In many respects, the film's portrayal of African Americans as standing on the margins of fast-moving events reflected commercial pressures which increasingly 'pulled the portrayal from its historical base and pushed it in the direction of fiction': '*Mississippi Burning* focused on whites for purposes of box office popularity ... the movie's primary audience was going to be whites (both in the United States and abroad)' (Toplin 1996b: 30, 36). Inevitably, the film excited lively contemporary debate in academia, the media and politics, as highlighted by *The Economist*'s (1989: 93) article headlined 'Facts for Burning'. For Harvard Sitkoff (1989: 1019), the author of *The Struggle for Black Equality* (1981), 'this film does such injustice to the events with which it deals that its ultimate lynching is of history itself'. Indeed, in 1994 a historical documentary *Freedom on My Mind* sought to set the historical record straight.

As happened with *Mississippi Burning*, history films have frequently unleashed considerable debate and controversy extending well beyond academia into the media and political worlds. Toplin (1996b: 47) credited Stone's *JFK* as particularly significant in this respect: 'Few movies have made as great an impact on public affairs as *JFK* did.' Both the film and the accompanying study guide attracted strong criticism from both the press and politicians. Thus, David Belin (quoted, Toplin 1996b: 69), counsel to the Warren Commission set up to investigate the assassination, attacked Stone's conspiracy theories and 'disinformation' campaign as 'brainwashing students through the power of commercial film and rewriting history the Hollywood way'.

Hollywood and History: Case Studies

The contrasting agendas of Hollywood filmmakers and historians are best discussed by case studies centred upon two history films, *Braveheart* and *U-571*, and one Hollywood television mini-series, *The Tudors*.

Braveheart

In September 1995 Neal Ascherson (1995), a leading Scottish journalist with a Cambridge history degree, visited the cinema to see a recently released film: 'Seeking heroes, I went the other day to see *Braveheart*. As an account of the real William Wallace, or of late 13th-century Scotland, it is a joke. The list of cultural howlers and historical distortions rolls on forever.' Even so, such criticism failed to prevent Mel Gibson's *Braveheart* (1995) proving a critical and commercial success as far as Hollywood was concerned. Apart from winning five Oscars, including awards for best picture and best director, worldwide box-office returns of $210 million placed the film among the year's top-grossing movies and more than covered production costs of $72 million (Box Office Mojo n.d. a). Premiered in Stirling, the site of the National Wallace Monument, the film proved extremely popular throughout Scotland, where it secured 28 per cent of the film's British box-office takings as compared to the usual 8 per cent (McArthur 2003: 125). Nor were all media commentators as critical as Ascherson. Accepting *Braveheart* as a Hollywood epic, *not* a history documentary, many newspaper reviewers (quoted, McArthur 2003: 179) seemed prepared to gloss over any historical shortcomings:

- 'It might be a dodgy history lesson, but it's riveting cinema' (*Film West*) ...
- 'Historians will no doubt tear *Braveheart* apart ... But it is not intended as a history lesson, any more than Shakespeare's *Macbeth* was' (*Scotsman*)
- 'You could quibble for a century about Gibson's view of the past ... He is out to make a movie that will sell' (*Guardian*) ...
- 'What I find most wearisome, however, is the bellyaching of those who are upset over the film's lack of historical accuracy ... What do they expect? This is Hollywood, not a BBC documentary' (*Scotland on Sunday*).

However pedantic and 'wearisome' it might be, historians felt compelled still to highlight the false history offered by a film apparently lacking any listed historical consultant. Unimpressed by the Oscar awarded for best picture, historians (Ewan 1995: 1219–21) have treated *Braveheart* as a prime example of the sins of Hollywoodisation. Unsurprisingly, the film, described as providing a 'massively inaccurate portrayal' of the life of the thirteenth-century hero William Wallace, figures prominently among the 'worst medieval movies' listed on the 'Medieval History in the Movies' website hosted by New York's Fordham University (2002). Sharon Krossa (2001; 2008), a American-based historian with a doctorate from the University of Aberdeen, dismissed *Braveheart* as 'fantasy', not history, when pointing to 18 historical errors in the film's first two and a half minutes:

> Basically, as an historian, my opinion of *Braveheart* is that it is a work of fantasy, not history. Any resemblance to actual persons or events, in other words to real history, appear (*sic*) to be purely accidental. My best advice, for anyone interested in the real story of William Wallace, Robert Bruce, and the Scottish Wars of Independence, is not to believe *anything*, whether major or minor, depicted in the film, but instead read some reliable history books about the period. Enjoy the film as a fantasy film, by all means – just as one enjoys *Star Wars* or any other work of the imagination – simply do not mistake it for history. The events aren't accurate, the dates aren't accurate, the characters aren't accurate, the names aren't accurate, the clothes aren't accurate – in short, just about nothing is accurate.

For Starkey (2001: 14), *Braveheart*, typifying Scottish identity's reliance upon the 'wilful misrepresentation of history', was 'tripe'.

Only a few examples of the film's numerous distortions can be outlined here:

- **factual inaccuracies** – at the start of the film, dated 1280, the king was said to be dead, yet King Alexander III (1249–86) did not die until 1286.
- **inventions** – an attempt to link together Scotland's two national heroes led the film to depict a meeting between Robert Bruce and Wallace after the 1298 Battle of Falkirk. Yet such a meeting never took place.
- **inaccurate compression of time lines** – at the Battle of Falkirk in 1298 William Wallace is depicted as having an affair with Princess Isabelle of France, the wife of Edward II of England (1307–27), thereby conceiving the future King, Edward III. In fact, Isabelle was only 3 years old in 1298, and did not arrive from France until 1308, that

is, three years after Wallace's death, with her child being born seven years later in 1312.

- **factual alterations** – On 11 September 1297, William Wallace led Scottish troops to victory at Stirling Bridge over the invading English forces under John de Warenne. Victory resulted in the withdrawal of English troops as well as in the appointment of Wallace as one of Scotland's Joint Guardians. In the film, this battle is fought in a field. Neither a bridge nor a river is shown in the battle scenes, yet the narrow bridge proved a decisive factor in Wallace's success (Michael Prestwich, quoted, History Channel 2001). Believing that a pitched battle in a field would work better visually, Gibson (quoted, 'Stirling history' 2006) decided that 'We had to get rid of it [the bridge]; it got in the way.'
- **images of Wallace** – having watched the film, audiences were likely to believe that they possessed a clear and fairly full impression of Wallace's life and contribution upholding Scottish independence against the English. Indeed, Andrew Fisher (quoted, History Channel 2001), author of a biography of Wallace, complained that Gibson portrayed Wallace as rather like '"Lethal Weapon" [the title of one of Gibson's films] in drag', a psychopath. Yet notwithstanding the film's visual certainties, Wallace's life is 'shrouded in mystery'; indeed, both his date (*c.*1270) and place of birth remain uncertain (Morton 2001: 18–50). Myths abound based largely on the writings of 'Blind Harry', whose poem, the 'Acts and Deeds of Sir William Wallace' was written in the 1470s, a long time after Wallace's death in 1305.

Inspired by the family link and a visit to Edinburgh's Wallace statue in 1983, Randall Wallace (quoted, History Channel 2001) wrote a film script blending Blind Harry's poem into a story presenting Wallace as a Scottish national hero in a way rendering it difficult to separate fact from either fiction or propaganda. As a dramatist, Randall Wallace was only too willing to draw upon any myths to fill in the numerous gaps in our knowledge of William Wallace's life. Reportedly, Gibson (quoted, 'Wallace' 2005) admitted that 'We adhered to history where we could but hyped it up where the legend let us.' In many ways, the black-and-white certainties conveyed by the film, like the tie-in book (1995), merely compounded the problem. Indeed, the film inspired Tom Church, a sculptor, to produce a bust of William Wallace depicted in the likeness of Mel Gibson for placement in the National Wallace Monument's car park (Morton 2001: Fig. 22). Of course, Church benefited from the fact that – to quote Schama (quoted, Bremner 2001: 73) – 'we've not a clue' what William Wallace looked like.

Notwithstanding historians' reservations, *Braveheart* was nominated for an Academy award as the best screenplay. Encouraging Scots to take a greater interest in their country's history, culture and heritage, *Braveheart* gave the Wallace story to a new generation of Scots, and boosted an ongoing resurgence of Scottish national pride. Unsurprisingly, the film was soon appropriated politically by the Scottish National Party, while the *Braveheart* factor is credited as contributing to the 75 per cent vote for devolution in the referendum held significantly on 11 September 1997, 700 years to the day after the Battle of Stirling Bridge. Thus, Scottish nationalism gained recognition from both Westminster and Hollywood (Anderson 2004). Representing a new international brand name, *Braveheart* was used also to promote Scottish tourism, and proved instrumental in boosting visitor numbers to Stirling Castle and the Wallace Monument.

In 2000 Mel Gibson reprised his anti-English message in Emmerich's *The Patriot*, which was attacked in Britain as an American *Braveheart* (Glancy 2005: 523–5, 531–9). However, a critique by Brandeis University's David Hackett Fischer (2000), echoing that by Roberts quoted above, showed that American historians were equally unimpressed by the film's claims to historical authenticity. Complaining about repeated errors, Fischer asserted that Emmerich failed the academic test of accuracy by making the 1776–83 American War of Independence 'appear so artificial': 'He would have done better if he had listened to history more closely.'

U-571

In 1945 Hollywood's Second World War epic *Objective, Burma!*, starring Errol Flynn, showed American forces recapturing Burma (now Myanmar) in a way overlooking the central role performed by British troops. Strong British press criticism – *The Times* (1945a; 1945b; Jarvie 1981: 120–8) complained that it 'leaves the audience to draw the conclusion that the Burma campaign was fought exclusively by American troops' – led the film to be withdrawn soon after its opening in London's West End, and it was not re-released in Britain until September 1952.

More recently a similar controversy about yet another Hollywood hijack of British wartime history arose regarding *U-571* (2000). Directed by Jonathan Mostow, this film told the gripping story of how an American ship captured an Enigma code machine and codebooks from a German submarine. Boosting Allied code-breaking efforts, the event was depicted as turning the tide of the war in the Atlantic, and hence playing a critical role in winning the Second World War. In 1942, the year in which the film is set, the Allies did seize Enigma codebooks from a U-boat, but the action, resulting in the loss of two naval personnel, was undertaken in October 1942 by Britain's *HMS Petard*. Nor was the German submarine involved *U-571*, but rather *U-559*. Moreover, already in May 1941, before the USA entered the war, *HMS Bulldog* had captured an Enigma machine and code and cipher books from *U-110*.

Daniel Lee (2006) summarised the film's fundamental historical problem: 'apart from depicting the wrong country capturing the wrong material at the wrong time from the wrong submarine, *U-571* is a good film'. Interviewed in 2006, David Ayer (quoted, BBC 2006b), one of the film's scriptwriters, stated that any detours from the historical record reflected 'a mercenary decision to create this parallel history in order to drive the movie for an American audience'. For Robert Harris (quoted, Lee 2006), the author of the historical novel *Enigma* (1996), *U-571* represented another manifestation of American 'cultural imperialism': 'No matter what the situation, or where the film is supposed to be set, an American has to be central, to be seen as the good guy, or to save the day in some way.'

Prior to the closing credits, a caption stated that the film was fictional but inspired by real events. Dedicated to Allied forces capturing Enigma materials, the credits cited the two British successes in May 1941 and October 1942 alongside that of US Navy Task Force 22.3 in June 1944. Reportedly, these dedications were added only because of an outcry from historians, the media and politicians in Britain while the film was still in production. Both the American president and British prime minister were drawn into the resulting controversy. Responding to a letter from Paul Truswell, a British MP, President Bill Clinton stated that the film was 'not intended to be an accurate portrayal of historical events', but would acknowledge the British role in the credits when the film was eventually released (Wainwright 1999; Sebag-Montefiore 2000). Interviewed on television on 4 June 2000 after the film was released, Chris Smith (quoted, Carrell 2000), the Secretary of State for Culture, Media and Sport (1997–2001), told viewers that he found the film 'a bit galling' because historical events had been rewritten by Hollywood in a manner playing down Britain's role. The dispute might harm, he feared, the 'special relationship' between Britain and the USA.

> One of the things we need to make clear to Hollywood is, yes, you're in the entertainment business, but people see your movies ... They're going to come away thinking that's information, not just entertainment. You've got to make it clear where the dividing line lies. It's something I'll be raising with colleagues in Hollywood when I next see them.

Speaking in the House of Commons a few days later, Tony Blair (2000: 283), the prime minister, claimed that *U-571* was an 'affront' to the British people, and particularly to the two British sailors who died during the episode: 'We hope that people realise that those were people who, in many cases, sacrificed their lives in order that this country remained free.' On 3 July Parliament returned to the issue. Responding to further pressure, Chris Smith (2000: 15) stated:

> I have received a number of letters from members of the public about historical misrepresentation in Hollywood films, and while it is not for the Government formally to intervene in the creative process of film-making, I have made my personal views on the subject clear and will do so again when appropriate occasions arise.

When interviewed on television a month earlier, Smith (Carrell 2000) had revealed that he had urged Spielberg to respect historical accuracy when filming *Band of Brothers* (2001) because of the way in which *Saving Private Ryan* (1998) had played down Britain's role in the Normandy landings.

Whether or not such ministerial arm-twisting impacts upon Hollywood remains debatable, particularly as compared to the much stronger commercial pressures compelling filmmakers to Americanise film scripts. In any case, complaints from historians, journalists and ministers are likely to be secretly welcomed by filmmakers in the light of the manner in which any resulting controversy secures visibility and free publicity for their films. Certainly, *U-571* proved a commercial success in the USA – 60 per cent of the gross return of $128 million as compared with a production budget of $62 million came from the USA (Box Office Mojo n.d. b) – but it performed surprisingly well also in Britain.

The Tudors

For many studying the Tudor period in schools and universities, the written histories of Geoffrey Elton, John Guy, David Loades, John Neale and J.J. Scarisbrick, among others, have proved, and remain, pre-eminent. Nor should one overlook the popularity of David Starkey's histories and television documentaries. However, for many present-day Britons and Americans, their knowledge and understanding of the Tudor years is more likely to have been moulded principally by historical novels, such as those written by Philippa Gregory (chapter 10) or Hilary Mantel, as well as by Hollywood films, like *Shakespeare in Love* (1998), *Elizabeth* (1998) and *Elizabeth: The Golden Age* (2007), and television mini-series, including *Elizabeth I* (2005) and *The Tudors* (2007–11). Gregory's novel *The Other Boleyn Girl* (2001) was made into both a BBC television programme (2003) and a film (2008). According to Cynthia Herrup (2009), the Tudors have become 'a hot dynasty' thanks to a range of stars, like Helen Mirren, Cate Blanchett, Anne-Marie Duff and Jonathan Rhys Meyers, featuring in films set in the Tudor period, not because of Tudor historians. For Herrup, Hollywood has rediscovered the Tudors' narrative possibilities arising from their use and abuse of power, political intrigue, war, religious conflict, domestic and marital strife, and powerful women.

Reportedly, by 2009 over 120 million people in 70 countries had already watched Showtime's *The Tudors*. Little imagination is required to predict historians' hostile reaction to *The Tudors*, first shown on BBC Two in October 2007 after receiving good viewing figures on the USA's Showtime Channel (April–May 2007). Occupying a top-ten spot in BBC Two's audience ratings throughout its run, this glossy series attracted some 3.2 million viewers. Certainly, the BBC adjudged the ten-programme series a popular success, warranting the commissioning of three further series. In this manner, *The Tudors* highlighted the fact that filmmakers/television broadcasters judge history films largely by reference to audience and commercial considerations, not conformity to historical standards. Unsurprisingly, *The Tudors*, prompting the usual range of divergent responses to any cinematic/televisual treatment of history, attracted its fair share of detractors in both academia and the media, who pointed to the exploitation of the Tudor past to fit dramatic purpose and to meet the perceived needs of television audiences on both sides of the Atlantic. Undoubtedly, the series' American origins – it was produced by Showtime, a CBS company – raised yet again concerns about the liberties taken by Hollywood with British history. Far from offering a drama documentary, *The Tudors* proved a highly authored, racy and entertaining soap opera.

Operating within a factional framework set during the 1520s, the first series revolved around key personalities and relationships, but employed storylines involving considerable amounts of fiction designed to sex-up history. Casting Jonathan Rhys Meyers as Henry VIII – a tight-fitting leather jacket accentuated the rock-star appearance of a young actor well known already for *Bend it like Beckham* (2002) – confronted stereotypical images of a corpulent king fostered by Hans Holbein's 1537 portrait and Charles Laughton's 1933 portrayal in *The Private Life of Henry VIII* (Freeman 2009b: 30, 44–5). Reviewing the opening programme, Caitlin

Moran (2007) pointed to the breakneck pace, overtly populist tone, and challenge to the image of Henry VIII as 'a fat tyrant in pointy shoes':

> Within the first 12 minutes of *The Tudors*, Henry VIII – played by Jonathan Rhys Meyers – has shagged a married woman, shagged his wife's maid, jousted, played a vicious game of tennis with improbably small, period-accurate bats, and then declared war on France. Oh, and a man has been stabbed to death on some parquet, just to razz things up a bit .... Henry was, like, totally hot back in the day – a swaggering, athletic, rock-star sex king. This was a man worth having your head chopped off for, ladies, is the clear message ... who wouldn't like a man driven enough to abolish the Catholic Church, just for a shag?

Far from being dull, Tudor history, it seemed, came down to 'either a) sex or b) horrific torture and death – or maybe sometimes c) horrific, torturey sex-death'.

In 2008 the second series, a testament to the popularity of the initial series, provoked considerable angst in Britain about yet more Hollywood distortions of British history. Casting Peter O'Toole as Pope Paul III, the king's prime antagonist, the series centred upon Henry VIII's attempt to annul his marriage to Catherine of Aragon in order to marry Anne Boleyn, the resulting rift with Rome, and the creation of the Church of England. For most viewers, the storyline, reinforced by the usual quota of sexual shenanigans, worked well. For Tudor historians, the series, set during the late 1520s and 1530s, raised serious issues concerning factual accuracy and inventions; the compression, even reversal, of time lines; and historical anachronism. For example, during the late 1520s and early 1530s the prime confrontation was between Henry VIII and Pope Clement VII, who refused the divorce and excommunicated Henry. In fact, Paul III, O'Toole's character, did not become Pope until 1534, by which time Anne Boleyn had become Queen. Additional points of concern centred upon the fact that O'Toole played the part clean-shaven whereas Paul III was bearded, a point of considerable historical significance. Following the Sack of Rome in 1527 and his subsequent imprisonment by Emperor Charles V, Pope Clement VII sported a beard as a sign of penitence and mourning, a practice followed by Paul III and his successors. Moreover, the series' apparent preoccupation with period costume was qualified by present-day priorities, with Rhys Meyer's rock-star attire complemented by the women's revealing necklines.

Once again, the series was well placed in BBC Two's ratings – the average audience was 2.27 million – but less well placed as far as many newspaper reviewers were concerned. Richard Woods (2008) praised *The Tudors* as entertainment: 'It's fun, it's sexy – but is this really history?' For professional historians, the answer was an emphatic 'No.' Historical accuracy matters, and hence *The Tudors* was criticised yet again as misconceived and a product of sloppy writing and research. Starkey (quoted, Martin 2008; Foster 2008), television's Tudor man, proved gratuitously rude about what he dismissed as a 'gratuitously awful' series dumbed down, in his view, 'so that even an audience in Omaha [Nebraska, USA] could understand it': 'It's a mid-West view of the Tudors.' In any case, as Starkey had already informed television viewers, the Tudor period had more than its fair share of real-life drama – for example, Henry VIII's reign alone claimed six wives, two of whom were executed – without any need for fictionalisation upon the part of present-day scriptwriters.

Media critiques prompted those involved in making the series to state the case for the defence. Michael Hirst (quoted, Woods 2008) – apart from being the series' creator and writer, he scripted *Elizabeth* (1998) and co-wrote *Elizabeth: The Golden Age* (2007) – pointed out that he was commissioned 'to write an entertainment, a soap opera, and not history'. Rhys Meyers (quoted, Naughton 2008) echoed this line when asserting that the aim was to provide compelling drama, *not a history lesson*: 'We're not making a documentary for universities.' Moreover, 'having actors with an appealing look is what an audience demands today – especially when there's quite a bit of sexual activity involved'. Elton, if still alive, would have been appalled. From this perspective, the Tudor past was merely the wallpaper for a present-day soap featuring the period's leading personalities.

Of course, there is also the argument – this is not easy to disprove – that such programmes, though flawed historically, might encourage some viewers to learn more about the period, even to study the Tudors in depth through books published by Elton and Starkey, among others, or at least to visit the locations and royal palaces shown in the programmes. Such beliefs encouraged Brett Dolman (quoted, Woods 2008), the curator of the Historic Royal Palaces, to adopt a more sympathetic view in terms of praising the series for 'opening out the Tudors' world to us today'. For Herrup (2009), Tudor filmography offers a useful tool for teaching centred around discussions about film form and content.

Subsequently, the third series, shown by the BBC in 2009, the year marking the 500th. anniversary of Henry VIII's accession, helped keep such debates going, even if a sense of perspective is provided by knowledge that Korda's *The Private Life of Henry VIII* (1933) was also accused of being 'a feeble history' (Beard 1934: 124–5; Freeman 2009b: 33) characterised by 'a hopeless ignorance' of the past. The fourth and final series was broadcast by the BBC in 2011.

Does Hollywood Always Get It Wrong?

Lest this sounds rather negative, and yet another example of a historian trashing historical films, does Hollywood sometimes get it right? Can any film be recognised as 'good history', as asserted by George MacDonald Fraser (1988: xi–xii), the author of the *Flashman* historical novels?

> There is a popular belief that where history is concerned, Hollywood always gets it wrong – and sometimes it does. What is overlooked is the astonishing amount of history Hollywood has got right, and the immense unacknowledged debt we owe to the commercial cinema as an illuminator of the story of mankind.

In fact, Fraser's (1988: 183–4, 241–2) attempt to justify this assertion was unconvincing, given his uncritical historical reviews of such films as *Gone with the Wind*, *The Longest Day* and *Objective, Burma!*

Reading the literature, it has proved difficult to identify specific historical films justifying the descriptor 'history'. Of course, by definition, any Hollywood-type film will fall short of accepted historical standards, given the need for such films to meet the distinctive agenda of the film-maker as compared to that of historians. Hollywood films are not made for historians. Even so, occasional films, though not necessarily regarded as 'good history', have been recognised as possessing some historical merit. Spielberg's *Schindler's List* (1993) is frequently mentioned in this connection. Based on Thomas Keneally's best-selling Booker prize-winning book (chapter 10), the film told the story of Oskar Schindler, a shady war profiteer who mixed in high Nazi circles and switched from exploiting Jewish labour to rescuing Jews from Auschwitz. The film won several awards, including Oscars for best director and film. Despite frequent praise as a historical document drawing moviegoers into the story of the Holocaust (Toplin 2002: 50–3, 120–3), Spielberg's film, like Keneally's book, was nonetheless basically a work of faction, not history. Other films mentioned in the literature as rating discussion include *Tora! Tora! Tora!* (1970), *All the President's Men* (1976), *Born on the Fourth of July* (1990), *Flags of our Fathers* (2006) and *Letters from Iwo Jima* (2006). Antony Beevor (quoted, Carey 2009) cited Pierre Schoendoerffer's *La 317ème section* ['The 317th. Platoon'] (1965), a little known French film set in Indochina, as the best war movie.

For James M. McPherson (1990: 22), Princeton's Pulitzer prize-winning author of *Battle Cry of Freedom: The Civil War Era* (1988), Edward Zwick's *Glory* (1989) is one Hollywood movie suitable for teaching history. Set in the American Civil War, the film tells the story of the 54th. Massachusetts Volunteer Infantry, a regiment of black combat troops commanded by Robert Gould Shaw, from its formation until the attack on Fort Wagner in July 1863. *Glory* was significant for being the first feature film foregrounding the role of black soldiers in the American Civil War.

Excepting Shaw, as McPherson (1990: 27) acknowledged, the principal characters were invented. Furthermore, the regiment, though depicted in the film as comprising former slaves, was recruited mainly from men who had always been free. Perhaps the most serious error concerned the fact that whereas in 1863 the regiment attacked the fort guarding the approach to Charleston, South Carolina, from the south, in the movie the charge was made in the opposite direction, seemingly for technical reasons. Even so, McPherson (1990: 22, 27) opined that *Glory*, though getting some of the historical details wrong, was 'the most powerful and historically accurate movie about that war ever made'. Telling 'the real story' of the Civil War, the film conveyed 'the underlying meaning of events' to moviegoers. Thus, the black soldiers, depicted as former slaves, were employed to relate 'the story of their transformation from an oppressed to a proud people' as part of a conflict bringing about the revolutionary transformation of America:

> If it wins a deserved popularity, it will go far to correct the distortions and romanticizations of such earlier blockbuster films as *Birth of a Nation* (1915) and *Gone with the Wind* ... *Glory* will throw a cold dash of realism over the moonlight-and-magnolias portrayal of the Confederacy.

Nor has McPherson been alone in singing the film's praises. Admitting the difficulties faced by any two-hour film in grappling with the past's complexities, Gerald Horne (1990: 1143) concluded that 'all we can ask is if the basic thrust of the film has been true to history. *Glory* easily passes this test.' Likewise, Rosenstone (2006: 40–8) has discussed the film positively in successive publications. By contrast, Ken Burns (quoted, Toplin 2002: 8–9) proved highly critical of the film's factual inaccuracies and stereotypical characters, perhaps in part to emphasise the historical merit of his American Civil War series (chapter 6) shown on television in 1990.

Moving on to 2011 Ben Macintyre (2011), the author of the best-selling popular wartime history *Operation Mincemeat* (2010), claimed that recent films – he mentioned Bryan Singer's *Valkyrie* (2008), Peter Weir's *The Way Back* (2010) and Tom Hooper's Oscar-winning *The King's Speech* (2010) – yielded evidence of a change of attitude upon the part of filmmakers: 'Where history was once regarded as a hoard of tales to be looted, melted down and refashioned for the screen, film-makers now feel an obligation to reflect the past as accurately as possible within the demands of the art.' Reportedly, Hooper confessed about being 'obsessed' with historical accuracy. Inevitably, his film's historical merit attracted media interest, including an editorial in *The Times* (2011), and controversy. Conceding that the film was not entirely free of errors, distortions and fabrications, most notably totally misrepresenting Churchill's attitude towards the abdication of Edward VIII, Macintyre opined that '*The King's Speech* is ... proof that respecting the detail of the past need not impinge on imagination and creativity. Historical veracity, so far from undermining drama, actually enhances it.' However, most historians, as reflected by Andrew Roberts's (2010) critique of *The King's Speech* as a historical record, have yet to be convinced that Hollywood filmmakers have changed course.

By contrast, Rosenstone (2006: 45) has always possessed a more positive view of historical films as history, as evidenced by his description of *Glory* as 'a powerful work of history'. However, whereas this chapter has targeted Hollywood, his focus has been the world cinema. For Rosenstone (2006: 50), European, Latin American and Asian filmmakers have often produced more serious and profound historical films, and hence provided much stronger material than Hollywood in support of his arguments about films as history. Nor have some of these filmmakers working outside the confines of Hollywood been as concerned with the bottom line.

Rosenstone on History Films as 'History'

In December 2007 five commentators came together for a Forum published in the journal *Rethinking History* to mark Rosenstone's contribution to the study of history and film. Apart from contributing the opening essay to a pioneering Forum on film and history in the *American Historical Review* in 1988 – in May 2011 this article was still among the journal's twenty most accessed online articles – he was the first editor (1989–92) of the journal's film reviews section. During the past 30 years or more Rosenstone has proved prominent in discussing history as film and film as history, with particular regard to film's role as a popular communicator presenting history to a mass audience in the cinema and on the television screen. His global impact has been enhanced by the fact that many of his studies have been published in translation.

As discussed above, within academia there exists still a relatively negative view of film as 'history', given the common perception that historical accuracy is of little or no concern to producers of historical films. However, Rosenstone, among others, has pushed for a more sympathetic attitude. Without disparaging the merits of traditional written histories, he has pressed the case for acknowledging that film establishes that there can be more than one way of understanding the past and more than one medium in which to present that understanding. Depicting the past visually, film, Rosenstone argued, can contribute to historical knowledge and understanding, offer broader insights into historical topics, and enhance the larger discourse of history.

Reviewing history films, such as for the *American Historical Review* and *Reviews in American History*, working as a historical consultant for Hollywood filmmakers, and watching filmmakers produce films (*Reds*; *The Good Fight*) based on his histories helped Rosenstone (2006: 158; 2009b) to understand not only the 'enormous' amount of fiction included in any history film but also how and why films presented things differently from, and sometimes better than, the written word. He gained insights also into dramatic practice and the possibilities of film as a medium:

> What seems clear is that too many academics critique film naïvely, unthinkingly – as I did in my first essay ['*Reds* as History']. Why? Because movies run against our notion of proper history ... but I have come to see ... that film is not history in our traditional sense, but it is a kind of history nonetheless.

Conceding that history films cannot compare with written histories in terms of 'informational content, intellectual density or theoretical insight', most notably in meeting the expository and analytical functions valued by academic historians, Rosenstone (2006: 159) claimed that historical films possess power through their visual and auditory qualities: 'moving images and soundscapes will create experiential and emotional complexities of a sort unknown upon the printed page'. Breaking down the 'confining walls' (Rosenstone 2006: 1) of words, film's multi-layered approach exposes the audience simultaneously to the past's other dimensions, 'colour, movement, sound, light, and life'. Acting like time machines, history films erode the gulf between past and present by plunging the audience into a vivid and multi-layered past. In particular, the dramatic techniques employed by filmmakers, combined with seamless camera work, skilful editing, the use of colour, the mix of sound and vision, and the visual authenticity arising from reproducing the material culture of the past, encourage viewers to believe that they are looking through a window at a real world rather than a carefully constructed one. It becomes all too easy for the audience to forget that they are watching a film and to believe what they see on the screen, that is, the illusion of reality enabling people to experience events through which they themselves did not live.

Moreover, some members of the audience might be encouraged to want to know more, such as by reading written histories elaborating topics covered in the film. Indeed, having watched Alex Cox's *Walker* (1987), Rosenstone (2006: 159) proceeded 'to read everything' about that nineteenth-century adventurer operating in Nicaragua. Far from putting history to the sword, history films can be presented as breathing life into the study of the past.

Within this context, Rosenstone has pointed to the need to view film histories and written histories as complementary methods of presenting the past, not as rivals for authority over the past. Given his literary background and postmodernist mindset, Rosenstone (2009a: 24–5) has sought to prioritise how films as text communicate meaning and are received by audiences. Pushing aside issues concerning authenticity, Rosenstone (2006: 8–9) has pressed the merit of studying history films in their own terms,

> as a separate realm of representation and discourse, one not meant to provide literal truths about the past (as if our written history can provide literal truths) but metaphoric truths which work, to a large degree, as a kind of commentary on, and challenge to, traditional historical discourse.

Points for Discussion

Taking advantage of *History on Film/Film on History* (2006) to develop his ideas at greater length, Rosenstone drew together the fruits of his lengthy career as a historian of film dating back at least to the mid-1970s, when he began teaching courses on history and film. Unsurprisingly, the book provided a series of useful debating points for historians, as highlighted in December 2007 by the *Rethinking History* Forum mentioned above. Even so, as Rosenstone pointed out at the start of the book, words on a page prove inadequate when seeking to understand how film presents the past, and particularly to evaluate its effectiveness in performing this role. Only moving images, supported by sound effects, can do this.

As ever, it proves easier to pose questions about film as 'history' than to provide agreed answers, but key points raised for discussion by Rosenstone included:

- **Can Hollywood's history films be treated as 'history' making a serious contribution to historical knowledge and understanding by offering an alternative visual way of presenting the past particularly outside academia? Or should history films continue to be viewed negatively in terms of fostering false and distorted images of the past?**
  Whether or not Rosenstone (2006: 9) is correct in depicting history films as 'a new form of historical thinking', prioritising metaphor and symbol over amassing data, critical analysis and logical argument remains debatable. On the one hand, Hughes-Warrington (2007: 9, 12), disputing the view that they offer 'only an impoverished or compromised' view of the past, claimed that 'films are not a form of history but are history'. Likewise Leen Engelen (2007: 555–6) used her contribution to the *Rethinking History* Forum to follow Higashi (1998: 87, 97) in challenging those espousing a negative view to forget disciplinary turf wars. Thus, it seemed 'no longer fruitful to continue defending historical fiction films against the criticism of zealous historians "of the old stamp" relentlessly trying to unmask fiction films as incomplete, historically inaccurate or completely false versions of history'. For Engelen, history films can, and do, represent one way of presenting the past as history, and deserve to be recognised by history's 'gatekeepers' as offering something more than a somewhat unsatisfactory complement to written histories. Just as film histories cannot hope to perform the same tasks as written histories, so the latter are unable to do everything achieved by history films. Moreover, as Engelen pointed out, there are 'good' and 'bad' examples of both genres.

  By contrast, Paul Smith (2008: 417), who edited the pioneering study on *The Historian and Film* (1976), acknowledged the merits of Rosenstone's approach, but argued that 'historical argument is a contrapuntal activity predicated on the existence of alternative or opposing views and deriving its structure and significance from its dialogue with them. Filmic forms are not well adapted for this.' Although few historians would go as far as Marwick (2001: 239) in dismissing Rosenstone's approach to film as history as an 'absurdity', most would incline towards Freeman's (2009a: 25) view that history films, like historical dramas, novels or paintings, are *artistic representations of the past*. As such, history films should *not* be treated as 'history': 'Reimagining the past is not the same thing as analyzing it ... Contrary to what some post-modernists maintain, one historical interpretation is not as good as another.'

- Can history films be studied in the same manner as written histories? In particular, can filmmakers be expected to operate under the demanding standards of historical scholarship? Or should history films be treated as a different medium, judged by what Rosenstone (1988: 1184; 2006: 7–8, 157–8) called different 'rules of engagement'?

Any attempt to push beyond existing boundaries should be qualified by an awareness of the need to remain true to historical standards, and to acknowledge, like Rosenstone, that filmmakers practising their art with a well-informed and sensitive appreciation of history can make useful contributions to public thinking about the past. For James Chapman (2007), Rosenstone's focus on film as a form of discourse glossed over archival-based 'nuts-and-bolts' history, situating films in their contexts, most notably studying historical veracity, the intentions of filmmakers, the sources used, the production process, and the reception of the final film. Responding to Chapman's critique, Rosenstone (2007b) restated their points of difference:

> He [Chapman] seems to care more for how a film comes to mean than for its meaning ... But the approach I have chosen to take is to deal with the history portrayed in the film not the history of the film. I place the finished work into the context of the larger discourse of history out of which it emerges, to which it refers, and upon which it comments.

In 2009 *Tudors and Stuarts on Film*, edited by Susan Doran and Thomas Freeman, echoed the Chapman line, stressing the need to treat history films no differently from any written history (Freeman 2009a: 2).

For Jeffrey Richards (2009: 74–5), these 'culture wars' reflected the divergent ways in which feature films have been viewed as history. On the one hand, the 'Film Studies' approach, as adopted by Rosenstone, developed out of literature and concentrated on film as a discourse, whose meaning was explored through theory independent of the prevailing cultural, economic, political and social contexts. On the other hand, the 'Cinema History' perspective, as espoused by Chapman and Freeman, emerged out of history, and hence prioritised context and archival research concerning production and audience reception. Welcoming signs of convergence, Richards conceded that there exists still 'unproductive hostility' between the two camps, resulting in the unthinking dismissal of films meriting more serious historical study.

- **Should we continue to differentiate the ways in which historians and filmmakers engage with the past?**
  Filmmakers like Oliver Stone (e.g. *JFK*, 1991; *Nixon*, 1995) and Andrzej Wajda (e.g. *Korczak*, 1990; *Katyn*, 2007) have returned repeatedly to the past, and might be interpreted as merely presenting history in a different way. As such, should they be studied as historians, or as 'cinematic historians', as Stone (Toplin 1996b: viii) has described himself, as much as filmmakers?

- **As Britain's past is continually being represented, frequently misrepresented, on film, what do these representations say, why and how? What impact do these representations have on audiences within and outside Britain? How far does watching history films provide a different historical experience from that of reading written histories?**
  Hollywood's history films, though intended primarily as commercial entertainment, present audiences with one simplified version of the past. Despite easily dismissed as 'transient entertainments' offering an account falling short of 'history', history films can exert enduring impacts upon popular views of the past, especially as they are frequently presented by filmmakers as not merely the products of artistic imagination but also an authentic reconstruction of actual events. The problem is that cinema audiences, though welcoming being told that they are watching 'a true story', do not always appreciate or necessarily care about the historical imperfections of any film, let alone have ready access to the views of professional historians thereupon as a corrective. As a result, Hollywood's seriously flawed presentations of the past can come to influence, even dominate, how people see their country's past, especially those who did little history at school or college and have never been made aware of the need to view any history in a critical and sceptical manner. As Richards (2003: viii) has pointed out, the general public's view of 'history' often follows Hollywood's lead:

> Hollywood has conquered and colonised the imagination of the rest of the world. In doing so, it has created celluloid images of other countries and other cultures filtered through its own ideological preoccupations and priorities. England, Scotland, Wales and

Ireland all have Hollywoodised images that exist alongside and interrelate with their own self-generated images.

Following on from chapter 1, the problem might be partially alleviated if people proved more historically literate, but in Britain this would require a considerable enhancement of history's place in the educational curriculum.

At the same time, the profession's suspicions about the treatment of history in film and television often blind us to the medium's possibilities. In particular, as Randall Wallace (quoted, Pendreigh 1998) argued in response to his many critics, history films have a track record of striking a chord with the general public, and fostering interest in the past:

> It's an interesting irony that *Braveheart* has created far more interest in history than anything any academic has written. I'm not the least bit troubled that they would say this isn't accurate or that isn't accurate. The great thing is to stimulate people to be interested in history.

• Given the contrasting, frequently conflicting, agendas of those involved, how far can filmmakers strike a balance between historical authenticity and the commercial pressures of the box office?

In 1935 Louis Gottschalk (quoted, Rosenstone 2002: 473–4), Professor of History at the University of Chicago, advised the president of Metro-Goldwyn-Mayer Studios that 'No picture of a historical nature ought to be offered to the public until a reputable historian has had a chance to criticize and revise it.' However desirable as an ideal, this strategy has never been, nor will it ever be, a practical possibility. Naturally, most historians have tended to discuss history films from a professional perspective, prioritising accepted historical standards. Hitherto, critiques articulated by so called 'historian-cops' (Sklar 1997: 346–50) have made little attempt to appreciate the other side of the coin, that is, the way in which Hollywood's systemic pressures relating to, say, the tyranny of 'the bottom line', perceived audience expectations, and the basic narrative template required of mainstream films combine to push aside any real priority for historical accuracy. Nor has Hollywood exhibited much, if any, embarrassment about its poor track record in taking liberties with history. Contrasting, even conflicting, agendas mean that filmmakers cannot be expected to tick all of the boxes required to enable a history film to be treated as 'history'. In any case, Hollywood must be allowed a reasonable degree of flexibility in terms of not allowing the historical facts to get in the way of telling a good story.

- **Does Hollywood discriminate specifically against British history?**
'Has Hollywood stolen our history?', as discussed by David Puttnam (2004) at the 2002 History and the Media Conference held at the Institute of Historical Research, London, remains an enduring topic for debate. Targeting principally American audiences, naturally Hollywood tells American-centred stories, even if no country's history, even that of the USA, has remained safe from creative Hollywood rewrites. For Freeman (2009a: 9): 'Hollywood's indifference to much of the past, partially stemmed from, and has been intertwined with, an indifference to the sensibilities of other nations and cultures as well as, for much of its existence, an indifference to the sensibilities of the non-white populations of America.'
- **Does Hollywood discriminate specifically against 'history'?**
In reality, the problem might be dismissed as merely a product of the Hollywood system. After all, there are many novelists who welcomed the money for their book's film rights but then complained that the film script bore little or no resemblance to the original manuscript.

Conclusion

Joining in the debates about Hollywood dramatics and history prompted by *Mississippi Burning, The Economist* (1989: 93) articulated the growing urgency of what had proved a long-running issue:

> What is an artist's responsibility to the historical record when he is using the entertainment media to convey his ideas? The question has been asked at least since Shakespeare's time; but now that television and films are fast displacing books as the chief sources of information, it has become more vexing.

Over two decades on, the fundamental problem remains. Indeed, today even more people watch history feature films and television mini-series than read history books. The question of film as history is now very much on the agenda for academic historians within and outside Britain. If nothing else, ongoing controversies have forced a growing number of historians to revisit the merits of existing ways of presenting the past, and particularly to appraise film critically as an acceptable alternative. Traditionally, empirically-based written histories have set the norm for the discipline of history, even discouraging the view within academia that there was any other method of adequately understanding and presenting the past. As Rosenstone (2006: 150) complained, 'criticizing the Hollywood historical film can be a kind of reflex action among academics'. Nor is this attitude confined to academia, as evidenced by the manner in which controversies sparked off by history films often spill over into the media, politics and the public consciousness.

Conceding that Hollywood's take on the past often conflicts with accepted notions of 'history', Rosenstone sees film still as providing an agreed way forward given the way in which history films have already changed the way we see and present the past. For those exploring new ways of doing and presenting history in an increasingly visual digital age, film offers one way of bringing – to quote Rosenstone (2006: 3, 158, 160; 2007a: 13–18) – 'the practice of history kicking and screaming into the twenty-first century'. In this vein, Champion (2003: 155) fears that fellow historians, though adept at exposing Hollywood's historical errors, have missed the bigger picture:

> One of the commonly-expressed anxieties about such error-strewn work is that such faulty representation of the past will mislead the viewer in to holding inaccurate beliefs about the past. This may be fair, but it is also premised upon a recognition that the medium of film is a powerful one. Repeatedly to dismiss it as an inadequate and improper medium for the 'serious' business of scholars is to ignore a resource that is now a dominant cultural form.

As Rosenstone warned, there is the risk that Hollywood's historical films will not only challenge written history but even replace it unless historians acknowledge, explore and exploit the presentational power of film. In particular, as argued by James McPherson (1990: 27) and Richard Bernstein (1989), does it matter if some of the historical details are wrong but 'the underlying meaning' of past events is accurate? But most historians, even those studying film, have yet to be convinced that film can deliver the same level of information and analysis as a written history. Thus, Chapman (2007) welcomed Rosenstone's *History on Film/Film on History* as 'an intellectually stimulating and even provocative read', but was not converted:

> Received wisdoms are not always wrong. A decade ago, when the postmodernist critique of history was at its height, this book would probably have been accorded more currency than it will now. I cannot help but feel, however, that methodologically it re-treads old

ground (much of it trodden by Rosenstone himself) rather than offering a genuinely new 'take' on the subject.

Clearly, the long-running debate about history films as 'history' looks set to continue, especially as future Hollywood releases are guaranteed to follow *Braveheart*, *U-571* and *The King's Speech* in prompting comment and criticism from historians, among others, about their presentation of the past.

Robert Allan Rosenstone (1936–): Select Bibliography

Histories

1969:   *Crusade of the Left: the Lincoln battalion in the Spanish Civil War* (rep.1980)
1975   *Romantic Revolutionary: a biography of John Reed*
1982   '*Reds* as History', *Reviews in American History*
1988   'History in Images/Images in History: reflections on the possibility of really putting history onto film', *American Historical Review*
1988   *Mirror in the Shrine: American encounters with Meiji Japan*
1992   'Walker: the dramatic film as historical truth', *Film Historia*
1992   '*JFK*: Historical Fact/Historical Film', *American Historical Review*
1995   *Visions of the Past: the challenge of film to our idea of history*
1999   'Reel History – With Missing Reels?', *Perspectives*
2000   'Oliver Stone as Historian', in R.B. Toplin (ed.), *Oliver Stone's USA*
2002   'The visual media and historical knowledge', in L. Kramer and S. Maza (eds.), *A Companion to Western Historical Thought*
2004   'Confessions of a Postmodern (?) Historian', *Rethinking History*
2006   *History on Film/Film on History*
2007   'Space for the bird to fly', in K. Jenkins, S. Morgan and A. Munslow (eds.), *Manifestos for History*
2009   'What's a nice historian like you doing in a place like this?', *Rethinking History*

Historical novels

2002   *The Man who Swam into History*
2003   *King of Odessa: a novel of Isaac Babel*
2010   *Red Star, Crescent Moon: a Muslim–Jewish love story*

→

Edited/co-edited histories

1994   (with Bryant Simon and Moshe Sluhovsky) 'Experiments in narrating histories: a workshop', *Perspectives*

1995   'The Historical Film', *Film Historia*

1995   *Revisioning History: film and the construction of a new past*

2004   (with Alun Munslow) *Experiments in Rethinking History*

2007   (with Richard Francaviglia and Jerry Rodnitzky) *Lights, Camera, History: portraying the past in film*

2012   (with Constantin Parvulescu) *The Blackwell Companion to Historical Film* (in press)

10
Philippa Gregory: The Historical Novelist

Reviewing Philippa Gregory's *The White Queen* (2009), Kate Saunders (2009) recognised that 'at the moment, we can't seem to get enough of the Tudors, and this is largely due to Gregory: *The Other Boleyn Girl* (televised and filmed) was hugely popular and widely imitated'. Likewise, John Guy (2009: 58) of the University of Cambridge, one of Britain's leading Tudor scholars, admitted that the present-day fascination for the Tudors owed much to Gregory's historical novels. *The White Queen*, though in fact offering a prequel to the Tudor period, confirmed Gregory's popularity on both sides of the Atlantic, presenting the past through bestselling historical novels offering 'a delectable mélange of history, fiction and female feuding' (Donahue 2008). In this vein, *The White Queen* raised the question of whether Gregory could do for the Plantagenets what she has done for the Tudors, that is, to spawn what Donahue (2009b) described in *USA Today* as 'a fertile entertainment cottage industry' capturing the attention of readers, television viewers and cinemagoers. Naturally David Starkey saw things rather differently. For Starkey (quoted, Mustich 2009; 2001: 12–13), the Tudors' enduring appeal derives from 'the sheer impress' of leading personalities and present-day recognition that 'the 16th century is the central century in English history'.

In fact, any explanation of the Tudor dynasty's present-day visibility on both sides of the Atlantic must range more widely, such as to acknowledge Gregory's contribution alongside Starkey's television series and books, the popular histories of Antonia Fraser and Alison Weir, television's *The Tudors*, and Hollywood films. Nor should the impact of other historical novelists, like C.J. Sansom, the writer of crime novels set in Henry VIII's reign; Suzannah Dunn, the author of *The Queen of Subtleties: a novel of Anne Boleyn* (2004) and *The Confession of Katherine Howard*

(2010); and Hilary Mantel, be overlooked. Indeed, following the award of the Man Booker Prize in October 2009 Mantel's *Wolf Hall*, centred upon Thomas Cromwell's rise to power under Henry VIII, joined *The White Queen* in Britain's top-ten fiction charts. By the close of the year *Wolf Hall* had sold over 208,000 hardback copies. Over 316,000 copies were sold in 2010 when the book was released in paperback.

Despite the continued prominence of Tudor history in schools and universities, a growing number of people draw their knowledge of the Tudor period directly from historical novels, television documentaries and Hollywood films. Hitherto, historical novels, though attracting increased academic interest as literature, have been largely ignored by nature of history-type publications – exceptions include those by Sam Merry (1994), Jerome de Groot (2009a: 217–25; 2010) and Beverley Southgate (2009) – even if they must figure in any discussion about public history.

Historical Novels as a Genre

Overviewing the history of the relationship between history and fiction from classical antiquity through Shakespeare to the present day, Southgate (2009: x, 1) concluded that the linkage has always been problematic, occasionally turbulent. Traditionally the two genres came to be seen as mutually exclusive opposites, given historical fiction's nature as an oxymoron. Indeed, historians, pointing to the disclaimer printed in novels to the effect that any resemblance to actual events, places or persons, living or dead, is entirely coincidental, defined and defended their subject primarily by reference to history's 'virtue of *not* being fictional', particularly following its Rankean-influenced professionalisation. As Schama (1993: 25) recorded, 'the "professionals" got on with the "serious work"' of history, leaving the general reader to historical novelists, filmmakers, and so on. Like literature specialists, historians treated historical fiction as a disreputable genre – to quote Melvyn Bragg (quoted, D. Wallace 2005: 227), it was 'the genre that dare not speak its name' – offering 'vulgar fiction, impure history' (Rehberger 1995: 59).

For historians, the prime problem centred upon the way in which historical novelists were viewed as following Sir Walter Scott in prioritising rose-tinted stories and invented mythologies over historical standards. Following on from chapter 7, much historical fiction is critiqued also as a form of 'What if?' writing in that the fictional elements never actually occurred. However, during recent decades historical novels, like counterfactual histories, have enjoyed a renaissance, regained gravitas following a transformation in their historical and literary standing, attracted a growing global audience on both sides of the Atlantic, achieved strong sales and library lending totals, and gained literary prizes. Thus, 2010 saw the introduction of the £25,000 Walter Scott prize for historical fiction and the HA/*BBC History Magazine* 'Young Quills' award for children's historical fiction. Also in 2010 *History Today* broke with tradition to begin reviewing historical novels. Inevitably, questions have been raised, such as by Derek Wilson (1999: 44–5), about whether academic historians and historical novelists are still as different from each other, as argued by Edmond de Goncourt, the nineteenth-century French writer: 'Historians tell the story of the past, novelists the story of the present.' Unsurprisingly, postmodernists have been to the fore in this debate.

What is a Historical Novel?

Founded in 1997, the Historical Novel Society (HNS) has proved instrumental in enhancing the profile of historical novels. Like any historical or literary genre, there are problems of definition, but the Historical Novel Society (n.d) adopted a fairly broad approach, even including counterfactual histories (chapter 7):

> To be deemed historical (in our sense), a novel must have been written at least fifty years after the events described, or have been written by someone who was not alive at the time of those events (who therefore approaches them only by research). We also consider the following styles of novel to be historical fiction for our purposes: alternate histories (e.g. Robert Harris' *Fatherland*), pseudo-histories (e.g. Umberto Eco's *Island of the Day Before*), time-slip novels (e.g. Barbara Erskine's *Lady of Hay*), historical fantasies (e.g. Bernard Cornwell's King Arthur trilogy) and multiple-time novels (e.g. Michael Cunningham's *The Hours*).

Alternatively, the Walter Scott prize specified a 60-year period. Despite providing useful working definitions, these rubrics raise serious questions for historians, most notably regarding, say, the proposed time limits as compared to the British archives' 30-year (projected 20-year) rule, the extent to which novelists adhere to historical methodology, and the acceptability of categories listed in the second sentence.

Generally speaking, historical fiction reflects three key elements: the genre's conventions; the balance between historical research and imaginative writing; and the author's attitudes.

The Genre's Conventions

As indicated by the HNS's definition, the genre's conventions prove relatively flexible, except that novels must focus upon the past. As a result, the genre embraces a diverse group of sub-genres, ranging on the one hand from serious, well-researched novels, like those written by A.S. Byatt and Hilary Mantel, to, on the other hand, bodice-rippers and Mills and Boon-type books paying little or no attention to history except in the sense of being set in the past. Moreover, Julian Barnes and Rose Tremain, among others, have moved the historical novel on beyond its conventional boundaries – to quote Philippa Gregory (2006) – 'with experiments in material, style, and psychological immediacy'.

The Balance between Historical Research and Imaginative Writing

The success of historical novelists in exploring and offering a convincing re-creation of past lives and times proves in part a function of their historical knowledge and understanding, especially as informed by research. In practice, the amount of research might vary from virtually nothing to in-depth study conducted over several years. Indeed, novels might have a stronger research base than that of some scholarly histories. Much depends on the priority attached by novelists to historical accuracy, as well as upon their skills in discovering and using sources, particularly the extent to which they are equipped and willing to adopt an informed and critical approach towards the evidence.

Even so, the research process must be treated as a means to an end, not an end in itself, as stressed by Kate Pullinger (2008):

> We've all had the experience of reading a novel where the research is too evident on the pages, where the writer feels compelled to jam in every last detail about what kind of buttons that regiment wore on their jackets and where, in fact, those buttons were made, and what, exactly, was the correct way to polish them. It's as though the writer is thinking, I took 10 years to learn all this stuff, so I'm going to damn well share it with you.

Echoing such advice, Sarah Bower (2006: 1), when co-ordinating editor of the *Historical Novels Review*, recalled a seduction scene ruined by detailed descriptions of the clothing being removed by the seducer:

> Historical novelists must remember they are novelists first and foremost, for whom history serves merely as a prop, a source of plots and

characters and intriguing curiosities. If the past is another country, historical novelists are not so much the tour guides as the PR people who create the alluring adverts which beckon us in.

The Authors' Attitudes

Like other presenters, historical novelists are influenced by a wide range of prejudices and assumptions. However, unlike historians, for whom the objectivity/subjectivity issue remains an enduring focus, historical novelists are recognised as presenting a subjective authorial interpretation of the past, even following Walter Scott – his Waverley novels helped invent and popularise Scottish nationalist mythologies – to propagate a present-day message.

Historical Fiction as Literature

In October 1982 the Australian writer, Thomas Keneally, won the £10,000 Booker McConnell Prize for *Schindler's Ark*. Awarded to fiction written in English, this well-established literary award, now called the Man Booker Prize, attracts a high media profile, impacts upon the public imagination, transforms literary reputations, and possesses considerable marketing power.

Unsurprisingly, the announcement sparked off the usual controversies regarding the subjectivity of literary judgements. For example, was Keneally's book about Oskar Schindler's efforts to save Polish Jews from Nazi Germany's genocidal policies better than other shortlisted titles like William Boyd's *The Ice Cream War*? But there were more fundamental questions. For example, did the award, following on from the previous year's success of Salman Rushdie's *Midnight's Children*, signal an emerging recognition of historical novels as literature, given the generally low esteem traditionally attached to this genre? Also, what did the book's avowedly fictional nature contribute to debates about historical novels as 'history'?

Reporting the award in *The Times*, Philip Howard (1982) claimed that Keneally's book was 'not really a novel at all', but rather 'a brilliantly detailed piece of historical reporting' best categorised as 'faction' combining the results of in-depth research with the novelist's imaginative reconstruction of the past. Indeed, Isabel Raphael (1982) questioned whether the book was eligible for a fiction prize:

> But is it a novel? ... I don't believe it is a novel at all. It lacks the novelist's eye to look deep into characters and the novelist's art to

bring them to life … I looked in vain for that flash of imagination and style that would … lift a workmanlike piece of reporting into a work of literature.

Praising its literary qualities, John Carey (quoted, Howard 1982), the prize panel chair and Professor of English at the University of Oxford, acknowledged that *Schindler's Ark* raised interesting questions about the borderline between fact and fiction: 'Of course, history is always a kind of fiction.' Nor did Keneally's (1982: 9–10) 'Author's Note' appease the critics:

> To use the texture and devices of a novel to tell a true story is a course which has frequently been followed in modern writing. It is the one I have chosen to follow here … I have attempted to avoid all fiction, though, since fiction would debase the record … Most exchanges and conversations, and all events, are based on the detailed recollections of the *Schindlerjuden* (Schindler Jews), of Schindler himself, and of other witnesses to Oskar's acts of outrageous rescue.

As mentioned in chapter 9, *Schindler's List* (1993), Spielberg's film based on Keneally's book, replayed this debate.

Moving forward to the 2009 Man Booker Prize, now totalling £50,000, the prominence of historical novels in the shortlist – it included A.S. Byatt's *The Children's Book* and Sarah Waters's *The Little Stranger* – yielded further evidence indicating the genre's present-day literary acceptability. Significantly, Mantel, the winning author, admitted that Keneally's *Schindler's Ark*, alongside Robert Graves's *I Claudius* (1934) and Gore Vidal's *Burr* (1973), inspired her to write a historical novel about the French Revolution at a time when the genre still possessed a problematic literary reputation. Moreover, for Mantel (quoted, Appleyard 2009), who had studied law at university, the French Revolution project proved an invaluable learning experience in terms of writing a lengthy research-based historical narrative eventually published as *A Place of Greater Safety* (1992): 'I turned myself from a person reliant on data to a person who would lean heavily on the facts, but would also apply her imagination.'

Reportedly *Wolf Hall* took around five years to complete, given Mantel's belief in historical accuracy: 'I don't believe there's a better story than the facts as they unfolded, and I think it's up to the novelist to shape the drama around those facts, not to shape the facts around the drama.' For Mantel, the major challenge was to deal with gaps in the evidence: 'I will apply my imagination and see how psychologically this might all fit together. The novelist goes on working where the biographer has to stop.' Despite denying any coded comment about today's world, Mantel's focus on domestic political manoeuvring and England's troubled relations with continental Europe provided scope for readers to draw their own contemporary parallels.

Historical Fiction as History

Generally speaking, academic historians ignore historical fiction. Few historical novels, if any, are reviewed by academic journals, let alone cited by academic historians, except to attract negative, even rude, comments. As James Goodman (2002: 503) remarked:

> Historians are not, by and large, interested in what most interests novelists: the sound of words, imagery, the shape of the story, voice. They approach fiction no differently than they approach history, discussing what the novelist got right and what he or she got wrong, the analytic ends but not the literary means, the content but not the form.

Typically Wilentz (2001: 38) complained that the 'renewed rage for historical fiction has produced ... books long on knowingness and minutiae and postmodern sampling, but only rarely containing any historical ideas of note'. Starkey (2010) has proved even more dismissive: 'The wonder of history is that you have to do it by the rules, and the rules are rigorous. You can only use what has survived in the great wastepaper basket of the past, whereas in historical fiction, you can invent anything. It's rather pointless.'

Clearly Starkey had Gregory's novels in mind when launching his well-publicised attack on feminised accounts of Henry VIII. Treating the Tudor period as 'a history of white males', the real power players, Starkey (quoted, Hironson 2009; quoted, Purvis 2009) stressed the need to present Henry VIII's reign through the king, not his wives and mistresses:

> [The] modern historical novel ... is largely written about women, written by women and read by women. Stuff like *The Other Boleyn Girl*. It's a quite amazing book, in the sense that the author, Philippa Gregory, has managed to write an historical novel based on four known facts. I think it's one fact per 75 pages. [the book has over 500 pages]

Nor was Starkey (quoted, Lay 2010: 2), who dismissed the book as 'historical tosh', impressed by Mantel's *Wolf Hall*.

Despite the continued indifference, even outright hostility, of academic historians towards historical novels, the past decade or so has witnessed a rising challenge to such 'disciplinary apartheid' (Southgate 2009: 45). Indeed, in many respects, Starkey's critique implicitly recognised that historical novels have emerged as – to quote Diana Wallace (2005: 3, 227–8) – 'one of the most important genres for women writers and readers', particularly as a tool for presenting feminist messages to a wide readership. More than any other genre, the historical novel has allowed women writers to override the constraints imposed by gender, re-imagine women's history, publish consciousness-raising politically radical texts under the guise of entertainment, and reach out to a large audience.

In 2005 *Rethinking History*'s Forum on history and fiction, introduced by Hayden White, highlighted the manner in which recent developments appertaining to historical theorising and practice have transformed what John Demos (2005: 329) called the history/fiction borderland. In particular, postmodernist depictions of history as a literary discourse based on evidence of questionable reliability challenged the supposed distinction between historical and fictional narratives, thereby fostering 'a new self-reflexiveness about the constructed nature of history' (D. Wallace 2005: 227; de Groot 2010: 108–13). Pointing to the erosion of what was once a distinct boundary, Southgate (2009: 20, 173–4) argued that today history and fiction have numerous meeting points, even becoming 'inseparably twinned'.

More recently, in 2009, when speaking at a conference on 'Talking Books – Novel History' at Birkbeck College's Institute for the Humanities, Joanna Bourke (2009a; 2009b: 54–5) admitted that as an academic historian she saw herself as sharing with historical novelists, like her fellow speakers, Sarah Dunant and Hilary Mantel, the fundamental problem of presenting the past as accurately as possible. After all, both academic historians and serious historical novelists rely upon extensive research as well as informed speculation to interpret across gaps in the evidence about something which is 'other' and unknown. Nor, Bourke claimed, could either grouping avoid viewing the past through the prism of the present.

Bourke's supportive views remain untypical of the profession as a whole, but over time a growing number of academic historians – examples include Saul David (*Zulu Hart*, 2009), Simon Schama (*Dead Certainties*, 1991) and Richard Slotkin (*The Crater*, 1980; *Abe: a novel of the young Lincoln*, 2000) – have used historical novels to present the past. Despite admitting that they were different genres – 'The truth the novel seeks is poetic rather than historiographical' – Slotkin (2005: 222, 225, 229, 231) stressed their mutually supportive nature, as evidenced by the manner in which he wrote *The Crater* (1980), a historical novel set in the American Civil War, alongside a scholarly history entitled *Fatal Environment* (1985). Following this pattern thereafter, Slotkin discovered that writing historical fiction proved 'a valuable adjunct' to his work as a historian, most notably enabling the coverage of people, like black soldiers, poor whites and Pennsylvanian coal miners in the American Civil War, lacking sufficient evidence for him to tell their story as a historian. For Slotkin, historical novels left writers and readers free to explore alternative possibilities, putting flesh on the bare bones of history. Significantly, Slotkin (2005: 222, 229), albeit acknowledging the risks posed to his professional credentials, refuses to view his historical novels as offering an inferior presentation of the American past:

> There is no reason why, in principle, a novel may not have a research basis as good or better than that of a scholarly history; and no reason why, in principle, a novelist's portrayal of a past may not be truer and more accurate than that produced by a scholarly historian.

Even so, Slotkin (2005: 232–3) has no desire for his novels to be read as factual histories, in spite of his willingness to defend his interpretation of events on scholarly grounds.

Philippa Gregory

Possessing a lengthy track record of writing well-researched, compellingly readable and commercially successful historical fiction, Philippa Gregory is represented as a 'popular' (D. Wallace 2005: 142–59, 187) historical novelist publishing in the family saga and erotic historical sub-genres. British sales of 2.57 million books meant that she occupied 72nd place in the list of bestselling authors of the 'Noughties' (*Daily Telegraph* 2010). However, for Saunders (2009), Gregory, though capable of winning such awards as the £10,000 Parker Romantic Novel of the Year prize in 2002 for *The Other Boleyn Girl*, is deemed unlikely to reach a Booker shortlist: 'This sort of historical fiction is about historical characters falling in love and having lots of sex, against a backdrop of the livelier and better-dressed events in history.' By contrast, Mantel's *Wolf Hall*, the winner of the 2009 Booker and 2010 Walter Scott prizes, is seen as offering a more serious take on the Tudor period, concerned not with the details of Henry VIII's sex life but rather with Thomas Cromwell's attempts to secure, use and retain political power.

Born in Nairobi, Kenya, in 1954, Gregory grew up in Bristol. Following a brief period working as a journalist, she went to the University of Sussex to study English. Whereas GCE 'A'-level history proved dull, Gregory was so inspired by her first-year history option that she switched subjects (Wignall 2004; Gregory 2008c): 'It was such a powerful experience that, really, it transformed my life. I was looking for something that would explain everything – I was that kind of earnest young woman! – and history seemed to be able to do that.'

Inspired by E.P. Thompson's *The Making of the English Working Class*, Gregory (1992) called herself a Marxist and joined the university's *Das Kapital* reading group. Subsequently, Gregory, who returned to the media briefly after graduation, enrolled for a doctorate on eighteenth-century popular fiction at the University of Edinburgh. Having successfully completed her doctorate, a dearth of academic opportunities led Gregory (quoted Zigmond 2003: 4; D. Wallace 2005: 187) 'to think of other ways of earning a living', and particularly to build upon her historical education and media experience to become a full-time writer focusing principally upon historical fiction.

Prior to publication, the British and US rights to *Wideacre* (1987), her first novel, sold for around £500,000 (Gregory 1987). In turn, the book's overnight success – it reached the *New York Times* bestseller list – reaffirmed Gregory's career choice. Further historical fiction followed – *The Other Boleyn Girl* (2001) sold over 800,000 copies – alongside contemporary novels, children's books, and an occasional academic publication (Gregory 1996; 2005). Media work has included television adaptations of *A Respectable Trade* (1998) and *The Other Boleyn Girl* (2003); appearances on BBC Radio 4's *Round Britain Quiz*, Channel 4's *Time Team* and BBC television's *Celebrity Mastermind*; and book reviewing for the press. During 2009 Gregory joined other historical novelists, including Mantel, and academic historians, like Guy and Starkey, to contribute to public lecture series mounted by the Historic Royal Palaces/*History Today* at Hampton Court Palace and the British Library to mark the 500th. anniversary of Henry VIII's accession to the throne. Also in 2009, Gregory was the University of Edinburgh's alumna of the year.

Gregory's Methodology

Acknowledging the popularity and improving scholarly quality of historical fiction, Bourke (2009a) urged historians to adopt a more positive attitude towards the genre, and particularly to consider what could be learnt from historical novelists about engaging with an audience. Within this context, what can be said about Gregory's method of presenting the past?

* Prioritising historical accuracy
  Although historical novelists are often accused of treating the historical record lightly, Gregory (2004: viii) believes that historical accuracy should never be sacrificed for the sake of a good story: 'the history has to come first'. Espousing 'a total commitment to history', Gregory (n.d. c) is on record as expressing concern about inaccuracies and distortions in historical novels, like Hugh Walpole's *Judith Paris* (1931), or television's *The Tudors*. Believing in the need to offer readers an intellectual challenge as well as entertainment, Gregory (2004: vii) claimed that:

> A good historical novel tells of characters who are entirely congruent with the known conditions of their time, and yet sufficiently independent in thought and action to stand out from the crowd, and for the modern reader to identify with them. They are rounded characters because they exist in a recognisable time and place and these circumstances work on them.

As a result, Gregory (2008b) adjudges it necessary that she 'should know more as an historian than I tell as a novelist' if readers were to feel as if they were living through the events narrated in any book. Drawing upon her postgraduate education as well as the example of such writers as Georgette Heyer and Anya Seton, Gregory (quoted, Wignall 2004) views her preparations for presenting a novel as *equivalent* to academic research, often taking twice as long as writing the manuscript: 'I read everything. I go to museums, I visit the places involved, I even know about the weather.' Thus, researching the life of Mary Boleyn for *The Other Boleyn Girl* 'was very much detective work reading one book after another for a reference to her, and piecing together different accounts' (Gregory 2008a):

> My Tudor books are specifically set in a place and a time, and that is accurate to the historical record when that is available. Sometimes, I can base a scene in the novel almost exactly on an account by a contemporary eye-witness. I took great pleasure in the colour of Mary Boleyn's dress at a masque since I had seen the accounts from the royal wardrobe that told me she was wearing green.

More importantly, Gregory acknowledges the need to treat sources critically:

> The historical research is a difficult quantity, since it is no more an objective account of the past than the novel that will be based, unsteadily, on it. It is no coincidence that our prejudiced opinions of women of the Tudor court are drawn from the devoted Victorian historians who were the first translators and publishers of original Tudor documents, but were deeply committed to their own view of women as either saints or whores.

Traditionally, historical novels, though containing a range of para-texts, have included neither a bibliography nor footnotes. Gregory (n.d. b) has no desire to destroy the illusion of the novel, let alone to pose as a scholarly historian, but remains anxious to influence the manner in which readers engage with and interpret her text by establishing that – to quote from *The White Queen*'s author blurb – 'her love of history and commitment to historical accuracy are the hallmarks of her writing', that is her books, based on solid research, are written by a historian. Thus, Gregory includes author's notes articulating issues relating to authenticity and imaginative writing, extracts from primary sources, bibliographies pointing readers towards sources and further reading, and a blurb informing readers about her expertise and doctorate. Additional information, including guidance for reading groups, is available on her website (http://www.philippagregory.com/). Reportedly Gregory (2008c) is considering other possibilities, like a DVD readers' guide or annotated editions citing sources. Hitherto, she has avoided footnotes, such as included in Katherine Christensen's *A Rib from Eve* (2007) or Adam Thorpe's *Hodd* (2009). More recently, her efforts to link up with readers have been reinforced by the use of twitter and an iPhone app for launching *The White Queen*.

- **Balancing fact and fiction**
  Gregory's (2008b) first rule is 'that it has to work as a novel, as well as be absolutely based on the history':

> The broad narrative of the history imposes the story of the novel, all I can choose is when to start and stop. The only time I invent an occasion in the life of an historical character is when we simply don't know what they were doing – and then I choose the most likely explanation.

As a result, much depends on Gregory's skills of imagination, empathy and informed speculation to write an engaging text accommodating history and fiction in an appropriate manner. In practice, the precise balance varies from book to book and from character to character therein, but most of 'what goes on in people's heads is invented, as it must be' (Gregory n.d. a):

> By and large the fiction fills in the gaps of the known historical record and brings it to life. In a story such as that of Elizabeth I when we know so much about what she thought and did the fiction animates the story that we know ... In a story like that of Mary Boleyn we know only the slimmest outline and the fiction fills in the gaps.

When writing *The Other Boleyn Girl*, Gregory (quoted, Blake n.d.) found gaps concerning, say, Mary's date of birth and relationship with her first husband, William Carey, but discovered a letter written by Mary revealing her 'concealed rivalry and resentment towards her sister': 'That letter gave me the key to Mary's character, as well as historical documentation for her passion and resentment.'

Recognising the risk of meticulously researched novels proving dull, even unreadable, Gregory (2008b) uses research findings only 'in service to the story-telling'. Thus, information about, say, table settings, food, and entertainment was included only 'if it really helps to set the scene, give the atmosphere, animate and illustrate the scene ... and ... if it adds to the understanding and enjoyment of the reader'.

- **Making Britain's past as real as the present**
  When asked to explain her popularity, Gregory (2008c; quoted, Ramaswamy 2008) pointed to the way in which she approached past events from 'the side of the stage', that is, relating a well-known story, such as the reign of Henry VIII, from an alternative perspective: 'people find that exciting, it makes the story new again'. In particular, her fictional biographies focus upon engaging but hitherto largely ignored female heroines, like Mary Boleyn in *The Other Boleyn Girl* or Elizabeth Woodville in *The White Queen*.

  Bringing the Tudors 'to glorious, soapy life' (Saunders 2006), Gregory's historical novels have struck a chord with a popular (largely) female audience. Tales of love, seduction, rape, incest, and so on have become Gregory's hallmarks. As Gregory (quoted, Blake 2009: 183) observed, the undoubted audience appeal of the erotic historical sub-genre is reinforced by sex's perceived significance for any story line focused upon power in both public and private life:

> I don't see sex as being different to any other activity and it's worth writing about because it sometimes works as a metaphor for the relationship. It can be an act of power or perhaps an act of absolute love, unity and tenderness, so you can show that.

• **Using contemporary language in dialogue**
Reviewing D.J. Taylor's *Kept: A Victorian Mystery* (2006), Gregory (2006) found the book a fascinating page-turner but asked why a modern author wrote in 'the dialect of Past-Shire'. Tortuous and verbose sentences, well-endowed with clauses and sub-clauses, predominated. Claiming to be inspired by Jane Austen to write as clearly and simply as possible, Gregory (2008c) favours modern language for conversations because of her belief that the reproduction of past conversational patterns detracts from the storyline.

• **Writing in the first person**
Adopting a first-person narrative for the Tudor series in preference to the third-person approach favoured by most historians, Gregory (n.d. a, n.d. b) views this 'very immediate style' as enabling readers to get into the head of characters, like Mary Boleyn in *The Other Boleyn Girl* or Hannah Green, a young Jewish girl eavesdropping on the innermost thoughts of Mary I and Elizabeth I, in *The Queen's Fool*: 'Readers understand that the books are fiction: we cannot know what someone, dead five centuries ago, was thinking and feeling. But this style is a doorway to the imagined consciousness of the period.' Alternatively, this technique allowed the story line to be told from contrasting personal perspectives, such as that of Anne of Cleves, Katherine Howard and Jane Boleyn in *The Boleyn Inheritance*. This approach was replicated for a fictional Elizabethan *ménage à trois* in *The Other Queen*, with Mary, Queen of Scots, placed in the keeping of George Talbot, the Earl of Shrewsbury, and his wife, Bess of Hardwick. At the same time, Gregory (2008c; Alperin 2009) admitted that this style possessed disadvantages. Apart from viewing events from a narrow personal perspective, 'I don't have the luxury (as I would writing as an historian) to say – on the one hand, this, on the other hand, that – perhaps this is what happened. I have to write "this happens to me this morning."'

- **Presenting alternative visual pasts**
  For Gregory (2008a), each historical novel 'has only one producer, one writer, one director and one actor: all me'. By contrast, the Hollywood version of *The Other Boleyn Girl* (2008) proved a very different beast in spite of being based upon Gregory's book and using her as a histori- cal consultant (but not a scriptwriter). As Gregory (2008c) admitted, filmmakers and historical novelists have different agendas: 'I feel very strongly that the film makers have to produce their work of art, and I produce mine ... I thought the film was visually very beautiful and strongly emotional – the book more complicated and thoughtful.'
  For Gregory (2008a), the film presented a new telling of the story:

  > Films, especially those with a huge budget, are bound to favour a conventional and popular view. It is assumed that the court of the king is of more interest than the house of the commoner, and undoubtedly it is a more beautiful setting ....
  >
  > My suggestion in the novel is that the interesting story after the rivalry, is Mary's choice to be an ordinary Tudor wife and mother. The film, however, focuses on the drama rather than the humdrum and ordinary.

  According to Gregory the story of Mary Boleyn as a woman who went against the social norm to live an ordinary life 'could be told only in a novel': 'The film is on the big screen, the novel is on the small page.'

- **Underpinning historical novels with a present-day message**
  Commenting about the ability of historical novelists to treat the past as a foreign country, Gregory (2006; quoted, Blake n.d.) concluded that 'I don't think one could write a novel about any period without reflecting on one's own time.' Indeed, far from representing herself as a historical novelist detached from contemporary concerns, Gregory (n.d. c; quoted, Alperin 2009) prefers to present herself as 'a gritty radical historian' inspired by E.P. Thompson, the historian responsible for introducing her to the English tradition of dissent viewing events 'with an opposite prejudice'. Pointing to *Wideacre*, Gregory (1992) claimed that 'everything I learned from Thompson is in that novel'. Disclaiming any attempt to present a definitive history, Gregory (2005: 242) admitted that her books offered 'just a view ... just the author's view. And it is a prejudiced, biased view – just like any history book.'
  In her doctoral thesis, Gregory recorded the perceived educa- tional utility of eighteenth-century historical fiction to propagate

contemporary messages (D. Wallace 2005: 193). In this vein, Gregory (2008c; quoted, Mackenzie 1991) has always seen her fictional writing as a vehicle for articulating her political beliefs, most notably concerning human rights in general and feminism in particular: 'my politics which are pro-women and pro-the common people means that I write novels which are not stuffy or snobbish but engage with real people's difficulties in a very difficult world'. Inevitably, Gregory views her strong focus on women as serving not only to make their history visible but also to challenge the masculinist nature of history. Pointing to *The Other Queen*'s focus on Mary I, Gregory (2008c; n.d. b) claimed that 'Mary has been treated very badly by the historical record, largely, I think because of the prejudices of male historians against women in power.' Unsurprisingly, Gregory has proved very critical of Henry VIII. Despite recognising the political imperatives imposed by the need for an heir, Gregory (2008c), a self-proclaimed republican, argued that over the course of his reign Henry VIII learned tyranny and increasingly harboured paranoid fantasies: 'His subsequent career taught him that he could execute people who displeased him and that nobody would stand against him effectively.'

Three brief case studies follow, outlining Gregory's purposive approach to historical fiction.

The Politics of the Wideacre Trilogy

Covering the period between 1760 and 1805, the Wideacre trilogy – *Wideacre* (1987), *The Favoured Child* (1989) and *Meridon* (1990) – appears at first sight to represent a typical family saga. Centred upon the Lacey family's ancestral estate at Wideacre Hall in Sussex, in fact the series traced three generations of the family through its women: Beatrice Lacey, her daughter Julia, and granddaughter Meridon (*née* Sarah Lacey).

Covers depicting provocative female figures alongside the text's inclusion of graphic scenes of sex, rape and incest meant that readers, as noted by Howard Jacobson (1987), could easily mistake individual titles as downmarket bodice-rippers. However, this would be misleading, as emphasised by Diana Wallace (2005: 186–7):

> Their popular appearance belies the political content of these texts and the seriousness of their engagement with history ... the ostensible artlessness of Gregory's texts conceals both her commitment to historical accuracy and the ways in which her texts subvert the conventions of the popular forms they borrow, smuggling in radical politics under the guise of entertainment.

According to Wallace (2005: 187), Gregory presented an eighteenth-century storyline underpinned by a present-day Marxist–feminist critique of the economic individualism of Margaret Thatcher's premiership (1979–90):

> This critique is at odds with both the conservative sexual politics of the typical family saga and the glamorisation of female suffering in the typical erotic historical ... Gregory presents the past as the political and economic prehistory of the present and connects a Marxist analysis of the growth of capitalism to a feminist analysis of the relationship between women, property and ownership.

The series highlighted both the sexual exploitation of women and the discrimination resulting from their exclusion from property ownership through primogeniture. Thus, Julia Lacey complained that her husband 'owned me as surely as he owned ... my land, my horse, my little box of trinkets, my gowns, even my own body' (Gregory 1989: 556). Subsequently Meridon moved on from complaining about the loss of common land through the agricultural revolution to articulate concern about the erasure of the history of women: 'the worst theft of all was to take someone's history from them' (Gregory 1991: 490).

Significantly, in the final book, Meridon opted for communality in preference to individualism. Rejecting a return to Wideacre Hall, she opted to live in the village with Will Tyacke, an eighteenth-century character used by Gregory (1991: 546) to critique twentieth-century Thatcherism:

> I don't think people can be happy unless they are well-fed and well housed and have a chance at learning ... And you'll never do that by opening the market place and saying it's all free to those with money to buy it. Some things are too important to be traded in a free market. Some things people should have as a right.

Subsequently, Gregory continued to engage with the past by exploring theories of political economy impacting adversely upon 'the people'. Thus, she critiqued Britain's responsibility for colonialism in *Earthly Joys* (1998) and *Virgin Earth* (1999) and the slave trade in *A Respectable Trade* (1995). For Gregory (quoted, E. Wallace 2000: 237), 'it is still important in historical terms that there is a recognition of that injustice'.

Presenting Mary Boleyn as a Feminist Heroine

Gregory's Tudor series comprises six books. Despite being set in the reign of Henry VIII, *The Wise Woman* (1992) is not normally categorised as part of this extremely popular series, whose first book, *The Other Boleyn Girl* (2001), remains Gregory's most successful book to date in terms of sales, visibility and impact. Providing a strong foundation for the series, the book was adapted for both a 2003 BBC television programme featuring Natascha McElhone and Jodhi May and a 2008 Hollywood film starring Scarlet Johansson, Natalie Portman and Kristin Scott Thomas.

Rescuing her from the footnotes of history books, *The Other Boleyn Girl* told the hitherto largely unknown story of Mary Boleyn, who became Henry VIII's mistress before making way for her sister, Anne. As Gregory (quoted, Chrisafis 2002) pointed out, Mary's story was that of 'a woman who overcame tyranny and patriarchy to dominate the royal court and eventually marry for love'. For Gregory, the choice of heroine resulted from research about the Tudor navy and the discovery that Henry VIII had named one of his ships *Mary Boleyn*. In turn, the research process transformed Gregory's (2008c; Blake n.d.) image of Mary: 'I started my research fearing that she was manipulative and overly romanticised by the historical record but the more I found out about her the more I admired her.'

Presenting readers with what she described as an 'unconventional take' on the public and private persona of Henry VIII, Gregory (2008a) acknowledged the present-day considerations prompting her to foreground Mary Boleyn as a feminist heroine standing up to the demands of a masculinist society:

> My own interest in women's history and my aversion to English snobbery led me to write *The Other Boleyn Girl* as a triumph of the common sense of Mary Boleyn over the ambition of her sister Anne ... The idea that a woman could be sexually experienced and not a 'bad' woman is a modern one .... Mary Boleyn ... could only be a heroine to a feminist, radical historian.

Focusing upon the dramatic possibilities offered by the rivalry of two sisters for the king's affections, Gregory forced readers to decide who was the real heroine, Anne or the other Boleyn girl? As indicated by the book's title, Gregory foregrounded Mary 'as she slowly realises that there is an interesting life to be had outside the glittering circle of the court, and this is both her realisation and also a revelation to the reader'. For Gregory (quoted, Blake n.d.): 'Mary gets what she wants because she makes what we think is the right choice – but the Tudors wouldn't have thought it the right choice when she decides to marry for love.' In the event, Anne gained only a pyr-rhic victory. Thus, she won the crown, but lost her head.

Another Powerful Woman in *The White Queen*

In 2009 *The White Queen* ushered in a new series focused on the Plan-tagenets. Going back to the pre-Tudor period, Gregory (2008c) discovered yet another family with an interesting story to be told: 'they are like the Tudors but much badder [*sic*], conspiratorial and in constant competition for the throne'. Taking readers back to an England divided between the Lancastrians and Yorkists, the book provided the usual quota of political rivalries, family tensions and sex plus a touch of witchcraft.

Once again, Gregory (n.d. d) concentrated upon 'the truly wonderful women' standing behind the great men of the period but hidden from history. Widowed by the War of the Roses, *The White Queen*'s heroine, Elizabeth Woodville, secretly married the Yorkist King Edward IV to become Queen of England:

> I am interested in powerful women. I think she will fascinate modern women in the same way that many historical women strike a chord: despite so many changes in the world, women are still trying to find happiness, manage their children, seek advantage, and avoid the persecution of misogynists. As women of any time, we have a lot in common. Despite the amazing advances in the rights of women (and I am so grateful for these myself), the struggle for women's freedom, independence, and the right to exercise power goes on.

As a Lancastrian, Elizabeth's position was far from secure. Thus, *The White Queen* centred upon Elizabeth's attempts to protect both her posi-tion and the interests of the two princes, whose disappearance from the Tower of London in 1483 challenged readers to think about where they stood regarding the guilt of Richard III.

Selling over 71,000 copies in hardback, *The White Queen* was placed in Britain's top 20 fiction titles for 2009. Over 266,000 copies were sold in 2010 when it was released in paperback; indeed, it was placed 33rd in Britain's bestsellers' list for 2010. Across the Atlantic, in August 2009 the book entered the *New York Times*'s fiction charts at second place, and remained in the top 20 titles until October. A six-book series is planned. In 2010 *The Red Queen* featured the Lancastrian Margaret Beaufort, Henry VII's mother, who spent her life determined to see him as king and then lived long enough to see her grandson inherit the throne as Henry VIII. *The Lady of the Rivers*, scheduled for publication in 2011, tells the story of Jacquetta of Luxembourg, the mother of Elizabeth Woodville.

Gregory's Audience

For over two decades Gregory has proved herself a bestselling author with a large and dedicated fan base in Britain, North America and beyond. Reportedly, her books have been published in over 60 countries. Claiming that she has always written 'to reflect my own view of the period', Gregory (n.d. c) has denied any attempt to write for a specific readership, even if sales figures suggest her sensitivity to market trends. Indeed, Gregory has acknowledged the fact that her novels benefited from being published 'at a time when people wanted a new sort of historical fiction: more realistic, more radical, more sexy, and harder edged'. In this vein, the concept of 'authentic fallacy' articulates the fact that many readers want to believe that what they are reading really happened. In particular, as Gregory (2006) asserted: 'The emergence of radical, working class and women's history gave new relevancy to the research while the return of narrative history, as told by historians such as Alison Weir, David Starkey and Simon Schama, has encouraged a readership that demands authentic historical background.' Moreover, like any historical novelist, Gregory has benefited from the cultural shift arising from history's present-day visibility and society's responsiveness to diverse representations of the past.

Lacking in-depth market research, we can only speculate about why Gregory's books have proved so phenomenally successful on both sides of the Atlantic. However, it is worth recalling that Gregory's (quoted, Alperin 2009) doctoral research investigated the hypothesis 'that what people read creates an imaginary world – it tells you what they think about the real world and what they want to think about the real world'. Anecdotal evidence, though needing to be treated with caution, offers guidance about readers' motives, which include:

- the search for a good escapist read set in the past and conforming to the predictable rhythms of present-day soap operas – during an online session conducted by Gregory (2008c) for the *Washington Post*, one contributor, based in Mobile, Alabama, praised the books 'immensely as entertainment', while another participant from Greensboro, North Carolina, claimed that Gregory's 'readable, exciting' books 'take me on a journey every time';

- **the demand for infotainment** – several other participants in this online session used Gregory's novels as a peg for raising more fundamental questions about the past, thereby highlighting the way in which such books satisfy, even encourage, a quest to acquire historical knowledge in an entertaining manner. In this vein, writing in *USA Today* Deidre Donahue (2009a) noted the impact of Gregory's novels as public history: 'Thanks to historical-fiction hits such as *The Other Boleyn Girl*, Gregory has turned millions of readers into rabid amateur historians fixated on Henry VIII's mating woes.' Unsurprisingly Gregory (quoted, Wignall 2004) welcomes reader feedback recording how her novels have provided a springboard for further study: 'A lot of people write to me to say that they got interested in history after reading one of my books';
- **the perceived contemporary appeal of messages pressed in Gregory's books** – for Carol Thurston (quoted, D. Wallace 2005: 154), historical literature acts as a kind of 'testing ground for women readers struggling to find new ways of seeing and thinking about themselves and their place in the world'. Arguably, for many readers the appeal of the Gregory brand arises from the manner in which her historical novels enable them to enter a fictional world through identification with individual characters, especially strong female characters, touching upon a range of present-day experiences central to everyday life and personal relationships. Certainly, Gregory (2004: ix; quoted, Blake n.d.) believes that *The Other Boleyn Girl*, like all her historical novels, speak directly to today's women torn between the desire to express themselves and the perceived pressures to conform:

> Any story about a woman who is confronted with a situation in which she has no power, where she has to figure out how to survive, will always be of interest to women in our society. Most women recognise the situation Mary [Boleyn] faces when she has few choices and few cards to play. The choice between your family's ambition, society's demands and your own emotional demands is a key one today.

In this sense, as stressed by de Groot (2009a: 12; 2010: 76, 96–7), Gregory's novels, though set in Britain's past, are present-day 'global texts' capable of resonating with a worldwide audience.

Of course, whereas academics might analyse in depth the content and underlying themes in Gregory's writings, there is no guarantee that readers merely seeking a good read will worry about, let alone respond to, such messages. However, Gregory's readership, like that for most historical novels (Wallace 2005: 3, 127), is assumed to be predominately female, attracted by her overt use of a feminist perspective to fictionalise the histories of women during a period when women were normally written out of history, merely footnoted, or presented in a shallow manner. Certainly, Gregory (2008c; quoted, Blake n.d.) believes that her pro-woman agenda explains her popularity with female readers.

What Makes a Good Historical Novel?

Given this book's focus on good history, what makes a good historical novel and how far does such a novel rate as 'history'? For Jenny Wormald (2008), the need is for:

> An author who takes *her* [my emphasis] subject seriously, investigates it thoroughly, understands its context, then uses *her* [my emphasis] skills to bring to life the principal players with more freedom than may be possible for historians. At its best, therefore, it can have a huge amount to offer. At worst, it is irritatingly sloppy, unnecessarily erroneous, and romantic after the fashion of Mills & Boon.

Wormald's use of 'her' was deliberate, given the fact that more women than men write historical novels (just as their readership is assumed to be mainly female). Gregory (2008c) ticks all the boxes in the first sentence of Wormald's quotation, most notably in terms of writing readable literary texts paying due regard to the historical record: 'I feel very strongly that as an historian it is my task to represent the history as accurately as I can. But as a novelist it is my job to make the story come alive.' Her writing is engaging and accessible, even to those with limited historical background. Imbued with present-day concerns and messages that women mattered in a male-dominated past, Gregory's books are characterised by, indeed renowned for, what Saunders (2009) describes as 'genteel pornography'. As 'history' her books might be deemed partial and uncertain, but as literature they offer wonderful stories about the past.

As one of Britain's most successful historical novelists, Gregory has developed a well-tried strategy for writing historical novels combining what she represents as 'well-researched history' with 'well-written fiction'. Buoyant sales, strong lending library figures, and enthusiastic responses from readers establish that this approach has worked well for over two decades in terms of presenting Gregory's version of the past to a vast audience outside academia. Generally speaking, academia has proved far less responsive, even if Diana Wallace, among others, has demonstrated that historical novels, such as those written by Gregory, merit serious critical literary attention.

By contrast, most academic historians have said little or nothing about Gregory's books – Starkey's blast was the exception that proved the rule – or, like Jenny Wormald, offered somewhat mixed messages. Despite praising the way in which *The Other Boleyn Girl* highlighted the ambitions and fears of those serving in Henry VIII's court, Wormald questioned details regarding, say, Gregory's account of the fall of Anne Boleyn because of the lack of evidence for both witchcraft and the monstrous birth of 1536. Inevitably, Jenny Wormald (2008), the author of *Mary Queen of Scots: Politics, Passion and a Kingdom Lost* (1988), took a close interest in Gregory's *The Other Queen*: 'What Gregory brings out well is the often overlooked fact that Elizabeth and her chief minister, William Cecil, contemplated finding a way of getting her (Mary) back to Scotland as queen. So the theme of "will she, won't she?" runs through the book.' On the other hand, Jenny Wormald was more critical of sketchy character development and historical inventions: 'It does not help us to get to grips with [the Earl of] Shrewsbury by having him fall in love with Mary, an entirely romantic invention. And why invent the thick, black hair that Mary certainly did not have?' Also she expressed reservations about Gregory's attempt to underpin *The Other Queen*'s historical credentials: 'There is a bibliography, but it is unsatisfactory. Omitting all recent studies of Mary seriously undermines Gregory's claim to have written a novel "heavily built on the historical record".' Revealingly, Jenny Wormald's biography of Mary was not listed therein.

Historians and Historical Novels

Popularising history, though treated more sympathetically within the historical profession, remains still a source of controversy. Fictionalising history through novels, like films, proves even more problematic. Notwithstanding continuing criticism of historical fiction for lacking an intellectual challenge, downplaying analysis and falling well short of 'history', the popularity and growing literary respectability of historical novels aimed at adults and children raises serious questions for historians. As detailed in chapter 11, Terry Deary, though best known for his 'Horrible Histories', has proved also a successful writer of children's historical fiction. Moreover, in 2009 Jacqueline Wilson, another popular children's writer, published her first historical novel, *Hetty Feather*, which was joint winner of the initial 'Young Quills' award in 2010.

Identifying significant issues for debate, the following section highlights the fact that, as with Hollywood history films, historians possess divergent views about historical novels. Key questions include:

- Should history and historical novels be treated still as either completely different (Wilentz 2001: 38; Starkey, quoted, Mustich 2009), complementary (Slotkin 2005: 222; Powell 1994: 15–16; Dunant 2009), or 'inseparably twinned' (Southgate 2009: 20)? Following Derek Wilson (1999: 45), should historians view historical novelists as allies, rather than as either saboteurs guilty of confusing readers through mixing fact and fiction, or rivals attracting higher sales and greater public visibility for their version of the past?
Just as the research of historical novelists benefits from what Dunant (2009) has described as the 'deep mining' of academic historians, so cultural and social historians treat the publications of Walter Scott and other historical novelists as primary sources reflecting the ideas and mores of their time (Merry 1994: 88–90; Southgate 2009: 7–8).
- What do historical novelists present about the past that cannot be provided by academic historians? How far can historical novelists fill gaps in the verifiable historical record, most notably by giving voice to those overlooked by academic historians or exploring people's inner experiences (Slotkin 2005: 232)?
For Mantel (2009), lack of evidence prevents historians detailing Thomas Cromwell's private life and inner thoughts, but enough material existed to enable informed speculation in *Wolf Hall*.
- Should historical novels be judged as 'history' in the same manner as academic histories, or, following Saunders (2009), be judged only as 'a form of entertainment – sometimes intellectual entertainment, mostly far less exalted'?
Bernard Cornwell (quoted, Teeman 2010), the author of the bestselling historical novels about Richard Sharpe, set in the Napoleonic Wars, disclaimed any pretensions about acting like a historian: 'I'd never be a historian. Too much responsibility to get things right.' By contrast, Mantel (2009) sees her books in part as revisionist historical texts prompting readers to think again about the past; thus, she claimed that her novels, though offering merely one version of the past, 'could be true'.
- What lessons can academic historians learn from the popularity of historical fiction, especially as the genre is no longer a niche

market? Following Bourke (2009a) and Dunant (2009), should historians investigate what historical novelists can teach them, most notably regarding methodology, imaginative writing, and engaging audiences?

Despite tending to denigrate their merits, academic historians should not underestimate the challenge of writing historical novels offering 'intellectual entertainment' (Powell 1994: 14–15; Saunders 2009);

- To what extent do historical novels serve as a form of public history, even enhancing levels of historical literacy? Alternatively, does the mix of fact and fiction characteristic of historical novels merely foster a confused and uncertain grasp of the past?

Pointing out that history speaks primarily to historians, Herbert Butterfield (1924: 23) conceded that 'everybody is not a historian; so historical fiction does the work for all the world; it fuses the past into a picture, and makes it live'. Within this context, John Sutherland (2009) claimed that historical 'fiction can't recover the past for us, but what it can do is of great importance – it defines our relationship with the past'. Antony Beevor (2009) has adopted a very different view. Deploring what he described as superficial 'histo-tainment' and 'faction-creep', he attacked historical novels for blurring fact and fiction. Paradoxically, he argued, the better the novel, the more dangerous it proved in terms of misleading readers.

- Do historical novels encourage readers to move on to discover the characters and events around which authors crafted their stories (Powell 1994: 15; Gregory 2008c; Senior 2009)?

Reportedly several historians and historical novelists – they include Bourke (2009a), Dunant (2009), Rosenstone (2004: 151) and Alison Weir (2003: 94–5) – admit being drawn initially to history through a love of historical novels. For example, Weir found history at school 'stultifyingly boring', 'a dreary succession of dates, acts and battles'. Reading historical novels opened up a new window on the past to reveal engaging personalities and stories, and led her to become 'hooked on Tudor history'. Ken Burns (n.d.), the documentary film-maker, claimed that *The Killer Angels* (1974), Michael Shaara's historical novel about the Battle of Gettysburg, inspired his television series *The Civil War* discussed in chapter 6. According to Diarmaid MacCulloch (2010: 60–2), Oxford's Professor of the History of the Church and biographer of Henry VIII and Thomas Cranmer, Mantel's 'startlingly accurate' *Wolf Hall* had encouraged him to contemplate writing a biography of Thomas Cromwell.

• What insights do historical novels provide about history's role and significance in contemporary culture?

Pointing to its role as a historical novel, historical romance fiction, television costume drama, and Hollywood film, de Groot (2009a: 12–13, 181–3) represented Gregory's *The Other Boleyn Girl* as drawing together the key themes articulated in *Consuming History*'s introduction. For de Groot, the story's multiple meanings, manifestations and uses highlighted the way in which history threaded right across contemporary popular culture in a society obsessed with the past.

Conclusion

Philippa Gregory (n.d. b) admits to being frequently approached by readers and cinemagoers about the fiction–history linkage, given the manner in which the 'historical' element – to quote David Mitchell (2010) – 'demands fidelity to the past' and the fiction part 'requires infidelity'. Inevitably, as acknowledged by David Harlan (2007: 108–23), this issue has always excited lively exchanges between historians. Overviewing recent trends in the 2005 *Rethinking History*'s Forum, Demos (2005: 329–30) claimed that the ongoing transformation in the borderland meant that 'the history/fiction boundary has never looked more interesting'. In many respects, this view is even more valid today, given claims about the rising literary and historical respectability of historical novels, surging sales thereof, the enhanced interest in public history, the vogue for counterfactual histories, and signs of a more pragmatic postmodernist dimension. Meanwhile, the enhanced historical quality and growing popularity of historical fiction are continuing to challenge existing ways of thinking about and presenting the past.

Finally, let us finish with a comment by Gregory (2005: 242), a university-trained historian with a doctorate and a historical novelist self-conscious about her practice, encouraging historians to revisit the way in which they patrol the boundaries between 'history' and fiction:

> People often ask me whether I am firstly a writer of fiction or a historian. It's an easy one to answer. I cannot help but be a story-teller, it is my way of describing the world; but I have learned to be a historian, it is my way of understanding the world. I am both.

Philippa Gregory (1954–): Select Bibliography

Historical novels: series

Wideacre trilogy, 1760s–1800s
1987   *Wideacre*
1989   *The Favoured Child*
1990   *Meridon*

Earthly Joys, seventeenth century
1998   *Earthly Joys*
1999   *The Virgin Earth*

The Tudor Court, 1485–1603
2001   *The Other Boleyn Girl*
2003   *The Queen's Fool*
2004   *The Virgin's Lover*
2005   *The Constant Princess*
2006   *The Boleyn Inheritance*
2008   *The Other Queen*

The cousins' war, late fifteenth century
2009   *The White Queen*
2010   *The Red Queen*
2011   *The Lady of the Rivers*

Projected (provisional titles)
The Kingmaker's Daughters
The White Princess
The Last Rose

Historical novels: other

1992   *The Wise Woman*
1993   *Fallen Skies*
1995   *A Respectable Trade*

11
Terry Deary: The Children's Historian

For young children as well as many older people, Terry Deary is the voice of history. As John Crace (2003) informed *Guardian* readers:

> It must niggle Simon Schama, David Starkey, Niall Ferguson *et al.* that the most popular historian in this country prefers to think of himself primarily as an entertainer rather than an academic. It must also niggle that there's a good chance that his name will mean little to most adults, though it will to their children.

For Alice Thomson (2007), 'Terry Deary's "Horrible Histories" have inspired more children than the most earnest of teachers.'

Parents and teachers might raise their eyebrows, but during recent decades Deary has proved one of the more popular writers for children whether judged by sales or borrowing figures for public and school libraries. Indeed, during the Noughties he ranked 33rd. in the list of bestselling authors in Britain (*Daily Telegraph* 2010). Featuring regularly in lists of children's non-fiction best sellers and claiming over 25 million sales worldwide of the 'Horrible Histories', Deary must count as one of the bestselling history presenters of all time. Apart from being translated into over 30 languages, including Chinese, Korean and Russian, for publication around the world, 'Horrible Histories' have reached a wide range of audiences through audio cassettes/CDs/DVDs, road shows, stage plays, television programmes, museum exhibitions, a computer game, and even a bus tour! Deary, whose 'Five Horrid Things' already publicised selected sites, has been used also by English Heritage to promote its 'Time Traveller's Passport' enabling children to time-travel to the nation's historic environment.

Pointing to his ability to view the past through the eyes of young people, Deary has been successful in presenting history to a demanding audience characterised by an increasingly limited attention span and faced by a growing range of rival distractions. For many people, and not only historians, children's access to history is important. Apart from the much publicised shortcomings in historical education in schools discussed in chapter 1, there is also the maxim about the advantage of catching people young in order not only to pass on the acknowledged benefits of knowing history for the purposes of identity, toleration, and so on but also to ensure the future health of the discipline. Despite achieving extensive media recognition for his bestselling 'Horrible Histories' series and emerging television presence, Deary's name means very little to most academic historians. In part, this reflects typical academic disdain about popularising history through what is seen as a bizarre mix of interesting facts, bad jokes, quizzes and illustrations. Thus, Harvard's Niall Ferguson (2006; quoted, Ebner 2010a), when admitting that he read the 'Horrible Histories' to his children, dismissed 'the product of Terry Deary's pen' as merely 'light-hearted introductions to historical subjects', 'quite funny', but falling well short of proper history. From this perspective, Deary should be viewed rather as a writer of children's literature set in the past, not a history presenter.

A Prolific Presenter

Born in Sunderland in 1946, Deary took time to find his true vocation after leaving school. Following an unhappy period working for the local electricity board, he studied drama at teacher-training college and then taught drama in primary and secondary schools. Subsequently Deary became an actor–teacher for *Theatr Powys*, a touring Welsh theatre company performing plays in schools and community theatres. A paucity of suitable material led him to begin writing plays for the company before moving on to write them down as stories. One play formed the basis for Deary's first novel, *The Custard Kid*. Following 24 rejections, the manuscript was eventually accepted, and published in 1978. Reportedly (Deary 2003), his next book was rejected 73 times! The first two 'Horrible Histories' did not appear until 1993, but their success means that today Deary is viewed primarily as a non-fiction history writer. In fact, he continues to write fiction, frequently combining the two genres, as in historical fiction series like 'The Time Detectives' in which a team of young investigators uncover the truth behind actual historical mysteries.

A fast-growing range of publications – the number of titles, which includes over 50 'Horrible Histories', passed 200 in 2009 – complemented by other outputs, like radio, television and theatre scripts, reflect Deary's productiveness, most notably his ability to complete several projects in any one year with no apparent loss of quality. Typically in 2007, when looking forward to the following year, Deary (n.d. a) stated:

> A book takes me between six hours and six weeks to write, depending on how long it is and how difficult it is to get the information together. Some authors take ten years or more to write a single book. I plan to write 10 in 2008 – one book every five weeks.

Any look at published or projected titles confirms that this was not an idle boast. Despite developing the original concept and researching the initial 'Horrible Histories' books himself, over time commercial considerations and publishers' schedules transformed the production process. Thus, recent projects have been developed and structured more consciously by the publisher in the light of topics adjudged likely to sell well. Moreover, the publisher provided the research ready for Deary's spin (Crace 2003). However, in 2010 Deary (quoted, Ebner 2010b) indicated that no new 'Horrible Histories' would be published apart from those already in production. Even so, his pursuit of alternative career directions will not halt the ongoing adaptation of existing titles into alternative formats.

Reportedly (Hammill 2009: 11), Deary, who lives in Burnhope, County Durham, writes in a room looking across fields towards his working-class roots in Sunderland. Like any author, he takes considerable pride in his work, and admits still the thrill of seeing his name on a new publication. In particular, Deary (n.d. a) welcomes letters from children saying how much they enjoyed his books: 'That makes it worthwhile.' Even so, Deary, albeit viewing himself as a natural writer, claims that he does not actually enjoy the writing process: 'I love writing two words . . . "The" and "End". It's a great feeling to complete a book, to have a letter from a publisher accepting it and seeing it finally in print. But the work of writing it is hard.' Unsurprisingly, he has often admitted reservations about his work, given the way in which initial worries about making enough money were overridden by the pressures of success, most notably repeated publication deadlines. In fact, Deary, whose acting has run alongside his writing career for over 30 years, claims to be happiest performing on stage, radio or television.

Developing 'Horrible Histories'

Having concentrated initially on writing fiction, Deary changed direction after being commissioned to write a Father Christmas joke book

(Unstead 2003: 3). Following its publication in 1990, he was asked for a history joke book. Finding the content more interesting than the jokes, Deary developed what became the 'funnies and facts' format employed for the 'Horrible Histories'. The initial titles, *The Terrible Tudors* and *The Awesome Egyptians*, were published in 1993. Other books followed, and within three years over one million 'Horrible Histories' had been sold (Attenborough 1997: 10). New titles continued to appear, but were not poured into an identical mould. On the contrary, books are characterised by their diversity, with subject matter dictating style and approach.

Deary (n.d. b; n.d. c) justifies his approach to the past in terms of responding to what he sees as wrong with history presented to young people in 'big, thick books': 'The trouble with history books is adults who can be pretty pompous write them. You can just hear them saying, "I am an expert. So sit there and listen to what I am saying!"' Certainly, Deary's (2002a) schooldays left much to be desired by way of presenting history:

> History was the most mind-numbingly boring, badly taught and pointless subject ever. Notes were dictated endlessly, and at the end of term we had to read and learn the notes so we could be tested on them. We learned one or two dates, one or two names, but nothing of any value to us in the real world.

In many respects, 'Horrible Histories', based upon the premise that history is horribly boring unless enlivened by the Deary formula involving generous helpings of blood and gore alongside jokes and illustrations, represent his revenge.

Despite presenting the past primarily through books possessing a strong authorial voice, Deary views himself as offering reader-friendly ways of reaching young people, especially those lacking in reading fluency or a long attention span. In brief, Deary (quoted, Sale 2006) claims to offer an 'alternative voice' for history, what has been described as 'a subversive, child's-eye take on the past'. Moreover, this approach is rooted in Deary's persona as a children's writer, not a historian. Rather than following academic historians by claiming to unearth new research, Deary (2002a) seeks to tell readers what happened, and particularly to share with them all the fascinating and horrible things he has discovered:

> I am a children's author, NOT a historian. The historian's voice is, 'Now sit down and listen to me and I will teach you something!'

My voice is, 'Hey! You'll never guess what I found out about this period in history!' I never preach or teach – I simply share my enthusiasm. Also, I am not bound by the National Curriculum to teach the boring bits. I offer an 'alternative' education, and so I can choose the facts that will appeal to my readers – something textbooks cannot do. The facts I choose are not really 'history', they are anecdotes about people.

As Sue Unstead (2003: 3) recorded, Deary's presentational style strikes the right note for his target audience:

His tone is conspiratorial – not 'I'm a grown-up so sit still and I'll tell you what I know', but 'I'm no expert but you'll never believe what I found out when I read this book'. His huge popularity, especially amongst boys, is undoubtedly a result of this genuine enthusiasm – a big kid who just wants to share the information with others kids, big or small.

At the same time, Deary (quoted, Crace 2003) fears that his much cherished subversive role risks becoming the victim of the series' success. In particular, he worries that his books might be perceived as establishment texts if used widely in schools: 'And then where will they go for the alternative voice?' In this vein, Deary (n.d. a) refuses school visits, as announced on his website: 'Teachers note: Terry will not set foot inside a school for any reason.' Indeed, Deary's (quoted, Crace 2003) sweeping critique of schools reflects in many respects his own educational experience: 'Everything I learned after 11 was a waste of time.' For Crace, Deary came across as someone 'proudly anti-establishment', as highlighted also by his refusal of invitations to meet either Tony Blair, the prime minister, at Downing Street or Queen Elizabeth II during her Jubilee visit to the north-east. For some, Deary might be viewed as a Wearsider with a social conscience, but Crace believed that 'at heart, he is a contradictory bloke: a paid-up member of the awkward squad': 'It's the profound mixed in with the absurd – much like his writing – but it's hard to tell how much of this he actually means, how much is just thinking aloud on the hoof and how much is just for effect.'

The 'Horrible Histories'

But why does Deary, the children's author, write histories? For Deary (2002a; 2006), the storyteller, the past provides wonderful stories about

ordinary people. Moreover, these stories possessed contemporary resonance: 'There is only one question worth seeking an answer to: "Why do
people behave the way they do?" History can help answer that, as can
fiction and real-life relationships.' Thus, 'Horrible Histories' focus upon
the people, not 'boring' historical facts, as emphasised in the introduction to *The 20th.Century* (Deary 1996: 4):

> History is horrible. Mainly because we have to learn it and then be
> tested on it. Nobody ever teaches you the interesting things because
> you can't be tested on those. Nobody ever asks you, 'What did people
> laugh at a hundred years ago?' or, 'What made people cry? What did
> they read? What did they eat? What games did they play? Were teach-
> ers just as cruel?' ... These are the sort of things that help you under-
> stand what life was like for people in those days. The history of this
> century *could* be just as boring as a history of the Middle Ages' monks.
> But it *should* be as interesting as your teacher's secret diary.

In addition, the series, though intended to be entertaining and funny,
reflects Deary's political beliefs, most notably the fact that the 'Horrible
Histories' are – to quote Thomson (2007) – 'anti any establishment at
all'. Deary (quoted, Duffy 2007) has proudly claimed that: 'I want to
open the eyes of the readers to the realities of the world so that they are
not hurt and so they can pick up my torch and go on opposing privilege
wherever they find it.' Unsurprisingly, this approach, rooted also in
the cynicism typical of present-day society, was foregrounded in *Rotten
Rulers* (Deary 2005: 5), which began: 'Some of the most horrible people
in history have been the people in charge. The bosses. The rulers ...
emperors, kings and queens, warlords and history teachers.'

Deary's formula

Pressing the need for history to be fun, exciting and engaging for
his young readers aged predominantly between 6 and 12. Deary has
employed a diverse range of presentational strategies to ensure that his
books meet these aspirations.

- **The prime focus is placed upon ordinary people**
  Pressing his anti-authority views, Deary's books have adopted a strong
  'history from below' position concentrating upon how ordinary
  people – they are represented always as just like Deary and his readers –
  actually lived in the past: what they ate, such as the 'rotten recipes', wore

or – critically for this age group – used for lavatories. Deary (1993: 8) set out his basic approach in the introduction to *The Terrible Tudors*:

> This book is about really horrible history. It's full of the sort of facts that teachers never bother to tell you. Not just the bits about the kings and the queens and the battles and the endless lists of dates – it's also about the ordinary people who lived in Tudor times. People like you and me. Commoners! (Well, I'm dead common, I don't know about you!) And what made them laugh and cry, what made them suffer and die.

- **A presentist approach strikes a chord upon the part of readers**
  Despite repeatedly stressing how the past differed from the contemporary world, 'Horrible Histories' view the past largely through present-day spectacles, as highlighted by Deary's critiques of the British empire and war – these are discussed below – and support for learning from history.
- **The past is presented in a striking, frequently light-hearted, and jokey manner**
  Avoiding the straight chronological and/or bland encyclopaedic approach of many histories targeted at the children's market, 'Horrible Histories' contain substantial amounts of information framed in a manner intended to give a vivid and engaging portrait of the past. Generally speaking, as befits the 'History has never been so horrible!' descriptor used on back covers, Deary's histories present the past 'with the nasty bits left in', the aspects appealing to young children – blood, executions, poison, puke, rats, seeping sewage and swearwords. Stories tell of monks chopped into chunks or of live slaves being fed to the lions in the Colosseum in Rome. Fighting and feuding take priority over facts and figures, and, perhaps surprisingly, also over sex, given Deary's (quoted, Thomson 2007) reluctance to confuse young children about the sexual dimension of human relationships.

A light-hearted, frequently humorous, approach helps offset the blood and gore; thus, every beheading is counterbalanced by a joke. *The 20th Century* illustrates the Deary (1996: 114–15) method in operation for the 1960s:

> 1964: Britain invades America ... with four young men called the Beatles! Their weapons? Pop music ... The Americans reply by sending the incredible Sindy Doll over here ... In

South Africa the government locks up a man called Nelson
Mandela and will keep him locked up for 25 years. His real
crime is to fight for equal rights for the black people in his
country.

1965   Shocking young women wear something called the 'mini-
skirt'. Sir Winston Churchill dies (no connection) ... Home
video-recorders are on sale and within 20 years some people will know how to use them properly ...

1968: The post office invents first- and second-class postage. One
is really slow but the other is incredibly slower.

- **The text is broken up by numerous illustrations**
  Designed to reinforce as well as to break up the text, illustrations are
  employed on almost every page to grab the reader's attention. Most
  are drawn still by Martin Brown, an Australian who worked with
  Deary in creating the series' basic framework.
- **The books are written in an accessible manner**
  What happened in the past is presented in familiar reader-friendly
  language. For example, Benito Mussolini is described as 'a mate of
  Adolf Hitler and nearly as nasty' (Deary 2005: 110). Likewise, Deary
  (1998: 7–8) presented the outbreak of war in 1914 as something
  akin to a 'punch-up' between rival street gangs rather than a conflict
  between rival alliances:

  > Why did the Great War start? Lots of big, thick history books
  > have been written to answer that question. But, to put it simply,
  > by 1914 the countries of Europe had formed themselves into two
  > big gangs ... like street gangs ... The two gangs started collecting
  > weapons, making threats and swapping insults, the way gangs do.
  > All it needed was for one gang member to throw the first punch
  > and a huge punch-up would follow.

- **An interactive approach engages the active attention of readers**
  Readers are involved repeatedly working on quizzes and things to do
  arising from the text. Apart from helping to engage their attention and
  active interest, this interactive approach avoids the top-down lecturing tone of academic historians. Deary (quoted, Hammill 2009: 11)
  provokes his young readers to think about people in the past and
  their behaviour by writing 'Look at that. Isn't that terrible? What
  would *you* have done?'

What I want to do is look at how human beings interact in traumatic situations and then ask the reader to measure themselves – 'How would I react in those situations?' ... It's the same if you're writing fiction or non-fiction. You take characters and put them through situations. The readers' job is to measure themselves against these people and find out *who they are* ... That's the whole purpose of children's literature for me ... discovery, challenge and change.

Fostering historical awareness

Despite seeking to differentiate 'Horrible Histories' from what he views as academic histories, Deary does in fact apprise his young readers, albeit often implicitly, about the nature of history as a subject:

- **The inclusion of numerous dates and facts**
  Building upon children's love of collecting facts, most notably those of the gruesome and lavatorial variety, Deary and his publisher have taken pains to ensure the factual accuracy of his books (Hislop 2002). As Deary (2003) told one of his readers, he obtained his facts from 'big fat boring history books': 'My skill is re-telling those facts.'
  Despite occasional narrative sections running across several pages, the fractured nature of the text has led some academics, like Anna Whitelock (quoted, Beck 2009: 71), to prefer an alternative approach, such as offered by Henrietta Marshall's *Our Island Story* (1905):

  > In principle, the 'Horrible Histories' are a good thing, at least as far as getting kids interested in and enthusiastic about history. However, I find the pick and mix approach of topics in the books rather limited and I think children would benefit far more from good narratives. The 'Horrible Histories' are certainly no replacement for a book like *Our Island Story* which was so popular with children of previous generations.

  Lamenting the absence of a more recent text possessing a similar narrative drive, Tristram Hunt (quoted, Beck 2009: 71) echoed Whitelock's praise for the 'very uncomplicated certainty' of Marshall's text: '"Horrible Histories" are as good as we've got at the moment, but I much prefer *Our Island Story*, which seems to offer more of the romance of history ... it would still be my first choice as a history book to enthuse a child about the subject.' In fact, Marshall's classic text was republished in 2005, but is inevitably dated, reflective of its times, and British-centred. Whether its format will appeal to today's children as much as to present-day academic historians remains questionable.

- **The role of evidence in knowing the past**
  Like most popular histories, the 'Horrible Histories' are not referenced, but some effort is made to reinforce the text through coverage of historical places, buildings and museums and the inclusion
  of primary sources. For example, extracts are included from, say,
  an account about force feeding by the suffragette, Lady Constance
  Lytton (Deary 1996: 17–18), or the 1915 British Army Field Almanac
  detailing wartime first aid (Deary 1998: 27–8).

- **The past as a process of continuity and change, with a speeding-
  up since 1900**
  Although his approach runs the risk of making it difficult for readers
  to see links between concentrated but detached blocks of information
  on specific periods, Deary (1996: 175) makes some attempt to outline
  long-term trends:

  > History is all about 'change'. But there has never been a century
  > quite like the 20th Century for change. There's probably been
  > enough history in the last 100 years to fill a million books ... And
  > you'll have seen that some things *never* change if you live to be a
  > million – births and deaths, wet weekends and school dinners ...
  > The weapons have changed but the people using them haven't.
  > They still want to kill each other to get what they want!

- **The value of knowing the past in order to learn from history**
  For Deary (1996: 175), it proves vital 'that we remember the horrible
  lessons of history and learn from them', particularly those concerning
  war, empire, unemployment, old age, and the damaging impact of
  prejudices based on class, race or gender.

- **The role of readers in living through and witnessing the history
  of the recent period**
  Deary (1996: 175–6; 2002b: 127) reminds readers that, far from being
  a dead subject, history is a living thing: 'The exciting thing is that *you*
  are part of it [history]. In your own lifetime you'll have seen satellite television, personal computers, the Channel Tunnel and trans-
  plants of mechanical hearts.' The twenty-first century will see further
  changes. Whether it is for the better or the worse 'really depends on
  you', the reader.

• **History is a matter of personal interpretation**
Deary's *'Horrible Histories'* are distinguished by a strong story line and make no more than a token effort to be detached and historically balanced. Undoubtedly academic historians will worry about the risk of exposing young minds to a somewhat loaded version of the past, but this approach serves not only to acquaint young readers with history's subjective nature but also to provide scope for informed comment and debate.

Deary makes some effort to acknowledge the positive features of a changing world, such as the way in which modern communications empower and help people, as well as to recognise those responsible for 'firsts'. Even so, the past is viewed largely in a jaundiced manner imbued with present-day concerns, even prejudices. Underpinned by the view that 'history can be truly horrible', the prime focus is directed towards the negatives, as befits Deary's (quoted, Duffy 2007) political agenda: 'My books ... show authority figures over the ages as being the villains. They are not balanced history books but demonstrations of how evil authority has been through the ages – a cautionary tale.' Pointing to his favourite historical character, Henry VIII, Deary (quoted, Hislop 2002) followed Starkey in seeking to dispel the myths, but adopted a somewhat different approach: 'When I was at school, Henry VIII was a hero. But when I did my own research, I discovered that he was a grotesque, psychopathic monster. If I go overboard knocking the Establishment view of history, it's because it's a redress.'

In *The Vile Victorians*, Deary (1994: 128) praised the Victorians' achievements:

> The Victorian age wasn't all vile, of course.
> The Victorians were energetic and inventive. By the time the old Queen died we had electric lights ... We had schools ... and teachers. We had the very, very rich ... and the very, very poor.

But this recognition of positives came only on the final page of the book, that is, after the preceding 127 pages had concentrated upon the 'vile' character of the Victorian period, and even then was mixed with negatives like the concentration of wealth in a few hands. In other titles, Deary pressed the case against war and empire. For instance, the conclusion of *The Frightful First World War* (Deary 1998: 127–8) was imbued with anti-war sentiments reflecting the numerous lives lost and the failure of a long war either to resolve the fundamental issues or to bring an enduring peace: 'Each of us should find our nearest war memorial, stand in front of it and read the names. Then say, "Never again".'

Nor has Deary shown himself to be an enthusiast for empire in general or the British Empire in particular. Indeed, Deary (2002b: 5–7, 126) adjudged Britain guilty of regularly sending in its 'bully-boys' to expand the Empire: 'Imagine what that must be like! You've lived in your house all your life and enjoyed it. You're sitting at home one day when in marches a bunch of soldiers.' Backed by guns, the British took over overseas territory: 'And that's how it was with the British Empire till about 1900 ... In fact, the history of the British Empire is full of horrible people and horrible deeds. Just the sort of stuff for a Horrible History.' For him, empire reflected the bullying character of 'a greedy grasping nation': 'Every day, somewhere in the British Empire, someone suffered.' Unimpressed by the reputed benefits of empire, as articulated in 2003 by what Deary (quoted, Ebner 2010a) criticised as Ferguson's 'deeply offensive right-wing' television series, *Empire* (chapter 7), he glossed over what happened after 1900. Only a few lines of *The Barmy British Empire* were devoted to the other side of the story, such as represented by the decolonisation process and the alleged political and economic benefits of being part of the British empire.

More than just books

The success of Deary's 'Horrible Histories' has inspired a range of initiatives designed not only to emulate the concept – for example, there is now a lengthy list of similar series covering topics like 'Horrible Science' or 'Horrible Geography' – but also to exploit the brand by recycling material under licence for presentation in an alternative format targeting both existing and new audiences. Like his publisher, Deary (2009c) is constantly searching for yet another way to present his stories about the past to young people. The principal formats include:

- Books
  Apart from the 'Horrible Histories' books, as discussed above, there are 'Horrible Histories' annuals, handbooks, pop-up books, 'high-speed' histories offering historical tales in a comic-strip format, and historical fiction like the 'Horrible Histories'' 'Gory Stories';

- 'Horrible Histories' part-work
  Between 2003 and 2005 the 'Horrible Histories' collection went on sale as a fortnightly 80-issue part-work. Benefiting from the strength of the 'Horrible Histories' brand, the magazine achieved a stable circulation of 200,000, well in excess of the norm for part-works. Maggie

Calmels (quoted, Matthews 2003), the publisher's editorial director, reported a mixed postbag from teachers. Most proved supportive, but there was the usual quota of complaints to the effect that – to quote from teachers' feedback – 'this sort of magazine cheapens and dumbs down what are highly significant historical events' by 'sensationalising or trivialising the great events of history', 'skirting around the crucial religious and political undercurrents', joking about executions and bloodshed, and relying upon 'toilet humour'.

- **'History roadshows' and audio recordings**
  Having begun his career performing and writing plays, Deary, the actor, has experimented with various ways of presenting history live to an audience, such as through the 'Terry Deary History Roadshows'. Apart from bringing the 'Horrible Histories' to life on the stage for family audiences, the shows inspired the concept of audio recordings designed to transport the listener to an old classroom, a Tudor tavern or a Victorian music-hall, where history becomes entertainment and dead people come to life. Recordings, albeit heavily reliant on the 'Horrible Histories' for content, were not straight readings of the books. Rather they told stories through drama, poetry, music, characters and role-play in a more vivid manner than possible through the printed word. As narrator, Deary linked the anecdotes with a personal commentary. Actors playing individual parts gave listeners a variety of voices, while sound effects, like the fall of the executioner's axe, heightened the sense of authenticity. In October 2002 BBC Worldwide launched ten 'Horrible Histories' CDs. Not only did these sell well, but between 2005 and 2007 millions were distributed free in Britain with Kellogg's cereals and the *Daily Telegraph*. The fact that a promotion was repeated highlighted the 'Horrible Histories'' perceived value as a brand for marketing purposes – these nationwide campaigns also enhanced Deary's public profile – as well as the utility of audio recordings as another way of engaging children with the past.

- **Television**
  Leading a session on children's history television programming at the 2010 History Makers Conference held in New York, Lion Television's production team shared their experience of bringing Deary's 'Horrible Histories' and 'Time Detectives' to the small screen for CBBC (Children's BBC) and the PBS, respectively. In 2009 13 30-minute 'Horrible Histories', covering the 'Savage Stone Age' onwards, offered British viewers 'a sense of the connections, continuities and layers of history' (BBC 2008b; Hickman 2011).

When asked to compare making a television series with the experience of writing a book, Deary (2009b) pointed out that: 'The television company have bought the "Horrible Histories" name so they can do what they like with it. With a book I am in control and I can argue with the editors. The television company listens to me but they don't have to.' In fact, the comedian Marcus Brigstocke was responsible for series development, with humorous sketches, based on Deary's books, contributed by a range of writers, including Jon Holmes and Steve Punt. Frequently, sketches drew upon familiar television formats such as *Historical Wife Swap* and *Victorian Dragon's Den*. *This is Your Reign* emulated *This is Your Life*, while a Roman gladiator school was based on *Grange Hill*. In the opening programme, broadcast on 16 April 2009, four King Georges, singing 'Born2 Rule Over You', performed as a boy band, in a clip attracting numerous hits on YouTube. In subsequent programmes Henry VIII's song, 'Divorced, Beheaded and Died; Divorced, Beheaded, Survived', offered children an easy way of remembering the names, order and fate of the king's six wives, while Charles II featured as a rapper who loved to party. Deary, the actor, featured in cameo roles playing, say, a Roman emperor or a grave robber.

Attracting positive reviews – for one reviewer, 'it was everything that "Blue Peter" [a popular children's TV programme] isn't: fun, filthy and genuinely engaging in a peer-to-peer way' (Jarvis 2009) – the series achieved strong audience ratings. By mid-June it proved the most watched children's television programme in Britain (Scholastic 2009). Reportedly nearly half of Britain's 6–12-year-olds tuned in. In 2010 the programme won the *Prix Jeunesse* children's non-fiction award for 7–11-year-olds and three Children's BAFTAs for the best writing, best comedy and best performer categories. Significantly, in 2010 the series received the British Comedy Award for the best sketch show, beating established prime-time television programmes. Subsequently, DVDs of the series were released for sale, and Scholastic republished several 'Horrible Histories' titles as television tie-ins. 'Horrible Histories' Interactive, an online mix of games and video material, provided support through a 'soft learning approach' to historical content. Following the success of the first series, CBBC commissioned two further series for 2010 and 2011, plus a spin-off game show called *Gory Games*. In July 2011 songs and music from the series featured in a '"Horrible Histories' Family Prom' held at the Royal Albert Hall, London, as part of the BBC Proms season.

- **Plays**

Writing for the stage has proved a longstanding interest for Deary, as evidenced by his work for Theatr Powys. More recently, since 2005 the

Birmingham Stage Company has conducted national tours performing plays based on such 'Horrible Histories' as *The Terrible Tudors, The Vile Victorians* and *The Frightful First World War*. Performances, staged at times geared towards school parties, epitomised the typical 'Horrible Histories' formula. As Benedict Nightingale (2005) reported, when reviewing *The Terrible Tudors* at Bromley's Churchill Theatre for *The Times*, the show prioritised 'the weird, the jokey and the gruesome – the hangings, head-choppings and burnings'. In 2011 the company conducted another lengthy national tour with two plays: *The Awful Egyptians* and *The Ruthless Romans*. For children, the plays' educational impact is reinforced by the provision of resource packs and workshops.

More importantly, over time newspaper reviewers, like Nightingale, have confirmed the manner in which the plays engaged the target audience and sold out at many venues. Reviewing *The Terrible Tudors* at Cardiff's New Theatre in June 2008, Abbie Wightwick (2008) provided a typical example:

> Heads and hands were chopped off with gay abandon to delighted shrieks at Cardiff's New Theatre. The Birmingham Stage Company's live version of Terry Deary's 'Horrible Histories' tells the story of the Terrible Tudors with a gleeful snub at squeamishness. Children in the audience loved it ... If this sounds unsavoury for school age children, just imagine how much more attention you would have paid if teachers had gone into gory details rather than intoned lists of kings and queens ... This is learning through fun and director Neal Foster kept the action racing along so there was no danger of getting bored.

Within this learning context, *The Terrible Tudors* juxtaposed 'horrible' Tudor realities alongside popular images of the era as a golden age. When the facts threatened to get in the way blood and guts were thrown in for dramatic effect. Or the audience was prompted to join in a football-type chant reciting the above mentioned mnemonic outlining the fate of Henry VIII's wives. For Wightwick, 'it was learning by rote but didn't feel like it' for the five children aged 5 to 10 accompanying her. For Susan Lee (2009), the plays, staged in New Brighton, presented 'history as it should be delivered – lively, engaging and highly creative': 'This wasn't a dry history lesson, just great entertainment.'

What proves extremely popular is 'Bogglevision', a video-screen device requiring theatre audiences to don 3-D glasses, and then duck, laugh and shout, as rocks, cannonballs and – as Wightwick (2008) discovered – the skull of the newly executed Mary Queen of Scots flew into the auditorium, courtesy of 3-D glasses and visual effects. The audience, composed chiefly of young children in school parties or with parents, proved equally responsive and excited when I visited the New Wimbledon Theatre to watch *The Vile Victorians* and *The Frightful First World War* in 2006 and 2009, respectively. In the former case a fast-moving series of sketches dramatised various aspects of Victorian life – these included the inevitable focus on toilets as well as railways, child labour, hospitals and war – while after the interval rats, cannonballs and other items flew into the audience in the Crimean War scene via 'Bogglevision'.

- **Computer game**
  In summer 2009 the launch of a *Ruthless Romans* computer game, produced by Slitherine Software, enabled Deary to tap yet another audience. Apart from writing the script, Deary is the 'voice' of the game. Lisa Edwards (quoted, Slitherine 2008; 2009), Scholastic's editorial director, was optimistic: 'We are delighted to have found the right home for our brand. Die-hard 'Horrible Histories' fans have been waiting for an exciting gaming extension of the brand – and if we can attract children who are primarily gamers to the books then that will indeed be a bonus.' Her references to the 'brand' proved equally revealing.

- **Museum exhibitions**
  Building upon the successful 'Frightful First World War' exhibition held at Imperial War Museum North in 2009–9, during 2009–10 London's Imperial War Museum (2009) staged the '"Horrible Histories": Terrible Trenches' exhibition, enabling all the family to 'Learn, see, smell and hear about the First World War through frightful facts, ropey rhymes, sad songs and sinister superstitions in a great day out.' In the longer term, Deary has hopes of developing a 'History Experience' theme park in north-east England.

- **Audio bus tour**
  In March 2007 an audio bus tour based on the 'Horrible Histories' was launched in Edinburgh.

Conclusion

Despite exerting minimal impact on the historical profession, Deary's 'Horrible Histories' have acquired a high profile in bookshops, public libraries, schools, theatres and on television, at least on this side of the

Atlantic. Growing media recognition was typified by Cassandra Jardine's (2006) article in the *Daily Telegraph* in 2006: 'Telegenic historians such as Simon Schama, Niall Ferguson and Starkey have been credited with the recent rise in demand for history, but the true hero is a lesser-known figure: Terry Deary, author of the Horrible Histories.' Quoting the number of 'Horrible Histories' sold, Alice Thomson (2007) informed the *Daily Telegraph*'s readers soon afterwards that 'All this makes Deary the most influential historian in Britain today, which must depress the likes of Simon Schama and David Starkey.'

Regardless of the academic pros and cons of his 'Horrible Histories', Deary has a proven track record of encouraging young people to take an interest in the past and hence to read, listen or watch history for interest and pleasure. As such, they have a greater chance of developing an enduring taste for the subject. As Virginia Matthews (2003) noted: 'The torture, murder and warfare that characterises much of human history is proving to be an irresistible cocktail for the *Harry Potter* and *Lord of the Rings* generation of children who until recently would have rated the past as about exciting as reheated sprouts.' Echoing comments made by several of my students with young families, Thomson (2007) reported how Deary's 'revolting version of *1066 And All That*' enthused her own children:

> My six-year-old son is entranced by *The Terrible Tudors, The Vile Victorians* and *The Awful Egyptians*. He now wants to spend his weekends at the Tower of London, looking for drops of blood from past executions. He stands on the battlements of Windsor Castle lecturing us on Queen Victoria's appalling attitude to children working in sweatshops and he insists on going to see the mummies at the British Museum once a month. My daughter loves the true stories of naughty princesses far more than any fairy tale and is currently trying to persuade us to go to the Colosseum rather than Disneyland.

The appeal of 'Horrible Histories' to their children has been admitted by a wide range of people, including Cherie Blair (Hodgson 2008), the wife of the former British prime minister, and Niall Ferguson (2006), even if many parents follow Emma Mahony (2008) in admitting that they 'don't "get" the "Horrible Histories" books', given their lavatorial humour, illustrations, corny captions, and so on. But Mahony conceded that 'Millions can't be wrong.' Indeed, her son, Humphrey, sought to persuade her that 'they're great': 'I usually skim-read normal history books, but with "Horrible Histories" I actually bother to read all of it.' Similarly, Amanda Craig (2006), *The Times*'s children's book critic, found it hard to object to the books because they did teach children the rudiments of history along with the rude, violent and disgusting bits.

During recent decades, Deary has made a significant contribution to popular history in general and to children's history in particular. Focusing on topics left out by history teachers, Deary (quoted, Ryan 2009), who has often proclaimed his lack of qualifications in history, has no desire to become part of the history mainstream, let alone to be described as a historian: 'I just don't know how I feel about being called a historian. I'm a children's writer – an entertainer.' Indeed, in 2010 Deary (quoted, Ebner 2010b) launched a strong attack on historians in general – most were deemed 'seedy and devious' – and Niall Ferguson in particular. Nor does academia seem anxious to embrace, let alone to study, Deary's 'Horrible Histories' or historical fiction, as recorded by Crace (2003): 'Most academic historians are happy to give him a wide berth: if they trash him, they look pretentious and if they take him seriously they are accused of dumbing down.' Hitherto, Champion, de Groot (2009a: 39–40, 42) and the author (Beck 2009) have proved lone academic voices urging a sense of perspective. According to Champion (2003: 157–8):

> One of the most popular historians, if we make the award by book sales alone, is the children's author Terry Deary .... These books are entertaining. They have cartoons, games and quizzes which all aid the digestion ... Convinced that history is a means of communicating with a variety of audiences, Deary does this on a bedrock of factual truth. His writing is passionate and entertaining, truthful and subjective: most importantly, it works. Academic historians no doubt have barely deigned to open a copy of the *Stormin' Normans* or the *Terrible Tudors*; if they did, they might well be struck by the depth of research and acuity of characterization. Quite clearly, Deary's books are designed for a particular audience and written in an appropriate style: who is to say that his volumes contain more or less 'truth' than the equivalent volumes of the *Oxford History of England*?

More recently, the success of the television series has forced a growing number of academics to sit up and take notice of the proven ability of 'Horrible Histories' to engage not only children but also adults, especially given the media's attempts to elicit historians' thoughts about this way of presenting the past (Hickman 2011; Midgley 2011). One other element of academic recognition, albeit not in the sphere of history, occurred in 2000 when Deary was awarded an honorary doctorate in education by the University of Sunderland.

Avoiding what Schama (quoted, *Daily Telegraph* 2002) described as 'the monstrous monotone' characteristic of many student textbooks, Deary's (quoted, Duffy 2007) populist treatment of the past has shown that young people want to be entertained as well as informed: 'If I can inform them by sneaking in a bit of information, fine. But first you have to engage them. A lot of parents say to me, "My child never read a book until he picked up yours, and now he reads regularly".' Certainly, Deary (2009a) sees himself as exerting more impact on young minds than academic historians: 'I sell rather more than they do and I probably have more influence because I get the young people before their minds are formed so I indoctrinate them with anti-authority.' Whether or not the undoubted interest generated in young people by Deary's books, plays and television series provides a springboard for the subsequent study of history at secondary school and university remains questionable. Even so, as indicated above, there is some anecdotal evidence concerning their positive impact.

In the meantime, Deary's histories ensure that the past is not totally ignored by children at a time when history is struggling to retain its place and identity in the school curriculum. Children's publishers and broadcasters have also been made aware of the fact that history packaged and presented in an appropriate manner proves highly marketable to children, as well as to many of their parents and teachers. Indeed, during the mid-1990s the success of the 'Horrible Histories' was instrumental in the expansion of Scholastic's non-fiction list and staffing (Attenborough 1997: 10). Nor should the role of the 'Horrible Histories' and Deary's historical fiction in encouraging young people to read, a vital historical skill, be underestimated, given contemporary concerns about the reluctance of young people to open a book as compared to using a computer keyboard or joystick. Despite claims that they often fail to share their pupils' or children's enthusiasm, many teachers and parents read 'Horrible Histories' for pleasure, perhaps awakening an interest in the subject for the first time or rediscovering an interest lost over time. In this vein, in summer 2011 BBC1 broadcast a six-programme 'Horrible Histories' series – the content was selected from the series shown already on CBBC – targeted at a prime-time adult audience with a limited grasp of history (Wynne-Jones 2010). Stephen Fry (2006) acted as host.

During the mid-1980s the editors (Benson *et al.* 1986: xviii) of a book about public history mentioned the 'academically shunned literary ghetto of children's history books'. Within this context, historians should consider what light Deary's approach casts on ways of popularising history, moving children's history out of the literary ghetto, and bridging the gap between history and the wider audience. In this vein, perhaps the last word should go to the small boy who paid Terry Deary (quoted, Unstead 2003: 4) what he describes as the best compliment for any presenter of the past: 'I don't like books, but I read yours.'

Terry Deary (1946–): Select Bibliography

'Horrible Histories' books

1993	*The Awesome Egyptians*
1993	*The Terrible Tudors*
1994	*The Vile Victorians*
1994	*The Rotten Romans*
1994	*The Vicious Vikings*
1995	*Cruel Kings and Mean Queens*
1996	*The Slimy Stuarts*
1996	*The 20th Century*
1997	*The Angry Aztecs*
1998	*Bloody Scotland*
1998	*Even More Terrible Tudors*
1998	*Frightful First World War*
1999	*The Savage Stone Age*
1999	*The Woeful Second World War*
2000	*Horrible History of Ireland*
2001	*The Stormin' Normans*
2002	*The Barmy British Empire*
2003	*A Wicked History of The World*
2004	*Villainous Victorians*
2005	*London*
2005	*Rotten Rulers*
2005	*Edinburgh*
2006	*Awful Egyptians*
2007	*Oxford*
2008	*Wales*
2010	*Britain and Ireland*

'Horrible Histories' handbooks

2006	*Knights Handbook*
2008	*WW1 Trenches Handbook*
2009	*WW2 The Blitz Handbook*

→

Radio and television broadcasts

[number of programmes given in brackets]

2001–2	*Horrible Histories* cartoon series (CiTV)	[26]
2005	*Henry VIII's Wives* (BBC Two)	[6]
2005–6	*Terrible Tales of Wales* (BBC Radio Wales)	[12]
2008	*Terry Deary's Five Horrible Things* (History Channel)	[5]
2009	*Horrible Histories* (CBBC)	[13]
2010	*Horrible Histories* (CBBC)	[13]
	Horrible Histories Christmas Show (CBBC)	[1]
2011	*Horrible Histories* (CBBC)	[13]
	Horrible Histories (BBC One)	[6]

12
Michael A. Bellesiles and Stephen Ambrose: Presenters in Trouble

Presenters produce histories of varying historical quality. Moreover, just as historians struggle to agree with each other, so listeners, readers, viewers and reviewers experience difficulty in reaching a consensus judgement about any history in terms of either its historical merit and/or ability to engage an audience. Flaws might result from a failure to take account of the existing historiography, incomplete research, shortcomings in content and analysis, plagiarism or poor literary style. Indeed, in certain cases, presentations might even be adjudged to fall short of the standard required for 'history'. Thus, an account using and abusing the past for a present-day purpose should be dismissed as propaganda, not 'history'.

Traditionally, any shortcomings in presentations by academic historians have been pursued within academia, most notably through procedures for refereeing manuscripts and reviewing books or historical revisionism. However, occasionally academic historians accused of presenting flawed versions of the past have become the unwilling subjects of media and public controversy, particularly if they are well known and/or working on topics possessing contemporary resonance. Two *causes célèbres* follow.

Michael A. Bellesiles

In September 2000 Michael A. Bellesiles, a Californian teaching at Emory University, Atlanta, published *Arming America*, a history of gun culture in the USA. Following its publication, *Arming America*, though targeted according to Bellesiles (2002b: 5) at an academic audience, attracted widespread media and public attention on both sides of the Atlantic because of its perceived challenge to the historical and legal validation traditionally employed to justify gun rights in the USA, as enshrined in the Second Amendment to the constitution.

248

Debating the history of the USA's gun culture

According to Bellesiles (2000: 5, 15, 72–82, 429–30, 445), in early America gun ownership was 'exceptional'. Between 1765 and 1790 he claimed that only 14.7 per cent of households possessed arms, many of which were either broken or defective. Far from dating back to early America, as claimed by the gun lobby and existing histories, Bellesiles (2000: 9, 13) argued that a gun culture did not emerge until mid-nineteenth century industrialisation and the 1861–5 Civil War. In effect, existing histories presenting the USA's gun culture as going back to early America were exposed as political constructs based upon an 'invented tradition' of a well-armed citizenry 'read from the present into the past': 'The nation's history has been meticulously reconstructed to promote the necessity of a heavily armed American public.'

At first sight, Bellesiles's revisionist groundbreaking thesis gained strength from the fact that *Arming America* was:

- a massively researched scholarly work referenced by over 1400 footnotes occupying 125 pages supported by a 10-page statistical appendix. Sources included literary and travel accounts, probate records recording wills and gun ownership inventories, and homicide statistics;
- written by a history professor based at a leading university, with a doctorate from the University of California at Irvine;
- followed the author's well-regarded book *Revolutionary Outlaws: Ethan Allen and the struggle for independence on the early American frontier* (1995), published by the University of Virginia Press; and
- published by a major publisher, Knopf.

As well as gaining strong initial praise from reviewers in the *New York Times* and the *New York Review of Books*, in 2001 Bellesiles received Columbia University's Bancroft Prize of $4000 awarded to 'distinguished' studies on American history.

Bellesiles's attack on a central feature of present-day American society and identity provoked extensive media and public debate about both the book's content and policy implications (Robin 2004: 8–10, 57–84; Wiener 2005: 73–93). In January 2001 Bellesiles was even interviewed for *Playboy* magazine. Inevitably, the book prompted a hostile reaction from the powerful gun lobby led by the National Rifle Association (NRA). Charlton Heston (2000), the NRA's President, dismissed Bellesiles's thesis as 'ludicrous'. In effect, the gun lobby, describing *Arming America* as an erroneously constructed 'exercise in presentism' (Robin 2004: 80), accused Bellesiles of academic fraud in support of a present-day anti-gun political agenda. Exploiting a scandal-hungry media, NRA campaigners used press releases and the internet to foster 'a powerful web of doubt' (Robin 2004: 66) about Bellesiles's sources, data and arguments.

A more scholarly tone to the exchanges was imparted by studies published in academic journals like the *William and Mary Quarterly*, the *William and Mary Law Review* and the *Yale Law Journal*. Their principal focus was Bellesiles's scholarship and methodology. For Ira D. Gruber (2002: 217, 219–22), the fundamental problem arose from Bellesiles's attempt 'to use the past to reform the present'. Thus, the resulting 'consistently biased reading of sources' reflected 'careless' use of evidence about the militia and arms in early America. Bellesiles's misuse of evidence was highlighted by other critics:

- Gloria Main (2002: 211) dismissed as 'nonsense' Bellesiles's claim that probate records offered a relatively complete listing of people's assets, including guns;
- James Lindgren (2002: 2198, 2201, 2230) accused Bellesiles of 'innumeracy' when arguing that his data on gun ownership was 'mathematically impossible'. Also Lindgren (2002: 2209, 2231) claimed that counting the wills of women, who held fewer guns than men, enabled Bellesiles to distort gun-ownership figures downwards; and
- Randolph Roth (2002: 233–4) asserted that Bellesiles's data on gun-related homicide was 'false'.

Shortcomings in referencing proved another focus:

- Lindgren and Justin Heather (2002: 1822–6) stated that inadequate referencing rendered it impossible to validate gun-ownership data for the period 1765–1859. A footnote listed probate records sourced from 40 counties, but gave no information about sample size, regional classification, or archival locations;
- Lindgren and Heather (2002: 1820) reported that 100 or more wills cited by Bellesiles for Providence, Rhode Island, did not exist. Lindgren (2002: 2210–11) recorded also that probate records referenced as used for San Francisco had been destroyed in the 1906 earthquake and fire.

In July 2002 an independent committee of investigation established by Emory University (2002: 19) reported no evidence of 'intentional fabrication or falsification', but raised serious questions about Bellesiles's scholarship. The report (2002: 6, 15, 18–19) highlighted 'abundant evidence of superficial and thesis-driven research'; 'unprofessional and misleading' research on probate records; 'serious failures and care-lessness in the gathering and presentation of archival records and the use of quantitative analysis'; and 'mathematically improbable or impossible' data. In October Bellesiles resigned his post at Emory University with effect from 31 December 2002. Meanwhile, the Bancroft Prize was rescinded on the grounds of 'scholarly misconduct' contravening the 'norms of historical scholarship'. Soon afterwards Knopf withdrew *Arming America* – 24,000 copies had been sold already – from sale.

The episode's broader significance

For historians, the case raised serious issues. According to Bellesiles (2002b: 1), academic discourse, not media confrontations, offered the most appropriate way of dealing with what he saw as fundamentally 'a scholarly disagreement' about historical content and interpretation. As Bellesiles (2002a: 262) remarked, 'we sometimes seem to read the evidence differently'. Having read many of the relevant records, Mary Beth Norton (quoted, Wiener 2005: 87, 92) concluded that his interpretation was 'just as plausible' as those advanced by critics. Most criticisms seemed to be like 'the usual sorts of disagreements historians always have about how to interpret documentary evidence, although those criticisms have been expressed more vehemently than is usual in the scholarly literature'.

The episode established the need for historians to conform to sound historical methodology, most notably to provide full and accurate referencing 'leaving a clear trail for subsequent historians to follow' (AHA 2005) when checking the research. Falling short of the standards expected of an academic historian, Bellesiles was guilty of – to quote Norton (quoted, Wiener 2005: 92) – 'slapdash and sloppy' research and referencing. Apart from citing evidence in Providence that did not exist, Bellesiles mistakenly listed probate records, held by the Contra Costa County Archives, as located in San Francisco (Lindgren 2002: 2210–11). Nor did his responses do much to satisfy critics. Apart from appearing confused about archival locations, Bellesiles did not help his case by claiming the loss of his research notes due to the flooding of his room at Emory University in 2000.

Despite Bellesiles's (2002b: 5) claim that *Arming America* was primarily 'written for an audience of historians' to prompt a rethink of early American history, the topic's contemporary political resonance ensured that his revisionist thesis, or garbled versions thereof, would engage a much larger audience. Moreover, the fact that Bellesiles presented a version of the past confronting that espoused by a powerful, vocal and well-organised constituency capable of mounting pressure on authors, publishers, the media and the historical profession ensured that *Arming America* was subjected to close and extensive public scrutiny. This placed a premium on ensuring that prior to publication the book's thesis and methodology were watertight in order to avoid providing critics with any openings. But Bellesiles failed to do this. Even so, the microscopic scrutiny of his text raised the question of how well any history would stand up to such treatment. Significantly, the 2000 Irving–Lipstadt trial (chapter 13) led Bellesiles (2002b: 1, 7) to represent himself combining with Deborah Lipstadt, an Emory University colleague, to defend academic freedom against extremists denying the validity of any history except their preferred propagandist version: 'I believe that if we begin investigating every scholar who challenges received truth, it will not be long before no challenging scholarly books are published.'

In addition, the controversy suggested a transformation in modes of historical discourse, given the emerging empowerment of lay persons in debating and presenting public history. Pointing to the internet as his nemesis, Bellesiles (quoted, Robin 2004: 67, 82) complained that there were 'no rules' demarcating historical expertise. Eroding the 'walls' separating academia from the wider public, the internet enabled individuals with an axe to grind about the past to bypass history's gatekeepers and to reach out directly to a wider audience: 'A once-invisible lay audience now critically and visibly challenged the professional historian's methodology, ethics, and politics' (Robin 2004: 82–3).

As Emory University's (2002: 1) report recognised, Bellesiles's revisionist presentation of early American history 'set off a controversy which, beginning to some degree as a debate involving hot political issues, became something else: a dispute over perceived failures of scholarly care and integrity in the documentation, presentation and analysis of archival sources'. For Bellesiles, the impact was traumatic, even transformational, casting aspersions on his integrity as a scholar, involving the loss of his tenured post, and undermining the credibility of his entire book. For other academics, the episode warned about the need to uphold historical standards, even when presenting the past to a public audience. Clearly, writing a popular history was capable of seriously harming an academic career in more ways than one.

In 2003 Bellesiles (2003: 1–16) used Soft Skull Press to publish a revised edition of *Arming America* in which both the text and tables were updated in the light of revisiting probate archives. Despite raising the gun-ownership figure for 1765–90 to 22 per cent and toning down the introductory critique of the NRA's presentation of the American past, Bellesiles reiterated his original thesis that America's gun culture was an invented tradition dating back no further than the Civil War era. Subsequently, Bellesiles sought to relaunch his career by co-editing *Documenting American Violence: a sourcebook* (2006), contributing to the History News Service, and teaching American history at Central Connecticut State University, New Britain. Significantly, Bellesiles (quoted, P. Cohen 2010) claimed that the subject of his latest history, *1877: the year of living violently* (2010), was chosen deliberately in order to avoid political controversy. Even so, the book has been closely scrutinised as regards the use of evidence, especially as – to quote Anthony Grafton (P. Cohen 2010) president-elect of the AHA and author of *The Footnote* – hitherto Bellesiles has proved 'pretty unrepentant' about his past failings.

Stephen Ambrose

Plagiarism, defined in chapter 2 as recycling someone else's words as your own, is a growing problem in higher education. Nor has the problem been confined to students. During recent decades, several historians, including Doris Kearns Goodwin, the Pulitzer prize-winning author of *The Fitzgeralds and the Kennedys* (1987) and *No Ordinary Time* (1995), and Stephen Oates, the biographer of Abraham Lincoln and Martin Luther King, Jr., have been accused of plagiarism in cases attracting considerable media visibility in the USA.

Popularising the American past

Perhaps the most high-profile case concerned Stephen Ambrose. By the late 1990s he had established himself as one of the USA's leading history presenters responsible for popularising the story of the American past through books, television, films, lectures, museums, and historical tours. Writing in *The Wall Street Journal*, Matthew Rose (2001) pointed to Ambrose's five million-plus sales when claiming that 'only a handful of authors – Stephen King, Tom Clancy and John Grisham among them – have bigger names and generate more cash for their publishers'.

During the mid-1990s Ambrose, who was Boyd Professor of History at the University of New Orleans until his retirement in 1995, emerged to become one of the USA's most popular historians regularly placed in the bestseller lists. Despite achieving public visibility for his role as associate editor of *The Papers of Dwight D. Eisenhower* and biographies of both President Eisenhower and President Nixon, for much of his career,

Ambrose, who was also a contributing editor for *MHQ: The Quarterly Journal of Military History*, targeted an academic audience. However, following sales of over 700,000 for *D-Day: June 6, 1944: the climactic battle of World War II* (1994), he switched to page-turning histories about the American West and the Second World War. Using *Undaunted Courage: Meriwether Lewis, Thomas Jefferson, and the opening of the American West* (1996) – it sold over one million copies – as an example, Ambrose (quoted, Bacon 1998) outlined his presentational strategy:

> I write a continuous narrative. I long ago learned ... to tell the story chronologically because that's the way it happened. And as soon as you do that you just get a driving force to your narrative. The characters don't know what's going to happen next, so I don't want the reader to know, either. If Meriwether goes around a bend in the river and nobody had ever been on the river before to write about it, I want my readers to be surprised just like Lewis was at what he saw.

Underpinned by a philosophy echoing that outlined by Hibbert in chapter 3, Ambrose's Second World War histories drew also upon extensive oral testimony from veterans to present war's story from below by foregrounding ordinary soldiers fighting on Rhine bridgeheads or on Normandy's beaches. Moreover, Ambrose (quoted, Bacon 1998), a self-confessed 'unabashed triumphalist' from Lovington, Illinois, viewing the USA as 'the best and greatest country that ever was', inclined towards Hollywood-type presentations centred upon the USA's principal responsibility for winning the war. As highlighted by the film *Saving Private Ryan* (1998) and the Emmy-winning *Band of Brothers* (2001) television mini-series – both were based on his publications – Ambrose assigned Britain and the Soviet Union only a marginal wartime role.

Apart from boosting book sales, film and television adaptations confirmed Ambrose's celebrity status, rubbing shoulders with Steven Spielberg and Tom Hanks, who were responsible for purchasing the rights of Ambrose's 1992 book to make *Band of Brothers* (2001) shown by HBO and the BBC. Ambrose, a captivating lecturer, contributed to numerous television programmes for the USA's PBS as well as the History and National Geographic Channels. For example, he acted as a 'talking head' and programme adviser for Ken Burns's *Lewis & Clark: The Journey of the Corps of Discovery* (1997). Also he founded the National D-Day Museum in New Orleans. Opened on 6 June 2000, in 2003 Congress designated it 'America's National World War II Museum'.

In turn, a range of activities, including 'Stephen Ambrose Historical Tours', formed in 1999, exploited his name to create 'a commodified historical enterprise' (Robin 2004: 8, 54; Kaminer 2002: 9), centred upon the family company, 'Ambrose–Tubbs, Inc.' [John Tubbs, the treasurer, was Ambrose's son-in law], based at Helena, Montana. Commentators (Stack 2002; Wiener 2005: 187–8) depicted Ambrose as heading up a multimedia franchise selling television/movie rights of his histories, operating battlefield tours, and churning out a succession of lucrative boilerplate histories to entertain a mass audience, on an assembly line from parts assembled by a workforce of researchers headed by his son Hugh. Reportedly (Rose 2001), Ambrose's annual earnings, boosted by royalties, $1 million in book advances, film rights, and speaking fees totalling $40,000 per engagement, amounted to at least $3 million.

Allegations of plagiarism

When Ambrose died in October 2002, one obituary (*National Geographic* 2002) recorded that his histories were based on far more than library research and oral testimony. Reportedly, when writing about Lewis and Clark, he followed their trail, just as he visited the Normandy beaches or flew in a B-24 bomber when researching D-Day or the air war over Germany. However, in January 2002 accusations of plagiarism suggested that his histories involved also stealing words from other presenters. The initial attack was launched in the USA's *Weekly Standard*, whose executive editor, Fred Barnes (2002: 27), claimed that Ambrose's current bestseller, entitled *The Wild Blue: the men and boys who flew the B-24s over Germany* (2001), copied text verbatim from Thomas Childers's *Wings of Morning: the story of the last American bomber shot down over Germany in World War II* (1995), but without using quotation marks:

> The only attribution Childers gets in 'The Wild Blue' is a mention in the bibliography and four footnotes. And the footnotes give no indication that an entire passage has been lifted with only a few alterations from 'Wings of Morning' or that a Childers sentence has been copied word-for-word.

Box 12.1 provides one example cited by Barnes

Ambrose's public profile, including the fact that *The Wild Blue* was currently ranked in the USA's top 20 non-fiction charts, ensured that Barnes's accusations sparked off extensive media and academic controversy as well as close scrutiny of both *The Wild Blue* and Ambrose's previous publications. Generally speaking, text published without quotation marks is presumed to be the author's, even if a footnote cites an information source. Thus, Ambrose appeared guilty of presenting text

---

Box 12.1   Barnes's allegations of Ambrose's plagiarism

Thomas Childers, *Wings of Morning* (1995): 83

> Up, up, up, groping through the clouds for what seemed like an eternity ... No amount of practice could have prepared them for what they encountered, B-24s, glittering like mica, were popping up out of the clouds all over the sky.

Stephen Ambrose, *The Wild Blue* (2001): 164

> Up, up, up he went, until he got above the clouds. No amount of practice could have prepared the pilot and crew for what they encountered – B-24s, glittering like mica, were popping up out of the clouds over here, over there, everywhere.

---

written by another historian as his own. Moreover, the media discovered and revealed that even Ambrose's early work suffered from varying levels of plagiarism in the sense that copied phrases and sentences, though footnoted, were not placed within quotation marks (Robin 2004: 47). For example, in 1970 Cornelius Ryan, the author of *The Longest Day* (1959), had complained that Ambrose's *The Supreme Commander* (1970) contained unattributed quotes from his book *The Last Battle* (1966). Similarly, Ambrose's *Crazy Horse and Custer* (1975) was shown to copy text verbatim from Jay Monaghan's *Custer: the life of General George Armstrong Custer* (1959).

Pointing to the way in which Ambrose's *Citizen Soldiers* (1997) plagiarised his history entitled *Beyond the Beachhead: The 29th Infantry Division in Normandy* (1989), Joseph Balkoski (quoted, Lewis 2002) identified the fundamental problem: 'The bottom line is, he's giving the reader that impression that the words on the page came out of his mind – but they came out of *my* mind. It's no understatement to say that I agonized over 90% of those sentences. Those words are *my* words.' For Balkoski, a footnote was inadequate compensation. Such revelations undermined the initial view that the plagiarism identified in *The Wild Blue* might be excused as a one-off event arising from what Eric Foner (quoted, Kirkpatrick 2002) called 'the sloppiness that comes with speed' for a book-a-year popular historian.

Ambrose (quoted, Robin 2004: 48, 55; Wiener 2005: 190–1) acknowledged the problem, but played down the issue as affecting only a few pages, especially as the allegedly copied passages were referenced: 'You would have to be some kind of fool to plagiarize somebody and then put a footnote on it and tell them where it came from.' Plagiarism, he argued, involved deliberate deception, that is, giving no credit at all in a footnote. Pointing to the contrasting approaches adopted by popular and academic historians, Ambrose (quoted, Kirkpatrick 2002) claimed that the absence of quotation marks was a matter of methodology, not wrong-doing: 'I tell stories ... I don't discuss my documents ... I am not writing a Ph.D. dissertation.' He won strong support from his publisher, Simon & Schuster, as well as from George McGovern (quoted, Robin 2004: 48), the subject of *The Wild Blue* and a former presidential candidate, who praised Ambrose as a 'superb historian'.

Academia, like the media, was divided. Was Ambrose guilty of deliberate deception, 'literary kleptomania', 'innocent oversight', or poor research (Stack 2002; Robin 2004: 32)? Had he made a fortune from the hard work of other scholars? Unsurprisingly, public debate about plagiarism soon moved on to broader issues such as celebrity historians, historical standards, and intellectual property. A key focus was the alleged manner in which Ambrose's role as an academic historian seeking to inform and entertain a vast popular audience led political and commercial priorities to override academic considerations, especially as the controversy gave historians jealous of his fame and wealth or uneasy about his flag-waving approach the opportunity for attack. For some commentators (Lewis 2002; Robin 2004: 46–7), Ambrose was acting less as an author-presenter but more as an editor, using material assembled by staff working for Ambrose historical enterprises from presentations written by other historians. As Wendy Kaminer (2002: 9) remarked, 'he doesn't author books, it seems, so much as he assembles them'. For Robin (2004: 49–50): 'Ambrose ... appeared to be the CEO [Chief Executive Officer] of a vast history factory in which a host of assembly-line workers put together a historical product comprising mass-produced platitudes, refurbished parts from the works of others, and recycled material from Ambrose's own previous studies.'

Whereas charges of plagiarism prove a cardinal sin for academic historians and potentially career-threatening, Ambrose's retired status and present-day image as a public historian rendered him immune from institutional sanctions. In the event, he apologised, while agreeing to insert quotation marks and full attribution in future editions and publications (Box 12.2; Ambrose 2002a).

It is difficult to say how far the episode tarnished Ambrose's reputation. In part, the problem went away, particularly as soon afterwards the press reported that Ambrose, a long-time smoker, had lung cancer. Despite intensive treatment, he died in October 2002, when most obituaries

---

Box 12.2   Ambrose's amended text

Stephen Ambrose, *The Wild Blue* (2002 ed.): 164

'Up, up, up he went, until he got above the clouds.' As Thomas Childers describes it, 'no amount of practice could have prepared the pilot and crew for what they encountered – B-24s, glittering like mica, were popping up out of the clouds' over here, over there, everywhere.

Note: The section containing these sentences was footnoted as based upon Childers's *Wings of Morning*: 82–91.

---

referred only briefly to the plagiarism scandal (Wiener 2005: 191). However, one wonders how far most of Ambrose's loyal and devoted readers really cared about missing quotation marks and attributions. For them, did the story line, whatever its origin, come first? Nor did Spielberg and Hanks discontinue collaboration with the Ambrose family. Thus, their Pacific War project, as discussed initially with Stephen Ambrose, went ahead, with his son, Hugh, writing the bestselling book accompanying the ten-part 2010 television mini-series *The Pacific* (Ambrose 2002b: 191; Whitworth 2010).

In 2010 a further challenge to Stephen Ambrose's scholarly integrity occurred when Tim Rives, deputy director of the Eisenhower Library, queried the interviews referenced in his biographies of Dwight Eisenhower (Rayner 2010: 19). Pointing to the manner in which mismatches with presidential appointment books were accentuated by vague referencing, Rives implied that Stephen Ambrose significantly exaggerated the extent and the frequency of his relationship with the former president. Commenting on the revelations, Eisenhower's son, John (quoted, Rayner 2010: 19), recalled 'Ambrose's fondness for embellishment and his tendency to sacrifice fact to narrative panache'. By way of defence, Hugh Ambrose (2010) conceded that his father was guilty of the occasional 'regrettable' exaggeration about his contacts with Eisenhower, but argued that they 'hardly outweigh a towering legacy' based on 'decades of scholarship'.

Conclusion

These controversies reaffirm the fact that today history is no longer confined to the ivory tower but represents a popular public enterprise presented by 'a new generation of media-savvy practitioners' (Robin 2004: 35–6). The continued blurring of the boundaries between academic writing and popular history, alongside the media hunger for news stories and the internet's empowerment of the lay public, has rendered it more difficult to deal with any cases of deviance through the profession's traditional rules and procedures. Presenters of the past risk becoming the focus of unwelcome media attention, especially if, as happened with Ambrose and Bellesiles, methodological and other shortcomings provide ammunition for critics within and outside the historical profession. Finally, these cases remind history presenters of the need always to conform to historical standards, particularly on aspects like referencing, as articulated by the AHA (2005): 'By practicing their craft with integrity, historians acquire a reputation for trustworthiness that is arguably their single most precious professional asset.'

Michael Anthony Bellesiles (1954–): Select Bibliography

Histories

1993   *Revolutionary Outlaws: Ethan Allen and the struggle for independence on the early American frontier*

1996   'The origins of a gun culture in the United States, 1760–1865', *Journal of American History*

2000   'Exploding the myth of an Armed America', *Chronicle of Higher Education*

2000   *Arming America: the origins of a national gun culture*

2001   'Disarming the Critics', *Organization of American Historians Newsletter*

2001   'The Second Amendment in Action', in Carl T. Bogus (ed.), *Law and History: historians and constitutional scholars on the right to bear arms*

2003   *Arming America: the origins of a national gun culture*, 2nd ed.

2003   *Weighed in an Even Balance*

2010   *1877: America's year of living violently*

Edited works

1999   *Lethal Imagination: violence and brutality in American history*

2006   (with C. Waldrep) *Documenting American Violence: a sourcebook*

Stephen Edward Ambrose (1936–2002): Select Bibliography

Histories

1962	*Halleck: Lincoln's Chief of Staff*
1967	*Eisenhower and Berlin, 1945: the decision to halt at the Elbe*
1970	*The Supreme Commander: the war years of General Dwight D. Eisenhower*
1975	*Crazy Horse and Custer: the parallel lives of two American warriors*
1981	*Ike's Spies: Eisenhower and the espionage establishment*
1983–84	*Eisenhower, 2 vols.: 1: Soldier, General of the Army, President-elect, 1890–1952; 2: The President*
1985	*Pegasus Bridge: June 6 1944*
1987	*Nixon: the education of a politician, 1913–1962*
1990	*Eisenhower: soldier and president*
1990	*Nixon: the triumph of a politician, 1962–1972*
1990	*Nixon: ruin and recovery, 1973–1990*
1992	*Band of Brothers, E Company, 506 Regiment, 101st Airborne: from Normandy to Hitler's Eagle's Nest*
1994	*D-day, June 6 1944: the climactic battle of World War II*
1996	*Undaunted Courage: Meriwether Lewis, Thomas Jefferson and the opening of the American West*
1997	*Citizen Soldiers: the U.S. Army from the Normandy Beaches to the Bulge to the surrender of Germany, June 7 1944–May 7 1945*
1997	(with Douglas Brinkley) *Rise to Globalism: American foreign policy since 1938*
1997	*Americans at War*
1998	*The Victors: Eisenhower and his boys — the men of World War II*
1999	*Comrades: brothers, fathers, heroes, sons, pals*
2000	*Nothing Like it in the World: the men who built the transcontinental railroad, 1863–1869*
2001	*The Wild Blue: the men and boys who flew the B-24s over Germany*
2003	*This Vast Land*

→

Edited works

1970   (with A.D. Chandler, Jr.) *The Private Papers of Dwight David Eisenhower: the War Years, vols. 1–V*

Autobiography

2002   *To America: personal reflections of an historian*

13
David Irving: On Trial as a Presenter

In 2000 David Irving, self-styled historian of Hitler's Third Reich, occupied centre stage in a three-month trial held at the High Court in London. Irving had issued a writ for libel against Deborah Lipstadt, Professor of Modern Jewish and Holocaust Studies at Emory University, Atlanta, and Penguin Books, her publisher. Lipstadt's *Denying the Holocaust: the growing assault on truth and memory* (1993), Irving contended, accused him of being a Nazi apologist and an admirer of Hitler guilty of distorting the facts and manipulating the evidence in support of Holocaust denial. For Irving, Lipstadt's book represented part of a concerted attempt to ruin his reputation and living as a professional historian. In effect, the High Court was asked to give a verdict on Irving's work as a presenter of the past, with particular regard to the extent to which his publications presented an accurate picture of events concerning Nazi Germany in general and the Holocaust in particular. Of course, anyone can claim to be a historian – there is no law against it – but this is not the same thing as being accepted by society in general and the historical profession in particular as acting in the manner expected of a historian rather than being dismissed as, say, an antiquarian, a chronicler, a propagandist, or even a fraud. Furthermore, the situation was complicated by the recent extension of legal constraints upon what could be said about the Holocaust.

The trial, though easy to characterise as a mere historical spat capable of resolution in the usual way through written and oral exchanges, raised substantial issues about the presentation of the past, most notably regarding historical standards and methodology. In particular, how can we tell whether presenters are providing an accurate history rather than a propagandist account using the past to support a present-day cause? When reading a history book, how many readers, particularly those outside academia, can be expected to detect deliberate manipulations, misinterpretations, omissions, and mistranslations of the evidence? Certainly, the impact of the historian's presentation upon the audience was a prime focus for the court, as admitted in legalese by Mr Justice Charles Gray (2000: 2.13), the High Court judge hearing the case: 'My task is to arrive, without over-elaborate analysis, at the meaning or meanings which the notional typical reader of the publication in question, reading the book in ordinary circumstances, would have understood the words complained of, in their context, to bear.'

The use and abuse of history proved a central issue, since Lipstadt accused Irving of presenting, over time, a deliberately distorted view of the past for present-day politico-ideological purposes. In this sense, the trial was as much about the present as the past, given the alleged manner in which Irving's presentation of Nazi Germany's past reflected his contemporary neo-fascist agenda, infringed present-day political and moral sensibilities about the Holocaust, and touched upon the emerging issue of memory crimes. As such, the episode offered useful insights into public history, especially as the focus was placed upon someone described by de Groot (2009a: 16, 27–30) as one of Britain's 'most famous – or infamous – "public" historians of the past few decades'. For Ludmilla Jordanova (2000: 20), the trial, exposing the clash between opposing value systems, established that the historical questions interesting the lay audience were often painful and controversial.

Irving's Claim to be a 'Reputable Historian'

Pointing to his authorship of nearly 30 books about Nazi Germany and the Second World War, Irving (quoted, Evans 2001b: 5) has always represented himself as a 'reputable historian'. During the 1960s and 1970s books like *The Destruction of Dresden* (1963) and *Hitler's War* (1977), plus articles in the British and German press reportedly based upon extensive research benefiting from his fluency in German, enabled Irving to build up a media reputation as an expert on the history of the Third Reich. Despite covering relatively specialised historical subjects, Irving targeted a general audience, not academia. Most titles sold well, even becoming bestsellers, thereby enabling him to pursue a lucrative career as a professional writer living in a Mayfair apartment and driving a Rolls Royce. Irving has never held an academic post. Nor does he possess a history degree. Admittedly, he enrolled at university twice, but he neither graduated nor read history; indeed, Irving (quoted, Evans 2001b: 5–6) claimed also to have 'flunked' history at school.

Against this background, the trial was represented in part as academia taking on Irving (quoted, Gray 2000: 2.5), who complained in his opening statement that Lipstadt had 'vandalised [his] legitimacy as an historian'. Lipstadt, a university-trained historian teaching at a leading American university and targeting her histories principally at an academic audience, was ranged against Irving, a so-called professional writer lacking a university degree, let alone any formal training as a historian, but attracting a wide readership for his popular histories. Reprinted frequently in revised editions, many of Irving's titles have been published in translation in France, Germany, Italy and Spain, among other countries, or serialised in newspapers such as *Der Spiegel*. Certainly, Irving's books, highlighting his qualities as a talented storyteller, had been read by more people than those written by Lipstadt. Apart from claiming sales of two million in Austria and Germany alone, Irving (2008: 20) welcomed finding German editions of his books in the prison library when imprisoned in Austria during 2005–6.

Irving (2001a: back cover; quoted, Evans 2001b: 21–2) has described himself repeatedly as a champion for what he calls objective truth-seeking 'Real History': 'My duty as an historian is to establish the truth ... What is "Real History"? It is History that travels straight from history-maker to document, and from the archives to the writer and his book, without political input and free of academic prejudice; it is History that cannot be bought and cannot be bought off.' Confronting those who have denounced him as a far-right apologist using and abusing history, he has described himself as a revisionist historian seeking to correct and improve existing histories about Hitler's Third Reich. Irving (quoted, Evans 2001b: 21) has consistently denied adopting any underlying purposive approach to the past: 'I don't have any kind of political agenda, and really, it's rather defamatory for people to suggest that I do have an agenda. The agenda I have is ... I like seeing the other historians with egg on their face.' In part, this assertion reflected both Irving's combative nature and low opinion of academic historians. Their laziness, he argued, results in unreliable histories under-using relevant archival sources, especially foreign-language documentation. Dismissing 'their Hollywood versions of history', Irving (2008: 91; quoted, Evans 2001b: 22) has taken pride in presenting himself as 'a non-conformist historian' ploughing a lonely furrow working outside academia. Refusing to cite the work of other historians, Irving has refrained from placing his publications in the existing historiography. More recently, this separation from academia, and hence from its qualitative control procedures, has been accentuated by the manner in which he has been ostracised by most publishers and banned from academic libraries and archives because of his stance on the Holocaust.

Born in 1938, Irving has also enjoyed a difficult relationship with his family. Indeed, Nicholas (quoted, O. Craig 2006), Irving's twin, deliberately distanced himself from his brother's views: 'David never wanted the little life: he embraced the big, the exciting, the shocking. I see what he does and listen to his outrageous views – none, I think, are genuine, merely designed to cause controversy – and I shake my head in despair.' Depicted by William Rubinstein (2004: 237 n.139) as 'a right-wing gadfly and contrarian', Irving has adopted a deliberately controversial line in his books. For example, in both *Accident: the Death of General Sikorski* (1967) and *Churchill's War: volume II* (Irving 2001a), he suggested that in July 1943 the plane carrying Wladyslaw Sikorski, prime minister of Poland's London-based government in exile, was sabotaged, possibly on the orders of Churchill's government.

Claiming a succession of sensational archival discoveries, Irving has skilfully courted publicity to ensure considerable media visibility for his publications. Occasional brushes with the law, such as in February 1970 when ordered by the High Court to pay £40,000 damages for libel in *The Destruction of Convoy PQ17* (1967), merely helped book sales by keeping his name in the public eye. Inevitably, Irving's global media reputation as a historian of Nazi Germany was boosted in 1983 by his high-profile contribution when helping to expose the Hitler diaries as a forgery, as well as in 1992 when the *Sunday Times* commissioned him to translate Goebbels's diaries. However, by the early 1990s Irving had become an extremely controversial figure because of his increasingly active role as a Holocaust denier, at a time when governments and opinion were becoming more sensitive about the topic in the wake of the ongoing Arab–Israeli problem, contemporary examples of ethnic cleansing in the former Yugoslavia and genocide in Rwanda, and the growth of memory-crime legislation.

The Holocaust

The Irving–Lipstadt trial centred upon the 'Holocaust', the descriptor for the systematic mass murder of between five and six million Jews and other 'inferior' races by the Nazi German state, particularly during the period 1941–5 (Rubinstein 2004: 147–93; Fritzsche 2008: 594–613). For most of the war, the facts, obscured by a massive German security effort, were either not known or dismissed as far-fetched Allied war propaganda. In any case, the Allied wartime coalition was too busy winning the war to devote scarce resources to investigating allegations. Subsequently, when pushed back during the war's closing stages, German forces attempted to destroy much of the physical and documentary evidence of the 'Final Solution', such as by dynamiting the gas chambers at Auschwitz. Following the end of the Second World War, the advent of the Cold War and the threat of what was described at the time as a 'nuclear holocaust' (the annihilation of human civilisation by nuclear warfare) contributed to the postwar silence about the Holocaust.

By contrast, today the Holocaust, presented as one of the defining events in world history, has become ubiquitous and, for most (but not all, as shown by Irving) people, an accepted historical fact. Writing in *The Holocaust in American Life* (1999), Peter Novick (1999: 1–15) sought to explain why the Holocaust became a mainstream issue: the gradual easing of the Cold War; the growth of neo-Nazism in Germany, among other countries; and the use of the Holocaust as a fundamental part of Jewish identity. The televised trial of Adolf Eichmann as a war criminal proved a key catalyst. For the first time, in 1961 the general public was confronted with details about the Holocaust distinct from the carnage of the Second World War. Moreover, the Holocaust has been enshrined increasingly in law as a historical fact, as recorded by Timothy Garton Ash (2008): 'More and more countries have laws saying you must remember and describe this or that historical event in a certain way, sometimes on pain of criminal prosecution if you give the wrong answer. What the wrong answer is depends on where you are.' Denying the Holocaust is 'the wrong answer', given the manner in which several governments, including those in Austria, France, Germany and Israel, *but not* Britain and the USA, have enacted laws stipulating that any denial of the Holocaust, along with other cases of genocide, is illegal.

In addition, over time, especially during recent decades, a range of developments have helped to preserve, even to renew, society's memory, and add to what we know, or think we know, about the Holocaust. These have included:

- **events:** introduction in Britain of 'Holocaust Memorial Day' in 2001;
- **films:** *The Diary of Anne Frank* (1959); *Sophie's Choice* (1982); *Schindler's List* (1993); *The Reader* (2008); *The Boy in the Striped Pyjamas* (2008);
- **documentaries:** Claude Lanzmann: *Shoah* (1985); Steven Spielberg: *The Last Days* (1998); Leslie Woodhead: *The Holocaust On Trial*

(2000); Laurence Rees: *Auschwitz – The Nazis and the Final Solution* (2005);

- **novels:** Thomas Keneally: *Schindler's Ark* (1982); John Boyne: *The Boy in the Striped Pyjamas* (2006);
- **diaries:** *Anne Frank: the diary of a young girl* (1952);
- **memoirs:** Primo Levi: *Se questo è un uomo* (1947; English trans. *If this is a Man*, 1959); Filip Muller: *Eyewitness Auschwitz: three years in the gas chamber* (1999); and
- **museums:** Holocaust Exhibition, Imperial War Museum, London; US Holocaust Memorial Museum, Washington, DC; Auschwitz–Birkenau State Museum, Poland.

Holocaust Denial

Despite the Holocaust's escalating global visibility and enshrinement in memory legislation, Holocaust denial remains a feature of present-day society. Lipstadt (1994: 51) was instrumental in showing that Holocaust denial has a long history going back to, say, Paul Rassinier during the late 1940s, and continued by Harry Elmer Barnes, Austin App (*The Six Million Swindle*: 1973) and Arthur Butz (*The Hoax of the Twentieth Century*: 1976), among others, as well as Irving.

In brief, Holocaust deniers:

- deny the accuracy of the evidence furnished by survivors, witnesses and documents;
- deny the existence of any systematic Nazi programme of mass murder of Jews and other races;
- deny claims about the death of five to six million Jews in the Second World War, and assert that numbers amounted to only a few hundred thousand;
- deny the use of gas chambers to exterminate Jews; and
- dismiss the Holocaust as a mere hoax perpetrated by the propaganda of an international Jewish conspiracy.

Deniers have sought to give intellectual respectability to their campaign by appearing to act like academic historians through published 'histories', research centres (e.g. the Institute for Historical Review), regular conferences, journals (e.g. the *Journal of Historical Review*), and websites. Similarly, the deniers' use of the descriptor 'historical revisionism' to describe their thinking is intended to represent themselves as part of a recognised historiographical tradition, as noted by

Box 13.1 'History' and 'usable history'	
'History'	'Usable history'
The aim is to understand what actually happened in the past.	Priority is given to telling a 'good story' to justify a specific present-day propagandist purpose.
Research is based upon the critical use of a wide range of relevant source materials and a sceptical approach towards mythologies.	Highly selective and uncritical use is made of sources, while undue weight is given to supportive inventions and mythologies.
Viewed in the context of existing historiography, interpretations follow from the evidence.	Overlooking existing historiography, the 'facts' are squeezed to fit a predetermined view.
Past developments should be treated in context, not through present-day spectacles.	The past is viewed in present-day terms and assumptions.
Any history is treated as providing a reasonably accurate view of the past, a somewhat grey version.	'History' is presented in black-and-white terms as a true version of events.
Any history is regarded as no more than an interim account, subject to revision in the light of new evidence, etc.	Presented as an immutable and unalterable view of the past, 'history' only changes when the present-day purpose is altered.
Enhancing historical knowledge and understanding, the resulting history feeds into existing historiography.	Intended to serve a present-day propagandist purpose, the 'history' will not contribute to the topic's historiography.
History, though targeted also at a popular audience, is presented principally to a limited academic audience in peer-reviewed publications and produced in accordance with accepted historical standards.	Presented in an accessible style, the 'history' is directed towards a broad audience through the media, internet and the group's PR materials without peer review or adherence to the usual academic qualitative control procedures.

Lipstadt (1994: 20): 'The deniers' selection of the name *revisionist* to describe themselves is indicative of their basic strategy of deceit and distortion and of their attempt to portray themselves as legitimate historians engaged in the traditional practice of illuminating the past.'

Lipstadt's (1994: 51) critique of Paul Rassinier's writings, such as collected together in *Debunking the Genocide Myth* (1977), as 'a mixture of blatant falsehoods, half-truths, quotations out of context, and attacks on the "Zionist establishment"' was applicable equally to many others. She dismissed deniers as part of an irrational, 'far from scholarly' movement whose academic pretensions obscured the fact that they produced *usable accounts* of the past masquerading as history (Box 13.1). Lacking academic rigour, they took advantage of failing memories and public ignorance. Deniers represented, Lipstadt argued, a clear and present danger, given the risk that the lessons to be learned by future generations from the terrible events of the 1930s and 1940s would be obfuscated by false 'histories' of events.

Denying the Holocaust

For Lipstadt (1994: 181), Irving proved 'one of the most dangerous spokespersons for Holocaust denial'. During recent decades, Irving's views about the Holocaust have attracted increasingly close attention, and resulted in restrictions on access to libraries and archives, arrest warrants, court cases, deportations and imprisonment. Despite claiming to be a Hitler historian – 'Hitler appointed me his biographer' – not a Holocaust historian, Irving (Hari 2009) frequently and increasingly touched upon the Holocaust, including Hitler's role or non-role therein, in both his writings and speeches.

Irving did not deny numerous Jews died in the Second World War, but he did:

- deny that they were killed in gas chambers at Auschwitz and other camps;
- deny that there was a systematic programme, ordained at a high level by Hitler, to exterminate European Jewry; and
- deny that the killings were in any significant way different from the war's other atrocities.

Writing in *Hitler's War* (1977), Irving claimed that, far from ordering the extermination of the Jews, Hitler had not known about such excesses until late 1943. Prior to this date, Hitler, he argued, attempted to mitigate the anti-Semitic excesses of his subordinates. In 1977 Irving even offered a $1000 reward to anyone who could provide a document proving that Hitler actually ordered the Holocaust.

Such views, including strong support for Holocaust denial, were expressed more frequently and more vigorously from the late 1980s onwards. Indeed, his thinking about the Holocaust underwent a sea-change after reading the 1988 *Leuchter Report*'s dismissal of the existence of gas chambers at Auschwitz. Overlooking Frederick A. Leuchter's lack of relevant technical expertise – in fact, his report was produced as expert evidence for a 1988 court case, but completely discredited, along with its author, in the trial – Irving (quoted, Gray 2000: 8.17ix, 8.17xvi) admitted: 'That's what converted me, when I read that in the report ... I became a hard core disbeliever. I thought, well, whatever the Nazis are doing to the Jews, they were not killing them on a conveyor belt system in gas chambers in Auschwitz.' As a result, most references to the extermination of the Jews in *Hitler's War*, published originally in 1977, were removed from the revised 1991 edition. Moreover, *Focal Point*, Irving's own publishing company, published the *Leuchter Report* together with a foreword written by Irving himself.

On 15 November 1991 Irving and Leuchter, the report's author, shared the platform at Chelsea Town Hall. However, Leuchter, who had been banned from entering the country by the British government after protests from Jewish groups, was soon removed by the police. Undeterred, Irving (quoted, Sereny 1991) continued speaking, even informing the audience that readers of the recently revised edition of *Hitler's War* would 'not find one line on the "Holocaust" ... Why dignify something with even a footnote that has not happened'. Subsequently, Irving (1995: 15; quoted, Guttenplan 2002: 120) aligned himself more closely with the denial movement, as evidenced in 1992 when dismissing Auschwitz's gas chambers as 'Hollywood legends' or in 1995 when reaffirming that 'we revisionists say that gas chambers didn't exist, and that the "factories of death" didn't exist'.

Already in June 1989 a House of Commons Early Day Motion, signed by 88 MPs, had condemned Irving as a 'Nazi propagandist and long-time Hitler apologist' (Van Pelt 2002: 50). During the late 1980s and 1990s growing criticism of the content and tone of Irving's publications and speeches was accompanied by evidence establishing his close links with neo-fascist and denial groups, such as those forged through regular speaking tours to the former East Germany.

Deported from Canada in 1992, refused entry to Australia (1993–4), subject to arrest warrants from Austria and Germany, excluded from many archives, Irving proved a frequent target for hostile demonstrators. Booksellers and libraries refused to hold or restricted access to his books. When preparing his report for Lipstadt's defence team, Richard Evans (Gray 2000: 5.14) recorded that he had been required by the British Library to read *Hitler's War* in the section reserved for pornographic materials! Ostracised by publishers, Irving (quoted, Sereny 1991) was forced to establish a publishing company, Focal Point Publications, to reach his audience and 'publish truths other people are too scared to print'.

Unsurprisingly, Irving's relationship with academia deteriorated further. However, Irving, who rejoiced in his status as a professional 'independent historian' working outside the academic mainstream, had always experienced an uneasy relationship with academia. Generally speaking, his presentations of the past had attracted a critical, frequently hostile, reception from academic historians, who rarely cited or listed his publications because of their perceived political nature. There were occasional book reviews. Typical was a critique of his *Göring: a biography* (1989) by Peter Hoffmann (1989) of McGill University, Montréal:

> Mr. Irving's constant references to archives, diaries and letters and the overwhelming amount of detail in his work, suggest objectivity. In fact, they put up a screen behind which a very different agenda is transacted ... Mr. Irving is a great obfuscator ... Distortions affect every important aspect of this book to the point of obfuscation ... It is unfortunate that Mr. Irving wastes his extraordinary talents as a researcher and writer on trivializing the greatest crimes in German history, on manipulating historical sources.

Allowing his political convictions to dominate the story line resulted in factual errors, misinterpretations, distortions, omissions and mistranslations, as highlighted also by Eberhard Jäckel's *David Irving's Hitler: a faulty history dissected* (1993). As Cannadine (2000: 226) complained, Irving's publications were 'perversely tendentious and irresponsibly sensationalist ... written in a tone which is at best casually journalistic and at worst quite exceptionally offensive'.

Evans (2001b: 15) summarised the situation:

> A picture emerged, therefore, of a man who had left no stone unturned in his search for new documentation about Hitler and his role in the

Third Reich, but whose use of that documentation raised many objections in the minds of those who knew the field well. Their criticisms raised real issues of objectivity, bias, and political motivation in the study of history that went far beyond the work of Irving himself.

Evans (1999: 4biii) pointed also to the way in which inadequate and vague referencing transgressed a 'basic convention of historical scholarship' by making it very difficult to check out the sources of Irving's claims and statements. To some extent, the resulting gulf might be interpreted as a function of Irving's (quoted, Evans 2001b: 5–6) confession that 'I am an untrained historian.' Even so, as Evans advised, 'Irving could not be dismissed just because he lacked formal qualifications.' Indeed, some of Irving's publications, most notably *Hitler's War*, attracted qualified praise from historians, like Sir John Keegan (2000), the military historian, and A.J.P. Taylor. However, any praise tended to be mixed; thus, Taylor (1977b; 1978), though commending Irving's 'unrivalled industry' and 'good scholarship', rejected his claim concerning Hitler's ignorance about the Holocaust as 'too silly to be worth arguing about'.

Although she was not the first scholar to question his historical credentials, Lipstadt brought the controversy about Irving's standing as a historian to centre stage, even if only a few pages of *Denying the Holocaust* devoted much attention to him personally. Identifying Irving as 'a discredited figure' as a historian, Lipstadt (1994: 20, 111, 180) accused him, like fellow deniers, of falling well short of accepted historical standards: 'Deniers count on the fact that the vast majority of readers will not have access to the documentation or make the effort to determine how they have falsified or misconstrued information.' Driven by his obsession with exonerating Hitler of any personal guilt for the Holocaust, Irving was adjudged guilty by Lipstadt (1994: 181) of falsifying history: 'Familiar with historical evidence, he bends it until it conforms with his ideological leanings and political agenda ... he is most facile at taking accurate information and shaping it to confirm his conclusions.' Lipstadt (1994: 161) argued that Irving, failing to exercise the detachment, rationality and judgement expected of historians, deliberately ignored what was revealed by the historical record:

> Scholars have described Irving as a 'Hitler partisan wearing blinkers' and have accused him of distorting evidence and manipulating documents to serve his own purposes. He is best known for his thesis that Hitler did not know about the Final Solution, an idea that scholars have dismissed ... His work has been described as 'closer to theology

or mythology than to history,' and he has been accused of skewing documents and misrepresenting data in order to reach historically untenable conclusions, particularly those that exonerate Hitler.

Prior to the trial, Lipstadt's book had sold only 2100 copies in Britain, and hence might be adjudged as unlikely to have inflicted much actual damage to Irving's reputation as a writer of history, at least as far as the general public was concerned. However, Irving, seeking to safeguard his freedom of expression in the face of what he saw as a campaign orchestrated by international Jewish interests, perceived the book as part of a long-standing concerted attempt to silence him. Unsurprisingly, he welcomed the opportunity for personal, political and financial reasons to check those opposing the Holocaust denial movement as well as to give global visibility to his publications.

The High Court Trial, 2000

In September 1996 Irving took out a libel writ in England, where libel laws – they assume that any defamatory statement is a falsehood unless proved otherwise by the defendants – favoured the plaintiff more than those in the USA, where the First Amendment's guarantee of free speech restricts the scope for such cases. Given that defamation involves making a false statement about another person either in writing (libel) or orally (slander) causing that person to suffer harm, Irving, who represented himself in court, had to prove:

- that Lipstadt had made a defamatory statement about him in her book published by Penguin;
- that the statement was false;
- that the statement was made to a third party through publication, and not kept to herself; and
- that he suffered harm, such as an injury to his reputation as a historian, or mental anguish.

By contrast, it was incumbent upon Lipstadt and Penguin to establish the '*substantial* truth' of her book's critique to the effect:

- that Irving was discredited as a historian;
- that he denied the Holocaust; and
- that he persistently distorted the historical record in order to depict Hitler in a favourable light.

In effect, Lipstadt (2005: 37–9, 41) saw her task 'to protect the historical record', 'to prove ... that what I wrote about Irving was correct', and particularly – to quote one of her supporters – 'to nail this guy's lies and distortions'. Significantly, part of her legal costs was met by the SHOAH Foundation (Survivors of the Shoah Visual History Foundation), established by Steven Spielberg in 1994 after making the film *Schindler's List*.

When preparing their case, the defence, led by Richard Rampton QC, recruited an international team of experts to present informed guidance about Irving's publications, speeches and politics. Richard Evans, professor of modern history at the University of Cambridge, was commissioned to review Irving's writings and speeches. In July 1999 Evans (1999; 2001a: 55) submitted a detailed 740-page report: 'What I found was astonishing. In every case, Irving had manipulated or twisted the documents almost out of recognition.' More importantly, 'it was also clear enough that he was a "Holocaust denier"'. Robert Jan van Pelt of the University of Waterloo, Ontario, submitted an equally lengthy report on Auschwitz totalling 767 pages.

Focusing upon Irving's presentation of the past, particularly in 19 cases cited by the defendants, Gray, the judge, sitting without a jury, conducted an in-depth investigation of Irving's claims. Several historians gave expert evidence, with both Evans and van Pelt each spending over three days in the witness box. Public and media interest soon forced the trial to be switched to a larger court.

Space rules out coverage of the whole trial held between January and April 2000, but three case studies will be used to illuminate the trial process:

- *Kristallnacht,* 1938;
- the bombing of Dresden in 1945;
- Holocaust denial.

Kristallnacht, 9–10 November 1938

For Evans (2005: 580–94), like other historians, *Kristallnacht* ('the night of broken glass') marked a vital stage in the evolution of Nazi policy towards Jews in Germany, even the harbinger of Holocaust. Numerous synagogues were set on fire and destroyed during a nationwide attack upon Jews and their property. At least 7500 Jewish-owned shops were destroyed. Many Jews died, 30,000 were arrested, and many transported to concentration camps.

For Irving, this episode proved a central part of his attempt to exonerate Hitler of responsibility for the Holocaust. Writing in *Goebbels* (1996),

Irving (1996: 275, 281; Evans 2001b: 70, 206–8) referred to the 'sole personal guilt' of Joseph Goebbels, the Minister for Propaganda, for conceiving and initiating this nationwide pogrom. By contrast, Hitler is presented as not knowing about, let alone approving, the action until it was well under way; in fact, Irving (1996: 276–7) claimed that Hitler, when informed, was 'livid with rage', made a 'terrible scene with Goebbels', and tried to stop the action. In court, the defence criticised Irving's presentation of *Kristallnacht* for the systematic distortion, suppression, and mistranslation of documentary evidence, including Goebbels's diary entries. He was accused also of the uncritical use of oral testimony based upon interviews conducted long after the war with Hitler's adjutants, who were not only recalling distant events but also were bound to slant their accounts in favour of Hitler, if only to exculpate themselves.

Regarding the alleged suppression of evidence, the court was told that Irving omitted a telegram sent at 2355 hours on 9 November 1938 by Heinrich Müller, head of the Security Police. Warning German police officials about forthcoming anti-Jewish measures and the need to prepare for the arrest of 20,000–30,000 Jews, the telegram ordered that the arrests 'are not to be interrupted'. According to the defendants the telegram was a vital document reflecting precisely what Hitler had ordered earlier that evening, since Müller was in effect answerable to Hitler and clearly acting on instructions from the highest level. Irving, the defence argued, compounded the problem by mistranslating a telex sent at 0256 hours on 10 November from the office of Rudolf Hess, Hitler's deputy, to local Nazi party leaders stating that – to quote Irving (1984: 277–8) – 'On express orders issued at the very highest level, there are to be no kind of acts of arson or outrages against *Jewish property* [author's emphasis] or the like on any account and under any circumstances whatsoever.' For Irving (1984: 275–6; 1996: 277; Gray 2000: 5.60), this telex established that 'Adolf Hitler himself has ordered that all this outrage has got to stop forthwith': 'Hess's staff began cabling, telephoning and radioing instructions to *Gauleiters* and police authorities around the nation to halt the madness.'

Despite agreeing that the order emanated from Hitler, that is, 'the very highest level', Evans (2001b: 60) pointed to a crucial error, that is, mistranslating *Geschäften* as property, not shops. Thus, the relevant section should have read, 'On the express command of the highest instance, fire-raising in Jewish shops or the like must in no case and under no circumstances take place.' For Evans, this order, needing to be read together with Müller's telegram, reflected Hitler's aim to prevent fire-raising in Jewish shops and the like because most were owned by ordinary Germans. *There was no intention to forbid attacks on Jewish property such as homes or synagogues.* Thus, there existed, Evans asserted, no grounds for

Irving's claim that this order shows that Hitler commanded 'the outrage' to stop forthwith. If he had so ruled, why did the violence continue? Far from ordering a cessation, Hitler was by implication authorising the pogrom's continuation.

According to Evans (2001b: 61, 70), Irving's political agenda led him to present an inaccurate account falling well short of good history: 'his scholarship was sloppy and unreliable and did not meet even the most basic requirements of honest and competent historical research'.

> This was not a mere case of carelessness or sloppy research on Irving's part. He surely decided to suppress information of which he was aware, deliberately misconstrue other information, and manipulate the material in order to serve his own purpose of absolving Hitler from blame for the anti-Jewish excesses of the night in question.

Moreover, Irving's German-language skills suggested that any mistranslations were calculated and wilful rather than the result of a weak grasp of the linguistic possibilities.

Gray's judgement

Reviewing the evidence placed before the court, Gray (2000: 5.53; 13.16–13.20; 13.31) concluded that Irving's methodology and account were seriously flawed:

i)   Ignoring 'clear evidence' of Hitler's involvement, his account was basically 'a whitewash': 'Irving's endeavour to cast sole blame for the pogrom onto Goebbels is at odds with the documentary evidence.'

> Given the significance of the events of *Kristallnacht*, an objective historian would in my view dismiss the notion that Hitler was kept in ignorance until a relatively late stage. Yet Irving pays little attention to the evidence which implicates Hitler. He gives a misleading and partial account of Goebbels's diary entry ...

> I cannot accept Irving's explanation for his omission to refer to Muller's telegram ... [the latter lends] support to the thesis that Hitler knew and approved of the violence ...

> To write, as Irving did, that Hitler was 'totally unaware of what Goebbels had done' is in my view to pervert the evidence ...

The claim that during that night Hitler did everything he could to prevent violence against the Jews and their property is in my judgment based upon misrepresentation, misconstruction and omission of the documentary evidence.

ii) Irving treated too uncritically oral testimony about Hitler's attitudes gained 'many years after the event' from officers closely attached to Hitler, while failing to check the results against the documentary evidence:

Whilst Irving is to be commended for his diligence in tracing and interviewing these witnesses, there is in my judgment force in the Defendants' contention that Irving is unduly uncritical in his use of their evidence especially when it runs counter to the evidence of contemporaneous documents .... In my view he ought to have approached their accounts with considerable scepticism and rejected them where they conflict with the evidence of the contemporaneous documents.

According to Gray, 'The contemporaneous documents created during the night of violence are likely to prove a far more reliable guide than the self-serving and untested accounts of Hitler's staff.'

iii) Irving's distortions derived in part from the deliberate mistranslation of key sources.

It is my conclusion that the Defendants are justified in their assertion that Irving has seriously misrepresented Hitler's views on the Jewish question. He has done so in some instances by misinterpreting and mistranslating documents and in other instances by omitting documents or parts of them. In the result the picture which he provides to readers of Hitler and his attitude towards the Jews is at odds with the evidence.

The Bombing of Dresden, 13–14 February 1945

Seeking to disrupt German military industrial production and transport, early in 1945 Allied bombing raids targeted large urban centres, like Dresden. Despite being glossed over in Lipstadt's book, Irving's presentation of the bombing of Dresden in February 1945 was raised at the trial as yet another example of his shortcomings as a historian (Lipstadt 2005: 40–1, 167–8), especially as this non-Holocaust topic was the subject of his first book, *The Destruction of Dresden* (1963), and exploited by Holocaust deniers to qualify negative wartime images of Nazi Germany. Selling well in Britain and the USA and published when he was only 25 years old, the book helped to make Irving's reputation as a popular historian within and outside Britain, with translations being published in France, Germany, Italy, Portugal and Spain.

In 1963 Irving (1963: 7, 9, 197, 210) proposed 135,000 as an 'authoritative' death toll for Dresden. Varying totals, ranging between 100,000 and 250,000, were given in subsequent editions as well as his other publications – *Hitler's War* (1977) mentioned 250,000 deaths – and speeches (Gray 2000: 11.6–11.7). It was not until 1995, when he published *Apocalypse 1945*, a retitled version of the original 1963 book, that Irving accepted a lower total between 50,000 and 100,000, which he repeated in the High Court trial (Gray 2000: 11.39). For Irving (1963: 234), Dresden established that the Nazi regime was not alone in causing large-scale loss of life; indeed, he adjudged the British bombing of Dresden as responsible for 'the biggest single massacre in European history'. Speaking in 1990, Irving (quoted, Lipstadt 2005: 168) claimed that 'the holocaust of Germans in Dresden really happened. That of the Jews in the gas chambers of Auschwitz is an invention.'

The manner in which Irving's presentation of the bombing of Dresden influenced popular thinking and memory was highlighted in 1969 by their citation in the bestselling novel *Slaughterhouse-Five* by Kurt Vonnegut (2000: 136–7), an American soldier captured in 1944 and imprisoned in Dresden during the raid. Moreover, Irving's enduring impact on public history was indicated in 2007 when the Revd Brian Cooper (2007) – he had been involved in Coventry's postwar twinning reconciliation project with Dresden – had a letter published in the *Independent* quoting his 1963 publication as an authoritative source confirming 135,000 deaths. In many respects, such beliefs were encouraged by the book's supportive foreword written by Air Marshal Sir Robert Saundby, the Deputy Air Officer Commanding Bomber Command (1943–5). Acting 'dispassionately and honestly', Irving, Saundby (Irving 1963: 5–6) claimed, had 'gathered together all the evidence, separated fact from fiction, and given us a detailed account as near to the truth, perhaps, as we shall ever get'.

At the trial, the defence focused primarily upon the way in which Irving's political agenda led him to give credence to unreliable sources as well as to his stubborn refusal to revise death totals after his evidence had been exposed as a blatant forgery. Having relied in 1963 on a 'shaky' (Evans 2001b: 152) source lacking documentary support, Irving (1963: 207–8) used a copy – or rather a copy of a copy – of a German Order of the Day TB47, dated 22 March 1945, as the key source in subsequent editions (Lipstadt 2005: 168). Irving acquired a copy of TB47, *not* the original document, in November 1964, that is, shortly after his book first appeared. Citing a figure of 202,040 dead, his copy of TB47 indicated that numbers might rise to 250,000 when more information became available. Despite being warned about its possible lack of authenticity, Irving used TB47 to justify 200,000-plus deaths. Nor did the eventual discovery in 1977 of the original TB47 – recording 20,204 deaths, this established that a nought had been added to the total on his copy – impact upon Irving's presentation of events. Only in 1995 did Irving admit that his copy was a forgery resulting from the attempt of Hitler's Propaganda Ministry to persuade the German people to make a stand against the Allies by exaggerating the death toll (Lipstadt 2005: 169).

Gray's judgement

Once again, Gray sided with the defence, and concluded that Irving's methods cast serious doubt on his *bona fides* as a historian. More significantly, the episode revealed that Irving had persistently misrepresented the facts from an early stage of his career for personal and political purposes, even refusing to revise his text in the light of relevant new evidence or the exposure of a forgery. Stating that Irving 'failed lamentably' to assess the authenticity, nature and meaning of sources, Gray (2000: 5.53, 13.118, 13.125) pressed the need for historical standards: 'Historical evidence cannot of course be compartmentalised into reliable and unreliable evidence. It is part of the skill of an historian to evaluate the degree of individual items of evidence, seeking to adopt a consistent approach throughout.' Irving's methods fell well short of what was deemed appropriate: 'In my judgement, there are serious criticisms to be made of Irving's use of this document' [TB47]. Gray's (2000: 13.119, 13.126) repeated use of the phrases 'he should' and 'he should not' highlighted Irving's perceived failings as a historian: 'He should have verified the *provenance* of the document ... In the meantime he should not have made use of so suspect a document':

> The evidence ... affords a very slender basis for the claim which Irving has made for the numbers killed in the raids ... In my judgment the estimates of 100,000 and more deaths which Irving continued to put about in the 1990s lacked any evidential basis and were such as no responsible historian would have made.

By way of postscript, in March 2010 the Dresden Historians Commission, which had conducted an exhaustive five-year official study, gave a maximum death toll of 25,000 (Low 2010).

A Holocaust Denier

Ranging widely across Holocaust-related matters, the trial offered numerous insights into the question of how far the picture given in court conformed to Lipstadt's depiction of Irving as a Holocaust denier. Drawing upon several expert witnesses, including Evans and van Pelt, the defence conducted an in-depth exposé of Irving's repeated denials – examples from his speeches and writings were mentioned earlier in this chapter – about the use of gas chambers at Auschwitz.

Gray's judgement

Yet again, Irving, albeit claiming not to be a Holocaust historian, failed to convince the judge that he had a case for libel. As Gray (2000: 8.15) admitted, there was nothing wrong with denying that any event had occurred unless it could be established 'that such a denial is to a greater or lesser extent contrary to the available historical evidence'. Acknowledging that he became really active on Holocaust issues during the late 1980s, Gray confirmed Irving's status as a Holocaust denier. Significantly, Gray (2000: 8.17ix; 13.94–13.95) pointed to the need also to 'make allowance for the fact that, when addressing live audiences as opposed to writing books, Irving needed to hold the attention of his audience by expressing himself in a vivid and colourful style':

> It appears to me to be incontrovertible that Irving qualifies as a Holocaust denier. Not only has he denied the existence of gas chambers at Auschwitz and asserted that no Jew was gassed there, he has done so on frequent occasions and sometimes in the most offensive terms. By way of examples, I cite ... his dismissal of the eye-witnesses en masse as liars or as suffering from a mental problem; his reference to an Association of Auschwitz Survivors and Other Liars or 'ASSHOLS'. (speech at Calgary, 29 Sept. 1991)

On Trial as a Historian

In effect, the trial drew together the key issues underlying the long-running debate about Irving's conduct as a presenter of the past. Lipstadt and Penguin Books were the actual defendants, but the trial was conducted – Lipstadt's decision not to give evidence helped this impression – as if Irving himself was on trial. As Rampton (quoted, Guttenplan 2002: 34–5) informed the court, 'the essence of the case is Mr. Irving's honesty and integrity as a chronicler – I shy away from the word "historian"'.

Fundamentally, the trial focused upon Irving's methodology, that is, the alleged way in which he used and abused the evidence through misquotation, suppression, distortion, manipulation, mistranslation and poor referencing, not what happened in the Second World War. Key questions faced by the court included:

- Were Irving's publications really 'history', let alone objective 'real history'?
- Was Irving a 'reputable historian', as he claimed?
- Was Irving guilty of using and abusing the past to serve a political agenda?
- More importantly, given recent legislation and a changing moral climate, was Irving a Holocaust denier?

On 12 April 2000 Gray delivered his 350-page judgement. Deciding in favour of the defendants, Gray (2000: 13.165, 13.167–13.168) asserted that Irving had no case for libel: 'My overall finding in relation to the plea of justification is that the Defendants have proved the substantial truth of the imputations, most of which relate to Irving's conduct as an historian.' Gray found the following charges to be 'substantially true':

- 'that Irving has for his own ideological reasons persistently and deliberately misrepresented and manipulated historical evidence';
- 'that for the same reasons he has portrayed Hitler in an unwarrantedly favourable light, principally in relation to his attitude towards and responsibility for the treatment of the Jews';
- 'that he is an active Holocaust denier; that he is anti-semitic and racist and that he associates with right wing extremists who promote neo-Nazism'.

By implication, Irving was adjudged guilty of the historical equivalent of fraud. The High Court judgement was reaffirmed upon appeal in July 2001. The dismissal of Irving's libel suit rendered him liable for legal costs amounting to around £2 million.

'A Victory for Historical Scholarship'

Commenting on the verdict, *The Times* (2000) claimed that 'History has had its day in court and scored a crushing victory against Mr Irving's ideologically motivated abuse' of the past. For Evans (2001a: 55), the outcome was 'a victory for historical scholarship' over political propaganda.

Having already been criticised and ostracised by academia, Irving was now adjudged to have failed the test required of good public history, at least as far as the criteria pronounced by the court, as guided by expert witnesses, were concerned: 'Irving has significantly misrepresented what the evidence, objectively examined, reveals' (Gray 2000: 13.9).

Gray (2000: 3.144, 3.162–3) concluded that Irving 'has a political agenda', which 'disposes him, where he deems it necessary, to manipulate the historical record in order to make it conform with his political beliefs':

> Mistakes and misconceptions ... appear to me by their nature unlikely to have been innocent. They are more consistent with a willingness on Irving's part knowingly to misrepresent or manipulate or put a 'spin' on the evidence so as to make it conform with his own preconceptions ... he has deliberately skewed the evidence to bring it into line with his political beliefs.

Gray adjudged Irving guilty of not only being a Holocaust denier but also in effect acting as Hitler's spin doctor. Indeed, on one occasion a slip of the tongue even led Irving to address the judge as '*Mein Führer*', much to the court's amusement (Lipstadt 2005: 263).

Contrary to what he had intended, the trial undermined, possibly destroyed, Irving's credibility and reputation as a historian, even if Gray (2000: 13.7) rejected as 'too sweeping' Evans's depiction of him as no historian. In the eyes of many, Irving had been publicly exposed as – to quote one *Daily Telegraph* (2000) editorial – 'the bad history man'. Exhaustive in-depth examination of Irving's work had established a long-standing and deliberate falsification of the historical record dating back to his early books like *The Destruction of Dresden*. Indeed, the court's verdict recalled the fact that in 1967, Patrick Brogan (1967), a book reviewer for *The Times*, had been highly critical of Irving's *Accident*: 'it is not proper history'. Then, in 1970, Irving was ordered by the High Court to pay £40,000 damages for libel, including £25,000 as exemplary damages because he 'knowingly and willingly *peddled untruths* [author's emphasis] for profit' (*Guardian* 1970) in *The Destruction of Convoy PQ17* (1967). At first glance Irving's books conformed to the accepted canons of historical scholarship. Numerous footnotes and lengthy bibliographies gave the impression of extensive archival and library research supported by the diligent gathering of oral testimony. However, notwithstanding his 'extravagant self-promotion as a discoverer of new historical material and his arrogant denigration of other researchers' (Evans 2001b: 103), the trial confirmed that Irving's presentation of the past was basically 'a house of cards, a vast apparatus of deception and deceit'.

The trial received widespread media coverage within and outside Britain, but it remains debatable whether or not the popular readership, Irving's prime audience, might either know or care about the judgement, particularly as media reporting not only gave Irving global visibility but also focused upon his racist and anti-Semitic attitudes rather than his less newsworthy unhistorical methodology. As revealed by Cooper's (2007) letter to the *Independent* cited above, the court's verdict failed to prevent Irving's flawed version of the Dresden raid retaining its hold upon at least one of his many readers. Nor are present-day readers of Vonnegut's *Slaughterhouse-Five* or neo-Nazis – in February 2010 over 6400 neo-Nazis rallied in Dresden to mark the raid's 65th anniversary – likely to view the episode any differently.

What impact did the court's verdict exert on Irving himself as a presenter of the past? On 12 April 2000 Matt's cartoon in the *Daily Telegraph*, imagining Irving's next book entitled *The Libel Trial Never Happened*, highlighted Irving's new status as a trial denier. This depiction was inspired by the fact that during an extensive round of post-trial media interviews, including BBC Two's *Newsnight* programme, Irving displayed little sign of changing course. On the contrary, he took the opportunity provided by the interviews to publicise his books, even to deny the negative outcome (Roberts 2000a). 'Welcome to the World of Real History', stated his website's home page soon afterwards. Irving (2000) advertised a forthcoming 'thorough revision' of *Hitler's War*: 'I have found it necessary to correct only one factual error in the light of this trial; and I have introduced the SS police decodes of December 1, 1941 as further proof that Hitler's headquarters were vigorously opposed to the liquidation of German Jews then beginning.' Moreover, when the revised edition was actually published in February 2001, Irving (2001b: xxxii; 2008: 67–8) remained defiant in a note added to the introduction: 'I am glad to say I have not had to revise my view as originally expressed.' If anything, Irving's opinions have merely crystallised, not changed. More recently, in March 2009 Irving attended a seminar at the German Historical Institute in London. The speaker, Peter Longerich, another expert trial witness, used his presentation to detail incontrovertible evidence about the Holocaust. Reportedly (Sherwin 2009) Irving, seated in the front row, shook his head repeatedly by way of dissenting from Longerich's line.

History has moved on, but, for Irving, nothing seems to have changed. More significantly, given the court's reliance upon expert witnesses, Irving (2001b: xxviii) retained his original complaint that: 'Most of my critics relied on weak and unprofessional evidence. For example, they offered alternative and often specious translations of words in Hitler's speeches ... and quotations from isolated documents that have long been discarded by serious historians as worthless or fakes.' Apart from taking a dig at Evans and company, Irving remains only too willing to present himself still as 'a serious historian' by repeatedly quoting a sentence or two from Gray's judgement praising his qualities. In fact, the judge's comments (Gray 2000: 13.7) – these were guided largely by evidence given by Keegan, whose performance as an expert witness failed to impress both Evans (2001b: 240–4) and Guttenplan (2002: 134–7) – were limited to his contribution as a military historian:

> My assessment is that, as a *military* historian, Irving has much to commend him. For his works of military history Irving has undertaken thorough and painstaking research into the archives ... his knowledge of World War 2 is unparalleled. His mastery of the detail of the historical documents is remarkable ... Moreover he writes his military history in a clear and vivid style.

A few other commentators joined Keegan in sympathising with Irving. Pointing to Eric Hobsbawm's recent receipt of the Order of Merit, the *Daily Telegraph*'s columnist, 'Peter Simple' (2000), complained about Irving's ostracism in a country honouring Hobsbawm, an acknowledged apologist for the Soviet regime. Quite apart from mistakenly naming the honour awarded to Hobsbawm, who became in fact a Companion of Honour, Simple's criticism ignored the fact that the court focused primarily upon Irving's flawed methodology, not his message. Far from being guilty of falsifying history, Hobsbawm has proved active in upholding sound historical practice and exposing invented histories, as detailed in chapter 5. Reviewing the judgement, Evans (2001b: 246) acknowledged that inevitably historians were often influenced unconsciously by their politics when selecting and interpreting the evidence and publishing their histories, whereas Irving's presentation of the past was consciously *dictated and distorted* by his right-wing attitudes.

Overviewing the Trial's Broader Impact

i) The courts and history
As stressed in chapter 2, there is nothing unusual about historians disagreeing about the past. Normally, historical debates and disagreements are pursued in print or orally at conferences and seminars. Rarely are

writs issued or do the courts become involved, even if over time Irving has proved no stranger to the courts as either a plaintiff or defendant. In 2000 Irving (2008: 97; Lipstadt 2005: 296), though representing himself and still able to call upon a range of financial supporters, discovered yet again that the courts are also an expensive place to argue about the past. Indeed, the trial verdict left him facing bankruptcy, and downsizing from his Mayfair apartment.

For many historians, the courts, staffed by lawyers and possessing their own agenda and rules about evidence, represent an inappropriate place to pronounce about the past. For Daniel Goldhagen (quoted, Moss 2000; Evans 2001b: 187), the Harvard-based author of *Hitler's Willing Executioners* (1996), 'The ruling of a court has no bearing on historical fact: the court is a place where legal issues are adjudicated according to the particular legal standards of a given country, not where historical issues are decided according to the different and well-established standards of historical scholarship.' David Cesarani (2000; quoted, Moss 2000) welcomed the trial's outcome, but also voiced doubts about taking history to the courts:

> Evidence in history is not like evidence in court ... In a court of law, context and circumstance are the least important evidence; they may be deemed inadmissible, not real evidence. The court wants physical evidence, a fingerprint that no one can argue with, but in history context and circumstance matter a great deal. The 'fingerprint' in this case was Irving's massaging of the sources; only by concentrating on his methodology could the case be contained.

Echoing these views, Peter Mandler (2007: 16) advised that historians, whose role was best confined to pronouncements about historical practice, should have no illusions about their place and authority in the courtroom. By contrast, Evans (2001a: 55; 2001b: 187–90), a leading player in events, concluded that the courtroom proved 'a good place' for debating history. Despite initial doubts, he was impressed by the trial process, most notably the manner in which it allowed the in-depth questioning of expert witnesses, lasting in his case 28 hours spread over three days.

Obviously, this debate has further to run, but it is worth noting Gray's (2000: 1.3) limited perception of the court's role and reluctance to encroach too far on the historians' territory:

> I do not regard it as being any part of my function as the trial judge to make findings of fact as to what did and what did not occur

during the Nazi regime in Germany ... it is not for me to form, still less to express, a judgement about what happened. That is a task for historians. It is important that those reading this judgment should bear well in mind the distinction between my judicial role in resolving the issues arising between these parties and the role of the historian seeking to provide an accurate narrative of past events.

Notwithstanding Gray's reticence, Tobias Jersak, who assisted Evans prior to the trial, has argued that the case marked the conclusion of the long-running Holocaust controversy between 'functionalists', favouring the dynamic impact of changing circumstances, and 'intentionalists', who claim that Hitler ordered the murder of European Jews. For Jersak (quoted, Fritzsche 2008: 597), 'almost all historians' now favour the intentionalist thesis.

ii) Remembering the Holocaust

Confronting, indeed demolishing, the 'fact' of Holocaust denial, the verdict foiled what Irving (quoted, Lipstadt 1994: 179) presented as his 'one-man intifada' against the official history of the Holocaust prescribed by governments and 'establishment historians'. Speaking after the trial, Goldhagen (quoted, Moss 2000) observed that it was ridiculous that Irving-type views had ever been taken seriously: 'The Holocaust is an established historical fact. That the deniers and their fellow travellers have gotten a discussion going at all is absurd; denying the Holocaust is like denying that there was slavery in the US or that the Second World War happened at all.' Even so, the episode highlighted society's need for an informed historical memory, given the Holocaust's complexities, the perpetrators' efforts to cover up their crimes, and the deniers' distorted propagandist 'histories'. Nor has the denial campaign gone away. Today, Holocaust deniers remain impervious still to reasoned argument, and only too ready to exploit failing memories and society's partial historical knowledge.

As a result, present-day societies need, it is argued, to preserve memories of the Holocaust through academic and popular histories written according to sound historical methodology, school and university teaching, film documentaries, museums, and special commemorative events. In this regard, during the past decade British governments, though dropping plans to implement a memory law against Holocaust denial, introduced Holocaust Memorial Day, to be celebrated annually on 27 January, the anniversary of the liberation of Auschwitz–Birkenau in 1945; incorporated the Holocaust in the national curriculum for history;

and supported the Holocaust Education Development Programme for teachers.

Meanwhile, debate continues about whether the story of the Holocaust's horrors can be adequately told in any medium at all. For Rosenstone (2006: 135), 'The problem of representing the Holocaust can also be seen as the core problem of history. Can we really represent the past, factually or fictionally, as it was?' Clearly, the situation has not been helped by false histories propagated by Irving-type deniers. Likewise, Evans (1997: 237–43), Robert Eaglestone (2004) and Kevin Passmore (2003: 134–6), among others, have warned about the manner in which postmodernism's extreme relativism left the door wide open to Holocaust deniers. As mentioned in chapter 5, Hobsbawm (1998: 363; quoted, Snowman 1999: 18) is among those worrying about this problem, even if 'whether or not the Nazi gas chambers existed ... can be established by evidence .... Because their existence has been established, those who deny their existence are simply not historians'. Evans (1997: 124) agreed, dismissing any postmodernist attempt to ignore the evidence and Auschwitz's historical reality: 'Auschwitz was not a discourse. It trivializes mass murder to see it as a text.'

iii) Using and abusing the Holocaust

Irving's failure to have Lipstadt's book withdrawn and pulped ensured that historians, among others, can continue to expose the way in which the Holocaust has been, and is still being, used and abused by deniers for political purposes. However, deniers are not alone in exploiting the Holocaust, as noted by Steve Paulsson (quoted, Moss 2000), the senior historian for the Imperial War Museum's Holocaust exhibition: 'The Holocaust has its uses and abuses. It has been used politically by various people. People in different countries read their own national agenda into it.' For example, the Holocaust has been turned into a legitimising event for the existence of the state of Israel. Memory laws, as discussed below, provide further manifestations of this point.

iv) Free speech and memory laws

For Evans (2001a: 55), the court's verdict was 'a victory for free speech' in the sense that Irving – reportedly (Lipstadt 2005: 293) he had other libel actions in progress, or had threatened historians like John Lukacs with legal action – had failed to silence his critics, past, present and future. For Irving, the outcome was interpreted as both a failure to curb Lipstadt's abuse of this freedom but also a restriction upon his freedom to challenge what has become the official version of the Holocaust's history.

Unsurprisingly, the verdict's implications for public history proved a central focus for post-trial press commentaries, especially as a growing number of countries, including France in 1990, have passed laws stipulating that the Holocaust must be remembered and presented in a specified manner. Also in 2005 and 2007 the United Nations (2005; 2007) adopted resolutions rejecting 'any denial of the Holocaust as an historical event, either in full or part'. For many historians, the problem was that legislation, though perhaps allowable for the Holocaust, established a precedent liable to be employed by governments for more controversial topics. Although a French law adopted in 2001 about the history of slavery was generally acceptable, during 2005–6 an attempt to prescribe that the history of the French imperial experience must be treated positively attracted considerable opposition and proved abortive.

Commenting after the trial, Lipstadt (2005: xx; quoted, BBC 2006a) voiced her opposition to laws against Holocaust denial on the grounds that they would not work and would merely make martyrs of deniers: 'The way of fighting Holocaust deniers is with history and with truth.' Despite acknowledging the efficacy of the trial process, *The Times* (2000) echoed Lipstadt's opposition to a legal ban on Holocaust denial. For a growing number of historians, the legislation of memory is viewed as a serious threat to not only freedom of speech and thought but also historical scholarship. Thus, in December 2005 several historians, working through the *Liberté pour l'histoire* (2005) grouping, published a petition in the French press protesting against growing political and judicial interference in history: 'In a free State, neither the Parliament nor the judicial courts have the right to define historical truth. State policy, even with best case will [although this phrase is included in the English translation on the group's website, 'however well intentioned' reads better], is not history policy.' In September 2007 the Council of the American Historical Association (2007) endorsed the general principle: 'Any limitation on research or freedom of expression, however well intentioned, violates a fundamental principle of scholarship: that the researcher must be able to investigate any aspect of the past and to report without fear what the evidence reveals.' Lawmakers and courts, the AHA urged, should steer clear of history: 'If any other body, especially a body with the right to initiate legal proceedings and impose penalties, seeks to influence the course of historical research, the result will inevitably be intimidation of scholars and distortion of their findings.' Pointing to the fact that any historical publication was subject to critical scholarly review by historians, the AHA argued that it was in the realm of free public debate that historians can and must work.

In October 2008 *Le Monde* published an *'Appel de Blois'* (2008) signed by a multinational group of historians and writers, including Hobsbawm, Jacques Le Goff, Heinrich August Winkler and Timothy Garton Ash, reaffirming the *Liberté pour l'histoire*'s principle that in a free country, 'it is not the business of any political authority to define historical truth and to restrict the liberty of the historian by penal sanctions'. Depicting memory laws as 'dangerous nonsense', one signatory, Garton Ash (2008), urged society to uphold the autonomy of historians in order 'to see off the nanny state and its memory police'. Excepting Irving-type deniers, there seems no real problem in treating Holocaust denial as a memory crime. But should any other official version of history be beyond question? Should historians have a right to freedom of expression, including the right to be wrong? Are most topics unsuitable for state-ordained truths, given history's uncertainties and the politically-inspired nature of most memory laws?

Conclusion

For Irving (1977: vii), 'To historians is granted a talent that even the gods are denied', that is, the ability to offer alternative versions of the past. However, as Gray (2000: 13.24) ruled, 'an objective historian is obliged to be even-handed in his approach to historical evidence: he cannot pick and choose without adequate reason'. Notwithstanding the way in which media coverage downplayed methodological issues, the High Court trial gave global visibility to the high standards expected of a presenter of public history as well as to the attempt of Irving and his fellow deniers to present propagandist versions of the past masquerading as 'history'.

In brief, the Irving trial raised fundamental historical issues: the test of a historian's detachment; the authenticity and use of sources, including those used in translation; the ability of historians to subordinate political beliefs to the demands of historical research; the emerging challenge posed by memory laws; and the role of the courts regarding history. Confronted by two people claiming to present accurate but conflicting versions of the past, the court helped to show – to quote Evans (2001b: xi) – 'how we can tell the difference between truth and lies in history'. In many respects, the judge, though conceding Irving's merits as a military historian, went a long way towards accepting the view expressed in Rampton's (quoted, Guttenplan 2002: 31; Lipstadt 2005: 257) opening and closing statements to the effect that 'Mr Irving calls himself a historian. The truth is, however, that he is not a historian at all but a falsifier of history. To put it bluntly, he is a liar.'

From this perspective, the trial was hailed as a victory for academic history and historical scholarship, even a watershed highlighting the historian's role in furnishing an informed and accurate public history on vital historical issues (Champion 2008: 181; de Groot 2009a: 29–30). For Tosh (2006: xiv–xv; 2010: 51), this high-profile episode highlighted public history's dependence upon historical expertise:

> The Irving case was obviously important in diminishing the credibility of Holocaust denial. But it had a wider significance. It showed that what professional historians do matters, that some events in the past can be authenticated beyond reasonable doubt, and that society has a vested interest in the maintenance of scholarly standards. Each of these propositions has been a matter of debate in recent years. History has been dismissed by Modernists as an antiquarian irrelevance, and by Postmodernists as a self-serving fiction. Historians have sometimes felt that the scholarly claims of their profession have been locked in a losing battle with sceptical voices from outside. The Irving case may well prove to be unique: perhaps no other historical issue could lead to such a sharply focused confrontation between scholarship and propaganda. But it nevertheless provides a sober reminder that the most accurate history possible is a social necessity.

In fact, the trial, though ruling that denial was in breach of the evidence, did not place the Holocaust beyond controversy for presenters of history, let alone end the Holocaust denial movement. Indeed, subsequently Irving-type deniers received high-level political support from the Iranian President Mahmoud Ahmadinejad (2005–), who continues publicly to dismiss the Holocaust as a myth. Moreover, in December 2006 an 'International Conference to Review the Global Vision of the Holocaust', held in Teheran, gave a global platform to deniers. In June 2009 Barack Obama, the American president (2009–), visited Buchenwald concentration camp. Responding to yet another denial of the Holocaust by Ahmadinejad – recently, he had dubbed it a 'big deception' – Obama (quoted, Squires 2009) claimed the site was the 'ultimate rebuke' to such deniers:

> To this day, there are those who insist that the Holocaust never happened, a denial of fact and truth that is baseless and ignorant and hateful ... This place is the ultimate rebuke of those thoughts – a reminder of our duty to confront those who tell lies about our history. These sites have not lost their horror with the passage of time.

As a result, Holocaust history retains substantial contemporary resonance. As Cesarani (2000) opined when looking back to the Irving trial, 'Holocaust denial is not just about the past; it's about now and it's about the future. It's about rehabilitating Nazism. It might appear academic for us, but in parts of Europe it's a vital issue.' Nor has Irving (2008: 130; M. Taylor 2007a), a self-confessed nonconformist claiming to present real history, stopped writing and lecturing about Hitler's Germany. Admittedly, during 2005–6 a 400-day imprisonment in Austria for trivialising and denying the Holocaust checked his progress, but ongoing projects include his memoirs, a final volume on Churchill, a biography of Heinrich Himmler, and an edited collection of Eichmann's documents. Moreover, his lectures, like his website, continue to find an audience on both sides of the Atlantic; indeed, reportedly (Hari 2009) much of his present-day funding comes from the USA. Throughout his career, Irving, who Weber (n.d.) described as 'living proof that the life of an historian need not be dull', has proved a divisive presenter of the past capable of attracting considerable media visibility and disruptive protesters. This remains true even today, as highlighted in November 2007 by the chaotic scenes prompted by his appearance at the Oxford Union alongside Nick Griffin, the leader of the British National Party (M. Taylor 2007b). As John Keegan (2000) remarked, 'nothing but trouble comes of taking sides over Irving. Decide against him, and his associates accuse one of prejudice ... Decide for him, and the smears start.' Also, as Lipstadt, among others, discovered, 'decide against him', and Irving is liable to take out a writ for libel.

However, the chief lesson of the Irving trial is public history's need for presenters of the past capable of both engaging the interest of a popular readership and providing high-quality history. This point is of special importance for the Third Reich and the Holocaust because of the continued popularity of histories of the Nazi regime for book readers, cinemagoers, radio listeners and television viewers (BBC 2011).

David John Cawdell Irving (1937–): Select Bibliography

Publications

1963 *The Destruction of Dresden* (1995: retitled *Apocalypse 1945: the destruction of Dresden*)

1964 *The Mare's Nest: the secret weapons of the Third Reich*

1967 *Accident: the death of General Sikorski*

→

1967	*The Destruction of Convoy PQ17*
1967	*The German Atomic Bomb: the history of nuclear research in Nazi Germany*
1973	*The Rise and Fall of the Luftwaffe: the life of Luftwaffe Marshall Erhard Milch*
1973	*The Night the Dams Burst*
1977	*Hitler's War*
1977	*The Trail of the Fox: the life of Field Marshal Erwin Rommel*
1978	*The War Path: Hitler's Germany, 1933–1939*
1981	*The War between the Generals: inside the Allied High Command*
1983	*The Secret Diaries of Hitler's Doctor*
1986	*Der Morgenthau-Plan 1944–1945*
1987	*Churchill's War, vol. 1: The struggle for power*
1987	*Hess: the missing years, 1941–1945*
1989	*Göring: a biography*
1990	*Deutschlands Ostgrenze*
1995	*Der unbekannte Dr. Goebbels – Die geheimgehaltenen Tagebücher des Jahres 1938*
1996	*Goebbels: mastermind of the Third Reich*
1996	*Nuremberg: the last battle*
2001	*Churchill's War, vol 2: Triumph in adversity*

Autobiography

2008	*Banged Up: survival as a political prisoner in 21st century Europe*

Part III
Conclusion

Overviewing points raised by the case studies in Part II, Part III highlights the need for historians to focus more than previously on presenting well-written, engaging and high-quality history to an audience. Within academia peer-reviewed monographs and journal articles prove, and will remain, central in advancing historical knowledge and understanding. Nevertheless, historians must not turn their back on society's demand for public history. Nor should historians and their students overlook and fail to reflect upon the alternative and increasingly varied aural, literary and visual ways of presenting the past to diverse audiences, at a time when historians have acquired a high public profile but academia's authority over historical knowledge is no longer unchallenged.

14

'Presentation, Presentation, Presentation'

In May 2004 Alan Bennett's *The History Boys* premiered at London's National Theatre. Two years later, the play opened on Broadway in New York. Quite apart from offering excellent entertainment, impressing theatre critics, and winning numerous awards, the play was developed into several other formats. Giving history high-profile cultural visibility on both sides of the Atlantic, *The History Boys* confronted, and today is still confronting, diverse audiences, whether cinema- or theatre-goers, radio listeners, television viewers or book readers, with issues centred upon the perennial 'battle for the hearts and minds of schoolboys' (Brantley 2006). Highlighting alternative ways of presenting history, *The History Boys* illuminated several themes explored by this book. Indeed, as the boys' headmaster asserted at the start of the play, for historians, 'presentation' is 'the word' (Bennett 2004: 8).

Pursued inevitably in somewhat black-and-white terms, debate was conducted primarily through two schoolteachers. On the one hand, Hector, an inspiring but somewhat eccentric classroom teacher, believed in the intrinsic merit of education. On the other hand, Irwin, a young newcomer recruited to coach potential Oxbridge entrants, advised boys always to say something contrary and controversial, even about the Holocaust: 'the wrong end of the stick is the right one' (Bennett 2004: 73–4, 79–80). For Irwin (Bennett 2004: 35), 'History nowadays is not a matter of conviction. It's a performance. It's entertainment.' Understandably, Hector (Bennett 2004: 72) was appalled by Irwin's relativism: 'It's ... flip. It's ... glib. It's *journalism*.'

For Bennett, Irwin, who subsequently became a television history presenter, represented all that was wrong about recent trends in presenting the past. Depicting television history presenters as 'the new breed of history boys', Bennett (2004: xxiv) adjudged them guilty of offering yet another present-day example of spin over substance in the interests of performance and entertainment. Reportedly Bennett (2004: xxiii–xxv), though acknowledging A.J.P. Taylor's pioneering role as a populariser, modelled Irwin largely on Niall Ferguson, Andrew Roberts and Norman Stone, as suggested by his praise for R.W. Johnson's critique describing Ferguson as 'a self-consciously clever, confrontational young don, determined to stand everything on its head'. Significantly, Schama (2004), described by Bennett (2004: xxiii–xxv) as 'the doyen of TV historians', was not only exempted from his critique but also invited to contribute an article, 'True Confessions of a History Boy', for the play's London theatre programme.

Far from being flattered by Bennett's reported use of their historical persona, both Ferguson and Roberts responded sharply. Irritated by the implication that he harboured even the 'slightest David Irving-ite tendencies', Andrew Roberts (2006: 20–1; quoted, Johnson 2004) dismissed Bennett's critique as an uninformed left-wing rant. Ferguson (quoted, Duff 2007) counter-attacked at the 2007 Hay Book Festival: 'Irwin got his boys into a top college, taught his boys to think independently. Hector says to imbibe and "pass it on", but they will pass on it. Irwin, not Hector, is the future of the past.' By way of support, Ferguson listed his achievements to date: 900,000 global book sales, a 2.3 million television audience and numerous newspaper articles: 'Anything you'd like to add, Mr Bennett?' Nor did Bennett's dated view of history appeal to David Greenberg. Indeed, Greenberg (2006) countered that 'contrarian impulses, counterintuitive thinking, dissent from established interpretations – in the wrong hands, these propensities can be offensively slick, but in the right hands they're the stuff of scholarship'. After all – to quote Daniel Johnson (2004) – 'History boys will always try to shock and supplant their elders.'

Although the Hector–Irwin debate occupied centre stage, Mrs Lintott, another history teacher, articulated the feminist critique of history, as pressed in the case studies by Philippa Gregory (chapter 10) and Joan Scott (chapter 8). For Lintott, history, invariably presented as 'women following behind with the bucket' (Bennett 2004: 85), revealed 'the various and continuing incapabilities of men': 'I just wonder whether it occurs to any of you how dispiriting it is for me to teach five centuries of masculine ineptitude?' (Bennett and Hytner 2006: 79). Such comments, complemented by hopes of 'an occasional nod' (Bennett 2004: 84–5; Bennett and Hytner 2006: 80) in a more feminist direction, explained Lintott's complaint – this touches upon an issue foregrounded in chapter 6 – about the lack of women television historians.

The 'Contemporary Lust' for History

Pointing to the 'contemporary lust' for public history, a demand fuelled by people's quest for roots, identity, perspective, information and entertainment, as well as to the subject's diverse audiences, Peter Mandler (2002: 1, 3–4, 9) welcomed history's high profile within contemporary culture: 'history seems to have infiltrated the contemporary consciousness at too many levels for it to be ignored'. De Groot (2009b) has proved prominent in echoing such thoughts. Moreover, despite historians' enduring preference for written scholarly histories targeted at their peers, recent decades have witnessed the emergence of a more open and flexible approach to the manner in which history is presented and accessed as public history. Indeed, one reason for history's present-day visibility results from the fact that the past is now being presented increasingly in more user-friendly aural, literary and visual modes reflecting and fitting in well with recent media trends.

But how far do these variants presenting the past through, say, historical novels, Hollywood films or television documentaries rate as 'history', let alone 'good history'? Recalling concerns expressed over fifty years ago about Taylor's journalism and television histories, Mandler (2002: 123) acknowledged that doubts about popular histories as 'history' linger 'among historians more than most'. The introduction of a tabloid element, it is feared, will make history merely another form of 'infotainment' and leisure, given the need for any popular history presenter to simplify, emphasise certainty, and entertain through an engaging personality-centred story. For historians working with film and television companies, there is the need to be prepared not only to recognise their alternative non-academic agendas, but also to work as part of a production team involving the possible loss of control over presentation mentioned by Deary, Gregory, Kershaw and Rosenstone, but denied by Schama and Starkey.

Has the emergence of public history improved society's historical literacy? Currently, the jury is still out, since history's present-day popularity and ubiquity has to be balanced against its uncertain place in the school curriculum and the frequently discouraging results of surveys about people's historical knowledge. Having been operational for over a decade, the USA's 'Teaching American History' initiative is now recognised as having exerted positive impacts upon both teaching quality and student achievement in American history (National Coalition for History 2010). By contrast, government efforts to transform historical education in

British schools – in part these appear intended to exploit Schama's presentational skills – remain at an early stage.

History's Presenters

Notwithstanding the *ego-histoires* inspired by Pierre Nora (Popkin 2005: 70–5, 277), the growing number of historians' autobiographies and biographies, and the availability of biographical reference publications (Boyd 1999; Daileader and Whalen 2010), James Banner, Jr. and John Gillis (2009: viii) concluded that 'much has been written about the history of history but little about historians themselves'. Perhaps this reflects the fact that – to quote Ferguson (2002) before his private life attracted media attention – 'the lives of historians are generally a bore. After all, any historian worth writing about spends most of his time ... just scribble, scribble, scribbling'. Even so, this book has sought to remind readers about the vital, hopefully far from boring, role performed by the past's presenters, and hence the value of studying their attitudes, methods and relationship with audiences. To some extent, John Kenyon's *The History Men* (1983) promised to do this by helping readers to a better understanding of history through knowledge of individual historians. In the event, Kenyon (1983: 188, 194, 213, 230-5, 271–2, 282), quite apart from questioning the need for academic histories to be readable and reaffirming the masculinist character of the historical profession, produced a book lacking focus and critical depth concerning presentation and audiences.

Hitherto, presenting history, albeit prompting what Elton (1959) described as some of 'the hoariest debates among historians and their readers', has attracted only limited coverage in 'nature of history' publications and occasional bursts of professional interest. Unsurprisingly, during one such debate, conducted over half a century ago in *The Times*'s letter pages, Elton and the other historians involved raised issues covered in this book, including the gap between the general public and professional historians; the distinction between academic and popular historians; the extent to which historians should assume a fair degree of ignorance upon the part of their readers; the frequent publication of what Oliver Warner (1959) called 'almost unreadable stodge' as 'history'; and the fact that even popular histories could be dull. Understandably, these exchanges glossed over the role of the visual media. Notwithstanding the fact that the late 1950s saw Taylor's pioneering television programmes, it was only during recent decades that the visual media began to launch a serious challenge to the traditional primacy of written presentations in carrying historical messages in our culture.

History Presenters' Reputations

Quite apart from impacting upon the way in which historians present the past, the passage of time affects also present-day images of individual historians. Like past events and personalities, historians' reputations and legacies are not immune from historical revisionism. Naturally, the scholarly impact of most historians proves a function of their current academic status and track record, as evidenced by the manner in which Irving's lack of a university post and historical training, among other well-publicised shortcomings, predisposed historians against his publications. Even so, during the 1960s and after academic and media opprobrium failed to prevent his books securing good sales from a popular audience.

But what happens when historians retire and finally lay down their pens or put away their word processors? Then, according to Cannadine (2006), 'the reputations of even the greatest of them are prone to precipitous collapse': 'Their books, previously best-sellers, suddenly become unread; and their names, once widely known, abruptly disappear from popular consciousness.' However, both Hobsbawm and Taylor have shown that retirement does not necessarily prevent historians making substantial contributions as presenters, through media work and publications drawing upon a lifetime's scholarship and wisdom. Indeed, for Hobsbawm (quoted, Crace 2007), 'one of the benefits of being a historian is there's no limitation on age ... In fact being old is almost an advantage as you have a lifetime of study and experience behind you'. Moreover, as shown by Namier (Colley 1989: 5) and Taylor (chapter 4), historians can influence, inspire and divide historical thinking in death as well as in life. Frequently, historians, even those discounting any interest in setting up a school of history, continue to shape the way in which the past is presented to future audiences through the work of admirers and former students. Just as Trevelyan, Plumb and Taylor led the way by taking history outside academia, so Taylor blazed a trail for today's 'journodons' and television historians.

Academia and Popular History

For Schama (2009b: 692), 'the scholarly community is surely at a crossroads in considering the forms by which history is communicated within and beyond the academy'. Warning that 'we are unquestionably at the beginning of the end of the long life of the paper and print history book', Schama urged historians to prepare for the fact that 'most history will be consumed, especially beyond the academy, in digital forms'. From this perspective, Rosenzweig's *Clio Wired: the future of the past in the digital age* (2011) proves essential reading.

Regardless of the pressure exerted by Schama, among others, to knock down the "walls" separating academia and the general public, 'academic histories' and 'popular histories' are perceived still as occupying separate spheres. But the gap is closing. As outlined in chapters 6, 9 and 10, professional historians have presented television histories, worked with Hollywood filmmakers, written historical novels, and shared conference platforms with filmmakers and historical novelists. Even so, the picture depicted in chapters 2 and 3 still rings true. Contemporary academic culture continues to encourage historians to prioritise writing specialist academic histories, and hence to cut themselves off from the wider listening, reading and viewing public. In part, this divide can be justified in terms of history's status as an academic discipline, the accumulative nature of historical knowledge, the need to break free from history as heritage, and the fact that in time academic histories reach a wider audience when used as building blocks by popular historians, historical novelists and television/film scriptwriters. In part, the problem reflects the difficulties experienced by academic historians in relating to the demands of the popular audience as regards presenting less specialist subjects in a descriptive and narrative format.

On the other hand, history's high public profile means that historians are expected increasingly to do something more than take refuge in their professional bunker, target a narrow academic audience, and make minimal effort to contribute directly to the process of educating, informing and entertaining the general public. As Wood (2010) warned, 'serious non-fiction written by trained scholars for the educated public is in greater danger than at any time in living memory'. Indeed, one session at the 2006 *World Congress of History Producers* ranged 'Producers Vs. Academics. Producers defend their role as legitimate shapers of history'. Certainly, the proven ability of Hollywood filmmakers (chapter 9), historical novelists (chapter 10), and television historians (chapter 6) to reach large and responsive audiences poses questions for professional historians about their voice in modern society, and particularly about their ability to ensure history's survival as a public craft capable of meeting the demands of government and the general public. Public history is too important to be left to historical novelists, journalists, filmmakers, television historians, and 'internet historians'. Already Ferguson, Hobsbawm, Kershaw, Schama, Starkey and Stone, among others, have shown that history can be presented successfully to both academic and lay audiences, whether as listeners, readers or viewers.

Nor despite occasional critiques has such bridge-building undermined their academic standing; indeed, university status enhanced their authority when addressing a popular audience.

Writing from personal experience of moving out of the ivory tower, Sandbrook (2007), formerly of the University of Sheffield, claimed that, whereas 'the classic fallacy is to imagine this as a dilemma between dull but worthy scholarship, and glib but distinctly lucrative popularisation', '"popular" does not necessarily mean "bad"'. Indeed, he complained that 'there is something badly wrong with the attitude that stigmatises popular writing as "coffee-table books", a label that presumably encompasses everyone from Gibbon to Kershaw'. After all, the longstanding Wolfson History prize recognises already the ability of historians – prize-winners have included Schama (1977), Hobsbawm (1996) and Beevor (1998) – to write 'histories combining high scholarly authority with accessibility to the widest possible readership'. For example, when honouring Hobsbawm, Sir Keith Thomas (n.d.) challenged his professional colleagues:

> At a time when many academic disciplines have retreated into a private hermetic world of their own, with a subject-matter and a language intelligible only to initiates, history remains a subject in which it is still possible to write in such a way as simultaneously to command the interest of both professional scholars and the intelligent reading public.

Final Words

History's enduring fascination and significance derives still largely from its focus upon real people, real events and real places in the past. 'History' is what historians do. In effect, as Michael Burleigh (2002) asserted, historians act as time travellers, professionally authorised guides to 'the past'. Taking advantage of the cultural authority arising from their perceived ability to furnish authoritative and informed accounts of the past, historians have to play multiple roles when studying the past: archivist, investigator, detective, critic, creative thinker, literary artist, and presenter-communicator (Stanford 1986: 151).

For most historians, written presentations remain the norm, but whatever the format the essence of being a successful presenter is to communicate history in a manner which not only meets appropriate historical standards but also engages the interest, imagination and intellect of the target audience(s). Within this context, there exists a clear need for historians to focus more directly than hitherto upon presentation and audiences. In this vein, Terry Deary (2009b), who has probably sold more history books than any presenter covered in this text, identified perhaps the crucial point for any history presenter when responding to a 12-year-old boy from Glasgow:

> The most important person is always you, the reader. When I am writing I always have you, the reader, out there in front of me. I am thinking, are you going to be interested in this, will this make you laugh? Did you know this amazing fact we have found? The most important thing to remember is don't write for yourself, write for the reader out there.

For Champion (2003: 155, 170; 2008: 181–2), historians need to undertake 'deep thinking' and 'intellectual retooling' concerning alternative ways of reaching diverse audiences as well as of responding to and taking advantage of the changing nature and expectations of the audience over time. As a result, it is no longer sufficient just to teach history students how to read and write academic history. As David Harlan (2007: 121) advised: 'We must teach them to be thoughtful, reflective and resourceful readers of *all* the forms in which their society represents the past to itself. Academic history is one of those forms, of course, but it is only one, and it is neither the most interesting nor the most important.' Following Carr (2001: 38), we need also to make history students aware of the need to study the presenters providing accounts of the past for listeners, readers and viewers.

All the presenters discussed in the case studies have proved successful in taking the past to an audience, even if certain presentations will be dismissed by historians as falling short of 'history'. Conformity to strict professional standards is vital for academic historians, but historical lapses will not necessarily prevent history filmmakers, historical novelists, television historians and writers of popular histories reaching a large audience, particularly given the public's incomplete grasp of history and the ability of popular histories to blur the divide between fact and fiction. After all, Ambrose's popular audience was unlikely to worry overmuch about alleged plagiarism, just as during the 1960s and after Irving's publications, boosted by his public relations activities, found a ready popular audience regardless of the manner in which he was criticised and ostracised by academia. Also, whereas the key reference points within academia prove of a qualitative nature, popular history presentations tend to be judged much more according to quantitative criteria such as book sales, box-office returns, library lending figures, and radio listening and television viewing totals, not historical standards. Even so, the case studies indicated that qualitative factors are not totally irrelevant when assessing the success of individual presenters. Returning to the *The History Boys*, any history presenter seeking to engage an audience is well advised at least in part to apply Bennett's example, as noted by Ben Brantley (2006) when reviewing the play's opening in New York: 'No matter what you do, Irwin counsels his exam-bound students, remember that history must be entertainment. Mr. Bennett, with less cynicism and more heart, applies the same rule to the teaching of history, with compellingly watchable results.' Nor should any presenter – to quote Plumb's advice to Schama (quoted, Grice 2010) – either be apologetic about the gift of communication or underestimate the impact of personality. As Starkey (quoted, Hironson 2009) asserted, histories are increasingly sold on the fame and trademark style of the historian:

> I think what you need to do is not be afraid to use personality. The historian is not, as some academics believe, some neutral figure. The historian is a storyteller. You're also a teacher ... There needs to be that trait of personality and singularity. There needs to be that tone of voice that people recognise. Whether they find it attractive or not they know exactly, 'Ah, that's Starkey', or 'Ah, that's Schama'.

This does not mean that historians should follow Schama and Starkey to become a brand. Rather, Starkey's sentiments, as expressed here, should be read as underpinning this book's central message, that is the vital role performed by presenters in taking history to diverse audiences. Presenters represent the crucial link between history's producers – normally, the 'producer' is also the 'presenter' – and consumers. Revealing the powerful manner in which messages communicated by historical novelists, Hollywood history filmmakers and television historians resonate with audiences, this book has established that not all presenters of the past are academic historians. Moreover, these alternative presentations might be readable, watchable, and listenable, but not necessarily 'history' as historians know it.

Within academia scholarly books, articles, chapters and theses will remain central in advancing historical knowledge and understanding. However, the fact that the story of the past is being provided increasingly outside academia by non-historians to a public audience demanding to know more requires historians and history students to do three things.

- Firstly, they must reflect regularly upon and appraise critically the historical quality of the competing pasts offered by alternative modes of presentation, most notably those popular outside academia. In particular, historians and history students, though professionally inclined to dismiss, even to trash, historical novels, history films and televisual histories, should consider what can be learnt from other presenters of the past about reaching and engaging audiences.
- Secondly, historians should think seriously about reaching out more to the general public in an accessible and scholarly manner, even if fellow academics and history students remain their principal target audience.
- Finally, whatever their choice, the guiding maxim for historians and history students should be 'The better their presentation of the past, the more effective their history will be in accessing, engaging and impacting upon the target audience.'

Bibliography

Citations record the edition used for referencing, not necessarily the book's initial date of publication, as recorded in square brackets. Some website addresses are no longer accessible.

Abelson, E., Abraham, D. and Murphy, M. 1989. 'Interview with Joan Scott', *Radical History Review*, 45: 41–59.

Addison, P. 1990. 'Wizard of Ox', *London Review of Books*, 8 Nov.: 3–4.

Addison, P. 2001. 'Reviews in History', June: http://www.history.ac.uk/reviews/paper/addisonPaul.html, accessed 19 June 2001.

Allen, J. 1987. 'Evidence and silence: feminism and the limits of history', in C. Pateman and E. Gross (eds.), *Feminist Challenges: social and political theory* (Boston, MA: Northeastern University Press): 173–89.

Alperin, M. 2009. 'Strong women, stolen secrets, silent stories', *U.S.1* (Princeton), 2 Sept.: 31.

Ambrose, H. 2010. 'Eisenhower and my father, Stephen Ambrose', 20 May, History News Network, http://hnn.us/articles/126907.html, accessed 30 Jan. 2011.

Ambrose, S.E. 2001. *The Wild Blue: the men and boys who flew the B-24s over Germany, 1944–1945* (New York: Simon & Schuster).

Ambrose, S.E. 2002a. *The Wild Blue: 741 Squadron – on a wing and a prayer over Occupied Europe* (rev. ed., London: Simon & Schuster).

Ambrose, S.E. 2002b. *To America: personal reflections of an historian* (New York: Simon & Schuster).

American Council of Trustees and Alumni. 2000. *Losing America's Memory: historical illiteracy in the 21st century* (Washington, DC: ACTA).

American Historical Association (AHA). 2005. 'Statement on Standards of Professional Conduct', 6 Jan.: http://www.historians.org/pubs/free/professionalstandards.cfm, accessed 20 April 2010.

American Historical Association (AHA). 2007. 'Statement on the Framework Decision of the Council of the European Union on the Fight against Racism and Xenophobia', Sept.: http://www.historians.org/Perspectives/issues/2007/0711/0711int3.cfm, accessed 20 Nov. 2008.

American Historical Review. 2008a. 'In this Issue', *American Historical Review*, 113(5): xiv–xv.

American Historical Review. 2008b. 'AHR Forum: Revisiting "Gender: a useful category of historical analysis": Introduction', *American Historical Review*, 113(5): 1344–5.

Anderson, C. *et alia*. 2006. 'Letters: History matters for our future', *Daily Telegraph*, 8 July.

Anderson, L. 2004. *Braveheart: from Hollywood to Holyrood* (Edinburgh: Luath Press).

Andrew, C. 2004. 'Intelligence analysis needs to look backwards before looking forward', *History & Policy Paper* 23, June: http://www.history andpolicy.org/archive/policy-paper-23.html, accessed 12 Nov. 2004.

'*Appel de Blois*'. 2008. *Le Monde*, 10 Oct.

Appleyard, B. 2006. 'Rocking all over the art world', *Sunday Times*, 24 Sept.

Appleyard, B. 2009. '"A novelist goes on working where the biographer has to stop"', *Sunday Times*, 11 Oct.

Arnold, M. 2000. 'The "What ifs" that fascinate', *New York Times*, 21 Dec.

Ascherson, N. 1995. 'Now is the time for official heroes to come to the aid of the party', *Independent on Sunday*, 24 Sept.

Attenborough, L. 1997. 'Publishing Profile no.1: The Non-Fiction Editor', *Books for Keeps*, 102: 10–11.

Attie, J. 1992. 'Illusions of history: a review of "The Civil War"', *Radical History Review*, 52: 95–104.

Avon, Lord. 1963a. Avon to Arthur Mann, 10 June, Avon Papers (AP) AP24/47/63B, Special Collections, Library, University of Birmingham.

Avon, Lord. 1963b. Avon to P. Emrys Evans, 6 Aug., AP23/31/12A.

Avon, Lord. 1964. Avon to Alec Cadogan, 28 July, AP23/15/26.

Avon, Lord. 1968. Avon to Lord Caccia, 28 Oct., AP23/14/45B.

Babal, M. 2010. 'Sticky History: connecting historians with the public', *Public Historian*, 32(4): 76–84.

Bacon, K. 1998. 'Tell it like it was: interview with Stephen Ambrose', *Atlantic Online*, 12 Nov.: http://www.theatlantic.com/unbound/book auth/ba981112.htm, accessed 14 Aug. 2009.

Banner, J.M., Jr., and Gillis, J.H. (eds.). 2009. 'Preface', in J.M. Banner, Jr., and J.H. Gillis (eds.), *Becoming Historians* (Chicago, IL: University of Chicago Press): vii–xvi.

Barnes, F. 2002. 'Stephen Ambrose, copycat', *Weekly Standard*, 14 Jan.: 27.

Bati, A. 1990. 'The English history man', *Sunday Times*, 8 July.

Baxter, S. 2001. 'Bloody good yarns make a tidy profit for History plc', *Sunday Times*, 2 Sept.

BBC. 1981. *A.J.P. Taylor, History Man*, BBC1, 22 March.

BBC. 1994. *Late Show Special*, BBC2, 24 Oct.

BBC. 1995. *Reputations: A.J.P. Taylor – an unusual type of star*, BBC2, 22 Jan.

BBC. 2001a. 'News: A History of Simon Schama', 15 June: http://news.
bbc.co.uk/1/hi/entertainment/1390893.stm, accessed 30 Aug. 2001.

BBC. 2001b. 'News: BBC rejects ITV chief's criticism', 25 Aug.: http://
news.bbc.co.uk/1/hi/entertainment/tv_and_radio/1508370.stm,
accessed 30 Aug. 2001.

BBC. 2006a. 'Holocaust denier Irving is jailed', BBC News, 20 Feb.: http://
news.bbc.co.uk/1/hi/world/europe/4733820.stm, accessed 1 Oct. 2008.

BBC. 2006b. 'U-571 writer regrets "distortion"', 18 Aug.: http://news.
bbc.co.uk/1/hi/entertainment/5263164.stm, accessed 4 Oct. 2008.

BBC. 2008a. Today, BBC Radio 4, 18 Oct.

BBC. 2008b. 'Press Pack', Nov.: http://sain.sunsite.utk.edu/cgi-bin/text
only/0122/www.bbc.co.uk/pressoffice/pressreleases/stories/2008/11_
november/25/childrens3.shtml, accessed 6 Feb.2009.

BBC. 2010. Archive on 4: AJP at the BBC, BBC Radio 4, 15 Feb.

BBC. 2011. 'Nazi Gold: publishing the Third Reich', BBC Radio 4,
17 March.

Beard, C. 1934. 'Why get it wrong?', Sight and Sound, 2(8): 124.

Beck, P.J. 1983. 'History goes public', Times Higher Education Supplement,
21 Jan.: 13.

Beck, P.J. 1988. The Falkland Islands as an International Problem (London:
Routledge).

Beck, P.J. 1998. 'Politicians versus historians: Lord Avon's "appeasement battle" against "lamentably, appeasement-minded" historians',
Twentieth Century British History, 9(3): 396–419.

Beck, P.J. 2006. Using History, Making British policy: the Treasury and the
Foreign Office, 1950–76 (Basingstoke: Palgrave Macmillan).

Beck, P.J. 2009. 'Horrible Histories', History Today, 60(9): 70–1.

Beevor, A. 2002. 'The past is personal', Sunday Times, 14 July.

Beevor, A. 2009. 'Real concerns', Guardian, 25 July.

Bell, E. 2007. 'Televising history: the past(s) on the small screen',
European Journal of Cultural Studies, 10(1): 5–12.

Bell, E. 2008. ' "No one wants to be lectured at by a woman": women
and history on TV', Women's History Magazine, 59: 4–12.

Bell, E. 2009. 'Where are the women historians on TV?', HerStoria
Magazine, 2: 11–15.

Bell, E. and Gray, A. 2007. 'History on television: charisma, narrative
and knowledge', European Journal of Cultural Studies, 10(1): 113–133.

Bellesiles, M.A. 2000. Arming America: the origins of a national gun culture
(NY: Alfred A. Knopf).

Bellesiles, M. 2002a. 'Exploring America's gun culture', William and
Mary Quarterly, 59(1): 241–68.

Bellesiles, M. 2002b. 'Statement on Emory University's Inquiry of *Arming America*', n.d. (Oct.): http://www.emory.edu/news/Releases/B_statement.pdf, accessed 12 Aug. 2009.

Bellesiles, M.A. 2003. *Arming America* (NY: Soft Skull Press).

Bennett, A. 2004. *The History Boys* (London: Faber & Faber).

Bennett, A. and Hytner, N. 2006. *The History Boys: the film* (London: Faber & Faber).

Benson, S.P., Brier, S. and Rosenzweig, R. 1986. 'Introduction', in S.P. Benson, S. Brier and R. Rosenzweig (eds.), *Presenting the Past: essays on history and the public* (Philadelphia, PA.: Temple University Press): xv–xxiv.

Bernstein, R. 1989. 'Can movies teach history?', *New York Times*, 26 Nov.

Billen, A. 2003. 'The man who made history sexy explains why it is also our freedom', *The Times*, 20 May.

Black, J. 2008. *What If?: counterfactualism and the problem of history* (London: Social Affairs Unit).

Blair, A. 2000. *Hansard Parliamentary Debates (Commons)*, 351, 7 June.

Blair, A. 2007. 'PM hails renaissance of British culture', Tate Modern, 6 March: http://www.number10.gov.uk/Page11166, accessed 5 March 2009.

Blake, F. n.d. [2001]. 'Philippa Gregory Q & A', *Mail on Sunday*: http://www.dailymail.co.uk/home/books/article-174532/Philippa-Gregory-Q-A.html, accessed 4 Nov. 2009.

Blake, F. 2009. 'One to One: Philippa Gregory', *Woman and Home*, Oct.: 183.

The Bookseller. 2010. 'Top 50', 'Review of 2009', 8 Jan.; 12, 20–1.

Bourke, J. 2009a. 'Introduction', *Talking Books–Novel History Panel*, Birkbeck Institute for the Humanities, University of London, 6 June: http://backdoorbroadcasting.net/2009/06/talking-books-novel-history/, accessed 3 Dec. 2009.

Bourke, J. 2009b. 'Historical Novels', *History Today*, 59(10): 54–5.

Bower, S. 2006. 'Letter from the Editor', *Historical Novels Review*, 35: 1.

Bown, J. 2008. 'Niall Ferguson', *Sunday Times*, 16 Nov.

Box Office Mojo n.d. a. 'Braveheart', http://www.boxofficemojo.com/movies/?id=braveheart.htm, accessed 1 Oct. 2008.

Box Office Mojo n.d. b. 'U-571', http://boxofficemojo.com/movies/?id=u-571.htm, accessed 1 Oct. 2008.

Boyd, K. (ed.) 1999. *Encyclopedia of Historians and Historical Writing, I-II* (Chicago, IL: Fitzroy Dearborn).

Boydston, J. 2008. 'Gender as a question of historical analysis', *Gender & History*, 20(3): 558–83.

Brantley, B. 2006. 'Rivals for young hearts and minds in Alan Bennett's "History Boys"', *New York Times*, 24 April.

Braudel, F. 1988. [trans. S. Reynolds] *The Identity of France: I, History and environment* (London: HarperCollins).

Bremner, I. 2001. 'History without archives: Simon Schama's "A History of Britain"', in G. Roberts and P.M. Taylor (eds.) *The Historian, Television and Television History* (Luton: University of Luton Press): 63–75.

Brivati, B. 1993. 'The historian as history: an interview with Adam Sisman, biographer of A.J.P. Taylor', *Contemporary Record*, 7(3): 594–611.

Brogan, P. 1967. 'The mystery lingers on', *The Times*, 14 Oct.

BTF (Banff Television Foundation). 2001a. 'Media Release: Banff Television Foundation with the support of top international players in history', 13 June: http://www.festivalproducts.com/IFFG/060801banfftv.html, accessed 12 Feb. 2002.

BTF 2001b. 'Media Release: History Programming is the "New Rock 'n' Roll"', 25 Oct.: http://history2001.com/media/011025.history.rocks. html, accessed 2 Nov. 2001.

Bunzl, M. 2004. 'Counterfactual history: a users' guide', *American Historical Review*, 109(3): 845–58.

Burk, K. 2000a. *Troublemaker: the life and history of A.J.P. Taylor* (New Haven, CT.: Yale University Press).

Burk, K. 2000b. 'Oxford Affairs', *Guardian*, 2 Sept.

Burke, J. and Wavell, S. 1995. 'Winston who? Pupils cannot name war heroes', *Sunday Times*, 30 April.

Burke, P. 2009. 'Invitation to historians: an intellectual self-portrait, or the history of a historian', *Rethinking History*, 13(2): 269–81.

Burleigh, M. 2002. 'The end of history is nigh', *Sunday Times*, 25 Aug.

Burns, K. n.d. [2002]. 'Why I decided to make *The Civil War*', http:// www.pbs.org/civilwar/film/, accessed 15 April 2010.

Burns, K. 1991. 'The Documentary Film: its role in the study of history', Lowell Lecture, Harvard University, 2 May, http://www.dce.harvard. edu/pubs/lowell/kburns.html, accessed 28 Dec. 2008.

Burrell, I. 2007. 'Simon Schama: my secret recipe to bring the past to life', *Independent*, 26 Nov.

Burrow, J. 2007. *A History of Histories: epics, chronicles, romances and inquiries from Herodotus and Thucydides to the twentieth century* (London: Allen Lane).

Butterfield, H. 1924. *The Historical Novel: an essay* (Cambridge: Cambridge University Press).

Cannadine, D. 1987. 'British history: past, present – and future?', *Past and Present*, 116: 169–91.

Cannadine, D. 1992. *G.M. Trevelyan: a life in history* (London: HarperCollins).

Cannadine, D. 1998. 'I wish I'd written', *Guardian*, 15 Aug.

Cannadine, D. 2000. [1998] *History in our Time* (London: Penguin).

Cannadine, D. 2002. 'Preface', in D. Cannadine (ed.), *What is history now?* (Basingstoke: Palgrave Macmillan): vii–xiv.

Cannadine. D. 2004. 'Introduction', in D. Cannadine (ed.), *History and the Media* (Basingstoke: Palgrave Macmillan): 1–6.

Cannadine, D. 2006. 'A point of view: a tale of two historians', 25 Aug.: http://news.bbc.co.uk/1/hi/magazine/5286894.stm, accessed 2 June 2009.

Cannadine, D. 2008. *Making History Now and Then: discoveries, controversies and explorations* (Basingstoke: Palgrave Macmillan).

Cannadine, D. 2009. 'Featured Scholar', *The British Scholar Newsletter*, March–April, http://britishscholar.com/scholarofthemonthmarch 2009.html, accessed 27 April 2009.

Carey, M. 2009. 'D-Day historian: "Ryan" not best war film', http://edition.cnn.com/2009/SHOWBIZ/books/11/11/beevor.movies.dday/index.html, accessed 2 Feb. 2011.

Carnegie Library. 1996. 'Three Rivers Lecture Series', 8 Jan.

Carnes, M.C. 1995. 'Hollywood history', *American Heritage*, 46(5): http://www.americanheritage.com/articles/magazine/ah/1995/5/1995_5_74.shtml, accessed 10 Feb. 2010.

Carnes, M.C. 1996. 'Introduction', in M.C. Carnes (ed.), *Past Imperfect: history according to the movies* (London: Cassell): 9–10.

Carr, E.H. 2001. [1961] *What is History?* (2nd.ed., Basingstoke: Palgrave Macmillan).

Carrell, S. 2000. 'Don't airbrush UK out of history, Smith urges Hollywood', *Independent*, 5 June.

Cesarani, D. 2000. 'The Holocaust on Trial', Channel 4, 29 April.

Champion, J. 2002. 'Reviews in History', Dec.: http://www.history.ac.uk/reviews/paper/championJ2.html, accessed 4 April 2003.

Champion, J. 2003. 'Seeing the Past: Simon Schama's "A History of Britain" and Public History', *History Workshop Journal*, 56: 153–74.

Champion, J. 2008. 'What are historians for?', *Historical Research*, 81: 167–88.

Chandos, Lord. 1962. Chandos to Lord Avon, 21 Nov., AP23/17/65B.

Chapman, J. 2005. *Past and Present: national identity and the British historical film* (London: I.B. Tauris).

Chapman, J. 2007. 'Reviews in History', Nov.: http://www.history.ac.uk/reviews/paper/chapman.html, accessed 14 Dec. 2008.

Chrisafis, A. 2002. 'Everyday story of courtly folk takes romantic fiction award', *Guardian*, 19 April.

Christy, D. 1999. 'Fighting Blackadder', *Guardian*, 30 Oct.

Clark, A. 1998. 'Butchered in the name of attrition', *Daily Telegraph*, 7 Nov.

Clark, J. 2004. *Our Shadowed Present: modernism, postmodernism and history* (Stanford, CA: Stanford University Press).

Clee, N. 2010. 'Most borrowed', *The Times*, 13 Feb.

Clinton, C. 1996. 'Gone with the Wind', in M.C. Carnes (ed.), *Past Imperfect: history according to the movies* (London: Cassell): 132–5.

Cohen, P. 2010. 'Scholar emerges from the doghouse', *New York Times*, 3 Aug.

Cohen, S.K. 2011. 'Interview with Robert A. Rosenstone', Caltech Archives Oral History Project, http://oralhistories.library.caltech. edu/176/01/Rosenstone,_R_OHO.pdf, accessed 10 May 2011.

Cole, R. 1993. *A.J.P. Taylor: the traitor within the gates* (New York: St Martin's Press).

Colley, L. 1989. *Lewis Namier* (London: Weidenfeld & Nicolson).

Collini, S. 2006. *Absent Minds: intellectuals in Britain* (Oxford: Oxford University Press).

Conquest, R. 2000. *Reflections on a Ravaged Century* (New York: W.W. Norton).

Cooper. B. 2007. 'Letter to Editor', *Independent*, 25 April.

Costello, H. 2001. 'Magnificent but is it history?', *BBC History*, 2(5): 17–18.

Cowley, R. 2001. [1999] 'Introduction', in R. Cowley (ed.), *What if?: military historians imagine what might have been* (London: Pan): xi–xiv.

Cowley, R. 2002. [2001] 'Introduction', in R. Cowley (ed.), *What If?2: eminent historians imagine what might have been* (New York: Berkley Books): xvii–xix.

Cowley, R. 2008. 'When do counterfactuals work?', in D.A. Yerxa (ed.), *Recent Themes in Historical Thinking: historians in conversation* (Columbia, SC: University of South Carolina Press): 115–19.

Cowling, M. 1999. 'The intelligent populist', *Spectator*, 30 Jan.: 17–18.

Crace, J. 2002. 'It's the way you tell it', *Guardian*, 17 Dec.

Crace, J. 2003. 'Writing history', *Guardian*, 12 Aug.

Crace, J. 2007. 'Living history', *BBK Magazine*, 22: http://www.bbk.ac.uk/ about_us/publications/bbk/bbk22/history, accessed 11 Jan. 2010.

Craig, A. 2006. 'Books parents hate and children love', *The Times*, 4 March.

Craig, O. 2006. 'David, what on earth would Mother think?', *Daily Telegraph*, 25 Feb.

Cripps, T. 1995. 'Historical truth: an interview with Ken Burns', *American Historical* Review, 100(3): 741–64.

Croll, A. 2003. 'Review', *Twentieth Century British History*, 14(1): 84–5.

Daileader, P. and Whalen, P. (eds.) 2010. *French Historians, 1900–2000: new historical writing in twentieth-century France* (Oxford: Wiley-Blackwell).

Daily Telegraph. 2000. 'Editorial: The bad history man', 12 April.

Daily Telegraph. 2002. 'Restore the magic by ditching the monotone of textbooks', 6 Oct.

Daily Telegraph. 2010. 'Bestselling authors of the decade', 2 Jan.

David, S. 2000. 'Perhaps historians should stick to the facts after all', *Daily Telegraph*, 1 April.

Davies, N. 1996. 'How I conquered Europe', *New Statesman*, 20 Dec.: 36–7.

Davies, N. 2007. 'A.J.P. Taylor', *History Today*, 57(6): 62–3.

Davies, S. 2003. *Empiricism and History* (Basingstoke: Palgrave Macmillan).

De Groot, J. 2009a. *Consuming History: historians and heritage in contemporary popular culture* (Abingdon: Routledge).

De Groot, J. 2009b. 'The power of the past: how historical fiction has regained its gravitas', *Guardian* Books Blog, 30 Sept.: http://www.guardian.co.uk/books/booksblog/2009/sep/28/historical-fiction-booker-prize-hilary-mantel, accessed 25 Feb. 2010.

De Groot, J. 2010. *The Historical Novel* (Abingdon: Routledge).

Deary, T. n.d. a. 'Talk to Terry': http://www.terry-deary.com/club/talk.htm, accessed 10 Feb. 2008.

Deary, T. n.d. b. 'History for Young People': http://www.terry-deary.com/shop/pages/timedetectives.htm, accessed 12 Feb. 2009.

Deary. n.d. c. 'Authors: Terry Deary': http://www.horrible-histories.co.uk/index.tao?PageId=authors_terry_deary, accessed 12 Feb. 2009.

Deary, T. 1993. *The Terrible Tudors* (London: Scholastic).

Deary, T. 1994. *The Vile Victorians* (London: Scholastic).

Deary, T. 1996. *The 20th.Century* (London: Scholastic).

Deary, T. 1998. *The Frightful First World War* (London: Scholastic).

Deary, T. 2002a. 'Spread the word: Terry Deary', Sept.: http://www.bbcworldwide.com/spokenword/interviews/deary.htm, accessed 12 Feb. 2009.

Deary, T. 2002b. *The Barmy British Empire* (London: Scholastic).

Deary, T. 2003. 'CBBC Live Star Chat', 25 Feb.: http://www.bbc.co.uk/cbbc/xchange/xpress/xclusive/terry_deary.shtml, accessed 5 Oct. 2003.

Deary, T. 2005. *Rotten Rulers* (London: Scholastic).

Deary, T. 2006. 'History written by the losers', *Guardian*, 3 Oct.

Deary, T. 2009a. *The Music Group*, BBC Radio 4, 14 April.

Deary, T. 2009b. 'Interview – Terry Deary', April: http://www.history-for-kids.com/terry-deary.html, accessed 10 Feb. 2010.

Deary, T. 2009c. 'Hotseat Terry Deary', 7 Aug.: http://news.bbc.co.uk/cbbcnews/hi/newsid_8050000/newsid_8052100/8052185.stm, accessed 12 Jan. 2010.

Demos, J. 2005. 'Afterword: notes from, and about, the history/fiction borderland', *Rethinking History*, 9(2–3): 329–35.

Ditchfield, S. 2001. 'Reviews in History', Oct.: http://www.history.ac.uk/reviews/paper/ditchfieldSimon.html, accessed 5 April 2009.

Donahue, D. 2008. 'Philippa Gregory's "Queen" rule with intrigue', *USA Today*, 15 Sept.

Donahue, D. 2009a. 'Gregory creates a "Queen" for a new era', *USA Today*, 24 Aug.

Donahue, D. 2009b. 'Mantel's "Wolf Hall": think Tudor "Gangster"', *USA Today*, 12 Oct.

Downs, L.L. 1993a. 'If "woman" is just an empty category, then why I am afraid to walk alone at night? Identity politics meets the post-modern subject', *Comparative Studies in Society and History*, 35(2): 414–37.

Downs, L.L. 1993b. 'Reply to Joan Scott', *Comparative Studies in Society and History*, 35(2): 444–51.

Downs, L.L. 2003. 'From women's history to gender history', in S. Berger, H. Feldner and K. Passmore (eds.), *Writing History: theory & practice* (London: Hodder Arnold): 261–81.

Duff, O. 2007. 'Your boys are history, Ferguson tells Bennett', *Independent*, 4 June.

Duffy, M. 2007. 'Balanced stories? No, I'm showing the evil of authority down the ages', *Herald* (Glasgow), 27 March.

Dunant, S. 2009. *Talking Books – Novel History Panel*, Birkbeck Institute for the Humanities, University of London, 6 June: http://backdoor broadcasting.net/2009/06/talking-books-novel-history/, accessed 3 Dec. 2009.

Dutton, D. 2001. *Neville Chamberlain* (London: Arnold).

Eaglestone, R. 2004. *The Holocaust and the Postmodern* (Oxford: Oxford University Press).

Ebner, S. 2010a. 'Historians are so horrible, they're almost as bad as politicians, says children's author', *The Times*, 31 May.

Ebner, S. 2010b. 'Interview: "I hate horrible historians (and terrible teachers)"' *The Times*, 31 May.

The Economist. 1989. 'Facts for Burning', 310, 7 Jan.: 93.

Edgerton, G.R. 2001. *Ken Burns's America* (NY: Palgrave).

Edgington, S.B. 2009. 'Reviews in History', May: http://www.history. ac.uk/reviews/paper/phillipsj.html, accessed 14 May 2009.

Eley, G. 2003. 'Marxist historiography', in S. Berger, H. Feldner and K. Passmore (eds.), *Writing History: theory & practice* (London: Hodder Arnold): 63–82.

Eley, G. 2005. *A Crooked Line: from cultural history to the history of society* (Ann Arbor, MI: University of Michigan Press).

Elizabeth II. 2011. 'The Queen's speech at the Irish State Dinner, 18 May 2011', http://www.royal.gov.uk/LatestNewsandDiary/ Speechesandarticles/2011/TheQueensspeechattheIrishStateDinner 18May2011.aspx, accessed 21 May 2011.

Elliott, G. 2010. *Hobsbawm: history and politics* (London: Pluto).

Elliott, M. 2004. 'Niall Ferguson', *TIME Magazine*, 26 April: 113.

Elton, G. 1959. 'Letter to the editor', *The Times*, 2 Dec.

Elton, G.R. 1986. *Thinking Aloud*, Channel 4, 4 Jan.

Elton, G.R. 1991. *Return to Essentials: some reflections on the present state of historical study* (Cambridge: Cambridge University Press).

Elton, G.R. 2002. [1967] *The Practice of History* (2nd.ed., Oxford: Blackwell).

Emory University. 2002. 'Report of the Investigative Committee in the matter of Professor Michael Bellesiles', 10 July: http://www.emory. edu/news/Releases/Final_Report.pdf, accessed 12 Aug. 2009.

Engelen, L. 2007. 'Back to the future, ahead to the past. Film and history: a status quaestionis', *Rethinking History*, 11(4): 555–63.

Evans, R.J. 1997. *In Defence of History* (London: Granta).

Evans, R.J. 1998. 'Postmodernism and the study of history', *History Review*, 32: 28–9.

Evans, R.J. 1999. 'David Irving, Hitler and Holocaust Denial': http:// www.hdot.org/en/trial/defense/evans/430biii/keyword/footnotes, accessed 22 Feb. 2010.

Evans, R.J. 2001a. 'Witness', *BBC History*, Jan.: 54–5.

Evans, R.J. 2001b. *Lying about Hitler: history, Holocaust and the David Irving trial* (New York: Basic Books).

Evans, R.J. 2002. 'Telling it like it wasn't', *BBC History*, Dec.: 22–5.

Evans, R.J. 2005. *The Third Reich in Power* (London: Allen Lane).

Evans, R.J. 2009. *Cosmopolitan Islanders: British historians and the European Continent* (Cambridge: Cambridge University Press).

Ewan, E. 1995. 'Braveheart and Rob Roy', *American Historical Review*, 100(4): 1219–1221.

Farthing, S. 1999. 'Historians of "Past and Present"': http://www.npg.org. uk/collections/search/portrait.php?search=as&grp=1045%3BHistorians &lDate=&LinkID=mp11750&rNo=0&role=sit, accessed 20 Oct. 2008.

Feldner, H. 2003. 'The new scientificity in historical writing around 1800', in S. Berger, H. Feldner and K. Passmore (eds.), *Writing History: theory & practice* (London: Hodder Arnold): 3–22.

Fenton, B. 2006. 'Lessons from the past show history has a future', *Daily Telegraph*, 8 July.

Ferguson, N. n.d. [2006] 'Niall Ferguson talks about his latest book': http://www.penguin.co.uk/nf/Author/AuthorPage/0,,1000003904,00. html?sym=QUE, accessed 12 July 2009.

Ferguson, N. 1997a. 'The alternative 20th.century', *Sunday Times*, 6 April.

Ferguson, N. 1997b. 'History is dead. Long live history!', *Sunday Times*, 21 Sept.

Ferguson, N. 1998a. [1997] 'Introduction', in N. Ferguson (ed.), *Virtual History: alternatives and counterfactuals* (London: Papermac): 1–90.

Ferguson, N. 1998b. [1997] 'The Kaiser's European Union: what if Britain had "stood aside" in August 1914?', in N. Ferguson (ed.), *Virtual History: alternatives and counterfactuals* (London: Papermac): 228–80.

Ferguson, N. 1998c. [1997] 'Afterword: a virtual history, 1646–1996', in N. Ferguson (ed.), *Virtual History: alternatives and counterfactuals* (London: Papermac): 416–440.

Ferguson, N. 1998d. *The Pity of War* (London: Penguin).

Ferguson, N. 1999. 'On media dons', in S. Glover (ed.), *Secrets of the Press: journalists on journalism* (London: Allen Lane): 206–20.

Ferguson, N. 2001. 'Response: Reviews in History', Oct.: http://www. history.ac.uk/reviews/paper/fergusonNiall.html, accessed 2 Dec. 2001.

Ferguson, N. 2002. 'What a swell party it was ... for him', *Daily Telegraph*, 22 Sept.

Ferguson, N. 2003. *Empire: how Britain made the modern world* (London: Penguin).

Ferguson, N. 2006. 'Home truths about famine, war and genocide', *Independent*, 14 June.

Ferguson, N. 2011a. 'Personal website': http://www.niallferguson.com/ site/FERG/Templates/General2.aspx?pageid=6, accessed 2 Jan. 2011.

Ferguson, N. 2011b. *Civilisation: the West and the rest* (London: Allen Lane).

Figes, O. 1997. 'Revolution in the head', *The Times*, 5 June.

Firth, C.H. 1938. *A Commentary on Macaulay's History of England* (London: Macmillan).

Fischer, D.H. 2000. 'Hubris, but no history', *New York Times*, 1 July.

Foner, E. and Sayles, J. 1996. 'A conversation between Eric Foner and John Sayles', in M.C. Carnes (ed.), *Past Imperfect: history according to the movies* (London: Cassell): 11–28.

Fordham University. 2002. 'Medieval history in the movies': http://www.fordham.edu/halsall/medfilms.html#listsworst, accessed 1 Aug. 2008.

Foster, P. 2008. 'David Starkey says raunchy drama has brought "shame" upon BBC', *The Times*, 17 Oct.

Foster, R.F. 2000. 'The Storyteller', *New Republic*, 4 Dec.: 48–52.

Fraser, G.M. 1988. *The Hollywood History of the World* (London: Michael Joseph).

Freeman, T.S. 2009a. 'Introduction: it's only a movie', in S. Doran and T.S. Freeman (eds.), *Tudors and Stuarts on Film: historical perspectives* (Basingstoke: Palgrave Macmillan): 1–28.

Freeman, T.S. 2009b. 'A tyrant for all seasons: Henry VIII on film', in S. Doran and T.S. Freeman (eds.), *Tudors and Stuarts on Film: historical perspectives* (Basingstoke: Palgrave Macmillan): 30–45.

Fritzsche, P. 2008. 'The Holocaust and the knowledge of murder', *Journal of Modern History*, 80(3): 594–613.

Fry, S. 2006. 'The future's in the past', *Observer*, 9 July.

Fulford, R. 2001. 'Niall Ferguson, Part 1', *National Post* (Toronto), 14 March: http://www.robertfulford.com/NiallFerguson1.html, accessed 20 Aug. 2001.

Gaddis, J.L. 2004. *The Landscape of History: how historians map the past* (Oxford: Oxford University Press).

Garner, R. 2001. 'Don't know much about history? You are not alone, says questionnaire', *Independent*, 10 Nov.

Garton Ash, T. 2008. 'The freedom of historical debate is under attack by the memory police', *Guardian*, 16 Oct.

Genovese, E.D. 1984. 'The politics of class struggle in the history of society: an appraisal of the work of Eric Hobsbawm', in P. Thane, G. Crossick and R. Floud (eds.), *The Power of the Past: essays for Eric Hobsbawm* (Cambridge: Cambridge University Press): 13–36.

Gewertz, K. 2001. 'Schama kicks off Tanner series', *Harvard University Gazette*, 1 Feb.

Geyl, P. 1964. [1949] *Napoleon: for and against* (rev. ed., London: Jonathan Cape).

Gibson, O. 2007. 'Hadlow in plea for "serious TV"', *Guardian*, 23 Jan.

Gill, A.A. 2009. 'Her steeliness and allure were done to a Mrs T', *Sunday Times*, 1 March.

Glancy, M. 2005. 'The war of independence in feature films: *The Patriot* (2000) and the "special relationship" between Hollywood and Britain', *Historical Journal of Film, Radio and Television*, 25(4): 523–45.

Goldstein, B. 1999. 'Books: Audio Special interview with Niall Ferguson', *New York Times*, 20 April: http://www.nytimes.com/books/99/05/09/specials/ferguson.html?_r=2&scp=4&sq=ferguson%20AND%20goldstein&st=cse, accessed 15 July 2001.

Gömöri, G. 1985. 'Doctored history books', *Index on Censorship*, 14(6): 7–10.

Goodman, J. 2002. 'Review', *American Historical Review*, 107(2): 503–4.

Gordon, L. 1988. 'What is women's history ...?', in J. Gardiner (ed.), *What is History Today ...?* (Basingstoke: Macmillan): 91–3.

Gove, M. 2008. 'Notebook', *The Times*, 27 Oct.

Gove, M. 2010. '2010 Conservative Party Conference: all pupils will learn our island story', 5 Oct., http://www.conservatives.com/News/Speeches/2010/10/Michael_Gove_All_pupils_will_learn_our_island_story.aspx, accessed 15 Oct. 2010.

Grafton, A. 1999. [1997] *The Footnote: a curious history* (Cambridge, MA: Harvard University Press).

Grainger, J.H. 1986. *Patriotisms: Britain 1900–1939* (London: Routledge & Kegan Paul).

Gray, C. 2000. Judgment of Mr. Justice Charles Gray, 11 April: http://www.hdot.org/trial/judgement, accessed 12 Dec. 2008.

Greenberg, D. 2006. 'Class warfare: why the villain of *The History Boys* is the better teacher', *Slate*, 24 July: http://www.slate.com/id/2146396/, accessed 6 June 2009.

Gregory, P. n.d. a. 'Your frequently asked questions': http://www.philippagregory.com/living-room/faq/, accessed 12 April 2010.

Gregory, P. n.d. b. 'Fact and fiction: The Other Boleyn Girl': http://www.philippagregory.com/work/tudor/the-other-boleyn-girl/fact-and-fiction-the-other-boleyn-girl/, accessed 12 April 2010.

Gregory, P. n.d. c. 'Meet the writers: Philippa Gregory': http://www.barnesandnoble.com/writers/writerdetails.asp?cid=934860, accessed 15 Nov.2009.

Gregory, P. n.d. d. 'A conversation with Philippa Gregory', encl.: http://search.barnesandnoble.com/The-White-Queen/Philippa-Gregory/e/9781416563914, accessed 15 Nov. 2009.

Gregory, P. 1987. 'Exit Kate Wedd – pursued by £500,000', *Guardian*, 23 May.

Gregory, P. 1989. *The Favoured Child* (London: Viking).

Gregory, P. 1991. [1990] *Meridon* (London: Viking).

Gregory, P. 1992. 'Heroes and villains: E.P. Thompson', *Independent*, 5 Dec.

Gregory, P. 1996. 'Love hurts', in S. Sceats and G. Cunningham (eds.), *Image and Power: women and fiction in the twentieth century* (London: Longman): 139–48.

Gregory, P. 2004. 'Foreword', in Anya Seton, *Katherine* (Chicago, IL: Chicago Review Press); vii–ix.

Gregory, P. 2005. 'Historic passion: born a writer: forged as a historian', *History Workshop Journal*, 59: 237–42.

Gregory, P. 2006. 'A voice from the past', *The Times*, 21 Jan.

Gregory, P. 2008a. 'Philippa Gregory watches as her bestseller "The Other Boleyn Girl" gets the Hollywood treatment', *The Times*, 15 Feb.

Gregory. P. 2008b. 'Research', *Guardian*, 20 Sept.

Gregory, P. 2008c. 'Book World Live: Philippa Gregory, novelist', *Washington Post*, 9 Oct.

Grice, E. 2010. 'Simon Schama: could I have multiple personality disorder?', *Daily Telegraph*, 28 July.

Grimes, W. 1994. 'An effort to re-classify a racist classic', *New York Times*, 27 April.

Gruber, I. 2002. 'Of arms and men: "Arming America" and military history', *William and Mary Quarterly*, 59(1): 217–22.

The Guardian. 1970. 'A judge speaks of captain's reputation', 17 Feb.

Gunn, S. 2006. *History and Cultural Theory* (Harlow: Pearson).

Guttenplan, D.D. 2002. *The Holocaust on Trial: history, justice and the David Irving libel case* (London: Granta).

Guy, J. 2008. 'All hail the young Henry', *Sunday Times*, 5 Oct.

Guy, J. 2009. 'Signposts: The Tudors', *History Today*, 59(5): 58–9.

Gwinn, M.A. 2000. 'Over coffee with Simon Schama', *Seattle Times*, 17 Nov.

Hall, S. 1980. 'Encoding/decoding', in S. Hall, D. Hobson, A. Lowe and P. Willis (eds.), *Culture, Media, Language: working papers in cultural studies, 1972–79* (London: Hutchinson): 128–38.

Hammill, E. 2009. 'Terry Deary', *Books for Keeps*, 175: 10–11.

Hari, J. 2009. 'David Irving: "Hitler appointed me his biographer"', *Independent*, 15 Jan.

Harlan, D. 2007. 'Historical fiction and the future of academic history', in K. Jenkins, S. Morgan and A. Munslow (eds.), *Manifestos for History* (Abingdon: Routledge): 108–30.

Hastings, C. and Chittenden, M. 2009. 'Leaked BBC list dismisses appeal of Michael Palin and Delia Smith', *Sunday Times*, 13 Dec.

Hastings, M. 2000. 'Letter to Editor', *Times Literary Supplement*, 1 Dec.

Hastings, M. 2009. 'How the West was won', *Sunday Times*, 31 May.

Herrup, C. 2009. 'The hot dynasty: the Tudors on film and TV', *Perspectives on History*, April: http://www.historians.org/perspectives/issues/2009/0904/0904fil2.cfm, accessed 27 May 2009.

Heston, C. 2000. 'Letter: Arming America', *New York Times*, 1 Oct.

Hickman, L. 2011. 'How Horrible Histories became a huge hit', *Guardian*, 17 March.

Higashi, S. 1998. 'Rethinking film as American history', *Rethinking History*, 2(1): 87–101.

Hill, P. 2005. 'Are you a historian with telly vision?', *Times Higher Education Supplement*, 18 Feb.

Himmelfarb, G. 1987. *The New History and the Old: critical essays and reappraisals* (Cambridge, MA.: Harvard University Press).

Himmelfarb, G. 1989. 'Some reflections on the new history', *American Historical Review*, 94(3): 661–70.

Hinds, K. 1985. 'Joan Wallach Scott: breaking new ground for women?', *Change: the magazine of higher learning*, 17(4): 48–56.

Hironson, P. 2009. 'Interview: David Starkey', 6 April: http://www.tvscoop.tv/2009/04/tv_scoop_interv_26.html, accessed 12 Nov. 2009.

Hislop, V. 2002. 'Fury of a horrible historian', *Daily Telegraph*, 19 Oct.

Historical Association. 2010. 'Survey of History in Schools in England 2010', 12 Sept.: http://www.history.org.uk/news/news_869.html, accessed 16 Oct. 2010.

Historical Novel Society. n.d. 'Defining the genre': http://www.historicalnovelsociety.org/definition.htm, accessed 30 Oct. 2009.

History Channel. 2001. 'The True Story of Braveheart', 22 Dec.

History Makers. 2009. Press Release: http://www.historymakers2009.com/archives/history2008/?p=88, accessed 14 May 2009.

Hobsbawm, E. 1962. *The Age of Revolution: Europe, 1789–1848* (London: Weidenfeld & Nicolson).

Hobsbawm, E. 1978. 'The Historians' Group of the Communist Party', in M. Cornforth (ed.), *Rebels and their Causes: essays in honour of A.L. Morton* (London: Lawrence & Wishart): 21–47.

Hobsbawm, E. 1987. *The Age of Empire, 1875–1914* (London: Weidenfeld & Nicolson).

Hobsbawm, E. 1988. 'History from Below: some reflections', in F. Krantz (ed.), *History From Below: studies in popular protest and popular ideology* (Oxford: Basil Blackwell): 13–28.

Hobsbawm, E. 1995. [1994] *Age of Extremes: the Short Twentieth Century, 1914–1991* (London: Abacus).

Hobsbawm, E. 1998. [1997] *On History* (London: Abacus).

Hobsbawm, E. 2002a. *Interesting Times: A twentieth-century life* (London: Allen Lane).

Hobsbawm. E. 2002b. *Breakfast with Frost*, BBC1, 26 May.

Hobsbawm, E. 2003. 'A historical retrospect', 7 Nov.: http://www.balzan.org/en/prizewinners/eric-hobsbawm/a-historical-retrospect_20_22.html, accessed 14 Oct. 2008.

Hobsbawm, E. 2004. 'Spreading Democracy', *Foreign Policy*, Sept./Oct.: http://www.foreignpolicy.com/story/files/story2666.php, accessed 14 Dec. 2004.

Hobsbawm, E. 2005. 'In defence of history', *Guardian*, 15 Jan.

Hobsbawm, E. 2006. 'Could it have been different?', *London Review of Books*, 16 Nov.: 3–6.

Hobsbawm, E. 2008. 'Diary: Memories of Weimar', *London Review of Books*, 24 Jan.: 34–5.

Hobsbawm, E. 2011. *How to Change the World: tales of Marx and Marxism* (London: Little, Brown).

Hodgson, B. 2008. 'Terry Deary: rebel with a cause', *Journal* (Newcastle upon Tyne), 26 Aug.

Hoff, J. 1994. 'Gender as a postmodern category of paralysis', *Women's History Review*, 3(2): 149–68.

Hoffmann, P. 1989. 'Hitler's Good Right Arm', *New York Times*, 28 May.

Hoffmann, S. 2003. 'Review of Empire', *Foreign Affairs*, 82(5): 178–9.

Holgate, A. 2009. 'On the trail of D-Day's ghosts', *Sunday Times*, 24 May.

Honan, W.H. 1998. 'Historians warming to games of "What If"', *New York Times*, 7 Jan.

Hoock, H. 2010. 'Public History in Britain: Introduction', *Public Historian*, 32(3): 7–24.

Horne, G. 1990. 'Film Review: *Glory*', *American Historical Review*, 95(4): 1141–3.

Howard, P. 1982. 'Keneally "faction" wins the Booker prize', *The Times*, 20 Oct.

Howsam, L. 2009. *Past into Print: the publishing of history in Britain, 1850–1950* (London: British Library).

Hudson, C. 2001. 'The real band of brothers', *Daily Mail*, 13 Oct.

Huggins, M. 2002. 'Review', *Journal of Social History*, 36(1): 234–6.

Hughes-Warrington, M. 2007. *History Goes to the Movies: studying history on film* (Abingdon: Routledge).

Hughes-Warrington, M. 2008. *Fifty Key Thinkers on History* (2nd.ed., Abingdon: Routledge).

Hunt, T. 2002. 'Interview: man of the extreme century', *Observer*, 22 Sept.

Hunt, T. 2004a. 'How does television enhance history?', in D. Cannadine (ed.), *History and the Media* (Basingstoke: Palgrave Macmillan): 88–102.

Hunt, T. 2004b. 'Pasting over the past', *Guardian*, 7 April.

Hunt, T. 2006. 'Reality, identity and empathy: the changing face of social history television', *Journal of Social History*, 39(3): 843–58.

Hutton, W. 2002. 'Great television, but is it great history?', *Observer*, 16 June.

Imperial War Museum. 2009. 'Horrible Histories: Terrible Trenches Exhibition': http://trenches.iwm.org.uk/home, accessed 17 July 2009.

Institute for the Public Understanding of the Past (IPUP). 2010. 'Televisualizing the Past Conference Report', http://www.york.ac.uk/ipup/events/schama/televisualizing-report.html, accessed 10 May 2011.

Irving, D. 1963. *The Destruction of Dresden* (London: William Kimber).

Irving, D. 1977. *Hitler's War* (New York: Viking).

Irving, D. 1984. 'On contemporary history and historiography', *Journal of Historical Review*, 5(2–4): 251–88.

Irving, D. 1995. 'Revelations from Goebbels' diary: bringing to light secrets of Hitler's propaganda minister', *Journal of Historical Review*, 15(1): 2–17.

Irving, D. 1996. *Goebbels: Mastermind of the Third Reich* (London: Focal Point).

Irving, D. 2000. 'The Lipstadt Trial': http://www.fpp.co.uk/trial/questions/index.html, accessed 28 Oct. 2000.

Irving, D. 2001a. *Churchill's War, vol.II: Triumph in Adversity* (London: Focal Point).

Irving, D. 2001b. *Hitler's War* (London: Focal Point).

Irving, D. 2008. *Banged Up: survival as a political prisoner in 21st .Century Europe* (Windsor: Focal Point).

Isaacs, J. 2004. 'All our yesterdays', in D. Cannadine (ed.), *History and the Media* (Basingstoke: Palgrave Macmillan): 34–50.

Jacobson, H. 1987. 'Sex on the syllabus', *Observer*, 28 June.

Jaggi, M. 2002. 'A question of faith', *Guardian*, 14 Sept.

Jardine, C. 2006. 'History most horrid', *Daily Telegraph*, 12 Oct.

Jarvie, I.C. 1981. 'Fanning the Flames: anti-American reaction to Objective Burma (1945)', *Historical Journal of Film, Radio and Television*, 1(2): 117–37.

Jarvis, A-A. 2009. 'Last Night's Television: Horrible Histories, BBC1', *Independent*, 17 April.

Jenkins, K. 1991. *Re-thinking History* (London: Routledge).

Jenkins, K. 1997. 'Introduction: on being open about our closures', in K. Jenkins (ed.), *The Postmodern History Reader* (London: Routledge): 1–30.

Jenkins, S. 2002. 'Why history is more popular than pornography', *The Times*, 5 July.

Jenkins, S. 2009. 'The American Future', *Sunday Times*, 5 July.

Johnson, D. 2004. 'Bennett has a stab at rewriting the history of celebrity academics', *Daily Telegraph*, 20 May.

Jordanova, L. 2000. 'Public history', *History Today*, 50(5): 20–1.

Jordanova, L. 2006. *History in Practice* (2nd.ed., London: Hodder).

Jordanova, L. 2008. 'How history matters now', *History & Policy Paper* 80, Nov.: http://www.historyandpolicy.org/papers/policy-paper-80.html, accessed 12 Feb. 2009.

Judd, D. 1997. 'Historical writing', in L.J. Butler and A. Gorst (eds.), *Modern British History: a guide to study and research* (London: I.B. Tauris): 1–13.

Juddery, M. 2008. 'Gone with the Wind', *History Today*, 58(8): 36–41.

Kagan, D. 1999. 'Lessons of the Great War', *Commentary*, Oct.: 48–52.

Kaminer, W. 2002. 'Heavy lifting', *American Prospect*, 13(1), 25 Feb.: 9.

Kaufman, G. 1985. *My Life in the Silver Screen* (London: Faber & Faber).

Kaye, H.J. 1984. *The British Marxist Historians: an introductory analysis* (Cambridge: Polity).

Keegan, Sir J. 2000. 'The Trial of David Irving – and my part in his downfall', *Daily Telegraph*, 12 April.

Keneally, T. 1982. *Schindler's Ark* (London: Hodder & Stoughton).

Kennedy, P. 1986. 'A.J.P. Taylor: "Profound forces" in history', *History Today*, 36(3): 9–12.

Kenyon, J. 1983. *The History Men: the historical profession in England since the Renaissance* (London: Weidenfeld & Nicolson).

Kershaw, I. 2004. 'The past on the box: strengths and weaknesses', in D. Cannadine (ed.), *History and the Media* (Basingstoke: Palgrave Macmillan): 118–23.

Kershaw, I. 2008. 'The writing life: sometimes history just depends on that next cup of coffee', *Washington Post*, 19 Oct.

Kirkpatrick, D.D. 2002. 'As historian's fame grows, so do the questions on methods', *New York Times*, 11 Jan.

Klepp, L. 1995. 'Simon Schama makes a mess of history – ably flamboyant storyteller', *New York Magazine*, 24 April: 54–7.

Krossa, S.L. 2001. 'Regarding the Film *Braveheart;* also known as "That Film Whose Name Shall Not Be Uttered"', 31 Oct.: http://mediev alscotland.org/scotbiblio/braveheart.shtml, accessed 29 Sept. 2008.

Krossa, S.L. 2008. '*Braveheart* Errors: an illustration of scale', 2 Oct.: http://medievalscotland.org/scotbiblio/bravehearterrors.shtml, accessed 29 Oct. 2008.

Lamont, W. 1998. 'Introduction', in W. Lamont (ed.), *Historical Controversies and Historians* (London: UCL Press): xi–xiii.

Lang, R. 1994. 'The Birth of a Nation: history, ideology, narrative form', in R. Lang (ed.), *The Birth of a Nation: D.W. Griffith, Director* (New Brunswick, NJ: Rutgers University Press): 3–24.

Lay, P. 2010. 'From the Editor', *History Today*, 61(10): 2.

Lee, D. 2006. 'U-571': http://www.channel4.com/history/microsites/H/history/e-h/film-u571.html, accessed 3 Oct. 2008.

Lee, S. 2009. 'Theatre review: Horrible Histories', *Liverpool Daily Post*, 16 Sept.

Lenman, B.P. 2001. 'Review', *H-Albion, H-Net Reviews*, May: http://www.h-net.org/reviews/showrev.php?id=5133, accessed 12 Dec. 2007.

Leonard, T. 2004. ' "Shocking ignorance" about 1066 and all that', *Daily Telegraph*, 18 Oct.

Levy, G. 2009. 'Eric Hobsbawm, useful idiot of the chattering classes', *Daily Mail*, 3 March.

Lewis, M. 2002. 'Did Ambrose write Wild Blue, or just edit it?', 27 Feb.: http://www.forbes.com/2002/02/27/0227ambrose.html, accessed 14 Aug. 2009.

Liberté pour l'histoire. 2005. 'L'appel du 12 décembre 2005': http://www.lph-asso.fr/index.php?option=com_content&view=article&id=2&Itemid=13&lang=en, accessed 20 Nov. 2008.

Lindgren, J. 2002. 'Review: Fall from Grace: "Arming America" and the Bellesiles scandal', *Yale Law Review*, 111(8): 2195–249.

Lindgren, J. and Heather, J.L. 2002. 'Counting Guns in Early America', *William and Mary Law Review*, 43(5): 1777–842.

Lipstadt, D.E. 1994. [1993] *Denying the Holocaust: the growing assault on truth and memory* (London: Penguin).

Lipstadt, D.E. 2005. *History on Trial: my day in court with David Irving* (New York: CCC).

Litwack, L.F. 1996. 'The Birth of a Nation', in M.C. Carnes (ed.), *Past Imperfect: history according to the movies* (London: Cassell): 136–41.

Low, V. 2010. 'German report says Dresden firebomb toll was exaggerated', *The Times*, 18 March.

MacCulloch, D. 2010. 'Summer reading', *History Today*, 61(6): 60–2.

Macintyre, B. 2008. 'War films: the great escape from the truth', *The Times*, 8 Aug.

Macintyre, B. 2011. 'At last Hollywood history is no longer bunk', *The Times*, 18 Jan.

Mackenzie, S. 1991. 'Romantically inclined', *Guardian*, 17 April.

Mahony, E. 2008. 'A whiz-bang day out,' *The Times*, 21 May.

Main, G. 2002. 'Many things forgotten: the use of probate records in "Arming America"', *William and Mary Quarterly*, 59(1): 211–16.

'Making History'. 2008. 'Interviews: Eric Hobsbawm', Institute of Historical Research, 17 June: http://www.history.ac.uk/makinghistory/resources/interviews/Hobsbawm_Eric.html, accessed 11 Jan. 2010.

Mallinson, A. 2009. 'D-Day: The Battle for Normandy by Antony Beevor', *The Times*, 23 May.

Mandler, P. 2002. *History and National Life* (London: Profile Books).

Mandler, P. 2007. 'The responsibility of the historian', in H. Jones, K. Östberg and N. Randeraad (eds.), *Contemporary History on trial: Europe since 1989 and the role of the expert historian* (Manchester: Manchester University Press).

Mantel, H. 2009. *Talking Books – Novel History Panel*, Birkbeck Institute for the Humanities, University of London, 6 June: http://back doorbroadcasting.net/2009/06/talking-books-novel-history/, accessed 3 Dec. 2009.

Marius, R. 1999. *A Short Guide to Writing about History* (3rd.ed., New York: Longman).

Marr, A. 2004. 'The original showman', *Daily Telegraph*, 11 Dec.

Marshall, L. n.d. 'Columbia interactive e-seminars: Schama to teach': http://ci.columbia.edu/ci/eseminars/0730_detail.html, accessed 27 Dec. 2008.

Marshall, L. 2001. 'Simon Schama to Teach Fathom Internet Lesson on British Empire This Summer', *Columbia University Record*, 24 June.

Martin, N. 2008. 'BBC period drama The Tudors is "gratuitously awful" says Dr. David Starkey', *Daily Telegraph*, 16 Oct.

Marwick, A. 1989. *Nature of History* (3rd ed., Basingstoke: Macmillan).

Marwick, A. 1995. 'Two approaches to historical study: the meta-physical (including "postmodernism") and the historical', *Journal of Contemporary History*, 30(1): 5–35.

Marwick, A. 2001. *The New Nature of History: knowledge, evidence, language* (Basingstoke: Palgrave Macmillan).

Mason, T.W. 1964. 'Some origins of the Second World War', *Past and Present*, 29: 67–87.

Matthews, V. 2003. 'Horribly successful', *Independent*, 8 July.

McArthur, C. 2003. *Brigadoon, Braveheart and the Scots: distortions of Scotland in Hollywood cinema* (London: I.B. Tauris).

McCabe, C. 1985. 'Himself', in J.M. Merriman (ed.), *For Want of a Horse: choice and change in history* (Lexington, MA; Stephen Greene Press): 1–3.

McNamara, R.S. with VanDeMark, B. 1995. *In Retrospect: the tragedy and lessons of Vietnam* (New York: Times Books).

McPherson, J.M. 1990. 'The "Glory" story', *New Republic*, 202: 8 & 15 Jan.: 22–7.

Meades, J. 1978. 'The week in view', *Observer*, 9 July.

Meléndez, M.L. 2008. 'Teaching American History', *Federalist*, 19: http://www.ed.gov/programs/teachinghistory/shfg-article.doc, accessed 10 May 2009.

Membery, Y. 2002. 'The Virgin Queen – that's a pub, innit?', *Sunday Times*, 18 Aug.

Merry, S. 1994. 'Historical novels', in P. Catterall and H. Jones (eds.), *Understanding Documents and Sources* (Oxford: Heinemann): 86–91.

Meyerowitz, J. 2008. 'A history of "gender"', *American Historical Review*, 113(5): 1346–56.

Midgley, C. 2011. 'Historical or hysterical?', *The Times*, 20 May.

Milner, C. 2002. 'Schama makes history with £3m book and TV deal', *Sunday Telegraph*, 4 Aug.

Mitchell, D. 2010. 'Past, imperfect', *Daily Telegraph*, 8 May.

Moran, C. 2007. 'Porn to be King', *The Times*, 29 Sept.

Morgan, P. 1992. 'From a Death to a View: the hunt for the Welsh past in the Romantic period', in E.J. Hobsbawm and T. Ranger (eds.), *The Invention of Tradition* (Cambridge: Cambridge University Press): 43–100.

Morgan, S. 2006a. 'Introduction: writing feminist history', in S. Morgan (ed.), *The Feminist History Reader* (Abingdon: Routledge): 1–48.

Morgan, S. (ed.) 2006b. *The Feminist History Reader* (Abingdon: Routledge).

Morris, T. 2002. 'From blood feuds to blood ties', *Sunday Times*, 14 July.

Morrison, B. 1995. 'Today's past master', *Independent on Sunday*, 9 April.

Morrison, H. 1946. *Hansard Parliamentary Debates (Commons)*, 431, 11 Dec.

Morton, G. 2001. *William Wallace: man and myth* (Stroud: Sutton).

Moss, S. 2000. 'History's verdict on Holocaust upheld', *Guardian*, 12 April.

Moss, S. 2001. 'Dial-a-don', *Guardian*, 1 March.

Munslow, A. 2006. *The Routledge Companion to Historical Studies* (2nd ed., Abingdon: Routledge).

Mustich, E. 2009. 'David Starkey: Renaissance man', *Varsity*, 6 Nov.: http://www.varsity.co.uk/features/1466, accessed 10 Nov. 2009.

National Coalition for History. 2010. 'History organizations fight to save Teaching American History grants', http://historycoali tion.org/2010/08/20/history-organizations-unite-to-save-teaching-american-history-grants/, accessed 2 Feb. 2011.

National Geographic. 2002. 'Historian Steven (*sic*) Ambrose dead at 66', *National Geographic News*, 15 Oct.: http://news.nationalgeographic.com/news/2002/10/1015_021015_ambrose.html, accessed 14 Aug. 2009.

National Trust. 2008. *Why History Matters* (Swindon: National Trust).

Naughton, J. 2008. 'Dressed to thrill', *Radio Times*, 26 July–1 Aug.

Nightingale, B. 2005. 'Horrible histories', *The Times*, 24 Oct.

Novick, P. 1999. *The Holocaust in American Life* (Boston, MA: Houghton Mifflin).

Oakeshott, M. 1933. *Experience and its Modes* (Cambridge: Cambridge University Press).

Ofsted. 2007. 'History in the Balance: History in English schools 2003–07', July: http://www.ofsted.gov.uk/Ofsted-home/Publications-and-research/Browse-all-by/Education/Curriculum/History/Primary/History-in-the-balance, accessed 10 Oct. 2010.

Ofsted. 2011. 'History for All: History in English schools 2007–10', March: http://www.ofsted.gov.uk/Ofsted-home/Publications-and-research/Browse-all-by/Documents-by-type/Thematic-reports/History-for-all, accessed 22 March 2011.

Origin Publishing. 2005. Letter to the author, 18 Jan.

Otte, T.G. 2000. 'Neo-Revisionism or the Emperor's New Clothes: some reflections on Niall Ferguson on the origins of the First World War', *Diplomacy and Statecraft*, 11(1): 271–90.

Overy, R. 2010. 'The historical present', *Times Higher Education Supplement*, 29 April.

Palmer, W. 2001. *Engagement with the Past: the lives and works of the World War II generation of historians* (Lexington, KY: University Press of Kentucky).

Passmore, K. 2003. 'Poststructuralism and history', in S. Berger, H. Feldner and K. Passmore (eds.), *Writing History: theory and practice* (London: Arnold): 118–40.

Peck, L.L. 2009. 'Schama's Britannia', *American Historical Review*, 114(3): 672–83.

Pendreigh, B. 1998. 'Man who rewrites history', *Sunday Times*, 8 March.

Perry, M. 2002. *Marxism and History* (Basingstoke: Palgrave Macmillan).

Pickering, P. 2011. 'Reviews in History', Feb.: http://www.history.ac.uk/reviews/review/1041, accessed 24 Feb. 2011.

Popkin, J.D. 2005. *History, Historians and Autobiography* (Chicago, IL: University of Chicago Press).

Porter, A. 2003. 'Reviews in History', April: http://www.history.ac.uk/reviews/paper/porterA.html, accessed 3 Feb. 2009.

Powell, D. 1994. 'The historical novel: history as fiction and fiction as history', *The Historian*, 43: 13–16.

Price, M. 2003. 'Eric Hobsbawm: the historian who won't say goodbye to all that', *Boston Globe*, 2 March.

Pryce-Jones, D. 2001. 'Stalin's Professor – the awful, influential career of E.J. Hobsbawm – communist and historian', *National Review*, 15 Oct.

Pryce-Jones, D. 2003. 'Eric Hobsbawm: lying to the credulous', *New Criterion*, 21, Jan.: 9.

Pullinger, K. 2008. 'Research', *Guardian*, 20 Sept.

Purvis, J. 2009. 'David Starkey's history boys', *Guardian*, 2 April.

Puttnam, D. 2004. 'Has Hollywood stolen our history?', in D. Cannadine (ed.), *History and the Media* (Basingstoke: Palgrave Macmillan): 160–6.

Radice, G. 2004. 'Taylor made', *History Today*, 54(11): 94–5.

Ramaswamy, C. 2008. 'Mary, Mary, quite contrary – Philippa Gregory interview', *Scotland on Sunday*, 24 Aug.

Raphael, I. 1982. 'But is it a novel?', *The Times*, 21 Oct.

Rayner, R. 2010. 'Channelling Ike', *New Yorker*, 26 April: 19.

Rees, L. 2010. 'No, children: Hitler came after 1066', *Sunday Times*, 25 April.

Rehberger, D. 1995. ' "Vulgar fiction, impure history": the neglect of historical fiction', *Journal of American Culture*, 18(4): 59–65.

Richards, J. 2000. 'General Editor's Foreword', in J.K. Walton, *The British Seaside: holidays and seaside resorts in the twentieth century* (Manchester: Manchester University Press): vi.

Richards. J. 2003. 'General Editor's Introduction', in C. McArthur, *Brigadoon, Braveheart and the Scots: distortions of Scotland in Hollywood cinema* (London: I.B. Tauris): viii–ix.

Richards, J. 2009. 'Film and television: the moving image', in S. Barber and C.M. Peniston-Bird (eds.), *History Beyond the Text* (Abingdon: Routledge): 72–88.

Riding, A. 1999. 'An Oxford historian whose vox is populi', *New York Times*, 6 March.

Ritscher. S. 2008. 'Historikerpreis: Dr. Eric J. Hobsbawm ausgezeichnet', *Münstersche Zeitung*, 30 Nov.

Roberts, A. 1994. 'An inadvertent history lesson', *Evening Standard*, 29 Oct.

Roberts, A. 1998. 'Yes it was bloody, but oh what a necessary war', *Sunday Times*, 11 Oct.

Roberts, A. 2000a. 'Irving's greatest triumph', *Sunday Telegraph*, 16 April.

Roberts, A. 2000b. 'Hollywood's racist lies about Britain and the British', *Daily Express*, 14 June.

Roberts, A. 2000c. 'History man', *Evening Standard*, 4 Sept.

Roberts, A. 2004. 'Introduction', in A. Roberts (ed.), *What might have been: leading historians on twelve "What Ifs" of history* (London: Weidenfeld & Nicolson): 1–14.

Roberts, A. 2006. 'Bennett's History Boys gets me wrong', *Spectator*, 7 Oct.: 20–1.

Roberts, A. 2007. 'What if we had lost the Falklands?', *Daily Mail*, 19 June.

Roberts, A. 2010. 'The king who couldn't speak', 20 Nov.: http://www.thedailybeast.com/blogs-and-stories/2010–11–20/the-kings-speech-good-movie-bad-history/, accessed 16 Jan. 2011.

Roberts, G. 1998. 'Geoffrey Elton and the philosophy of history', *The Historian*, 57: 29–31.

Roberts, G. 2001. 'Geoffrey Elton: history and human action', in G. Roberts (ed.), *The History and Narrative Reader* (London: Routledge): 130–4.

Roberts, L. 2010. 'Simon Schama's appointment as history tsar is an insult, says Mary Beard', *Daily Telegraph*, 8 Oct.

Robin, R. 2004. *Scandals and Scoundrels: seven cases that shook the academy* (Berkeley, CA: University of California Press).

Rose, J. 2002. [2001] *The Intellectual Life of the British Working Classes* (New Haven, CT: Yale University Press).

Rose, M. 2001. 'History Inc.: as a professor's books become bestsellers, a big business is born', *Wall Street Journal*, 20 Aug.

Rosenfeld, G. 2002. 'Why do we ask "What If?": reflections on the function of alternate history', *History and Theory*, 41(4): 90–103.

Rosenstone, R.A. 1988. 'History in images/History in words: reflections on the possibility of really putting history into film', *American Historical Review*, 93(5): 1173–85.

Rosenstone, R.A. 1995. 'Introduction', in R.A. Rosenstone (ed.), *Revisioning History: film and the construction of a new past* (Princeton, NJ: Princeton University Press): 3–13.

Rosenstone, R.A. 2002. 'The visual media and historical knowledge', in L. Kramer and S. Maza (eds.), *A Companion to Western Historical Thought* (Oxford: Blackwell): 466–81.

Rosenstone, R.A. 2004. 'Confessions of a postmodern (?) historian', *Rethinking History*, 8(1): 149–66.

Rosenstone, R.A. 2006. *History on Film/Film as History* (Harlow: Pearson Longman).

Rosenstone, R.A. 2007a. 'Space for the bird to fly', in K. Jenkins, S. Morgan and A. Munslow (eds.), *Manifestos for History* (Abingdon: Routledge): 11–18.

Rosenstone, R.A. 2007b. 'Response: Reviews in History', Nov.: http://www.history.ac.uk/reviews/paper/chapmanresp.html, accessed 14 Dec. 2008.

Rosenstone, R.A. 2009a. 'What's a nice historian like you doing in a place like this?', *Rethinking History*, 13(1): 17–25.

Rosenstone, R.A. 2009b. 'Letters', *Oregon Historical Quarterly*, 110(1): 155–7.

Rosenzweig, R. 2011. *Clio Wired: the future of the past in the digital age* (New York: Columbia University Press).

Roth, R. 2002. 'Guns, gun culture and homicide: the relationship between firearms, the uses of firearms, and interpersonal violence', *William and Mary Quarterly*, 59(1): 223–40.

Rowan, D. 2004. 'Interview: Janice Hadlow', *Evening Standard*, 16 June.

Rubin, M. 2009. 'The BBC's "A History of Britain"', *American Historical Review*, 114(3): 664–71.

Rubinstein, W.D. 2004. *Genocide: a history* (London: Pearson Longman).

Rusbridger, A. 2007. 'A counsel of despair', 27 May: http://www.guardian.co.uk/commentisfree/2007/may/27/isitallover/print, accessed 12 Nov. 2008.

Rüsen, J. 2002. 'Preface to the Series', in J. Rüsen (ed.), *Western Historical Thinking: an intercultural debate* (Oxford: Berghahn): vii–xiii.

Ryan, A. 2009. 'Terry Deary', *Cambridge News*, 22 Oct.

Sale, J. 2006. 'My first job: actor and Horrible Historian Terry Deary worked as a butcher's boy', *Independent*, 12 Oct.

Samuel, R. 1991. 'Analysis: The History of Nations', BBC Radio 4, 7 Feb.

Samuel, R. 1999. [1998] *Theatres of Memory, Volume 2: Island Stories: Unravelling Britain* (London: Verso).

Samuel, R. and Stedman-Jones, G. 1982. 'Preface', in R. Samuel and G. Stedman-Jones (eds.), *Culture, Ideology and Politics: essays for Eric Hobsbawm* (London: Routledge & Kegan Paul): ix–x.

Sandbrook, D. 2007. 'Don't stand off – reach out over the coffee table', *Times Higher Education Supplement*, 3 Aug.

Sandbrook, D. 2011. 'He'll always have Marx', *Sunday Times*, 9 Jan.

Saunders, K. 2006. 'Fiction in short', *The Times*, 26 Aug.

Saunders, K. 2009. 'The prances in the tower', *The Times*, 8 Aug.

Schama, S. 1989. *Citizens: a chronicle of the French Revolution* (London: Viking).

Schama, S. 1993. 'History now: a room with no view', *History Review*, 16: 23–6.

Schama, S. 1995. *Landscape and Memory* (London: HarperCollins).

Schama, S. 1998. [1991] *Dead Certainties (Unwarranted Speculations)* (London: Granta).

Schama, S. 1999a. 'Shooting *Britannia*', *Perspectives Online*, April: http://www.historians.org/Perspectives/issues/1999/9904/9904FIL2.CFM, accessed 2 Nov. 2001.

Schama, S. 1999b. 'And What if ...', *Talk*, Dec.: 152.

Schama, S. 2000a. 'Live Chat', 4 Oct.: http://www.bbc.co.uk/history/programmes/hob/chat_transcript.shtml, accessed 12 Dec. 2000.

Schama, S. 2000b. 'Live Chat', 8 Nov.: http://www.bbc.co.uk/communicate/archive/simon_schma/page1.shtml, accessed 4 Jan. 2009.

Schama, S. 2000c. *A History of Britain vol.1: At the Edge of the World?, 3000BC–AD1603* (London: BBC).

Schama, S. 2001a. 'Live Chat', 22 May: http://www.bbc.co.uk/history/programmes/hob/chat_transcript3.shtml, accessed 22 Feb. 2002.

Schama, S. 2001b. 'The Burden of Television History', Oct.: http://www.history2001.com./pdf/history.keynote.doc, accessed 12 Jan. 2002.

Schama, S. 2001c. 'Obituaries: Professor Sir John Plumb', *Independent*, 27 Oct.

Schama, S. 2002a. *Breakfast with Frost*, BBC1, 26 May.

Schama, S. 2002b. 'Television and the trouble with history', *Guardian*, 18 June.

Schama, S. 2002c. 'Letter to the Editor', *Observer*, 23 June.

Schama, S. 2002d. 'Television and the Trouble with History, Pt.1', *BBC History*, July: 42–4.

Schama, S. 2002e. 'Television and the Trouble with History, Pt.2', *BBC History*, Aug.: 40–3.

Schama, S. 2002f. 'Michael Caine inspired me to cook (and not a lot of people know that)', *Guardian*, 19 Sept.

Schama, S. 2004. 'True Confessions of a History Boy', *History Boys Theatre Programme*, May: 4pp.

Schama, S. 2008. 'The American future: a history', BBC Two, 17 Oct.

Schama, S. 2009a. 'Baseball and me', BBC Radio 4, 7 March.

Schama, S. 2009b. '"A History of Britain": a response', *American Historical Review*, 114(3): 692–700.

Schama, S. 2010a. *Scribble, Scribble: writings on ice cream, Obama, Churchill and my mother* (London: Bodley Head).

Schama, S. 2010b. 'David Cameron talks to Simon Schama', *Financial Times*, 1 Oct.

Schama, S. 2011. 'Five minutes with Simon Schama', BBC Arts, http://www.bbc.co.uk/news/entertainment-arts-12864555, accessed 26 March 2011.

Schofield, P. 2004. 'History and Marxism', in P. Lambert and P. Schofield (eds.), *Making History: an introduction to the history and practices of a discipline* (Abingdon: Routledge): 180–91.

Scholastic. 2009. 'Press Release: Horrible TV series back at the top', 15 June: http://www.scholastic.co.uk/department/home/blogs/7741, accessed 25 June 2009.

Schwarz, B. 1982. '"The people" in history: the Communist Party Historians' Group, 1946–56', in R. Johnson, G. McLennan, B. Schwarz and D. Sutton (eds.), *Making Histories: studies in history-writing and politics* (London: Hutchinson): 44–95.

Scott, J.W. n.d. [2008]. 'Dear Joan, Call Me "Chuck"', *Tributes to Charles Tilly (1929–2008)*, SSRC: http://essays.ssrc.org/tilly/scott, accessed 18 Oct. 2009.

Scott, J.W. 1974. *The Glassmakers of Carmaux: French craftsmen and political action in a nineteenth century city* (Cambridge, MA.: Harvard University Press).

Scott, J.W. 1983. 'Women in history: the modern period', *Past and Present*, 101: 141–57.

Scott, J.W. 1986. 'Gender: a useful category of historical analysis', *American Historical Review*, 91(5): 1053–75.

Scott, J.W. 1988. *Gender and the Politics of History* (New York: Columbia University Press).

Scott, J.W. 1989a. 'History in crisis? The others' side of the story', *American Historical Review*, 94(3): 680–92.

Scott, J.W. 1989b. 'The new history and the old', *American Historical Review*, 94(3): 699–700.

Scott, J.W. 1993. 'The tip of the volcano', *Comparative Studies in Society and History*, 35(2): 438–43.

Scott, J.W. 1996a. 'Academic freedom as an ethical practice', in L. Menand (ed.), *The Future of Academic Freedom* (Chicago, IL: University of Chicago Press): 163–80.

Scott, J.W. 1996b. 'Introduction', in J.W. Scott (ed.), *Feminism and History* (New York: Oxford University Press): 1–13.

Scott, J.W. 2001. 'Women's history', in P. Burke (ed.), *New Perspectives on Historical Writing* (London: Polity Press): 43–70.

Scott, J.W. 2004. 'Feminism's history', *Journal of Women's History*, 16(2): 10–29.

Scott, J.W. 2007. 'History-writing as critique', in K. Jenkins, S. Morgan and A. Munslow (eds.), *Manifestos for History* (Abingdon: Routledge): 19–38.

Scott, J.W. 2008. 'Unanswered questions', *American Historical Review*, 113(5): 1422–9.

Scott, J.W. 2009. 'Finding critical history', in J.M. Banner, Jr., and J.H. Gillis (eds.), *Becoming Historians* (Chicago, IL: University of Chicago Press): 26–53.

Scott, J.W. 2010. 'Gender: still a useful category of analysis?', *Diogenes*, 57(225): 7–14.

Scott, J.W. and Hobsbawm, E. 1980. 'Political shoemakers', *Past and Present*, 89: 86–114.

Scott, J.W. and Tilly, L. 1978. *Women, Work, and Family* (New York: Holt, Rinehart & Winston).

Seal, J. 2011. 'A new take on Turkey today', *Sunday Times*, 13 March.

Sebag-Montefiore, H. 2000. 'Enigma variations', *Guardian*, 25 May.

Senior, A. 2009. 'Fictional history is best. And that's the truth', *The Times*, 9 Oct.

Sereny, G. 1991. 'David Irving resells Hitler's war', *Sunday Times*, 27 Nov.

Shankleman, M. 2008. 'Still working at 90', BBC News, 11 April: http://news.bbc.co.uk/1/hi/business/7340623.stm, accessed 6 Nov. 2008.

Shepard, A. and Walker, G. 2008. 'Gender, change and periodisation', *Gender & History*, 20(3): 453–62.

Sherwin, A. 2009. 'People', *The Times*, 5 March.

Sherwin, A. and Owen, G. 2002. 'History at A Level a farce, says Schama', *The Times*, 10 Oct.

'Simple, P.' 2000. 'History', *Daily Telegraph*, 21 April.

Sisman, A. 1994. *A.J.P. Taylor: a biography* (London: Sinclair-Stevenson).

Sisman, A. 2010. *Hugh Trevor-Roper: the biography* (London: Weidenfeld & Nicolson).

Sitkoff, H. 1989. 'Mississippi Burning', *Journal of American History*, 76(3): 1019–20.

Sked, A. 1996. 'Speaking volumes', *Times Higher Education Supplement*, 20 Dec.

Sklar, R. 1997. 'Historical films: scofflaws and the historian-cop', *Reviews in American History*, 25(2): 346–50.

Slitherine Software. 2008. 'Press Release: Slitherine signs Horrible Histories', 26 Aug.: http://www.slitherine.com/forum/viewtopic.php?p=62682, accessed 25 May 2009.

Slitherine Software 2009. 'Press Release: 'Horrible Histories™ Ruthless Romans Announced!', 12 March: http://www.slitherine.com/forum/viewtopic.php?p=81364, accessed 25 May 2009.

Slotkin, R. 2005. 'Fiction for the purposes of history', *Rethinking History*, 9(2–3): 221–36.

Smith, B.G. 2010. 'Women's history: a retrospective from the United States', *Signs: Journal of Women in Culture and Society*, 35(3): 723–47.

Smith, C. 2000. *Hansard Parliamentary Debates (Commons)*, 353, 3 July.

Smith, M. 2003. 'History and the media: are you being hoodwinked?', *History Today*, 53(3): 28–30.

Smith, P. 2008. 'History on Film', *English Historical Review*, cxxiii, 501: 416–17.

Smither, R. 2004. 'Why is so much television history about war?', in D. Cannadine (ed.), *History and the Media* (Basingstoke: Palgrave Macmillan): 51–66.

Snowman, D. 1999. 'Eric Hobsbawm', *History Today*, 49(1): 16–18.

Snowman, D. 2004. 'Simon Schama', *History Today*, 54(7): 34–36.

Snowman, D. 2007. *Historians* (Basingstoke: Palgrave Macmillan).

Soffer, R.N. 2009. *History, Historians, and Conservatism in Britain and America: from the Great War to Thatcher and Reagan* (New York: Oxford University Press).

Southgate, B. 2009. *History Meets Fiction* (Harlow: Longman).

Spalding, R. 2002. 'Reviews in History', http://www.history.ac.uk/reviews/paper/spaldingR.html, Oct. 2002, accessed 6 April 2009.

Spongberg, M. 2002. *Writing Women's History since the Renaissance* (Basingstoke: Palgrave Macmillan).

Squires, N. 2009. 'Barack Obama condemns "ignorant and hateful" Holocaust deniers', *Daily Telegraph*, 5 June.

Stack, M. 2002. 'For Historian Ambrose, it's time for a "Love Song"', *Los Angeles Times*, 11 May.

Stanford, M. 1986. *The Nature of Historical Knowledge* (Oxford: Basil Blackwell).

Stansky, P. 2009. 'Simon Schama: "A History of Britain"', *American Historical Review*, 114(3): 684–91.

Starkey, D. n.d. 'Behind the scenes': http://www.pbs.org/wnet/sixwives/about/behind_int_starkey.html, accessed 3 July 2009.

Starkey, D. 2001. 'The English historian's role and the place of history in English national life', *The Historian*, 71: 6–15.

Starkey, D. 2010. 'What I've learnt', *The Times*, 2 Oct.

Stern, F. 1999. 'Family values', *The New Republic*, 8 Feb.: 34–7.

'Stirling history'. 2006. http://www.stirlinglife.com/stirlinghistory.php, accessed 1 Oct. 2008.

Stone, N. 1990. 'Katyn: the heart of Stalin's darkness', *Sunday Times*, 15 April.

Stone, N. 1991. 'The man who played history's ace', *Guardian*, 13 June.

Stone, N. 1998. 'Left right out of the gong show', *Sunday Times*, 4 Jan.

Stone, N. 2011. *Turkey: a short history* (London: Thames & Hudson).

Suid, L.H. 2002. *Guts & Glory: the making of the American military image in film* (rev. ed., Lexington, KY: University Press of Kentucky).

Sunday Times. 1996. 'Editorial: Forgetting ourselves', 26 May.

Sutherland, J. 2009. *Talking Books – Novel History Panel*, Birkbeck Institute for the Humanities, University of London, 6 June: http://backdoorbroadcasting.net/2009/06/talking-books-novel-history/, accessed 3 Dec. 2009.

Taylor, A. 2000. 'The history man: Simon Schama is the media don who is poised to bring history into our living rooms', *Sunday Herald* (Scotland), 24 Sept.

Taylor, A.J.P. 1936. 'History and biography', *Manchester Guardian*, 4 Dec.

Taylor, A.J.P. 1950. 'History in England', *Times Literary Supplement*, 25 Aug.: iv–v. Despite being anonymous, this was written by Taylor (Wrigley 1980: 141–2).

Taylor, A.J.P. 1951. [1945] *The Course of German History: a survey of the development of Germany since 1815* (London: Hamish Hamilton).

Taylor, A.J.P. 1954. 'Could the war of 1914–18 have been averted?', *The Listener*, 12 Aug.: 233–4.

Taylor, A.J.P. 1956. *Englishmen and Others* (London: Hamish Hamilton).

Taylor, A.J.P. 1957. 'Another version of the same', *New Statesman*, 30 Nov.: 743.

Taylor, A.J.P. 1960. 'Namier the Historian', *Observer*, 28 Aug.

Taylor, A.J.P. 1962. 'Eden in the Thirties', *Observer*, 18 Nov.

Taylor, A.J.P. 1964. [1961] *Origins of the Second World War* (rev. ed, Harmondsworth: Penguin).

Taylor, A.J.P. 1967. [1955] *Bismarck: the Man and the Statesman* (New York: Vintage).

Taylor, A.J.P. 1969a. *War by Timetable: how the First World War began* (London: Macdonald).

Taylor, A.J.P. 1969b. [1957] *The Troublemakers: dissent over foreign policy 1792–1939* (London: Panther).

Taylor, A.J.P. 1971. 'How to Quote: exercises for beginners', in E.M. Robertson (ed.), *The Origins of the Second World War* (London: Macmillan): 100–4.

Taylor, A.J.P. 1977a. 'Accident prone, or what happened next', *Journal of Modern History*, 49(1): 1–18.

Taylor, A.J.P. 1977b. 'The Fuehrer as Mohican', *Observer*, 12 June.

Taylor, A.J.P. 1977c. 'In defence of small nations', *The Listener*, 4 Aug.: 138–40.

Taylor, A.J.P. 1978. 'Hitler the opportunist', *Observer*, 18 June.

Taylor, A.J.P. 1983. *A Personal History* (London: Hamish Hamilton).

Taylor, M. 2007a. 'Discredited Irving plans comeback tour', *Guardian*, 29 Sept.

Taylor, M. 2007b. 'Irving and Griffin spark fury at Oxford Union debate', *Guardian*, 27 Nov.

Taylor, P.M. 2001. 'Television and the future historian', in G. Roberts and P.M. Taylor (eds.) *The Historian, Television and Television History* (Luton: University of Luton Press): 171–7.

Teeman, T. 2010. 'Bibles and beatings: life at the Sharpe end', *The Times*, 9 Oct.

Thelen, D. 1994. 'The moviemaker as historian: conversations with Ken Burns', *Journal of American History*, 81(3): 1031–50.

Thomas, H. 1975. 'Get me Stalin', *The Listener*, 24 April: 537.

Thomas, K. 1966. 'The tools and the job', *Times Literary Supplement*, 7 April: 275–6.

Thomas, Sir K. n.d. [1997]. 'Wolfson Speech', n.d. (15 May), encl. Simon Fourmy, Wolfson Foundation, to author, 15 Jan. 2009.

Thompson, E.P. 1978. *The Poverty of Theory and Other Essays* (London: Merlin).

Thompson, J. 2004. 'Simon Schama: academic history is dull!', *Independent*, 22 Feb.

Thompson, W. 2004. *Postmodernism and History* (Basingstoke: Palgrave Macmillan).

Thomson, A. 2007. 'History as it bloody well was', *Daily Telegraph*, 11 May.

Thomson, G., Dobb, M., Hill, C. and Saville, J. 1954. 'Foreword', in J. Saville (ed.), *Democracy and the Labour Movement: essays in honour of Dona Torr* (London: Lawrence & Wishart): 7–9.

The Times. 1945a. 'Editorial: films and the allies', 25 Sept.

The Times. 1945b. '"Objective Burma" suspended', 26 Sept.

The Times. 1960. '60,000 in bomb protest demonstration', 19 April.

The Times. 1990. 'Obituary: A.J.P. Taylor', 8 Sept.

The Times. 1996. 'Europe: a history', 5 Oct.

The Times. 2000. 'Editorial: History and Bunk', 12 April.

The Times. 2008. '50 greatest British writers 1945', 5 Jan.

The Times. 2011. 'Editorial: Speaking the Truth', 10 Jan.

Toplin, R.B. 1996a. 'Preface', in R.B. Toplin (ed.), *Ken Burns's The Civil War: historians respond* (New York: Oxford University Press): v–x.

Toplin, R.B. 1996b. *History by Hollywood: the use and abuse of the American past* (Urbana, IL: University of Illinois Press).

Toplin, R.B. 2002. *Reel History: in defense of Hollywood* (Lawrence, KS: University Press of Kansas).

Tosh, J. 2008a. *Why History Matters* (Basingstoke: Palgrave Macmillan).

Tosh, J. 2008b. 'Why History Matters', *History & Policy Paper 79*, Nov.: http://www.historyandpolicy.org/papers/policy-paper-79.html, accessed 12 Feb. 2009.

Tosh J. 2010. *The Pursuit of History: aims, methods and new directions in the study of history* (5th ed., Harlow: Pearson).

Tosh, J. with Lang, S. 2006. *The Pursuit of History: aims, methods and new directions in the study of history* (4th.ed., Harlow: Pearson).

Trevelyan, G.M. 1968. [1913] *Clio, a Muse: and other essays* (Manchester, NH: Ayer Publishing).

Trevor-Roper, H. 1981a. 'History: professional and lay', in H. Lloyd-Jones, V. Pearl and B. Worden (eds.) *History & Imagination: essays in honour of H.R. Trevor-Roper* (London: Duckworth): 1–14.

Trevor-Roper, H. 1981b. 'History and imagination', in H. Lloyd-Jones, V. Pearl and B. Worden (eds.) *History & Imagination: essays in honour of H.R. Trevor-Roper* (London: Duckworth): 356–69.

Trevor-Roper, H. 2008. *The Invention of Scotland: myth and history* (New Haven, CT.: Yale University Press).

Truss, L. 2000. 'Do we love to be by the seaside?', *Sunday Times*, 27 Aug.

Tyrrell, I. 2005. *Historians in Public: the practice of American history, 1890–1970* (Chicago, IL: University of Chicago Press).

United Nations. 2005. General Assembly Resolution A/RES/60/7, 1 Nov.: http://www.un.org/holocaustremembrance/docs/res607.shtml, accessed 2 May 2009.

United Nations. 2007. General Assembly Resolution A/RES/61/255, 22 March: http://www.un.org/holocaustremembrance/docs/res61.shtml, accessed 2 May 2009.

Unstead, S. 2003. 'Terry Deary – horribly successful author', *Books for Keeps*, 141: 3–4.

van Pelt. R.J. 2002. *The Case for Auschwitz: evidence from the Irving trial* (Bloomington, IN: Indiana University Press).

Vickery, A. 2011. 'Making an impact on television', *Royal Historical Society Newsletter*, 7 (May): 3.

Vincent, N. 2000. 'Charm offensive', *Times Literary Supplement*, 24 Nov.

Vinen, R. 2006. 'More than stylish', *Times Literary Supplement*, 22 Dec.

von Maier, R. and Glantz, D.M. 2008. 'Questions and Answers: Antony Beevor', *World War II Quarterly*, 5(1): 48–59.

Vonnegut, K. 2000. [1969] *Slaughterhouse-Five* (London: Vintage).

Wainwright, M. 1999. 'Clinton makes peace over Hollywood hijack of history', *Guardian*, 4 Sept.

'Wallace'. 2005. 'Wallace, Man and Myth': http://www.wallace-manandmyth.org/man_and_myth/, accessed 1 Oct. 2008.

Wallace, D. 2005. *The Woman's Historical Novel: British women writers, 1900–2000* (Basingstoke: Palgrave Macmillan).

Wallace, E.K. 2000. 'Telling Untold Stories: Philippa Gregory's "A Respectable Trade" and David Dabydeen's "A Harlot's Progress"', *Novel: A Forum on Fiction*, 33(2): 235–52.

Walsh, J. 2000. 'Celebrate the land of bad complexions and snaggly teeth', *Maxim Online*, n.d. (Nov.): http://www.maxim.com/tv/reviews/28823/history-britain.html, accessed 21 Oct. 2003.

Warner, O. 1959. 'Letter to the editor', *The Times*, 27 Nov.

Warren, J. 1998. *The Past and its Presenters: an introduction to issues in historiography* (London: Hodder & Stoughton).

Weber, M. n.d. 'David Irving': http://www.ihr.org/other/authorbios.html, accessed 2 May 2009.

Weir, A. 2003. 'The allure of Anne', *History Today*, 53(5): 94–5.

Weisberger, B.A. 1990. '"The great arrogance of the present is to forget the intelligence of the past": an interview with Ken Burns', *American Heritage*, 41(6): http://www.americanheritage.com/articles/magazine/ah/1990/6/1990_6_96.shtml, accessed 12 Dec. 2008.

Wells, M. 2002. 'Starkey makes history with £2m TV deal', *Guardian*, 4 March.

Wheatcroft, G. 2006. 'Portrait: A.J.P. Taylor', *Prospect*, 120, March: 46–9.

Whitworth, D. 2010. 'This was more than war. It was annihilation', *The Times*, 6 March.

Wiener, J. 2005. *Historians in Trouble: plagiarism, fraud, and politics in the ivory tower* (New York: The New Press).

Wight, M. 1953. 'Contentious but creative', *Spectator*, 15 May: 639–40.

Wightwick, A. 2008. 'Horrible histories – Terrible Tudors', *Western Mail*, 26 June.

Wignall, A. 2004. 'Philippa Gregory', *Guardian*, 3 Feb.

Wilentz, S. 2001. 'America made easy: McCullough, Adams and the decline of popular history', *New Republic*, 2 July: 35–40.

Williamson, S.R,. Jr. and May, E.R. 2007. 'An identity of opinion: historians and July 1914', *Journal of Modern History*, 79: 335–87.

Willis, J. 2001. 'Past is Perfect', *Guardian*, 29 Oct.

Wilson, D. 1999. 'Stronger than fact?', *History Today*, 49(1): 44–5.

Wilson, J.E. 2003. 'False and dangerous', *Guardian*, 8 Feb.

Wolfson Foundation. 2010. 'History Prize': http://www.wolfson.org. uk/grant-applicants/history-prize/, accessed 9 March 2010.

Wood, G. 2010. 'In defense of academic history writing', *Perspectives on History*, April: http://www.historians.org/Perspectives/issues/2010/1004/1004art1.cfm, accessed 12 April 2010.

Woods, R. 2008. 'It's fun, it's sexy – but is this really history?', *Sunday Times*, 27 July.

Woodward, W. 2003. 'History on TV a mixed blessing, say academics', *Guardian*, 21 July.

Wormald, J. 2008. 'Mary Queen of Scots defeats author Gregory', *Sunday Times*, 10 Aug.

Wormald, P. 2001. '1066 and All That: Simon Schama chronicles Britain from its beginnings through the Elizabethans', *New York Times*, 4 Feb.

Wormell, J. 2001. 'Reviews in History', Oct.: http://www.history.ac.uk/reviews/paper/wormellJeremy.html, accessed 2 Dec. 2001.

Wrigley, C. (ed.). 1980. *A.J.P. Taylor: a complete annotated bibliography* (Brighton: Harvester).

Wrigley, C. 1997. 'From Disraeli to Callaghan: Britain 1879–1979', *The Historian*, 55: 21–2.

Wrigley C. (ed.). 2000. *A.J.P. Taylor: British prime ministers and other essays* (London: Penguin).

Wrigley, C. 2006. *A.J.P. Taylor: radical historian of Europe* (London: I.B. Tauris).

Wynne-Jones, J. 2010. 'BBC hopes Horrible Histories will throw a new spin on the past', *Daily Telegraph*, 5 Dec.

Yapp, M.E. 1990. 'The history that was hijacked', *Daily Telegraph*, 25 Aug.

Yeoman, F. 2009. 'POWs remember lost comrades – and that "silly" Steve McQueen', *The Times*, 25 March.

Zigmond, S. 2003. 'Historically accurate page-turners: how does she do it?', *Historical Novels Review*, 26: 4–6.

Index

Dates of birth and, if relevant, death for presenters mentioned in the text have been recorded *on a selective basis*, given this book's emphasis upon the value of studying individual presenters of the past. For today's presenters such information often proved difficult to discover, let alone check for accuracy, and hence their dates should be treated as *for guidance only*. Dates for public figures have been included also.